BEST VALUE

Law and Management

NICHOLAS DOBSON

Solicitor,
Partner, Head of Local Government Law
Pinsent Curtis

JORDANS

2000

Published by
Jordan Publishing Ltd
21 St Thomas Street
Bristol BS1 6JS

British Library Cataloguing-in-Publication Data
A catalogue record for this book is available from the British Library.

ISBN 0 85308 618 4

Typeset by Mendip Communications Ltd, Frome, Somerset
Printed by MPG Books Ltd, Bodmin, Cornwall

BEST VALUE

Law and Management

DEDICATION

To Martin and Maureen

ACKNOWLEDGEMENTS

I am very grateful to all who have given help and support in connection with this project. Amongst the many are: Pinsent Curtis for their generous commitment; John Jackson of the DETR; Frances Carter of the Improvement and Development Agency; Tony Kilner of Bradford Council; Philip Wilson-Sharp of Canterbury City Council; David Carter of Warwickshire County Council and other colleagues from ACSeS (Association of Council Secretaries and Solicitors) and the Law Society's Local Government Group for their constructive comments on the Best Value Healthcheck material included in the appendices; Melvyn Hughes, Stephen Edwards and colleagues at the DETR for kindly supplying Government publications; Robert Whittaker of the DETR and Davy Jones of the Audit Commission for assisting in the continuing development of the legal services performance indicators; Bob Niblett of the DTI, Jack Dromey of the TGWU, Charles Nolda and Joan Seaton of the Employers Organisation for Local Government for their support in connection with the TUPE Forum; Will Werry of CIPFA for good-humouredly reading an early draft of material in Chapter 11 and Ackvinder Baines and her colleagues at CIPFA Information. I am also grateful to my wife and children for their support during the project. However, any shortcomings or errors in any part of the book are of course entirely my responsibility.

NICHOLAS DOBSON

FOREWORD

Of Onions, Millefeuilles, and Lasagne

What should we make of best value? What is its meaning for modern local government? At an early stage in Torfaen as a best value pilot, a colleague introduced best value at staff seminars using shopping and supermarket analogies (around choosing washing-up liquid, as I recall). It worked as well as anything at a point when none of us was very sure what to make of it – including those who invented it at short notice as a fig leaf to cover the policy gap where compulsory competitive tendering (CCT) once resided.

Since then, I've seen best value from many vantage points, both within Torfaen and in national policy, and what is abundantly clear is that best value is of fundamental importance. It is no mere CCT replacement or Audit Commission fad. Three things stand out.

First, it is a central part of a much wider programme of local government reform and transformation which is likely to continue (and even, perhaps, quicken) for the next five years or so. It has not been very well connected to the other parts of that programme, as reflected in the separate legislative segments. But it is still at the core, for it will drive change and service improvement across the board at a time when e-possibilities are emerging which will expand the scope of choice in methods of service delivery in a very radical way. Best value will be the handmaiden to their introduction in local government.

Secondly, it applies across the range of services and in such a way as to amount to a change in culture and in mind-set. It challenges the practices and attitudes of elected members and of managers and staff, and it places responsibility for change and improvement back where it belongs, on local government itself.

Thirdly, in case anyone does fail to get the message, it brings with it a powerful machinery of planning, inspection and intervention, accompanied by a clear willingness (relish, even) to use it to drive improvement.

But, behind this pen picture, there is much which needs to be understood and applied, and Nicholas Dobson has done an outstanding job in doing that. There will be many books about best value, but there will be none better than this in conveying the meaning, relevance, content, and implications of this powerful new force in public services. He explains it through a style which combines clear prose with careful analysis. The treatment is accurate and acute, and also enjoyable to read.

There are many layers to work through in getting to grips with best value, and this book is an excellent guide in that. Think of best value, perhaps, in terms of food – lasagne, millefeuilles, and onions, for example. It's a dish which is very

rich, and which can be fulfilling, but which may also cause a tear or two. Food
for thought and a recipe for action!

CLIVE GRACE
Chief Executive, Torfaen County Borough Council
Honorary Secretary, SOLACE
(Society of Local Authority Chief Executives and Senior Managers)
Torfaen, May 2000

PREFACE

The duty of best value which started in full on 1 April 2000 will be testing for authorities and those doing business with them. It will demand a radical and creative approach. And whilst (unlike compulsory competitive tendering (CCT) before it) the focus of best value is transformational rather than technical, all those concerned with best value will still require ready access to the legal and practical material necessary to function effectively within the regime.

This book is designed to meet this need by having core information, material and commentary on best value and related issues portably 'under one roof'. It is hoped that it will be helpful not only to members and officers in best value authorities but also to others concerned with best value, in the private and voluntary sectors and in the trades unions. To all, best wishes with making best value happen.

The law is stated as understood at 24 April 2000.

NICHOLAS DOBSON
Partner, Head of Local Government Law
Pinsent Curtis

24 April 2000

CONTENTS

TABLE OF CASES

References are to paragraph numbers.

TABLE OF STATUTES

References are to paragraph numbers.

TABLE OF STATUTORY INSTRUMENTS

References are to paragraph numbers.

TABLE OF EUROPEAN MATERIALS

References are to paragraph numbers.

TABLE OF CIRCULARS, NON-STATUTORY CODES OF PRACTICE AND OTHER MATERIAL

References are to paragraph numbers.

TABLE OF ABBREVIATIONS

ADC	Association of District Councils
ACPI	Audit Commission performance indicators
BVH	best value in housing
BVPI	best value performance indicators
BVPP	best value performance plan
BVR	best value performance review
the Plans and Reviews Order	Local Government (Best Value) Performance Plans and Reviews Order 1999, SI 1999/3251
CBI	Confederation of British Industry
CCT	Compulsory competitive tendering
CIPFA	Chartered Institute of Public Finance and Accountancy
CRE	Commission for Racial Equality
DETR	Department of the Environment, Transport and the Regions
ECJ	European Court of Justice
ESEW power	power to promote or improve economic, social and environmental well-being
the 4Cs	challenge, compare, consult and compete
the Framework Document	DETR *Best Value in Housing Framework* (January 2000)
GOR	Government Office for the Regions
the Guidance	DETR Circular 10/99
HIP	Housing Investment Programme
HMIC	HM Inspectorate of Constabulary
HRA	Housing Revenue Account
I&DeA or IDA	Improvement and Development Agency for Local Government
LEXCEL	Law Society's Practice Management Standard Certification Scheme
LGA	Local Government Association
LGA 1988	Local Government Act 1988
LGA 1999	Local Government Act 1999
LGCnet	the internet service of the *Local Government Chronicle*
LSVT	Large Scale Voluntary Transfer
PFI	Private Finance Initiative
PPP	Public/Private Partnerships
PI	performance indicator
RSL	Registered Social Landlord
the 3 'E's	economy, efficiency and effectiveness
TMO	Tenant Management Organisation
TUPE	Transfer of Undertakings (Protection of Employment) Regulations 1981, SI 1981/1794
VFM	value for money
the Wales Commencement Order	Local Government Act 1999 (Commencement) (Wales) Order 1999, SI 1999/2815

So, naturalists observe, a flea
Hath smaller fleas that on him prey,
And these have smaller fleas to bite 'em.
And so proceed *ad infinitum*

On Poetry

Jonathan Swift (1667–1745)

Chapter 1

INTRODUCTION AND BACKGROUND

LEAD UP TO BEST VALUE IN THE *ANCIEN RÉGIME*

1.1 'Best value' shouts from every high street and shopping centre as a retail war cry. But for local government and similar bodies, the rather different and more complex duty to deliver best value now seems to be a time-weathered feature of the landscape. And whilst in some ways the idea is as old as the fiduciary duty[1] upon local authorities to those who finance them, the concept of best value as a radical performance management approach requiring cultural change, community re-engagement and a fresh service vision is relatively recent.

1.2 For the previous (Conservative) Government[2] the development of compulsory competitive tendering of specified local authority services (CCT)[3] was a key to local authority accountability and operational economy, efficiency and effectiveness. But whilst CCT should also have been popular with the commercial Conservative Party constituency base,[4] this was not universally so since the policy was widely seen as divisive and ineffective.[5]

---

1   A duty in the nature of that owed by a trustee to his beneficiary. An oft-quoted passage on fiduciary duty is that of Lord Atkinson in *Roberts v Hopwood* [1925] AC 578:
    'A body charged with the administration for definite purposes of funds contributed in whole or in part by persons other than the members of that body, owes, in my view, a duty to those latter persons to conduct that administration in a fairly businesslike manner with reasonable care, skill and caution, and with a due and alert regard to the interest of those contributors who are not members of the body. Towards these latter persons the body stands somewhat in the position of trustees or managers of the property of others.'

2   1992–1997: defeated at the General Election of 1 May 1997.

3   Compulsory Competitive Tendering (CCT) refers to previous obligations in (amongst other places) Part III of the Local Government, Planning and Land Act 1980 and Part I of the Local Government Act 1988 (LGA 1988) which required local and certain other public authorities to subject certain work to competitive tender as prescribed before they may undertake it in-house. These, with related provisions, were repealed on 2 January 2000 – see Local Government Act 1999 (LGA 1999), s 21.

4   This was traditionally regarded as the heights of industry and commerce. However, what were once atavistic verities can no longer be so regarded.

5   Giving evidence on Tuesday 28 April 1998 to the Select Committee on Environment, Transport and Regional Affairs, Norman Rose, Director General of the Business Services Association, said, 'We do not support CCT, we believe it is something which has long outlived its usefulness and we welcome the introduction of Best Value'. And he looked for private sector engagement with local authorities 'where there is a spirit of partnership, where the local authority, as the client, wishes to talk with us about ways in which service delivery can be improved or changed; and that is what we look forward to in Best Value'. Also, Stelio Stefanou, (amongst other things) Chair of the CBI Local Government Procurement Panel, giving evidence on the same occasion said, 'Our experience of CCT is that it was not an ideal procurement mechanism, because very often it led either to services

The reaction of the former administration was to make the regime ever tighter. But no sooner would one loophole be plugged than another would open in a continuing negative cycle. Some of the best local authority brains seemed to be engaged in a sterile (if often successful) cold war to avoid or mitigate CCT. With many in local government feeling demoralised, those whom authorities were set up to serve seemed to be forgotten in an increasingly inward focus.

1.3 On 6 June 1996, Hilary Armstrong, as shadow Local Government Minister, addressed the Association of Direct Labour Organizations Annual Seminar,[1] observing that:

> 'CCT is driven by legalistic rules and regulations drawn up by the centre. It is anachronistic, failing to reflect the modern relationships which have been developed by forward thinking councils and forward looking companies ... A Labour government will encourage and enable local authorities to use a range of mechanisms to provide value for money, quality services. The key factor is the outcome. Competition and tendering are and will remain important mechanisms to achieve our objectives. But they are not sufficient mechanisms across all service areas, which is why we need to develop performance indicators, benchmarking and other mechanisms further.'

Also in June 1996, the former Association of District Councils (ADC)[2] in launching a series of discussion papers about the future of local government at its annual conference included one which charted a duty to pursue best value for the public, which would replace CCT. The ADC Chair, Peter Greenwood stated:

> 'The government's mechanistic process of CCT must go. Let us put fair employment and fair trading conditions in place and then make sensible use of competition to get best value for our communities ... I suggest this needs to be shown by a clear statutory duty on local authorities to pursue best value for the public we serve.'[3]

1.4 Speaking as Leader of the Opposition, Tony Blair made it clear in an address to the shadow assembly of the Local Government Association (LGA) on 23 July 1996 that because the CCT regime was 'inflexible, bureaucratic and inefficient' and 'because we understand the need for more flexible, longer-term relationships of trust ... we wish to replace the current system with a new system where councils have a firm duty to secure best value for the public'. Mr Blair indicated that the emphasis should be on 'the best possible outcome in service delivery regardless of who actually delivers the service'.

> 'Councils will be required to introduce local performance programmes against which they can be judged. These will outline their targets for service delivery, their performance in the previous year, and their targets for improvement. Performance

---

not being competed for fairly, or sometimes, when they went out, they went out purely on the basis of price and not on the basis of quality of the proposals or the employment record of the firms that were involved'.

1   LGCnet (the internet service of the *Local Government Chronicle*).
2   Together with the Association of Metropolitan Authorities and the Association of County Councils, the Association of District Councils ceased to operate on 1 April 1997 upon the launch of the new Local Government Association.
3   *Local Government Chronicle*.

will also be assessed against the national indicators published by the Audit Commission. There will be continued pressure for efficiency ...'

In addition:

'Whilst an assumption that private provision is always best would be wrong it would also make no sense to suggest that a local service should be kept in-house for ideological reasons if it would be more efficient and would serve the public interest better to deliver it in another way ... We want to give choice [to] local councils as to how this is achieved but we will of course reserve the right to intervene in the public interest where there is a failure to meet that objective ... We want the Audit Commission to have increased powers in this regard and ultimately to allow the secretary of state to step in if a service is failing badly.'

And:

'With the minimum wage which [we] will introduce, and the proper enforcement of TUPE[1] regulations, councils will no doubt put some services out to tender and to use fair competition to achieve best value. It is right that they should do so. But they should be able to do so without the rigidity and red tape built into the current arrangements.'[2]

This speech set out clearly Government intentions. These have now been (and are being) implemented by the Local Government Act 1999 (LGA 1999)[3] together with related statutory material and initiatives. Part I of the LGA 1999, which deals with best value, is reproduced at Appendix 1.

THE DEVELOPMENT OF BEST VALUE UNDER THE LABOUR ADMINISTRATION

1.5 Following the May 1997 election of the Labour Government under the leadership of Tony Blair, Hilary Armstrong,[4] on 2 June 1997 announced to Parliament that the Government was 'pressing ahead with its Manifesto commitment to replace the failure of Compulsory Competitive Tendering (CCT) with a new duty for local authorities to ensure best value for the public'.[5] Ms Armstrong also indicated that:

'Achieving Best Value will not just be about economy and efficiency, but also about effectiveness and the quality of local services. The new framework will be a demanding challenge to local authorities, seeking continuous improvements in

---

1   'TUPE' refers to the Transfer of Undertakings (Protection of Employment) Regulations 1981, SI 1981/1794. These Regulations were brought in in 1982 to implement Council Directive 77/187/EEC (the Directive) 'on the approximation of the laws of the Member States relating to the safeguarding of employees' rights in the event of transfers of undertakings, businesses or parts of businesses'. In essence, where there is a relevant transfer, they provide for the employee to transfer to the transferee employer upon the same terms and conditions of employment except (at the time of writing) for pensions. However, the Government is also examining options for pension provision on transfer using powers contained in the revised Article 3 of the Directive introduced by Council Directive 98/50/EC. See also Chapter 12.
2   LGCnet/The Labour Party.
3   The Local Government Act 1999 received Royal Assent on 27 July 1999.
4   Local Government Minister from May 1997.
5   DETR Press Release.

service costs and quality. It will be a permissive framework which emphasises local choices and local accountability. But it will also ensure that every local authority makes improvements'.

1.6 She was also then 'writing to the Local Government Association to consult them on a draft statement of principles about Best Value which encapsulate these points'. The principles were:

'1. The duty of Best Value is one that local authorities will owe to local people, both as taxpayers and the customers of local authority services. Performance plans should support the process of local accountability to the electorate.

2. Achieving Best Value is not just about economy and efficiency, but also about effectiveness and the quality of local services – the setting of targets and performance against these should therefore underpin the new regime.

3. The duty should apply to a wider range of services than those now covered by CCT. Details will be worked up jointly with Departments, the Audit Commission and the LGA.

4. There is no presumption that services must be privatised, and once the regime is in place there will be no general requirements for councils to put their services out to tender, but there is no reason why services should be delivered directly if other more efficient means are available. What matters is what works.

5. Competition will continue to be an important management tool, a test of Best Value and an important feature in performance plans. But it will not be the only management tool and is not in itself enough to demonstrate that Best Value is being achieved.

6. Central government will continue to set the basic framework for service provision, which will in some areas as now include national standards.

7. Detailed local targets should have regard to any national targets, and to performance indicators and targets set by the Audit Commission in order to support comparative competition between authorities and groups of authorities.

8. Both national and local targets should be built on the performance information that is in any case needed by good managers.

9. Audit processes should confirm the integrity and comparability of performance information.

10. Auditors will report publicly on whether Best Value has been achieved, and should contribute constructively to plans for remedial action. This will include agreeing measurable targets for improvement and reporting on progress against an agreed plan.

11. There should be provision for intervention at the direction of the Secretary of State on the advice of the Audit Commission when an authority has failed to take agreed remedial action, or has failed to achieve realistic targets for improvement.

12. The form of intervention should be appropriate to the nature of failure. Where an authority has made limited use of competition, and as an exception to the usual rule, intervention may include a requirement that a service or services should be put to competition. Intervention might also take the form of a requirement that an authority should accept external management support, and may relate either to specific services, or to the core management of the council.'[1]

1   DETR Press Release, 2 June 1997.

1.7 On 12 February 1998, Hilary Armstrong, at a London conference, 'challenged the private sector to bring new approaches to partnerships with local authorities to provide Best Value in local services'.[1] She indicated that, amongst other ideas:

> '... firms might look at ... whether under-utilised facilities or assets could be used to help deliver quality local services. Examples might include car parks or canteen facilities ... Can local authorities and the firms concerned make better use of these facilities to mutual benefit? Could works canteens provide meals-on-wheels services? Could banks provide technology, expertise and investment in council tax collection or housing benefit payments? Could private sports grounds provide more sports facilities for schools?'

This charts the innovative 'joined-up'[2] approach which is a key feature of strategic best value.

BEST VALUE PILOT PROGRAMME

1.8 Following an invitation to all council leaders and chief executives sent out by Hilary Armstrong in July 1997 for their authorities to bid to be best value pilots to 'test the provisional framework for best value', on 4 December 1997 the 37 successful authorities were announced. A further 16 authorities which reached the final shortlist were also to be given 'selective exemptions from CCT in order to facilitate the implementation of their proposals'.[3] The Department of the Environment, Transport and the Regions (DETR) indicated in announcing the pilots that:

> 'The projects are intended to deliver measurable improvements in the value for money of provisions across a group of services. Therefore ... the proposals should demonstrate:
>
> – good consultation with service users and other members of the local community;
> – use of measurable local performance indicators and targets to manage performance;
> – a willingness to share information with other authorities;
> – rigorous and transparent examination of the options for delivery'.

---

1   DETR Press Release, 12 February 1998.
2   Joined-up or cross-cutting services may be described as those which, focusing on outputs, now provide a more economic, efficient and effective unified service by way of a partnership or other joint working arrangements between two or more organisations who had previously provided their services separately. See below for further information.
3   These authorities are listed in Annex A to DETR Circular 10/99. Summaries of each of the pilot projects appear there and also (at the time of writing) on the DETR's internet Website: http://www.local.detr.gov.uk/research/bvsummar/preface.htm List.

The DETR also commissioned a team from the Local Government Centre of the Business School at Warwick University to evaluate the best value pilot programme. The study includes a range of local authorities, together with police and fire authorities from across England and Wales and will provide feedback regularly to the ministerial Evaluation Panel.

1.9   In November 1999, the DETR published *Good Practice, Best Value – Improving Local Public Services.*[1] This gives examples of best value which are 'designed to illustrate the achievements of a selection of the pilots in the national Best Value Pilots Programme since April 1998'. The examples have 'been provided by the pilot authorities themselves and in their own words' and 'have been selected to cover all types of council in the pilot programme, and illustrate approaches to all stages of the best value process'.[2] Contributions cover material in respect of: taking an overview; performance review; consultation; comparison; competition; collaboration and performance planning.

Local Government Minister, Hilary Armstrong stated:

> 'I feel strongly that it is not enough for the Department to develop a legislative framework for best value. We also need to do what we can to assist and advise local authorities that are seeking to implement best value. In this task, the work of the best value pilot authorities is very important.'

> 'The pilot programme was designed to test a range of approaches to best value. They have tackled cross cutting issues, service integration, working in partnership with other organisations and involving the community. These snippets are designed to illustrate some of the approaches they have adopted. They are not intended to represent the only approach to best value. We are not even holding them up as the best approach. They are however, approaches that have been tried and found to work. I would recommend them to you'.

1.10   The Improvement and Development Agency has also produced a useful publication in the 'Approaches to Best Value' series: *The best value pilots – in our own words*[3] which authorities will no doubt wish to consider with care in developing their own best value strategies.

BEST VALUE CONSULTATION PAPER

1.11   On 3 March 1998, the Government issued its Consultation Paper: *Modern Local Government Improving Local Services through Best Value.* This contained the following features:

'–   Standards of performance will be set for all council services. Some will be set locally and some nationally;

–   each year councils will have to review a proportion – around a quarter – of their services to see how they can improve performance. They will have to set themselves both short-term and long-term improvement targets at the end of each review;

---

1   See http://www.local-regions.detr.gov.uk/bestvalue/pilot/pdf/bvpilot.pdf.

2   See introductory section in *Good Practice, Best Value – Improving Local Public Services.*

3   Improvement and Development Agency for Local Government and the Local Government Association ISBN 1 84049 123 X (£50 including postage: available from IDeA Publication Sales, Layden House, 76–86 Turnmill Street, London EC1M 5LG. Tel: 0207 296 6600).

  - as part of every service review, councils will:
    - challenge the reason for providing a particular service to ensure that it is properly justified;
    - consult local people through surveys and panels, and reflect employees' suggestions, about the quality and range of local services;
    - compare the performance of their council with other local authorities of the same type;
    - compete to show that a service is being delivered at a cost and to a standard that bears comparison with the best. Competition will play a key part in demonstrating that best value is being achieved;
  - local auditors and inspectors will report annually to the council and to the public on how well councils are meeting best value requirements;
  - central government will have powers to intervene in serious cases where councils fall short of acceptable standards, refuse to consult people, shy away from competition or are just plain inefficient. These powers will include a requirement for councils to make a specific improvement within a fixed time, put out a service to tender, accept the support of an external management team and, as a last resort, hand over a service to another authority or agency. The best value framework will be underpinned by a legislative duty, codes of guidance from the Secretary of State and a revised set of performance indicators drawn up by the Audit Commission.'[1]

LOCAL GOVERNMENT WHITE PAPER

1.12   The Consultation Paper was followed on 30 July 1998 by the Government's White Paper, *Modern Local Government In Touch with the People*, Chapter 7 of which dealt with best value. This opened with the statement:[2]

> 'A modern council – or authority – which puts people first will seek to provide services which bear comparison with the best. Not just with the best that other authorities provide but with the best that is on offer from both the public and private sectors. Continuous improvements in both the quality and cost of services will therefore be the hallmark of a modern council, and the test of best value'.

It indicated that: 'Best value will be a duty to deliver services to clear standards – covering both cost and quality – by the most effective, economic and efficient means available. In carrying out this duty, local authorities will be accountable to local people and have a responsibility to central government in its role as representative of the broader national interest'.[3]

An essential feature of best value is that 'Best value will also help councils to address the cross cutting issues facing their citizens and communities, such as community safety or sustainable development,[4] which are beyond the reach of a single service or service provider. These issues can be tackled successfully only with co-operation between partners and a shared understanding of the

---

1   DETR Press Release, 3 March 1998
2   *Modern Local Government In Touch with the People*, para 7.1.
3   Ibid, para 7.2.
4   Sustainable development is generally defined as 'economic and social development that meets the needs of the current generation without undermining the ability of future generations to meet their own needs'. This definition was formulated in 1987 by the World

outcomes that need to be achieved'.[1] This is important since best value expects authorities to focus innovatively upon outputs rather than the traditional, narrow provider-centred approach.

1.13 The White Paper followed the essential features of the earlier Consultation Paper. In the course of this, it restated the Performance Management Framework first charted at consultation stage, namely:

–   establishment of authority-wide objectives and performance measures;
–   agreement of a programme of fundamental performance reviews to be set out in the local performance plan;
–   undertaking of fundamental performance reviews of selected areas of expenditure;
–   setting and publishing performance and efficiency targets in the local performance plan;
–   institution of arrangements for independent audit/inspection and certification;
–   referral to the Secretary of State of areas requiring intervention.

Reviews are expected to be comprehensive and robust encompassing the '4Cs', namely that they will:

–   **challenge** why and how a service is being provided;
–   invite **comparison** with others' performance across a range of relevant indicators, taking into account the views of both service users and potential suppliers;
–   **consult** with local taxpayers, service users and the wider business community in the setting of new performance targets; and
–   embrace fair **competition** as a means of securing efficient and effective services.[2]

1.14 The White Paper also[3] announced the Government's intention of developing in consultation with the Audit Commission, local government and others, a 'new set of national performance indicators' with an output focus (ie on what is achieved rather than upon the manner and resourcing of service delivery). The set of indicators is to:

> 'include a small number of council-wide "general health" indicators that will reflect the underlying capacity and performance of local authorities as both democratic institutions and bodies responsible for managing a significant share of public expenditure. For each of the major services there will be key indicators reflecting the effectiveness and quality of local services. Each authority will be

---

Commission on Environment and Development (known as the 'Brundtland Commission' from its Chairperson, Gro Harlem Brundtland, then Norwegian Prime Minister). The Government's Sustainable Development Strategy, *A Better Quality of Life – A Strategy for Sustainable Development for the UK*, was launched by John Prescott, Deputy Prime Minister on 17 May 1999. It indicated the four main aims of the Strategy, namely: social progress which meets the needs of everyone; effective protection of the environment; prudent use of natural resources; maintenance of high and stable levels of economic growth and employment.

1   *Modern Local Government in Touch with the People*, para 7.3.
2   Ibid, para 7.18.
3   Ibid, paras 7.9–7.12.

expected to set targets in respect of these indicators and to publish both their targets and subsequent performance against them in annual local performance plans'.[1]

1.15 As to the new best value inspectorate, this will be empowered 'in common with the specialist inspectorates, to trigger swift and energetic action where an authority's performance falls short of reasonable expectations'.[2] The Secretary of State will be given powers 'to support flexible and constructive intervention . . . wherever there is serious or persistent failure in the delivery of services'.

1.16 The best value regime continues to unfold rapidly at the time of writing. As indicated, the LGA 1999 (which contains the entire legislative framework) received Royal Assent on 27 July 1999 and the general duty of best value in s 3(1) of the LGA 1999 (best value authority to make arrangements to secure continuous improvement in the way in which its functions are exercised, having regard to a combination of economy, efficiency and effectiveness) came into force on 1 April 2000.[3] On 14 December 1999 the Government issued DETR Circular 10/99 (Best Value Guidance)[4] and on 23 December 1999 *Best Value and Audit Commission Performance Indicators for 2000/2001*[5] was published. In addition, CCT was abolished on 2 January 2000,[6] and the Local Government (Best Value) Performance Plans and Reviews Order 1999[7] came into force on 4 January 2000.

As the LGA 1999 received Royal Assent, Hilary Armstrong[8] observed:

'... There is real momentum for change in local government. We are making excellent progress in delivering our programme for modern, effective councils, in touch with the needs and concerns of local people ... The new Act is an important step towards improved local services, focused on the people's needs, concerns and aspirations.'[9]

---

1   *Modern Local Government in Touch with the People*, para 7.10.
2   Ibid, para 7.41.
3   Section 3(1) came into effect fully in England on 1 April, 2000 and in respect of Wales only so far as concerns police or fire authorities – see the Local Government Act 1999 (Commencement No 1) Order 1999, SI 1999/2169. In respect of Wales, on 23 September 1999, the National Assembly for Wales approved the Local Government Act 1999 (Commencement) (Wales) Order 1999, SI 1999/2815, which was made on 28 September 1999 and which brought the general duty of best value into force in relation to Wales from 1 April 2000 and commenced a number of provisions from 1 October 1999 and others from 1 April 2000 (see Chapter 2: Commencement Issues in Wales). The Wales Commencement Order is reproduced in Appendix 3.
4   Throughout this book, unless the context otherwise requires, the term 'the Guidance' will refer to DETR Circular 10/99. See Appendix 4.
5   These followed the issue on 20 September 1999 of Draft Consultation Guidance on Implementing Best Value and (jointly with the Audit Commission) a consultation paper (*Performance Indicators for 2000/2001*) detailing proposals for both the Government's set of national best value performance indicators (in accordance with powers in the Local Government Act 1999) and those of the Audit Commission under its continuing duty to set local authority performance indicators pursuant to the Audit Commission Act 1998.
6   See LGA 1999, s 21.
7   SI 1999/3251, made under ss 5 and 6 of the LGA 1999 – see below.
8   Minister for Local Government.
9   DETR Press Release 28 July, 1999.

At a National Best Value Conference on 22 November 2000, organised jointly by the DETR with the Local Government Association, the Improvement and Development Agency and the CBI, Prime Minister Tony Blair in a letter of support to delegates said:

> 'Best Value drives up standards, encourages innovation and promotes competition. It strengthens partnership by recognising the contribution made by the private and voluntary sector. Above all, it ensures local people and local communities are put first.'

THE DEVELOPING BEST VALUE REGIME

1.17 The best value regime is a key component of arguably the most radical reconfiguration of local government in modern memory. One of its results (if not its primary aim) will be to generate something of the pressure for high quality performance, innovation and continuous improvement which market disciplines yield for those outside the public sector. For if a private undertaking fails to respond positively to these pressures then it will quickly go out of business.

1.18 If the scheme is detailed and prescriptive, this is more in structure than substance. It differs from CCT in that local authorities are given much more discretion in how they apply the duty in the best interests of their communities. Best value makes available building blocks which authorities may use as they may reasonably determine in fulfilling their duty of best value. Unlike CCT, the duty applies strategically across authorities (rather than to a narrow band of services) and facilitates service provision across traditional boundaries – what is often termed a 'cross-cutting'[1] or 'joined-up' approach. This book will examine the best value framework in some detail and will also consider some practical and management issues arising from it.

---

1   Cross-cutting services may be described as those which, focusing on outputs, now provide a more economic, efficient and effective unified service by way of a partnership or other joint working arrangements between two or more organisations which had previously provided their services separately. On 2 February 2000, the DETR published a report entitled *Cross-cutting Issues in Public Policy and Public Service* which was 'prepared and written by a team of six from the University of Birmingham's School of Public Policy'. This (amongst other things) concluded that 'Cross-boundary working will be a characteristic feature of the new paradigm or system, since no one structural solution can solve all the problems. It will have a tight-loose framework – tight on outcomes, loose on the means of achieving them in particular circumstances. The new system will have direction setting at the centre, local judgment and planning on how best to deliver the outcomes, audit of the results, with help and assistance to do better made available for service providers.' (See Executive Summary.) The February 2000 report of the Cabinet Office Perfomance and Innovation Unit – *Reaching Out: The Role of Central Government at Regional and Local Level* – recommended (amongst other things) strengthened Government Offices for the Regions with clearer accountability for cross-cutting issues and 'Strengthened Ministerial and Whitehall co-ordination of policy initiatives and of Government Offices.' (See Executive Summary.)

Chapter 2

THE DUTY OF BEST VALUE

INTRODUCTION

2.1 Lord Nelson, before the Battle of Trafalgar in 1805, indicated that 'England expects every man will do his duty'. And, following the death of CCT on 2 January 2000,[1] the Government no doubt expects the same of best value authorities in translating the duty of best value into positive practice.

2.2 On 14 December 1999 the Government issued in DETR Circular 10/99 'guidance to best value authorities in England and to police and fire authorities in Wales on how they might meet the requirements of Part I of the Local Government Act 1999' (the Guidance).[2] Paragraph 5 of the Guidance highlights the five main themes of the Government's White Paper *Modernising Government*[3] as being relevant to best value authorities. These themes are:

– ensuring that public services are responsive to the needs of citizens, not the convenience of service providers;
– ensuring that public services are efficient and of a high quality;
– ensuring that policy making is more joined-up and strategic, forward looking and not reactive to short-term pressures;
– using information technology to tailor services to the needs of users;
– valuing public service and tackling the under-representation of minority groups.

Paragraph 6 of the Guidance points out:

'Best value is about delivering these commitments at the local level. It has been designed to make life better for people and for business, and will be mirrored in the way in which policies and programmes are developed amongst other public bodies responsible for delivering public services locally'.

---

1 Under s 21(1) of the LGA 1999, the following provisions ceased to have effect on 2 January 2000:
    (a) Part III of the Local Government, Planning and Land Act 1980 (direct labour organisations);
    (b) Part I of the Local Government Act 1988 (competition);
    (c) s 32 of and Sch 6 to that Act (direct labour organisations);
    (d) ss 58 to 11 of and Sch 1 to the Local Government Act 1992 (competition).
2 The National Assembly for Wales has issued its own Best Value Guidance following a consultation exercise. See National Assembly for Wales Circular 14/2000.
3 *Modernising Government* – presented to Parliament by the Prime Minister and the Minister for the Cabinet Office by Command of Her Majesty, March 1999 (Cm 4310).

2.3   The basic Best Value Performance Management Framework has been well charted. It appeared in the Consultation Paper[1] of 3 March 1998 and in *Modern Local Government In Touch with the People.*[2] This also appears as follows in the Guidance at Figure 1:[3]

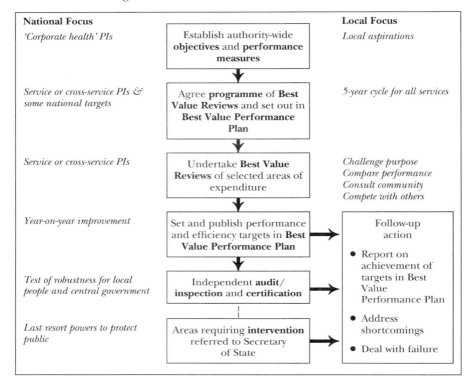

Figure 1. The Best Value Performance Management Framework

2.4   The Government has stated its commitment to this outcome which:

'... matters far more than who is providing the service or indeed how it is provided. What matters is what works. What works will depend critically on whether local services are able to respond quickly and imaginatively to peoples' needs and aspirations on the one hand, and to technological and organisational change on the other.'[4]

In addition, rising public expectations of 'efficient, high quality services, together with significant advances in the way in which services can be delivered, make it unlikely that any one provider can guarantee best value by itself'.[5] So:

'... authorities should draw from the best providers, whether in the public, private or voluntary sector, and plan positively for **diversity**: diversity in the way in which

---

1   *Modern Local Government Improving Services through Best Value.*
2   (30 July 1998), Chap 7, Fig 7.
3   Crown Copyright, reproduced with the permission of the Controller of HMSO.
4   DETR Circular 10/99, para 10.
5   Ibid.

services are delivered; and diversity in their choice of provider. In this way, real flexibility can be built into local services, making them better able to respond to the demands and opportunities of the future.'[1]

2.5 Those used to the CCT regime which was highly prescriptive as to process are exhorted that 'Best value is much more than a statutory framework'.[2] And:

'It will succeed insofar as it produces significant and continuous improvements to every service for which authorities are responsible. Without such improvements the processes that give effect to the framework will wither. The performance management framework around which the new statutory regime is structured will, in the Government's view, only deliver real improvements if it is followed imaginatively and in the spirit in which it has been designed. If it is used as a technical device operated by specialists it will fail to live up to its potential for delivering substantial change.'[3]

Consequently, best value needs the engagement of the political leadership of authorities as well as that of other members and officers.[4]

THE STATUTORY DUTY – PART I OF THE LGA 1999

2.6 Whilst the best value framework is familiar, it is, as noted above, the LGA 1999 which translates the concept into legislative reality. Part I of the LGA 1999 deals with best value[5] and the general duty of best value is contained in s 3(1). This requires a best value authority to:

'. . . make arrangements to secure continuous improvement in the way in which its functions are exercised, having regard to a combination of economy, efficiency and effectiveness.'

This came into force in England on 1 April 2000.[6]

Commencement Issues in Wales

2.7 Apart from the fire and the police services (and housing and council tax benefits) for which the Government retains responsibility, the National Assembly for Wales is responsible for best value in Wales. Consequently, following approval by the National Assembly on 23 September 1999 (and

---

1   DETR Circular 10/199, para 10.
2   Ibid, para 13.
3   Ibid.
4   Ibid.
5   Reference throughout this book to statutory best value duties will refer to the various duties on best value authorities contained in Part I of the LGA 1999.
6   See the Local Government Act 1999 (Commencement No 1) Order 1999, SI 1999/2169, which is reproduced in Appendix 2. Section 3(1) came into effect fully in England on 1 April 2000 and in respect of Wales only so far as concerns police or fire authorities. In respect of Wales, on 23 September 1999, the National Assembly for Wales approved the Local Government Act 1999 (Commencement) (Wales) Order 1999, SI 1999/2815 which was made on 28 September 1999 and which brought the general duty of best value into force in relation to Wales from 1 April 2000 and commenced a number of provisions from 1 October 1999 and others from 1 April 2000 (see above). The Wales Commencement Order is reproduced in Appendix 3.

pursuant to s 27(3) and (4) of the LGA 1999), the Local Government Act 1999 (Commencement) (Wales) Order 1999, SI 1999/2815 (C70) (W16) (the Wales Commencement Order) was made on 28 September 1999.

2.8   Pursuant to the 1999 Order, the following provisions of the LGA 1999 came into effect in relation to Wales as follows:

1 October 1999
Section 1(1)(a), (b) and (g), (3) and (5)(a); s 2(1)–(3) and (5); s 3(2)–(4); s 4(1)–(4); s 5(2), (4)–(7); s 6; s 8(2)–(7); s 10(4); s 12(1) and (4); s 19(1), (2) and (4); s 20; s 22; s 23; s 25(1), (2)(a), (d), (e), (f), (g) and (h) and (3); s 26.

1 April 2000
Section 3(1); s 4(5); s 5(1) and (3); s 7; s 8(1); s 9; s 10(1)–(3); s 11; s 12(2) and (3); s 13; s 15;

Many of these provisions are dealt with in the text below. In addition, Part I of the LGA 1999 is reproduced in full in Appendix 1.

Economy, Efficiency and Effectiveness (the 3 'E's)

2.9   These 3 'E's have long been a major part of the performance management vocabulary of local and other public authorities and have been a central feature of much Audit Commission[1] literature. This has followed from the general duty of auditors of local authorities and similar public bodies to satisfy themselves 'by examination of the accounts and otherwise' that 'the body whose accounts are being audited has made proper arrangements for securing economy, efficiency and effectiveness in its use of resources'.[2]

2.10   The former *Code of Audit Practice for Local Authorities and the National Health Service in England and Wales*[3] in its Explanatory Foreword[4] indicated that value for money depends on economy, efficiency and effectiveness in the use of resources. This was to be achieved by an appropriate mix of:

'–   Economy which means acquiring human and material resources of the appropriate quality and quantity at the lowest cost.

---

1   By s 22(1) of the LGA 1999, a reference within the 1999 Act to the Audit Commission is a reference to the Audit Commission for Local Authorities and the National Health Service in England and Wales.

2   See now s 5(1)(e) of the Audit Commission Act 1998 and formerly s 15(1)(c) of the Local Government Finance Act 1982.

3   Circular 14/95 prepared by the Audit Commission and approved by Parliament in accordance with s 14 of the former Local Government Finance Act 1982 (now governed by s 4 of the Audit Commission Act 1988) came into force on 21 July 1995. However, Circular 14/95 has now been replaced by a new Code of Audit Practice for Local Authorities and the National Health Service in England and Wales following approval by the House of Lords on 23 March 2000 (see *Hansard* cols 486–488). The revised Code came into effect on 29 March 2000. Transitional provisions are set out in the Annex to the Code which apply to audit work relating to financial years ending on or before 31 March 2000. These 'comprise the provisions of the *Code of Audit Practice* that came into effect on 21 July 1995, and which has now been replaced, updated to include references to the Audit Commission Act 1998 and to the National Assembly for Wales'. These provisions lapse with effect from 1 January 2001. (See Annex to the Code 'Transitional Provisions'.)

4   Under the heading: *'Value for money (VFM)'*

- Efficiency which means producing the maximum output for any given set of resource inputs or using the minimum inputs for the required quantity and quality of service provided.
- Effectiveness which means having the organisation meet citizens' requirements and having a programme or activity achieve its established goals or other intended aims.'

However, as we shall see, best value, whilst retaining these meanings, also aims completely to reconfigure the notions of 'economy, effectiveness and efficiency' in a substantial departure from traditional approaches to public services and functions so as to 'make a real and positive difference to the services which local people receive from their authority'.[1] This requires a change in mindset and approach from everyone in best value authorities from top to bottom.

2.11   On 29 March 2000, following Parliamentary approval, a revised *Code of Audit Practice* came into effect. It comprises five sections: general principles; the audit framework; reviewing the financial aspects of corporate governance; auditing the accounts and reviewing aspects of performance management. A box on the contents page indicates that 'External audit is an essential element in the process of accountability for public money and makes an important contribution to the stewardship of public resources and the corporate governance of public services.' The Code can be viewed on the Audit Commission's Website on http://www.audit-commission.gov.uk.

Best Value Authorities

2.12   Best value applies to the authorities specified in s 1(1) of the LGA 1999.[2] These are:

- local authorities;
- National Park authorities;
- the Broads Authority;
- police authorities;
- fire authorities constituted by a combination scheme and metropolitan county fire and civil defence authorities;
- the London Fire and Emergency Planning Authority;
- waste disposal authorities;
- metropolitan county passenger transport authorities;

---

1   See DETR, *Implementing Best Value – A Consultation Paper on Draft Guidance* (September 1999), para 9.

2   Section 1(1)(a), (b), (c), (g), (h), (2)(a), (b) and (c) and (5) (definition of best value authorities) came into force fully in England (and in Wales in relation to police and fire authorities) on 10 August 1999. Sections 1(1)(d), (e), (4)(a) and (b) came into force in England and Wales on 10 August 1999: see the Local Government Act 1999 (Commencement No 1) Order 1999, SI 1999/2169 which is reproduced in Appendix 2. Generally in respect of Wales, on 23 September 1999, the National Assembly for Wales approved the Local Government Act 1999 (Commencement) (Wales) Order 1999, SI 1999/2815, which was made on 28 September 1999 and which brought the general duty of best value into force in relation to Wales from 1 April 2000 and commenced a number of provisions from 1 October 1999 and others from 1 April 2000 (see earlier in this chapter: 'Commencement Issues in Wales'). The Wales Commencement Order is reproduced in Appendix 3.

–   Transport for London; and
–   the London Development Agency.

Section 1(1) refers to an authority which is subject to the duty of best value as 'a best value authority'. A 'local authority' in England is defined[1] as:

'(a) a county council, a district council, a London borough council, a parish council or a parish meeting of a parish which does not have a separate parish council;
 (b) the Council of the Isles of Scilly;
 (c) the Common Council of the City of London in its capacity as a local authority;
 (d) the Greater London Authority so far as it exercises its functions through the Mayor.'

And in relation to Wales the term 'local authority' means 'a county council, a county borough council or a community council'.

A police authority is defined by s 1(4) as being:

'(a) a police authority established under section 3 of the Police Act 1996;
 (b) the Common Council of the City of London in its capacity as a police authority;
 (c) the Metropolitan Police Authority'.

A waste disposal authority is such a body for the purposes of Part II of the Environmental Protection Act 1990 or a statutory 'joint arrangements' body established for this function in Greater London or a metropolitan county by the Secretary of State under s 10 of the Local Government Act 1985.[2]

2.13 As to best value authorities, the Government has also reserved power[3] to the Secretary of State[4] to provide by order that certain authorities and bodies are best value authorities (with power for those purposes to make specified modifications to the provisions for audit of best value performance plans[5] – see below). These are:

–   a local precepting authority within the meaning of s 39(2) of the Local Government Finance Act 1992. These include parish or community councils;[6]
–   a levying body within the meaning of s 74(1) of the Local Government Finance Act 1988. These include Passenger Transport and certain National Park Authorities;[7]

---

1   LGA 1999, s 1(2).
2   Ibid, s 1(5).
3   Ibid, s 2(1).
4   By s 29(1)(a) of the LGA 1999, in relation to Wales, 'for each reference to the Secretary of State there shall be substituted a reference to the National Assembly for Wales'. However, by s 29(2) of the LGA 1999, this does not apply to police or fire authorities or to 'any of sections 14, 16 to 18, 24 and 27' (see below for these sections).
5   LGA 1999, s 2(3). LGA 1999, s 7 provides for the audit of best value performance plans.
6   Others are: the Sub-Treasurer of the Inner Temple; the Under-Treasurer of the Middle Temple; the chairman of a parish meeting; and charter trustees. The scheme of the Local Government Finance Act 1992 is that local precepting authorities may each financial year issue to the relevant billing authority a precept in accordance with statutory requirements.
7   Levying bodies are empowered to issue a levy against either a billing authority or a precepting authority. The levy is paid directly by the relevant authority to the levying body. See s 74 of the Local Government Finance Act 1988.

- a special levy body under s 75 of the Local Government Finance Act 1988. An example of such a body is an internal drainage board.[1]

Parish Councils

2.14   Regarding parish councils, Hilary Armstrong, in launching the Consultation Paper *The Application of Best Value to Town and Parish Councils*, said:[2]

> 'Best value is central to the Government's plans to modernise local government. It will enable councils to deliver the quality services local people actually want and at a price they are willing to pay ... The Government intends that best value will apply to town and parish councils with an annual budgeted income of £500,000 or more. It remains in the interests of everyone that all local councils embrace best value – good management practices and the pursuit of excellence should be universal across the public sector.'

On 10 April 2000, the DETR issued its *Guidance on Best Value for town and parish councils.*[3]

Amongst the key elements of the Guidance are:

- an application threshold of £500,000 based on annual budgeted income (ie entire exemption from best value for town and parish councils with a budgeted income below this figure 'for any of the financial years commencing in 1997, 1998 or 1999');
- best value town and parish councils will (amongst other things) be subject to performance plans (see Chapter 5 below) and best value reviews incorporating the 4Cs (see also Chapter 4 below). However, the Government does not intend to prescribe a review programme for such councils;
- there will be no national performance indicators for best value town and parish councils, but they will be expected to set their own local indicators and targets in the light of local priorities and draw up action plans to meet these targets; and
- such authorities will also be subject to audit and inspection and sanction powers on the part of the Secretary of State (see Chapter 8 below).

Other Provisions Regarding Best Value Authorities

2.15   As noted above, the Greater London Authority is a local authority insofar as it exercises its functions through its Mayor. Section 2(4) enables the Secretary of State (with power for these purposes to make specified modifications) to provide by order for the Greater London Authority to be a 'best value authority' under Part I of the LGA 1999 in relation to specified Authority functions which it does not exercise through the Mayor and to specified functions which are not functions of the Greater London Authority but are functions of another best value authority.

There is also provision in s 2(5) for the Secretary of State by order to relieve a specified best value authority (or category of authority) of the duty of best

---

1   Under s 118 of the Local Government Finance Act 1988, the Secretary of State may by regulations remove or modify statutory rights to levy a rate, eg under private or local statutes. Where this power has been exercised, the Secretary of State may by, and subject to, regulations confer power on the body affected to issue a special levy.

2   DETR Press Release, 5 August 1999.

3   See http://www.local-regions.detr.gov.uk/bestvalue/legislation/tpguid.htm.

value under Part I of the LGA 1999 to the extent and in respect of such functions as are specified in the order.

All orders under s 2 (power to extend or disapply best value) are subject to the affirmative resolution procedure under s 2(6) which provides that 'No order shall be made under this section unless a draft has been laid before, and approved by resolution of, each House of Parliament'.

Consultation

2.16   In deciding how to fulfil the general duty of best value under s 3(1),[1] best value authorities must consult those who have a financial, service delivery or other interest (or stake) in the functions of the authority.[2] Such persons (who can also be referred to as stakeholders) are:[3]

'(a)   representatives of persons liable to pay any tax, precept or levy to or in respect of the authority,

(b)   representatives of persons liable to pay non-domestic rates in respect of any area within which the authority carries out functions,

(c)   representatives of persons who use or are likely to use services provided by the authority, and

(d)   representatives of persons appearing to the authority to have an interest in any area within which the authority carries out functions.'

This is a deliberate move to bring governance at local level more (as the title of the July 1998 Government White Paper put it) 'In Touch with the People'. The local government *ancien régime* (still in some places a *régime actuel*) generally took the view that representative democracy made *The Compleat Council*.[4] But once the electorate has exercised its franchise there can be dangers of an effective dictatorship until the next exercise of democratic empowerment. In practice, this has often been considered to result in an autocratic and non-responsive approach to local government and a failure to recognise that power is conferred for the benefit of those over whom it is exercised rather than the personal aggrandisement of those upon whom it has been bestowed.

2.17   Tony Blair pointed to such dangers of power when in May 1997, as a new Prime Minister, he told his 418 MPs as they gathered at Westminster for the first time that they were not there to enjoy 'the trappings of power' but to uphold the highest standards. He said that:

---

1   As noted above, this is that a best value authority must make arrangements to secure continuous improvement in the way in which its functions are exercised having regard to a combination of economy, efficiency and effectiveness.

2   Section 3(2)–(4) (consultation, definition of 'representatives' and guidance) came into force fully in England (and in Wales in relation to police and fire authorities) on 10 August 1999: the Local Government Act 1999 (Commencement No 1) Order 1999, SI 1999/2169, which is reproduced in Appendix 2. In respect of Wales, on 23 September 1999, the National Assembly for Wales approved the Local Government Act 1999 (Commencement) (Wales) Order 1999, SI 1999/2815, which was made on 28 September 1999 and which brought the general duty of best value into force in relation to Wales from 1 April 2000 and a number of provisions from 1 October 1999 and others from 1 April 2000 (see earlier in this chapter: 'Commencement Issues in Wales').

3   LGA 1999, s 3(2).

4   With apologies to *The Compleat Angler, or the Contemplative Man's Recreation* by Izaak Walton (1st edn, 1653).

'The people are the masters. We are the servants of the people. We will never forget that and, if we ever do, the people will very soon show that what the electorate gives, the electorate can take away'.[1]

And in March 1998, Tony Blair (through the Institute for Public Policy Research) wrote a document entitled *Leading the Way – A new vision for local government*. Here Mr Blair pointed out:[2]

'The new ways of working should ... involve council officers as well as council members. Senior managers must provide clear vision and leadership to their staff. They need to challenge and break down those professional and departmental barriers that hold back innovation and modernisation. They must engage with the leaders of the local community – both inside and outside the council. And, most crucial of all, they must not get so remote from the front line that they get out of touch with the day-to-day service that ordinary people experience'.

This theme was echoed in the Government's consultation paper *Local Leadership, Local Choice* issued in March 1999, accompanying the draft Local Government (Organisation and Standards) Bill.[3] That Consultation Paper[4] indicated that:

'The starting point to modernise how a local community is to be governed is for that community to be directly engaged in debate and discussion about the options for change ... Every council is therefore to be required to consult its local community – local electors and other interested parties, including business, other public bodies, and the voluntary sector – about how that community is to be governed, and what new form of local governance will be best suited to give it the leadership it needs to prosper and to provide its people with a good quality of life.'

2.18 So, in this context, s 3(2) requires consultation with those who have a financial or other stake in the authority and its outputs for 'the purpose of deciding how to fulfil the duty'. This does not of course mean that the authority should abdicate responsibility and follow blindly what those consulted demand. It is clearly for the authority to exercise governance in its particular functional area and the section makes it clear that it is the authority which is to decide how to fulfil its duty. What is happening is a reframing of the concept of local democratic government from 'elective dictatorship'[5] to a more partici-

---

1   There is perhaps an echo of the observation in the 26 January 1830 speech by US statesman, Daniel Webster (1782–1852): 'The people's government, made for the people, made by the people, and answerable to the people'.
2   At p 17.
3   This was issued for consultation in March 1999. The proposals (as amended) appear in the Local Government Bill 1999 which was introduced into the House of Lords on 25 November 1999.
4   At paras 2.1 and 2.2.
5   This refers to the famous comment by Lord Hailsham on the substantial power enjoyed by governments once elected until the next election: 'We live in an elective dictatorship, absolute in theory, if hitherto thought tolerable in practice. How far it is still tolerable is the question I want to raise for discussion.' And resonantly, and still relevantly, at both central and local levels: '... the government controls Parliament, and not Parliament the government. Until recently, debate and argument dominated the parliamentary scene. Now, it is the whips and the party caucus. More and more, debate, where it is not actually curtailed, is becoming a ritual dance, sometimes interspersed with catcalls'. The Richard Dimbleby Lecture, *The Listener*, 21 October 1976.

patory democracy. This means that those for whom local democratic power is exercised should have a greater input into decisions taken for and about them.

2.19 The Guidance[1] refers to consultation in the context of best value reviews (dealt with below at Chapter 4). This indicates[2] that authorities should 'engage with users and potential users of services' and:

> 'It is important that authorities seek out the views of all potential users, especially those who have traditionally been under-represented. Those that fail to engage local people fully from the outset – including hard-to-reach groups – will carry little conviction when it comes to explaining decisions on service targets and selected providers, and invariably overlook real opportunities to bring about lasting change'.

Also, there should be noted 'the importance the Government attaches to the place of the citizen – as user and taxpayer – in best value, and to the role of the private and voluntary sectors in contributing to the overall health of the local community'.[3] And in the best value performance plan (see Chapter 5[4]) there will need to be 'a consultation statement' which explains:

> '... how the authority has complied with its duty to consult under Sections 3 and 5 of the 1999 Act. This could usefully comment on the forms and types of consultation carried out over the previous year, the numbers or types of groups, bodies and individuals involved and an analysis of the results. The statement could refer to previous consultations that have informed the Performance Plan, include contact details for those who wish to make representations, and provide information on how or where local people can remain involved or provide feedback. Any changes planned over the coming year to secure improved results from consultation should be highlighted.'[5]

2.20 Performance indicators issued by the DETR, the Audit Commission and the Home Office in December 1999[6] (see Chapter 3) which set out the Government and the Audit Commission's 'performance indicators for local services for 2000/01' also contain the following concerning *Customers and the Community* in the 'Proposed Corporate Health Indicators':[7]

BV code	Indicator	Target	Definition
BVPI2	The level of the Commission for Racial Equality's 'Standard for Local Government' to which the authority conforms.	Local	Levels are defined in the CRE document 'Racial Equality means Quality' and 'Auditing for Equality' pages 15, 33 to 37. Authorities should report the level they have reached as follows:

1   DETR Circular 10/99, 14 December 1999.
2   Paragraph 17.
3   DETR Circular 10/99, para 33.
4   The statutory base for best value performance plans is s 6 of the LGA 1999. See also the Local Government (Best Value) Performance Plans and Reviews Order 1999, SI 1999/3251.
5   DETR Circular 10/99, para 54.
6   *Best Value and Audit Commission Performance Indicators for 2000/2001*, Audit Commission, DETR, Home Office, December 1999.
7   Paragraph 6.1.

BV code	Indicator	Target	Definition
			Level 1: The authority has written a racial policy statement.
			Level 2: The authority has an action plan for monitoring and achieving its racial equality policy.
			Level 3: Results of ethnic monitoring against equalities and consultations with local communities are used to review overall authority policy. [*Emphasis added.*]
			Level 4: The authority can demonstrate clear improvements in its services resulting from monitoring, consulting with local communities, and acting on its equal opportunities policy. [*Emphasis added.*]
			Level 5: The authority is an example of best practice in the way that it monitors and provides services to ethnic minorities, and is helping other authorities/forces to achieve high standards. Confirmation that the authority has reached this level must have been provided by the CRE.
			To report these levels, an authority must have adopted the CRE's 'Standard for Local Government'. If the authority has not adopted this standard, it should report the following:
			'This authority has not adopted the CRE Standard for Local Government'.
BVPI3	The percentage of citizens satisfied with the overall service provided by their authority.	Local	Percentage of citizens stating that they are very or fairly satisfied with the way the authority carries out its duties.
			See Chapter 14 for further guidance and the requirements for carrying out the survey.
BVPI4	The percentage of those making complaints satisfied with the handling of those complaints.	Local	The percentage of citizens stating that they are very or fairly satisfied with the way in which the complaint was handled.
			See Chapter 14 for further guidance and requirements for carrying out the survey.

BV code	Indicator	Target	Definition
BVPI5a	The number of complaints to an Ombudsman classified as Maladministration	Local	As recorded, classified and reported to authorities by the Commission for Local Administration in England. Maladministration refers to those cases classified as 'MI' or 'M'.
BVPI5b	The number of complaints to an Ombudsman classified as Local settlement.	Local	As recorded, classified and reported to authorities by the Commission for Local Administration in England. Local settlement refers to those cases classified as 'LS'.
BVPI6	The percentage turnout for local elections.	Local	Turnout is defined as the proportion of the electoral roll voting in any election in the year except individual by-elections. Where there is no election in the year, authorities should report the turnout from the most recent election.
BVPI7	The percentage of electoral registration form 'A's returned.	Local	Number of electoral registration form 'A's that were returned at the end of the last canvass divided by the number sent out at that canvass. Forms returned following reminders and follow-up visits should be included.

Table 1: Corporate Health BVPIs – Customers and the Community[1]

Indicators which specifically mention consultation have been highlighted. However, all the above indicators will require active community engagement of which consultation is just one element. So even authorities which are less enthusiastic in this area will have to demonstrate that they are following the principles of consultation and community engagement.

2.21 But it is important that authorities are not merely going through the form whilst ignoring the substance of consultation. The input must always be suitable to the output desired. This means considering carefully what manner of consultation is going to add value to the area in question. And the starting proposition must be that the consulter actually does want to find out what the consultee group really thinks! And whilst consultation on specific functional or service areas may be necessary (for example where support services consult their users), mechanisms and information to enable strategic, cross-cutting consultation should also be put in place. For it is the outcomes from services rather than mysterious internal processes which concern the public.

By s 3(3), 'representatives' in s 3(2) 'in relation to a group of persons means persons who appear to the authority to be representative of that group'. And in

---

1   Crown Copyright, reproduced with the permission of the Controller of HMSO.

deciding on those to consult and 'the form, content and timing of consultations, an authority must have regard to any guidance issued by the Secretary of State'.[1]

2.22   The Government has indicated that it has no current plans to issue s 3(4) guidance since it 'takes the view that authorities are best placed to decide whom to consult and in what way, taking account of other statutory requirements as well as good practice'.[2] However, the Government considers that authorities should adopt a strategic consultation approach and ensure that adequate arrangements are in place to meet their statutory responsibilities in this area both under s 3 and under s 5 (best value review process – see Chapter 4). The Government indicates that the arrangements under s 5 will need to address the following.

'–   **co-ordination with other best value authorities and other public bodies undertaking consultation at the same time.**[3] This will be particularly important where there is a two-tier structure of local government, and/or where there is a well-developed network of partnership working. Maximum use needs to be made of existing consultation exercises, and new forms of consultation should be designed with regard to economy and corporate priorities. Without such an approach there are risks of alienating those whose views have been sought and of incurring substantial cost to little effect.

–   **within a broad framework of general principles, a mix of techniques available for the full range of services and consultees.** It will be important to develop techniques appropriate for the different services and for communicating with groups within the local community that are typically hard-to-reach, whether because written English is not their usual or favoured mode of communication or for a variety of other reasons.

–   **a process for selecting the appropriate approaches for each specific Review.** Each Review is likely to require a different approach to consultation depending upon its focus and projected outcome.

–   **arrangements for informing consultees of the purpose of the consultation, how the information they supply will be used, details of the timetable and decision-making process, and feedback on the outcome and the reasons for it.** It is important that Reviews are not embarked upon without a clear indication being given to local people and potential partners as to what they should expect at the different stages, including feedback.'[4]

The Guidance indicates that practical advice on 'how to consult in different circumstances is best provided from within the local government community itself'.[5] For instance 'Advice on consultation techniques . . . is available from the I&DeA[6] and from the joint DETR/Democracy Network publication *Guidance on Enhancing Public Participation* (October 1998)'.[7] The Government also

---

1   LGA 1999, s 3(4).
2   See DETR Circular 10/99, para 34.
3   This is consistent with joined-up government and an economic, efficient and effective deployment of resources. Avoiding 'consultation fatigue' if not 'consultation irritation' is also important. Otherwise, consultation can become like uncoordinated roadworks on the same spot from a succession of different contractors.
4   DETR Circular 10/99, para 34.
5   Ibid, para 35.
6   Improvement and Development Agency for Local Government.
7   DETR Circular 10/99, para 35.

mentions that experience in consultation on Local Agenda 21 strategies will also be valuable.[1]

Help from the Police in Consultation Enquiries

2.23 A short but useful résumé of some strategic consultation issues appears as follows in *Best Value: Briefing Notes for the Police Service* issued by the Home Office on 21 September 1999:

> '– Is a robust consultation process in place?
> – How are users involved or their views taken into account in developing policy?
> – How are partners consulted and partnership plans aligned with each agency's plans?
> – How is feedback gained from the recipients of services?
> – How are the views of service users included in service improvement?
> – What information has consultation produced in the past – about the consultation process – about performance?
> – How are staff consulted and involved?
> – How is an annual cycle of consultation managed?
> – Does consultation take place jointly with partners?
> – Is a range of consultation methods employed as part of a targeted consultation programme?'

And, in the same document, some suggested means of consultation are detailed including:

- satisfaction surveys;
- opinion polls;
- interactive Websites for on-line feedback;
- referenda;
- community needs analysis;
- citizen's panels;
- citizen's juries;
- co-option of representatives onto review teams;
- consultation documents;
- surgeries;
- service user forums;
- focus groups;
- public meetings;
- partnership meetings.

Best Value Performance Plans: Practice and Procedures[2] – Consultation

2.24 Some extremely useful practical guidance and case-study material on consultation is to be found in Chapter 8 of the DETR publication (which can also be found on the DETR'S Best Value Website at http://www.local-regions.detr.gov.uk/bestvalue/performance/ppindex.htm). This reports on research commissioned by the DETR into the performance

---

1   DETR Circular 10/99, para 35.
2   DETR, *A Review of Early Experiences within eight local authorities*, 24 November 1999.

planning process on the basis of a case study of eight local authorities[1] 'drawn from a matrix of variables to reflect: regional location, type of authority, Best Value pilot status and political control'. It points out[2] that to 'be effective, consultation needs to include elements of both informing and involving'. And 'genuine dialogue requires that authorities provide people with sufficient information on which to base decisions *and are then prepared to alter what they do on the basis of opinions expressed.*' (Emphasis added.)

Whilst the document indicates that most of the authorities studied 'had not differentiated, explicitly or implicitly, between the different types of "public" ' despite the fact that 'Each of these different groups has varying needs and abilities to participate',[3] nevertheless the authorities did indicate that 'they felt they needed to carry out a range of different approaches to consultation in order to try and reach a range of different individuals and groups' and as 'one respondent phrased it, *"the methods of consultation need to be as varied as the uses to which the information is put"*[4]. It gives[5] some specific examples of consultation methods employed by the authorities studied:

- public meetings with open agendas in strategic venues including elderly people housing schemes, schools and homeless hostels (Carrick);
- conferences and panel meetings for specific user groups, to identify areas of concern and development of policies (Carrick Tenants Conference; Southampton's Older People Community Action Strategy);
- residents survey on local concerns and priorities (Hackney's 'put your mouth where your money is' survey; Northamptonshire's Public Opinion Survey; Torfaen's telephone consultation exercise);
- development of a cross-agency partnership for determining strategic priorities and potential areas of shared service delivery (Telford and Wrekin Partnership);
- development of area-based panels and forums (Hackney Neighbourhood Committees; Bradford Area Panels);
- Citizen's panels and forums – a statistically drawn sample of people who the Council is able to consult regularly via surveys and meetings (Bradford 'Speak Out' Panel; Northamptonshire Citizen's Panel);
- newsletters and magazines, articles in local media (Telford and Wrekin's Insight programme).

2.25 As mentioned above, given that one of the key purposes of best value is to provide continuously improving, coordinated and seamless services to the public, it will be necessary for consultation also to follow this strategic approach. This will also help avoidance of 'consultation fatigue'[6] where consultees are subjected to a high volume of consultation exercises. So, for

---

1   Cambridgeshire County Council (non-pilot); Northamptonshire County Council (pilot); City of Bradford Metropolitan Council (pilot); London Borough of Hackney (non-pilot); Southampton City Council (pilot); Torfaen County Borough Council (pilot); Telford & Wrekin Council (non-pilot); Carrick District Council (pilot).
2   At para 8.1.
3   Paragraph 8.2.
4   Paragraph 8.3.
5   At para 8.4.
6   See para 8.5.

example, Northamptonshire County Council has 'placed a corporate priority upon developing an authority-wide approach to consultation'[1] and Telford and Wrekin Council designated 1999 as a 'listening year' in which they were 'utilising all the avenues in which people are in contact with the Council to conduct a high profile request for information'. Whilst the case studies recognised that the corporate centre 'could not completely "remove" the consultation function from service areas' since 'the issue of "ownership" of the process and its findings, aside from any logistic or legal impediments, make it important that the function remains partially within their remit', it seemed that the solution lay in the scope for 'combining consultation approaches wherever possible, particularly since the public tend to perceive "issues" and not nominal departments'.[2] Further, cross-agency consultation (with the production of a cross-agency community plan) might also beneficially be considered.[3]

Best Value and Contracted-Out Services

2.26 How are best value authorities to fulfil their general duty when the responsibility for a specific function is contracted out? Particular issues arise here over the very long contractual arrangements for the provision of serviced assets which are a feature of PFI (private finance initiative) or PPP (public/private partnership) transactions.[4] The key is for authorities to ensure that their contractors comply with the duty of best value so far as possible co-extensively with themselves. Some factors to consider are:

- Since best value merely builds on what authorities should in any event reasonably expect in accordance with their fiduciary duty[5] to maximise the return on public investment, reasonable contractors and their financiers should not object to best value principles being integrated into the contract architecture. On this basis, there can be contractual obligations for continuous improvement having regard (amongst other things) to:
  - technological developments;
  - external service-relevant developments;
  - new ways of performing the service/delivering service outputs;
  - changing service output needs on the part of the end-users;
  - changing social and cultural expectations.
- The key parameters for assessing improvement should be set out clearly in the contract documentation.
- Bearing in mind that authorities are likely to have consulted their key relevant stakeholders before embarking upon the project (in addition to any strategic consultation needed as part of the corporate best value process), authorities will need to consider whether any additional

---

1   Paragraph 8.6.
2   Ibid.
3   Paragraph 8.7.
4   See the Local Authorities (Capital Finance) Regulations 1997, SI 1997/319 (as amended), made under the Local Government and Housing Act 1989 and *Local Government and the Private Finance Initiative – An explanatory note on PFI and Public/Private Partnerships in local government* (updated September 1998).
5   See Chapter 1.

consultation is necessary in respect of the particular project in line with the duty under s 3 of the LGA 1999.

- As indicated above, there should be a contractual duty of best value on contractors co-extensive (so far as reasonable and practicable) with the duty on the authority.

- There should also be a contractual duty for the contractor and the contracted services to be integrated fully into the authority's best value processes and for the contractor fully to co-operate and comply with all the statutory processes including inspection and review.

- The contractor will also need to comply with and/or assist the authority in complying with national and local performance indicators.

- Provisions for regular performance reviews of the contracted services with reasonable targets should be integrated into the contract.

- Default provisions should operate if the authority fails in its duty of best value because of the contractor's performance. The default penalties should be proportionate to the degree of contractor culpability.

- The contractor's duty of best value should encompass a duty to search out innovation and to respond positively to innovatory ideas from the authority.

- The regular best value review meetings should be conducted in a spirit of partnership but with hard-edged performance measures where necessary.

- Provisions for benchmarking or market testing should be considered to ensure that the services remain competitive.

- The best value expectations of the authority from the contractor should be demanding but reasonable. 'Reasonableness' in this context could be what any reasonable and reputable contractor of standing in the relevant sector would consider to be reasonable. Appropriate professional and trade associations can no doubt assist in charting the parameters of reasonableness.

BEST VALUE PARTNERSHIPS

2.27   Partnerships are a concept at the heart of best value which expects authorities to 'plan positively for diversity: diversity in the way in which services are delivered; and diversity in their choice of provider' so that ' real flexibility can be built into local services, making them better able to respond to the demands and opportunities of the future'.[1] However, within best value, partnership is very much a concept defined by the parties.

Partnerships can therefore encompass a spectrum of possibilities from formal contractual arrangements such as a joint venture (perhaps through a joint venture company or a formal partnership under the Partnerships Act 1890[2]) or co-operative outsourcing to a loose collaborative set of principles bringing mutual benefit to the parties and enhancing corporate and community outputs. The width of the concept was accepted by Newchurch & Co Ltd who conducted research on behalf of the DETR and indicated that:

1   DETR Circular 10/99, at para 10.
2   'Partnership is the relation which subsists between persons carrying on a business in common with a view of profit': Partnership Act 1890, s 1(1).

'Our review of published material has so far failed to find a completely satisfactory definition. There is no single definition which captures the totality of the local authority partnership phenomenon'.[1]

Consequently Newchurch presented 'the various definitions that have been advanced' and combined 'the best elements of these' into the following working definition:

'A local authority partnership is a process in which a local authority works together with partners to achieve better outcomes for the local community, as measured by the needs of the local stakeholders, and involves bringing together or making better use of resources. This working together requires the development of a committment [sic] to a shared agenda, effective leadership, a respect for the needs of the partners, and a plan for the contributions and benefits of all the partners. The dynamic aspect to be evaluated, and the assessment of the continuing fit between partnership activities and community needs and priorities'.

Some useful practical material on partnerships within best value also appears within Annex A to the Guidance.

2.28   Hilary Armstrong, Local Government Minister, in a Best Value Conference speech on 12 February 1999 indicated that 'Neither the public or private sectors can deliver the best quality and cost effective local services on their own'. However:

'The "Win Win" solution which we all seek is about making the most of existing skills and experience in the public sector, the private sector and the voluntary sector.

The different sectors all have skills, experience and other essentials to bring to the party. The private sector has brought welcome finance, new technology, a market discipline and a results orientated culture to bear on public service provision. Many people who work in local government and in the voluntary sector bring a passion and commitment to public service which has always been essential to their successes'.

She went on to illustrate the point:

'Let us suppose for a moment that a capital investment in IT or some other capital asset – refuse collection trucks or whatever – requires a certain volume of business to make that investment really pay. But that the volume does not match the volume of business in one particular local authority area. Does the private sector firm who might think of making that investment take the risk that they can pick up other business to optimise the use of that asset? How much of a premium on prices does that risk demand? Or does the investment go somewhere else leaving the local service under resourced?

What if the business in 3 or 4 or 5 local authorities can use the full capacity and those 3 or 4 or 5 authorities will sign up to the service at the time the investment decision is made? Is there scope here for a "Win Win" scenario? If so, what do we need to do to make this happen?'

Whilst the development of best value has moved on apace since this speech, the underlying message remains loud, clear and relevant. Lateral thinking[2] is the

---

1   DETR, *A Working Definition of Local Authority Partnerships*, 2 November 1999.
2   Essentially, approaching a problem with a completely fresh mind, freed from preconceptions. See Edward Francis Charles Publius de Bono, *The Use of Lateral Thinking* (1967) (see now (1990, Penguin Books Ltd)).

order of the day and unchallenging adherence to the old orthodoxies is deleterious as well as unorthodox.

2.29 Finally on partnerships, on 5 April 2000, the Deputy Prime Minister, John Prescott, delivered a speech[1] to the Institute for Public Policy Research on Public/Private Partnerships. Amongst his key observations were:

> 'Some thought that the public sector was always best – and in some cases pursuit of profit was immoral. Others thought the private sector was always best and that the sole pursuit of profit and self interest the best way to secure the public interest. For a long time, I have been determined to reject both of these approaches.'

> 'Part of the reason for the success of PPP is that there is no one single formula for a successful public private partnership. One definition of PPP makes clear that "a PPP can exist wherever the public sector and the private sector work together with a common purpose". It's horses for courses'.

> 'Our case is not that PPP is always best in every single case. Just that it can be best in the right conditions. There will always be services which are best provided by the public sector – the police and the core provision of the National Health Service being two obvious examples. And of course, there will always be a major commercial area where the state should play only a basic policing role. But where it does work, PPP can harness private finance and skills to improve public services. By creating partnerships between public and private sectors we get both sides doing what they do best.'

PROCUREMENT

2.30 Public service procurement has come to have a specialised meaning encompassing the substantial body of law, policy and practice which underpins sound purchasing and contracting practice both nationally and across the European Union. In this context it is a highly specialised area, coverage of which is beyond the scope of this book. Consequently, those requiring information on it are recommended to consult a specialist text. Nevertheless it is useful to note the following important EU Directives and consequent domestic regulations which govern this area:

Council Directive	UK implementation	Date UK Regulations came into effect
Public Works Directive 93/37/EEC Public Supply and Public Works Contracts Compliance Directive 89/665/EEC	Public Works Contracts Regulations 1991 (SI 1991/2680)	21 December 1991
Public Supplies Directive 93/36/EEC	Public Supply Contracts Regulations 1995 (SI 1995/201)	21 February 1995

---

1 See http://www.detr.gov.uk/ppp/dpmippr.htm.

Council Directive	UK implementation	Date UK Regulations came into effect
Public Service Contracts Directive 92/50/EEC and Public Works Contracts Compliance Directive 89/665/EEC	Public Services Contracts Regulations 1993 (SI 1993/3228)	13 January 1994
Utilities Directive 93/38/ EEC and the Utilities Compliance Directive 92/13/EEC	Utilities Contracts Regulations 1996 (SI 1996/2911)	12 December 1996

Table 2: Implementation of relevant EU Directives in the UK

These measures prescribe detailed rules governing the entire lifecycle of relevant procurement exercises above the requisite financial threshold.[1] The essential aim is to secure fair and non-discriminatory procurement across the European Union.

Authorities will also need to comply with their own internal procurement processes – for example, standing orders and financial regulations. These are designed to promote fairness, transparency, probity and integrity in public sector procurement.

Best Value and Procurement Handling of Workforce Matters in Contracting

2.31 This 'Consultation Paper on Draft Guidance' issued by the DETR on 11 April 2000[2] contains some valuable material on procurement in the above context. This contains (amongst other things) good practice guidance on: contract procedures (including service specification; pre-qualification; invitation to tender; tender evaluation and contract management); and related matters (equal opportunities and health and safety). Some 'common principles of good procurement' applicable 'in all circumstances' are highlighted as follows (at paragraph 12):

'–   there must be a balance between the needs of the client and the service provider. The procurement process should give the contracting authority sufficient information to form a view of potential service providers' competence but without placing an undue burden on them;

–   potential service providers should understand clearly from the outset what categories of information and general standards may be expected. They should be provided with adequate, accurate and timely information at all relevant stages of the procurement process;

---

1   The thresholds applying from 1 January 2000 to 31 December 2001 can be seen on HM Treasury's Website at http://www.hm-treasury.gov.uk/pub/html/docs/cup/ecpro/main.html.

2   This Paper is also looked at in Chapter 10 below. Consultation closes on 26 May 2000. The Paper can be viewed on: http://www.local-regions.detr.gov.uk/consult/bv/proc/index.htm#part1.

– all potential service providers, including any in-house bid teams, should be subject to the same requirements;

– care should be taken to avoid taking a too narrow view of how the service may be delivered as this may deter potential providers;

– in order to be able to demonstrate that procurement has been undertaken in an open and transparent manner, authorities should ensure that at all stages the procurement process can be audited satisfactorily with reference to a clear, written policy on evaluating tenders and awarding contracts.'

HM Treasury Material

2.32   There is a variety of useful material on HM Treasury Website (Procurement Guidance) at: http://www.hm-treasury.gov.uk/pub/html/docs/cup/main.html. This includes the detailed and useful *Government Construction Procurement Guidance* which encompasses: essential requirements for construction procurement; value for money in construction procurement; appointment of consultants and contractors; teamworking, partnering and incentives; procurement strategies; and financial aspects of projects.

Also available are the *Procurement Policy Guidelines* for Government Departments. The 'Key Points for Senior Management' at the beginning of the document contains the following sound general guidance:

'**Policy objective**
All public procurement of goods and services, including works, is to be based on value for money, having due regard to propriety and regularity.

Value for money
Value for money is the optimum combination of whole-life cost and quality (or fitness for purpose) to meet the user's requirement.

Legal framework
Departments and other public bodies are responsible for ensuring they comply appropriately with their legal obligations.

The user's requirement
The purpose of procurement is to meet the user's requirement. The requirement, including any specific level of quality or standard of service must, however, be tested critically for need, cost-effectiveness and affordability under whatever arrangements are in place for financial approval and separation of functions.

Competition
Goods and services should be acquired by competition unless there are compelling reasons to the contrary. Competition promotes economy, efficiency and effectiveness in public expenditure. Competition will also contribute to the competitiveness of suppliers, contractors and service-providers.

Relationships with suppliers
In all their dealings, purchasers should do their best to preserve the highest standards of honesty, integrity, impartiality and objectivity.

Legal advice
Departments should seek advice from their own legal advisers in the first instance.'

2.33   Also worth looking at is the July 1998 Cabinet Office publication *Efficiency in Civil Government Procurement*. This was a study commissioned by the

Ministerial Cabinet Committee on Public Expenditure with the following terms of reference:

> 'To work with departments and others to assess how central government can secure continuous improvement in value for money from their civil procurement of all goods and services over the lifetime of this Parliament and beyond, and to report by April 1998.'

Action recommendations include: reviewing the effectiveness of financial monitoring systems, a 'phased introduction of electronic commerce so that, within 3 years, electronic procurement by government becomes standard' and departments 'to adopt a policy of favouring collaboration with others, wherever this offers equal or better value for money'.

The Wider Procurement Concept

2.34   Although the specialised meaning of procurement has been noted, the term within best value, however, needs some 'rebranding'. For, in a broader sense, procurement will accommodate the entire strategic best value *challenge*[1] process to enable authorities to decide (having regard to their partner authorities and agencies and the existence of relevant public, voluntary and private sector providers) just what they need to achieve and how they can most economically, efficiently and effectively do so. When the strategic procurement process determines that external commissioning of goods or services is required then the formal 'procurement' rules will govern the process. However, authorities will need to ensure that they have the capacity for the type of strategic procurement (including cross-cutting solutions) which best value requires. This is likely to require organisational change and a recasting of standing orders and financial regulations.[2] The Improvement and Development Agency publication in the 'Approaches to Best Value' series *To buy or not to buy*[3] contains some valuable material on strategic procurement.

THOROUGH COMMITMENT TO CHANGE

2.35   The duty of best value is easier to state than fulfil. It demands positive commitment to change within the strategic framework set by the authority from *all* within the organisation be they chief officer, front line staff, administrative personnel, policy supremo or elected member. The scope of the duty and some practical approaches to meeting it will be examined in succeeding chapters.

---

1   This is in the sense of the 4Cs (challenge, compare, consult, compete) – see Chapters 1 and 3.
2   Paragraph 47 of DETR Circular 10/99 advises authorities to 'revisit their standing orders on procurement and tendering to ensure that they are consistent with the statutory provisions of the 1999 Act and the requirements of this guidance'.
3   Improvement and Development Agency for Local Government and the Local Government Association ISBN 1 84049 126 4 (£50 including postage: available from IDeA Publication Sales, Layden House, 76–86 Turnmill Street, London EC1M 5LG Tel: 0207 296 6600).

Chapter 3

PERFORMANCE INDICATORS AND STANDARDS

INTRODUCTION

3.1 If best value authorities wish to avoid a negative judgment on their service performance they will clearly have to ensure that they are responding positively and actively to the principles of best value in a way which is co-ordinated and integrated. Performance indicators provide structure and encouragement for this as well as providing performance information for authority stakeholders, managers and employees.

THE STATUTORY POSITION

3.2 Following a modern trend, the LGA 1999 provides only a skeleton and enabling outline to be filled and clad with statutory regulations and guidance. Whilst this provides legislative flexibility to enable adaptation to changing circumstances, it is not without constitutional implications since secondary legislation is not subject to the same rigorous parliamentary scrutiny as primary law, and guidance is subject to no substantive parliamentary scrutiny.

3.3 Section 4 of the LGA 1999[1] is one of the provisions enabling the Secretary of State to specify performance indicators and performance standards. Local and certain other public authorities have for some years been subject to the duty to publish performance information.[2] Now in addition, by s 4(1)(a) the Secretary of State has power to specify by order factors (referred to as performance indicators) by reference to which a best value authority's performance in exercising functions can be measured; and by s 4(1)(b) the

---

1 Section 4(1) and (2) (performance indicators and standards orders) came into force fully in England (and in Wales in relation to police and fire authorities) on 27 September 1999; s 4(3) and (4) (performance indicators and standards: consultation and specification requirements) came into force fully in England (and in Wales in relation to police and fire authorities) on 10 August 1999; and s 4(5) (best value authority duty to meet performance standards) came into force fully in England (and in Wales in relation to police and fire authorities) on 1 April 2000: the Local Government Act 1999 (Commencement No 1) Order 1999, SI 1999/2169, which is reproduced in Appendix 2. In respect of Wales, on 23 September 1999, the National Assembly for Wales approved the Local Government Act 1999 (Commencement) (Wales) Order 1999, SI 1999/2815, which was made on 28 September 1999 and which brought the general duty of best value into force in relation to Wales from 1 April 2000 and commenced a number of provisions from 1 October 1999 and others from 1 April 2000 (see Chapter 2 of this work: 'Commencement Issues in Wales'). The Wales Commencement Order is reproduced in Appendix 3.
2 See, for example, Local Government Act 1992 now superseded in this area by the Audit Commission Act 1998.

Secretary of State may by order set standards (performance standards) to be met by best value authorities in relation to performance indicators specified under s 4(1)(a).

Section 4(2) gives the Secretary of State the flexibility to specify different performance indicators or standards (which may apply at different times) for different functions and different authorities. However, before specifying any indicators the Secretary of State must consult those appearing to him to represent the best value authorities in question and anyone else he thinks fit to consult.[1] This consultation has taken place with the publication in September 1999 of the DETR, Audit Commission and Home Office Consultation Paper: *Performance Indicators for 2000/2001*. By s 4(5), in 'exercising a function a best value authority must meet any applicable performance standard specified under subsection (1)(b)' (power for Secretary of State by order to specify performance standards to be met by best value authorities in relation to specified performance indicators).

Under s 4(4), the Secretary of State has a duty in specifying performance indicators and standards and in deciding whether to do so to aim 'to promote improvement of the way in which the functions of best value authorities are exercised, having regard to a combination of economy, efficiency and effectiveness'. So the performance indicators and standards directly support and systemically feed into the general duty of best value on best value authorities set out above namely to 'secure continuous improvement in the way in which its functions are exercised, having regard to a combination of economy, efficiency and effectiveness'.[2] The Secretary of State must also in his specifications and decisions have regard to any Audit Commission Recommendations.[3]

BEST VALUE AND AUDIT COMMISSION PERFORMANCE INDICATORS FOR 2000/2001[4]

Introduction

3.4 Following the September 1999 consultation mentioned above,[5] on 23 December 1999 the above publication was issued in two volumes. Volume 1 contains the performance indicators for the period in question, whilst Volume 2 contains feedback following the consultation exercise.[6]

---

1   LGA 1999, s 4(3).
2   Ibid, s 3(1).
3   Ibid, s 4(4)(b).
4   Audit Commission, DETR and Home Office, 23 December 1999.
5   DETR, Audit Commission, Home Office, *Performance Indicators for 2000/2001*, 20 September 1999.
6   The documents can be viewed at the DETR Website: http://www.local-regions.detr.gov.uk/ bestvalue/indicators/indicatorsindex.htm

Feedback

3.5 Authorities will note the feedback on both the best value performance indicators (BVPIs)[1] and the Audit Commission performance indicators (ACPIs)[2] which it would be impracticable (and not particularly useful) to summarise here. However, some general observations are noted.

First, as to the Best Value Performance Indicators in general, the Feedback identified 'three overarching themes':[3]

(1) **Too many indicators are proposed.** Whilst the 'Government notes the concern over numbers of indicators ... [it] ... has been at pains not to create an excessive burden in specifying its BVPIs and recognises that there is a balance to be struck: too many BVPIs is a burden, but too few has potential to skew performance. Having reflected, the Government considers that the BVPIs set out in Volume one of this paper strike the right balance'.

(2) **There was concern that having separate Audit Commission and best value performance indicators was confusing.** In addition to the observation at (1), the 'Government is also of the view that the indicators are a means by which authorities can celebrate their successes and by which they and local people can compare their performance with other authorities, leading to improvements in knowledge and performance'.

(3) **Concerns regarding the cost of surveys and the comparability of data secured from these.** The Government indicates that essentially 'it has tried to prescribe the minimum amount of information (the essential parameters of each survey) which is compatible with ensuring comparable information'.

3.6 The feedback concerning the ACPIs is contained in Chapter 2 of Volume 2 within *Best Value and Audit Commission Performance Indicators for 2000/2001*. In *General Comments*[4] the Audit Commission made the point that although 'for most authorities the proposed overall number of BVPIs and ACPIs combined was only marginally more than the total previously set by the Commission alone, local authorities argued that there were too many, if they were also expected to establish a large number of local indicators'. And whilst the Audit Commission sympathised with this concern, from experience it knew that 'it is very hard to measure local authority services adequately with only a handful of indicators for each service'.[5] Therefore, subsequently the Commission has 'carefully assessed whether each remaining indicator can be justified' taking into account 'the burden on councils in the first year of Best Value and the need for ACPIs and BVPIs to complement each other'.

---

1   *Best Value and Audit Commission Performance Indicators for 2000/2001*, Vol 2 – Feedback, Chapter 1.
2   Ibid, Chap 2.
3   See Vol 2, Chap 1 (General Themes), para 1.1.
4   *Best Value and Audit Commission Performance Indicators for 2000/2001*, Vol 2 Chap 2, para 2.1.
5   Ibid.

Therefore, 'we are proposing to make further significant reductions to our suite of indicators. In addition, we will not introduce some of the new indicators we proposed in the consultation document. Overall, we proposed to reduce our number of indicators from 241 to 75 in the consultation document, and we have removed a further 21 indicators. The issues covered by the omitted indicators remain important, but we feel that their value has to be balanced against the concerns expressed by consultees'.[1] It is gratifying when regulatory organisations demonstrate a 'listening' approach to consultation.

3.7   There was also a desire expressed by consultees for a 'seamless set of PIs[2]'. Whilst the Audit Commission defended its particular role with performance indicators, nevertheless, it is intending in 2000 to initiate a wide-ranging review of its role in performance indicators. And in so doing the Commission will 'consult local authorities, national and consumer organisations, government departments and other stakeholders about what role ... [it] ... should play in future in specifying and analysing performance indicators for local authorities'.[3]

Detailed feedback is then supplied for the remainder of Chapter 2, following 'the main headings and issues identified in the original consultation document'.

Performance Indicators for 2000/2001

3.8   Volume 1 of *Best Value and Audit Commission Performance Indicators for 2000/2001* contains the Government and Audit Commission's performance indicators for local services for 2000/2001 (the performance indicators). Although pruned slightly following consultation, this remains a comprehensive collection of indicators encompassing (amongst others) the corporate health of authorities, education, social services, housing, housing benefit and council tax benefit, environmental services, transport and planning, cultural and recreation services and emergency services. As for the Crime performance indicators in Chapter 12,[4] both police authorities and local authorities are to report on and set targets in respect of domestic burglary, robbery and vehicle crime.[5] The indicators can be viewed via the DETR's Best Value Website (performance indicators index) at: http://www.local-regions.detr.gov.uk/bestvalue/indicators/indicatorsindex.htm.

---

1   Vol 2 – Feedback, para 2.1.
2   Performance Indicators.
3   Vol 2 – Feedback, para 2.1.
4   Paragraph 12.1.
5   This reflects the statutory responsibility for local crime and disorder reduction strategies shared between police and local authorities under s 5 of the Crime and Disorder Act 1998.

The Government indicated that it would specify BVPIs by an order under s 4 of the LGA 1999 early in 2000. However, 'for the purposes of helping authorities to prepare for best value, the Government considers it appropriate to let authorities know in advance, without prejudice to the Order, the indicators which it intends to set'.[1]

As to the ACPIs, these are prescribed by Direction in accordance with ss 44 and 46 of the Audit Commission Act 1998. A copy of *The Publication of Information Direction 1999 (England)* appears in Chapter 3 of Volume 1 of *Best Value and Audit Commission Performance Indicators for 2000/2001*. This provides the statutory authority for the ACPIs.

3.9 The selection of both the Government and the Audit Commission performance indicators has been on the basis that 'the two sets of indicators are complementary and present a coherent whole'.[2] Whilst the BVPIs 'focus on key national interest issues . . . the ACPIs reflect other areas of interest to the public or information that provides a context for the BVPIs'.[3] In all, following the consultation exercise referred to above,[4] there are 170 best value national performance indicators and 54 Audit Commission performance indicators (as compared with 241 indicators 'currently prescribed by the Audit Commission').[5]

As to navigation, the contents section is well signposted and in Chapter 13 of Volume 1[6] there is a useful table indicating which performance indicators relate to which type of authority (for example, metropolitan, London boroughs, unitary). There is also in this table some sophisticated sub-categorisation (for example, distinguishing between metropolitan authorities and London boroughs which are both waste collection and waste disposal authorities and those which are waste collection but not waste disposal authorities).

3.10 Although in general BVPIs are specified in England by the Government and in Wales by the National Assembly for Wales, since the UK Government retains responsibility for housing and council tax benefit and for police and fire authorities in Wales, it is therefore responsible for establishing BVPIs for Wales in those areas. Therefore, the BVPIs in *Best Value and Audit Commission Performance Indicators for 2000/2001* will apply to England only for all services other than police, fire and housing benefit and council tax benefit administration. The National Assembly for Wales will be giving information about the BVPIs for Wales 'in due course'.[7] Consequently, following a consultation paper issued on 18 November, 1999 by the National Assembly on its proposed BVPIs (responses to have been returned by 7 January 2000), in March 2000

---

1   *Best Value and Audit Commission Performance Indicators for 2000/2001*, Vol 1, Chap 1, 'Summary'.
2   Ibid.
3   Ibid.
4   DETR, Audit Commission, Home Office, *Performance Indicators for 2000/2001*, 20 September 1999.
5   *Best Value and Audit Commission Performance Indicators for 2000/2001*, Vol 1, Chap 1, 'Summary'.
6   Ibid, para 13.1.
7   Ibid, para 1.1.

National Assembly for Wales Circular 15/2000 was issued, entitled: Local Government Act 1999; *Guidance on Best Value Performance Indicators in Wales, 2000–2001*. The accompanying letter to (amongst others) Chief Executives of best value authorities in Wales from Peter Law, Assembly Secretary for Local Government and the Environment, stated that this Guidance 'now includes both the Assembly's performance indicators and those set by the Audit Commission'. It went on to indicate that the performance indicators 'can be a powerful tool in improving services and in comparing performance with other authorities across Wales and England'. These indicators can be viewed at: http://www.wales.gov.uk/polinfo/local_gov/bestvalue/152000.htm.

Defining Moment

3.11 Some key terminology is explained as follows in paragraph 4.4 of the *Best Value and Audit Commission Performance Indicators for 2000/2001*:

> 'Performance indicator: means the measure of a best value authority's performance in exercising a function.
> Performance standard: means the minimum acceptable level of service provision which must be met by a best value authority in the exercise of a function and measured by reference to a performance indicator for that function. A failure to meet a performance standard will be judged as failing the test of best value for that service or function.
> Performance target: means the level of performance in the exercise of a function that a best value authority is expected to achieve, as measured by reference to the performance indicator in relation to that function.'

Purpose of the Indicators

3.12 The Introduction to the *Best Value and Audit Commission Performance Indicators for 2000/2001*[1] reminds us that 'best value is a key element of the Government's programme to modernise local government'; and at 'the heart of best value is the statutory performance management framework' which 'provides for a set of national performance indicators and standards set by the Government'.

The set of performance indicators contained in Volume 1 has 'been designed to provide for a rounded view of performance, reflecting as far as possible service users' experience of service delivery (outputs and outcomes) rather than the resources devoted to them (inputs)'.[2] Nevertheless, the input level can be important in some circumstances, 'principally in measuring efficiency'.[3]

Meet the Family

3.13 The extended family of performance indicators consists of the following:

– local performance indicators;
– best value performance indicators;

---

1 *Best Value and Audit Commission Performance Indicators for 2000/2001*, Chap 2.
2 Ibid.
3 Ibid.

- Audit Commission performance indicators;
- other indicators set by government departments.

To look at the Government's proposals for each in turn:

Local Performance Indicators

3.14 In addition to those specified by the Government and the Audit Commission, authorities are also encouraged to 'develop and use local performance indicators' which will 'allow authorities to reflect local priorities and tailor best value to suit local circumstances'[1] as well as providing better management information. Improvement targets should be 'set and monitored' for local as well as national indicators. Authorities are also referred to the Audit Commission's February 1999 Management Paper: *A Measure of Success: Measuring and monitoring local performance targets*.[2]

Whilst the Audit Commission has removed some indicators which appeared at consultation stage from those which are formally specified for 2000/2001, nevertheless, the Commission recommends authorities to adopt those as local indicators. It indicates that if these are adopted, 'authorities will be able to maintain comparability with other authorities and monitor changes in their performance over time'.[3]

In practice, authorities will no doubt wish to set performance indicators and targets for their senior managers and their departments which as a management tool support the strategic and corporate national, best value and other performance indicators. Some suggested local performance indicators for the legal services function appear in Appendix 6.

Best Value Performance Indicators (BVPIs)

3.15 These have been set by the Government. The *Best Value Corporate Health Indicators* (see below) will 'provide a snapshot of how well the authority is performing overall' and 'will reflect the underlying capacity and performance of local authorities and others as both democratic or locally accountable institutions and bodies responsible for managing a significant share of public expenditure'.[4]

However, the *Best Value Service Delivery Indicators* within the BVPIs 'will reflect the national interest in the delivery of local services' and are designed to facilitate performance comparisons between different authorities, different

---

1   *Best Value and Audit Commission Performance Indicators for 2000/2001*, para 2.1.
2   Management Paper, ISBN 1 86240 146 2, February 1999. Of this publication, the Audit Commission indicates that: 'Setting robust, measurable targets that make sense to the public, to authority members and to staff is a challenging task. This paper is intended to help local authorities to put good local systems in place in time for the introduction of best value and is aimed at all those involved in setting local targets in councils, police forces and fire brigades. It may also be of interest to consumer organisations, government departments and others with an interest in local performance issues'. (See http://www.audit-commission.gov.uk/ac2/SSfirst.htm.)
3   *Best Value and Audit Commission Performance Indicators for 2000/2001*, para 2.1.
4   *Best Value and Audit Commission Performance Indicators for 2000/2001*, Chap 2.

types of authorities and of the same authority over time. Authorities will be required to set targets in respect of *all* the indicators which apply to the services which they provide.

The Government is using the following five performance dimensions to achieve a balanced view of authorities' performance. Together with the 4Cs[1] these provide useful signposts for management reviews and are:

'–   **strategic objectives**: why the service exists and what it seeks to achieve
–   **cost/efficiency**: the resources committed to a service; the efficiency with which they are turned into outputs
–   **service delivery outcomes**: how well the service is being operated in order to achieve the strategic objectives
–   **quality**: the quality of the services delivered, explicitly reflecting users' experience
–   **fair access**: ease and equality of access to services.'

Audit Commission Performance Indicators

3.16   As is pointed out in Chapter 4 of Volume 1 of *Best Value and Audit Commission Performance Indicators for 2000/2001:*[2] the 'Audit Commission is an independent body with a duty under sections 44 and 46 of the Audit Commission Act 1998 to set performance indicators'. Also, the 'Commission has been specifying and collecting performance indicators for local authorities since 1993/4 and has been updating its set following consultation with local authorities and other bodies'. The statutory duty to set indicators will remain 'to enable a comparison of performance both between different authorities and within an authority over time'. The Audit Commission's aim in specifying its indicators 'has been to facilitate a rounded view of an authority's performance'. The ACPIs are to complement the BVPIs, dealing with activities which the BVPIs do not cover (for example environmental health) or in providing information which will help the BVPIs to be interpreted.[3] The Commission has thoroughly reviewed the 'number and scope' of the ACPIs for 2000/2001 in the light of consultees' comments and intends to do so again for 2001/2002.[4]

Other Indicators

3.17   The information traditionally required by Government Departments for 'planning and resource allocation purposes' will continue. The BVPIs have regard to these and 'Departments will keep under review the demands placed on authorities for information outside the set of BVPIs'.[5]

The Application of Performance Indicators, Standards and Targets

3.18   As will be seen in Chapter 5 (and to ensure 'clear accountability'), best value authorities are required to publish performance information 'as

---

1   See, for example, Chapters 1 and 4 and also para 16 of DETR Circular 10/99.
2   At para 4.1.
3   *Best Value and Audit Commission Performance Indicators for 2000/2001*, Vol 1, para 2.1.
4   Ibid.
5   Ibid.

illustrated by performance indicators, standards and targets, in their annual Best Value Performance Plan'.[1] The first performance plan was to have been published by 31 March 2000. *Best Value and Audit Commission Performance Indicators for 2000/2001* points out[2] that indicators will play 'an important comparative role in the best value review process'[3] which will 'help to highlight areas needing particular attention'; and to improve inter-authority comparability, performance information will need to be reported consistently. Consequently, CIPFA[4] is 'modernising the local authority accounting framework to account for best value[5] and will codify proper practice in a "Best Value Accounting – Code of Practice"'.[6] The Government 'anticipates that authorities will be expected to follow this Code'.[7]

External auditors in their audit of best value performance plans (see below) will also need to pay close attention to performance indicators since they will be an 'important component' of such plans.[8]

3.19 As to publication of performance information, the Government wishes to align publication of BVPIs and ACPIs 'to provide local people with a rounded view of performance'.[9] Whilst performance plans will need to be published by 31 March annually (commencing 31 March 2000), ACPIs are (at the time of writing) to be published by 31 December following the end of the financial year. However, following the consultation, 'the Government intends to make an Order to move the date for publication forward to October 31 each year, with effect from the year 2000'.[10] *Best Value and Audit Commission Performance Indicators for 2000/2001* advises authorities to set out their BVPIs alongside the ACPIs on publication of the latter since this 'will help to focus public attention on authorities' performance at a time when consideration of the best value performance plan for the following year is under way.'[11] Publication is therefore seen as 'an important means of informing consultation' on the performance plan. It also suggests that it would be sensible for the two systems (BVPIs and ACPIs) to be audited in tandem 'to ensure that the two make a seamless set'.[12]

Beacon Councils

3.20 How authorities perform against BVPIs and the ACPIs will also 'play an important and growing role in the selection of Beacon Councils'.[13] The concept of Beacon Councils was first introduced in the Government's July,

---

1   *Best Value and Audit Commission Performance Indicators for 2000/2001*, Vol 1, para 4.2.
2   Ibid.
3   See Chapter 4 below.
4   Chartered Institute of Public Finance and Accountancy.
5   See Chapter 11 below.
6   CIPFA's *Best Value Accounting – Code of Practice* has now been published.
7   *Best Value and Audit Commission Performance Indicators for 2000/2001*, para 4.2.
8   Ibid.
9   Ibid, para 4.3.
10 Ibid.
11 Ibid.
12 Ibid, para 4.3.
13 Ibid.

1998 White Paper: *Modern Local Government In Touch with the People.*[1] These were envisaged as: 'the very best performing councils ... [which] ... will set the pace of change and encourage the rest to innovate and to modernise'. And the Government 'will establish a scheme to identify and select these beacon councils as recognised centres of expertise and excellence to which others should look'.

The Beacon Scheme was formally launched in May 1999 and on 17 December 1999, the Government announced the appointment of 42 Beacon Councils 'recognized as centres of excellence in the seven services areas chosen as the focus for the first year of the Beacon Scheme.' These service areas are: community safety, education, housing, modernising planning, modern service delivery, social services and sustainable development.[2] The Beacon Councils are set out in *The Beacon Council Scheme – Where to go and what to see*[3] and they will retain Beacon status until April 2001. During their 'tenure', the Beacon Councils are arranging various events and activities so that all authorities can benefit from their experience. These include roadshows, open days and other 'dissemination activities'.

The 'Year 2' Beacon Council Scheme Themes were announced by the DETR in March 2000. They can be viewed at http://www.local-regions.detr.gov.uk/beacon/year2/index.htm and are:

– competitiveness and enterprise – better regulation of business to protect consumers and encourage enterprise;
– education – increasing the attainment of underachieving groups;
– health – effective local strategies to tackle the wider causes of ill health;
– local environmental quality – maintaining a high quality local environment;
– making the most of culture, sport and tourism – stimulating economic and social regeneration through culture, sport and tourism;
– modern service delivery – good access to council services;
– older people – supporting independent living for older people;
– planning – town centre regeneration;
– social services – improving standards for children in foster care;
– younger people's issues – tackling drug misuse.

As to Wales, LGCnet reported on 2 March 2000 that Peter Law, the Local Government Secretary of the National Assembly for Wales:

'... announced that the beacon council scheme in Wales, still not up and running, would be delayed until an unspecified date in 2001. The first 42 English beacons

---

1   At para 2.18.
2   Sustainable development is generally defined as 'economic and social development that meets the needs of the current generation without undermining the ability of future generations to meet their own needs'. This definition was formulated in 1987 by the World Commission on Environment and Development (known as the Brundtland Commission from its Chairperson, Gro Harlem Brundtland, then Norwegian Prime Minister). The Government's Sustainable Development Strategy, *A Better Quality of Life – A Strategy for Sustainable Development for the UK*, was launched by John Prescott, Deputy Prime Minister on 17 May 1999. It indicated the four main aims of the Strategy, namely: social progress which meets the needs of everyone; effective protection of the environment; prudent use of natural resources; maintenance of high and stable levels of economic growth and employment.
3   DETR, December 1999.

were named in January. "We had originally intended to bring in a beacon scheme this year," he said. "However, authorities are currently under a good deal of pressure from competing priorities ... [The delay] should enable local authorities to make progress in introducing best value, the new management arrangements, ethical framework and community planning," he said.'

Performance Targets and Standards

3.21 Authorities will be expected to set performance *targets* for some of the BVPIs, but will not be obliged to do so in respect of the ACPIs (although this is suggested to be good practice).[1] The Government indicates that:

> 'Performance targets will indicate to local people how an authority intends to improve its performance in future. Targets will need to be challenging yet realistic, and will need to take into account the formal guidance'.[2]

The following is the framework for 'setting performance targets against the BVPIs for 2000/01':

–   All targets are to be set locally by authorities having regard to guidance under s 5 of the Local Government Act 1999 on the factors to be taken into account by authorities when setting targets. This guidance (dealing with performance targets, top quartile values and prompt payment of invoices) is contained in Chapter 15 of Volume 1 of *Best Value and Audit Commission Performance Indicators for 2000/2001*.[3] All nationally specified performance indicators should, wherever possible, 'have targets attached' taking account of 'any relevant national priorities and targets'.[4]

–   'For some indicators, the Government is requiring authorities to set targets that are consistent with reaching, over five years, the performance level of the top 25% of authorities at the time the targets were set. **Annual targets will still be a matter for local authorities, within this framework.** This approach is intended to put most pressure on those authorities that are performing poorly and will, over time, narrow the range of performance and improve the level of performance overall. Those authorities which are already in the top 25% will of course still need to seek continuous improvement'.[5]

The 'top quartile targets' should be 'fair but challenging' since local people 'should expect comparable service quality to be achieved no matter where they live'. However, 'national comparisons will not always be appropriate, particu-

---

1   *Best Value and Audit Commission Performance Indicators for 2000/2001*, para 5.1.
2   Ibid.
3   This indicates (at para 15.1) that whilst it will not be possible for authorities to set targets against new indicators for 2000/01, since 'there will be no historical data on which to base those targets', the Government 'proposes that authorities should set targets against new indicators from 2001/02 based upon estimated data from 2000/01'. And this information 'should be published in their best value performance plans for year two of best value, i.e. by 31 March 2001.' Paragraph 28 of DETR Circular 10/99 indicates that these targets will 'reflect an authority's position in relation to other authorities nationally, and in respect of cost and efficiency in relation to similar types of authority ...'.
4   *Best Value and Audit Commission Performance Indicators for 2000/2001*, para 5.1.
5   Ibid.

larly where there are good reasons for cost variations between types of authority'.[1] Therefore the Government proposes to categorise authorities into similar types (for example, metropolitan or district councils) 'for the purpose of setting top quartile targets for cost and efficiency indicators' as is Audit Commission and other inspectorate practice.

3.22   But where the 'top quartile approach' is inappropriate or insufficiently challenging, as indicated, the Government has set out by way of statutory guidance[2] in Chapter 15 of Volume 1 of *Best Value and Audit Commission Performance Indicators for 2000/2001* 'the specific levels of performance to which the relevant authorities should have regard when setting their targets'.

> 'In setting all targets, authorities will need to have regard to the duty to achieve continuous improvement. Authorities will need to take a corporate-level approach to target setting, considering particularly the balance between cost and quality improvements, and the wishes of local people, in delivering improvements across the three factors of economy, efficiency and effectiveness. As well as better services, authorities will be expected to achieve significant efficiency improvements'.[3]

The tablified BVPIs make it clear whether 'a local or top quartile target is expected for each performance indicator'.[4]

For those BVPIs where there is historical data (for example those taken from existing ACPIs), authorities will be expected to set targets and detail these in their 2000/01 performance plan. For all new indicators (where clearly historical data will not exist) the Government will expect authorities 'to set targets, which they should publish in their best value performance plan, against new indicators from 2001/02, based on estimated data from 2000/01'. Authorities will also be expected to set targets for other BVPIs 'where there is relevant historical data from other sources on the basis of existing data'.[5]

3.23   Where authorities are expected to set BVPI 'targets consistent with the top quartile over five years', in respect of existing indicators (ie ACPIs which have become BVPIs) the Government has specified the 2000/01 top quartile information in the guidance referred to above in Chapter 15 of Volume 1 of *Best Value and Audit Commission Performance Indicators for 2000/2001*.[6] These cover: corporate health, personal social services, housing, waste, police and fire services. As an example, BVP19 (under corporate health – derived from ACPI H1) sets a top quartile indicator for the proportion of Council Tax collected. The requisite percentages are: London boroughs 95.1; metropolitan boroughs 96.6; unitaries 96.7; district councils 98.2 and all England 97.9. And concerning 'performance', in the 'Notes on Definitions' in Chapter 13 it is stated that:

> 'Where an authority has a percentage target e.g. "to answer 90% of letters in ten days", performance should be given in absolute terms – the percentage of letters actually answered in ten days and not a percentage of the 90% target'.

---

1   *Best Value and Audit Commission Performance Indicators for 2000/2001*, para 5.1.
2   See LGA 1999, s 5.
3   *Best Value and Audit Commission Performance Indicators for 2000/2001*, para 5.1.
4   Ibid, para 5.1.1.
5   Ibid.
6   At para 15.3.

As to performance standards, failure to meet any which are specified by the Secretary of State under s 4 of the Local Government Act 1999 'will normally be judged as a failure to achieve best value for that particular service'.[1]

3.24 At consultation stage the Government indicated that there are several ways in which it could introduce performance standards. For instance it could:

> '... specify from a certain point in time a certain level of performance to be achieved. Or it could set out in statutory guidance a level of performance in respect of which authorities will be expected to set **targets** for future achievement and then, to ensure performance does not slip it could specify a performance **standard** to peg performance at the desired level'.[2]

However, although it is considered that standards 'can be a powerful and useful tool to drive up performance' the Government has indicated that it will 'use them sparingly and where there is a legitimate national interest in so doing'.[3] There is no intention to specify standards for the first year of best value but the issue will be reconsidered for later years.[4]

Corporate Health Indicators

3.25 Authorities will clearly need to study all relevant indicators with care in setting their corporate and departmental strategies and have processes in place to meet relevant targets. However, the corporate health indicators[5] are worth particular mention since they address some key strategic themes. These indicators 'are designed to provide local people with a snapshot of the performance of their authority as an institution and service provider'[6] and have undergone a number of changes in the light of the consultation process. The corporate health BVPIs cover: planning and measuring performance; customers and the community; management of resources and staff development. There are also specific corporate health BVPIs for police authorities, single-service fire authorities, National Parks and National Broads authorities and joint waste disposal authorities. The Chapter also contains the ACPIs.

3.26 The BVPIs include the following.

– As a local target under *Planning and measuring performance* whether the Authority adopted a Local Agenda 21 Plan (as set out in *Sustainable local communities for the 21st Century*) by 31 December 2000 – Yes/No.[7] Under the 'Definition' heading: 'Document developed with the participation of the local community and containing: a vision statement identifying sustainability issues and aims for the area and indicators for the quality of life and state of the environment; a plan of prioritised actions allocated to

---

1   Paragraph 5.2.
2   DETR, *Performance Indicators for 2000/2001* (September 1999).
3   DETR, *Best Value and Audit Commission Performance Indicators for 2000/2001* (December 1999).
4   Ibid, para 15.4.
5   Set out ibid, Chap 6.
6   Ibid, Vol 2, para 1.2.
7   BVPI1.

named individuals or bodies; implementation mechanisms including evaluation and review'.

–   Those dealing with *Customers and the community*[1] (as set out in full in Chapter 2 above concerning consultation).

–   Under *Management of resources* (and as a local target subject to the statutory guidance in Chapter 15, referred to above) the 'percentage of undisputed invoices which were paid in 30 days'.[2] Also under this heading is the proportion of Council Tax collected,[3] and 'the percentage of business rates which should have been received during the year that were received'.[4]

–   The *Staff development* indicators include the 'percentage of senior management posts filled by women'.[5] Following consultation (where a clear definition of 'senior management' was sought) this has been defined (in respect of the position as at 31 March 2001) as the number of 'women in post at senior management level as a percentage of all staff in post at senior management level, where "senior management" is defined as the top three tiers of management in the authority'.

–   Also included under *Staff development* is, as a top quartile indicator, the 'proportion of working days/shifts lost to sickness absence'[6] (including 'authority staff in schools'). The Government intends to publish early in 2000 top quartile data for this indicator to enable authorities to set targets from 2000/2001. Under 'Definition': the 'numerator is defined as the aggregate of working days lost due to sickness absence irrespective of whether this is self certified, certified by a GP or long term. The sickness of all permanent local authority employees, including teachers, staff employed in schools and staff employed in DLOs and DSOs should be included. Exclude the sickness of temporary or agency staff. Exclude staff on maternity or paternity leave. The denominator is the average number of FTE staff calculated by reference to the 1/4/00 and 1/4/01 (ie (FTE 1/4/00 + FTE 1/4/01)/2). For staff who work part time, the authority should calculate the FTE equivalent for both the numerator and denominator on a consistent basis. "Working days/shifts" means days/shifts scheduled for work after holidays/leave days have been excluded'.

–   The approach of authorities to meeting their obligations under the Disability Discrimination Act 1995 is tested by BVPI16 (as a local target) again under *Staff Development*: 'The number of staff declaring that they meet the Disability Discrimination Act disability definition as a percentage of the total workforce'. This is the number of 'disabled staff, divided by the total number of authority staff × 100'. Under the 1995 Act 'a person has a disability for the purposes of this Act if he has a physical or mental impairment which has a substantial and long-term adverse effect on his ability to carry out normal day-to-day activities.'

---

1   BVPI2–BVPI7
2   BVPI8.
3   BVPI9.
4   BVPI10.
5   BVPI11.
6   BVPI12.

– Also under *Staff Development* as a local target is BVPI17: 'Minority ethnic community staff as a percentage of the total workforce'. This is the number of 'minority ethnic community staff, divided by the total number of staff in the authority × 100', using the 2001 census classification detailed.

3.27 Regarding the Audit Commission corporate health performance indicators, these include:

– The number of the authority's buildings open to the public,[1] ie 'buildings from which the local authority provides a service, of which at least a part is usually open to members of the public, but excluding public conveniences which are not integral to such buildings, and schools and educational establishments'; and at AC-A1b the 'number of such buildings in which all public areas are suitable for and accessible to disabled people'.
– There is a new indicator at AC-A2a: the 'number of racial incidents recorded by the authority per 100,000 population' where racial incidents are any which are 'regarded as such by the victim or anyone else'. The indicator 'applies to all an authority's services including schools and to employment by the authority'. In addition (at AC-A2b) is the 'percentage of racial incidents that resulted in further action'. The 'Definition' indicates that:

> '**Further** action must be recorded in writing and would entail such things as:
>
> (i) detailed investigations, eg interviews with alleged perpetrator(s)
> (ii) referral to the police or other body (Commission for Racial Equality, Citizens Advice Bureau etc.)
> (iii) mediation
> (iv) warning to the perpetrator, which if oral must be recorded at the time
> (v) relocation of the victim
> (vi) removal of graffiti.'

Another new Audit Commission performance indicator (at AC-A3) is the 'number of domestic violence refuge places per 10,000 population which are provided or supported by the authority'. Here:

> '**Places** means the number of rooms providing bedspaces for a woman and her children. Rooms not normally designated as bedrooms cannot be counted towards the total. Figures should reflect the situation as at 31 March 2001.
>
> If the authority part funds an establishment then it can claim credit pro-rata to its contribution to the facility's running costs. Support can be financial or in kind e.g. a building or staff.
>
> **Refuge** means emergency accommodation for a woman and her children who have been referred for help having experienced threats to their physical safety and it must provide help, advice and advocacy support as well as being part of an integrated local approach involving partnership with other local and statutory bodies.'

And finally, AC-A4 is the total net spending per head of population where spending by the authority means (to the extent this clarifies matters): 'Net

---

1   AC-A1a

expenditure for 2000/01 per head of population as defined by 1998/99 RS form Line 67 less Line 35 (parish precepts), but figure must be outturn for 2000/01.'

User Satisfaction Performance Indicators

3.28   In keeping with the essential principle of best value as a duty owed to local people it is clearly most important for user satisfaction to be tested within the process. At consultation stage[1] the Government expressed its belief that 'users' views of local services are an essential resource to inform service planning' since those 'views are also a measure of success in service delivery'.[2] At that stage the Government proposed to set the following user satisfaction indicators for corporate health, social services, housing, benefits, waste, litter, planning, transport, cultural services and police:

Service	Proposed Indicator	Survey
Corporate health	The percentage of citizens satisfied with the overall service provided by their authority, and with its handling of complaints	General or specific
Social services	Users/carers who said they got help quickly	Specific
	Users/carers who said that matters relating to race, culture or religion were noted	
Housing	Tenants' satisfaction with arrangements for participation in management and decision making, including the local Tenant Participation Compact	Specific
	Tenant satisfaction with overall housing service provided by the landlord	Specific
Benefits	User satisfaction survey covering issues of accessibility, staffing issues (helpfulness etc.) and communications/ information (understandability etc.)	Specific

---

1   DETR, *Performance Indicators for 2000/2001* (September 1999).
2   Ibid, Chap 13.

Service	Proposed Indicator	Survey
Waste	Percentage of survey respondents expressing satisfaction with recycling facilities, household waste collection and civic amenity sites	General
Litter	Percentage of survey respondents satisfied with cleanliness standards	General
Planning	Percentage of applicants and those commenting on planning applications satisfied with the service	Specific
Transport	Percentage of users satisfied with local provision of public transport information	General
	Percentage of users satisfied with local bus service	Specific
Culture	The percentage of library users who found the book(s) they wanted and/or the information they needed	Specific
	Percentage of residents by targeted group satisfied with the local authorities cultural and recreational activities	General
Police	Feelings of public safety using agreed survey	General
	Level of crime using agreed survey	General
	Fear of crime using agreed survey	General
	Public confidence in the criminal justice system or its component parts, using agreed survey	General
	Percentage of victims and witnesses satisfied with overall treatment by the police in the course of the case	Specific

Table 3: User satisfaction indicators at consultation stage

3.29 While most of the above consultation indicators have been retained,[1] they have been amplified considerably by way of general requirements designed to achieve comparability and statistical integrity and consequent specified requirements underpinning each indicator.[2]

The view taken in the *Best Value and Audit Commission Performance Indicators for 2000/2001* is that the services which are 'provided by best value authorities have a direct effect on the quality of life of local residents'.[3] Since it is 'important that the best value performance indicators address levels of satisfaction with these services ... a number of "quality" BVPIs have been specified by the government to explicitly reflect users' experience of services'.[4] In the light of 'careful consideration to the consultation responses on user satisfaction performance indicators, the Government has decided to prescribe what it believes to be the minimum amount of survey detail consistent with obtaining comparable data across authorities'.[5] Chapter 14 also 'constitutes initial guidance to best value authorities on the approach to be taken to user satisfaction surveys arising out of BVPIs'.[6]

3.30 Authorities will clearly need to study these indicators and the require-ments very carefully and make sure that they have the systems in place and the necessary expertise (whether by in-house or external provision) to meet their obligations in this area. Some of the salient issues are as follows.

The requirements will cover (amongst other things) the following.[7]

- **Target population**: the group of people from which a sample will be extracted.
- The **sampling frame**: the set of people or households that have a chance to be selected. Depending upon the circumstances and requirements this can be 'all of the target population' or 'all the users of a service within a well defined time period'.
- **Specific questions to be asked**: To ensure comparability of results it is important that local authorities ask the same 'satisfaction' questions of service users for each service area. Whilst questions additional to those on BVPIs and in connection with another consultation exercise are in order, 'it is important that additional questions should be added after or before each of the modules (not incorporated as part of modules) of best value indicator questions (and before the socio-economic questions – gender, age, occupation and so on), so that question ordering does not affect

---

1   Except for police and social services functions where 'the Home Office and the
    Department of Health respectively will establish the parameters of the relevant surveys early
    in' 2000: see *Best Value and Audit Commission Performance Indicators for 2000/2001*, Vol 1,
    Chap 14.
2   For the present approach to User Satisfaction Performance Indicators *Best Value and Audit
    Commission Performance Indicators for 2000/2001* Vol 1: Table 14.1 (Social subgroups for all
    surveys); Table 14.2 Social services survey and General police survey; Table 14.3 General
    survey.
3   *Best Value and Audit Commission Performance Indicators for 2000/2001*, Vol 1, Chap 14.
4   Ibid.
5   Ibid.
6   Ibid.
7   Ibid.

responses too much'. Questionnaires should also be 'non-political in context and, ideally, reasonably short to encourage a better response rate'. Authorities are advised to seek expert advice if they are unsure in this area.

The relevant modules of questions for each of the user satisfaction BVPIs 'should always be asked in the same questionnaire'. Subject to this (and the other survey requirements) authorities are free to conduct a specific survey about a particular functional area or to carry out a multi-functional survey.

–   **Probability sampling**: This (together with other technical statistical issues) is a complex area on which authorities may wish to take appropriate expert advice. It is recommended as what is 'often considered to be the most reliable way to ensure a sample is statistically representative of the target population under study'. A 'probability sample' is defined as 'one in which each person in the target population has an equal, or at least a known, chance (probability) of being selected'; and the 'surest way of providing equal probability of selection is to use the principle of random selection'. The Government takes the view that since the results need to be compared across local authorities, 'all of the indicators must be collected using probability sampling'.

–   **Output** (sample size and confidence intervals around the estimates): Since statistical outputs are estimates, they are presented with a $\pm$ x% margin of error. This margin of error is the 'confidence interval'. The Performance Indicators document points out that the 'desired confidence interval is key to working out the ideal sample size for a survey and authorities might need expert advice in drawing the sample, working out the sample size and design if they do not have the expertise in-house'. Authorities will be required to provide the 'confidence interval' and the number of respondents on which the statistic is based (the base number) when reporting the results. However, where the term *confidence level* is used this refers to the degree of confidence that the outcome estimate was not arrived at by chance: eg a 'confidence level set at 95% indicates that we can be 95% confident that we did not arrive at the estimate by chance'.

–   Authorities will also have to detail their efforts to 'improve response rates and to make the results as representative of the target population as possible'. As to calculation of the sample size: 'An authority which normally gets a 70% response rate to their surveys as well as considering a wide variety of methods to improve the response rate will also need to take the likely response rate into consideration when calculating the sample size (the actual number of people who should be selected). Thus, if the confidence interval desired is $\pm 3\%$ (1,100 achieved responses) and the average response rate is 70% the authority should aim to send question-naires or interview 1,572 residents (1,100 $\times$ 100/70). The results should then be checked for representativeness of the target population as a whole'.

–   However, for 'service areas (or authorities) where the target population is too small to allow for a statistically valid sample, a census (100% sample) of the target population will be required'.

– Concerning social subgroups, to enable 'comparability across authorities and for authorities to be able to check the representativeness of their survey responses, all surveys will be required to contain questions on gender, age, employment status, occupation, ethnicity, disability and postcode'. Authorities which consider their local circumstances to require it are 'encouraged to ask more questions on socio-economic issues'.

– There are two timing issues. The first is the time of the year for fieldwork which refers to 'the period within which the questionnaires are administered to the sample selected'. The second is the timing of surveys. In the absence of some 'major change or new initiative in the authority or service area which would affect the residents significantly' any output changes are unlikely to be identified by carrying out a survey annually. Therefore, although authorities may wish to conduct surveys more frequently, the 'tables for each of the user satisfaction indicators specify the minimum intervals at which data for each of the indicators needs to be collected'.

– The method of calculating a **final rating** (outcome statistic from the survey) is included in each of the indicator tables. The final rating should exclude those who have failed to respond to particular questions or added an additional comment and should consequently 'be based on the total number of respondents who answered the question appropriately'.

– And as to **confidentiality**, 'all questionnaires will need to specify a confidentiality statement in their covering letter explaining that 'all of the data will be treated in the strictest confidence and will only be used to monitor the local authority's services'. The letter/statement will also need to explain that 'anonymised responses may be passed on to the Local and Regional Government Research Unit which will use the data to study national patterns of service satisfaction.'

– To enable collection of data at national level, authorities will be required to send a data file for each of the indicators to: 'Local and Regional Government Research Unit at the DETR, User Satisfaction BVPIs, 5/D5 Eland House, Bressenden Place, London, SW1E 5DU'. The data file 'should be in a format that allows for mathematical calculations to be carried out with the data. For example, simple frequency counts, working out means and percentages'. The data file should contain in anonymised format all of the survey responses, setting out for each respondent the specified social subgroup characteristics[1] including the respondent's postcode and their answers to all of the questions asked in connection with the indicator(s). The 'data file will need to be carefully labelled with the authority name, service area that the data covers and an authority contact name'.

---

1   See *Best Value and Audit Commission Performance Indicators for 2000/2001*, Vol 1, Chap 14: 'User Satisfaction Performance Indicators', Element 6 (Details of Requirements).

Guidance

3.31 There is intended to be guidance on the above and other related issues published on the DETR's Website[1] in Spring 2000.[2] Authorities are encouraged to consider 'getting expert advice in survey research methods if they do not have the expertise in-house'. This is likely to be good news for commercial statisticians since many authorities will not have the requisite capability.

3.32 Finally, in specifying the user satisfaction indicators, *Best Value and Audit Commission Performance Indicators for 2000/2001* indicates that there should be specific surveys conducted for council tenants, Housing and Council Tax Benefits claimants, planning applicants and library visitors. However, questions on the following should be asked in the same general survey since they all have the same target population of all local authority residents. These are: the percentage of citizens satisfied with the overall service provided by their authority (BVPI3); the percentage of satisfied complainants (BVPI4); litter – percentage of people satisfied with cleanliness standards (BVPI89); waste – percentage satisfied with waste and recycling facilities (BVPI90); percentage satisfied with local public transport information (BVPI103); percentage satisfied with local bus services (BVPI104); and the percentage of targeted group residents satisfied with local authority cultural and recreational activities (BVPI119).

If a general survey is conducted, 'BVPI 3 and 4 should be asked after all of the questions on BVPI89, 90, 103, 104 and 119'.[3]

Local Legal Services Indicators

3.33 To assist Legal Services Departments to prepare for best value and to provide some specific performance focus, through Pinsent Curtis the writer has devised a suite of locally adoptable performance indicators for this area. However, the indicators should also be readily adaptable to other support service departments. These indicators are set out fully in Appendix 6 and cover:

Outcomes
Corporate Value
Community Value
Service Outcomes

Enabling and facilitating outcomes
Operational Performance
Client Satisfaction
People Satisfaction
Innovation
Service Review

---

1   www.local-regions.detr.gsi.gov.uk/bestvalue/bvindex.htm.
2   See *User Satisfaction Performance Indicators: Guidance on Methods of Data Collection* which 'concerns those indicators which involve user satisfaction surveys. It aims to provide an overview of the different methods that can be followed for the collection of data. As well as aiming to help authorities to meet the requirements set out in the Order the guidance offers useful tips on how the User Satisfaction surveys can be used by the authority to consult with the public on other issues which they perceive as relevant to their authority.' It can be viewed on: http://www.local.detr.gov.uk/research/bvpi.htm.
3   *Best Value and Audit Commission Performance Indicators for 2000/2001*, Vol 1, Chapter 14.

CONCLUSION

3.34   The BVPIs and ACPIs are challenging but positive in that they provide sample tests for both management and public of the health and wellbeing of the various parts of the corporate body against best value fitness criteria. *The Guardian* did refer to the draft indicators at consultation stage as something which 'could tax the patience of the most dedicated bureaucrat with yet more paperwork'.[1] And whilst there is some substance in the concern that too much focus on process will extinguish the creativity which drives best value, nevertheless the indicators do provide an accountability framework as well as a constant spur to continuous improvement. In addition, following consultation, the indicators have been refined and streamlined somewhat. As the Deputy Prime Minister, the Home Secretary and the Audit Commission Chair[2] indicate in their signed Foreword, this process is to continue:

> 'These performance indicators are very much a start. We recognise that they will need to be refined in future years in the light of experience and the emergence of new priorities. We are committed to continued working with best value authorities, their partners and consumers in making those improvements, and in seeking to rationalise the overall number of indicators which local authorities are required to report against. The best value performance management framework offers local people a real opportunity to assess their authority's performance. It also provides best value authorities an incentive to improve their services for the local community. We look forward to working with them to turn these opportunities into a reality.'

---

1   'A Clean Sweep?' by Peter Hetherington, *The Guardian*, 6 October 1999.
2   Respectively John Prescott, Jack Straw and Dame Helena Shovelton.

Chapter 4

THE BEST VALUE REVIEW

THE STATUTORY FRAMEWORK

4.1   The best value review is a cornerstone of the statutory regime. It is covered by s 5 of the Local Government Act 1999[1] which, considering the range and depth of its implications, is misleadingly short.

The basic duty is contained in s 5(1) which requires best value authorities to 'conduct best value reviews of its functions in accordance with the provisions of any order made under' the section. By s 5(2) the Secretary of State may by order specify a period 'within which an authority is to review all its functions'. Such an order can be flexible in that it may:[2]

'(a)   apply to one authority or more;
(b)   make different provision in relation to different authorities;
(c)   require specified functions to be reviewed in specified financial years.'

4.2   A best value authority in conducting reviews has a duty to 'aim to improve the way in which its functions are exercised, having regard to a combination of economy, efficiency and effectiveness'.[3] It must also have regard to any statutory guidance issued by the Secretary of State under s 5(5).[4] Such guidance may cover:

–   the timetable for a review;
–   the procedure for a review;
–   the form in which a review should be recorded; and
–   the content of a review.

Guidance may also state that authorities should:

'(a)   specify performance indicators in relation to functions;

---

1   Section 5(2), (4), (5), (6) and (7) (Best Value Reviews: orders and guidance) came into force fully in England (and in Wales in relation to police and fire authorities) on 27 September 1999 and the duty on best value authorities to conduct reviews in s 5(1) and (3) came into force fully in England (and in Wales in relation to police and fire authorities) on 1 April 2000: the Local Government Act 1999 (Commencement No 1) Order 1999, SI 1999/2169, which is reproduced in Appendix 2. In respect of Wales, on 23 September 1999, the National Assembly for Wales approved the Local Government Act 1999 (Commencement) (Wales) Order 1999, SI 1999/2815, which was made on 28 September 1999 and which brought the general duty of best value into force in relation to Wales from 1 April 2000 and commenced a number of provisions from 1 October 1999 and others from 1 April 2000 (see Chapter 2: 'Commencement Issues in Wales'). The Wales Commencement Order is reproduced in Appendix 3.
2   LGA 1999, s 5(2).
3   Ibid, s 5(3)(a).
4   See ibid, s 5(3)(b).

(b) set targets for the performance of functions ('performance targets') by reference to performance indicators specified under section 4[1] or under paragraph (a);

(c) set a plan of action to be taken for the purposes of meeting a performance target.'[2]

In addition, guidance may 'state the matters which should be taken into account in setting performance targets'. And 'these may include the range of performances expected to be attained by best value authorities'.[3]

4.3 Section 5(4) enables the Secretary of State by order to specify matters which an authority must include in a functional review under s 5 of the LGA 1999. In particular, such an order may require an authority to:

– consider whether it should be exercising the function;
– consider the level at which and the way in which it should be exercising the function;
– consider its objectives in relation to the exercise of the function;
– assess its performance in exercising the function by reference to any performance indicator specified for the function under s 4 or under subs (6)(a);
– assess the competitiveness of its performance in exercising the function by reference to the exercise of the same function, or similar functions, by other best value authorities and by commercial and other businesses;
– consult other best value authorities and commercial and other businesses about the exercise of the function;
– assess its success in meeting any performance standard which applies in relation to the function;
– assess its progress towards meeting any relevant performance standard which has been specified but which does not yet apply;
– assess its progress towards meeting any relevant performance target set under subs (6)(b).[4]

The provisions in s 5(4) of the LGA 1999 together with relevant parts of the Local Government (Best Value) Performance Plans and Reviews Order 1999[5] are at the heart of the review process and will be considered in some detail below.

THE BEST VALUE REVIEW

Review Programming

4.4 Best value authorities (other than fire authorities) will be required to conduct the first best value review of all their functions by 31 March 2005.[6] Fire

---

1　See Chapter 3.
2　LGA 1999, s 5(6).
3　Ibid, s 5(7).
4　Section 5(4).
5　SI 1999/3251.
6　See art 5(1) of The Local Government (Best Value) Performance Plans and Reviews Order 1999, SI 1999/3251. See also para 18, DETR Circular 10/99 which points out that:

authorities[1] will be required to conduct their first best value review in accordance with the following timetable:

- communication and control functions by 31 March 2001;
- procurement functions by 31 March 2002;
- training functions by 31 March 2003;
- all other functions by 31 March 2005.[2]

Thereafter, all best value authorities must carry out a further best value review of all their functions by 31 March 2010.[3] Authorities must then conduct similar reviews 'by the end of each successive period of five years (ending on 31 March 2015, 31 March 2020 and so on)'.[4]

As a general rule, the Government is not intending to set a common review timetable since that would constrain the needs of the timetable to 'be practical and realistic and take into account the resources available to the authority, the opportunity for tackling cross-cutting issues,[5] and the demands placed on it by other statutory, financial and contractual requirements.[6] The Government gives an example concerning fire authorities where it is 'intending to set a prioritised programme of Reviews in the early years of the first cycle for the specific functions of communications and control, training and procurement, in order to promote joint working and co-operation between authorities'.[7]

'Authorities need to include in their Performance Plans a programme of Reviews in accordance with SI 1999/3251, which stipulates that best value authorities conduct Reviews of all functions within a 5 year period ending 31 March 2005, and within consecutive five year cycles thereafter'.

1   These are: '(a) a fire authority constituted by a combination scheme; (b) a metropolitan county fire and civil defence authority; (c) the London Fire and Emergency Planning Authority; (d) a county council acting as the fire authority for its area under the provisions of section 4 of the Fire Services Act 1947' – art 5(4), ibid.

2   Ibid at art 5(2). By art 5(4): ' "procurement functions" means the securing by fire authorities of such equipment as may be necessary to meet efficiently all normal requirements for the discharge of their duties, as set out in section 1 of the Fire Services Act 1947; "communication and control functions" means securing efficient arrangements for dealing with calls for the assistance of the fire brigade and for summoning members of the fire brigade, as mentioned in section 1(1)(c) of the Fire Services Act 1947; "training functions" means securing the efficient training of members of the fire brigade as mentioned in section 1(1)(b) of the Fire Services Act 1947'.

3   Article 5(3), ibid.

4   Ibid.

5   Cross-cutting services may be described as those which, focussing on outputs, now provide a more economic, efficient and effective unified service by way of a partnership or other joint working arrangements between two or more organizations who had previously provided their services separately. On 2 February 2000 the DETR published a report entitled *Cross-cutting Issues in Public Policy and Public Service* which was 'prepared and written by a team of six from the University of Birmingham's School of Public Policy'. This (amongst other things) concluded that 'Cross-boundary working will be a characteristic feature of the new paradigm or system, since no one structural solution can solve all the problems. It will have a tight-loose framework – tight on outcomes, loose on the means of achieving them in particular circumstances. The new system will have direction setting at the centre, local judgment and planning on how best to deliver the outcomes, audit of the results, with help and assistance to do better made available for service providers' (see Executive Summary).

6   DETR Circular 10/99, para 18.

7   Ibid.

- cost
- potential for market-testing
- strategic fit with Council objectives
- quality accreditation'.

For the first review year the services selected were those which were:

'– relatively important to the public
- poor performers (and publicly seen as such)
- relatively high cost
- a major part of the budget
- central to the Council's objectives and priorities
- and open to market-testing'.

And as noted below, Brighton and Hove Council (one of the best value pilot authorities[1]) has involved the public through the Council newspaper in choosing the areas to be reviewed with the aid of a prize draw incentive: 'Give us your Best Value priorities – and win a computer'![2]

The Joined-Up Approach

4.6 Essential to best value with its focus on fresh ways of providing user-centred outcomes is the cross-cutting (or joined-up) approach to service delivery.[3] This can be challenging to those managers who have traditionally been tribally protective of their narrow service areas. However, an atavistic attitude to promotion and defence of service territory does nothing for the public and leads to those who contact the authority being sent on a frustrating and circular journey (actual or virtual) with consequent frustration and the poisoning of potential goodwill. It will therefore be essential for authorities to consider the scope for 'joined-up' service delivery when conducting service reviews.

4.7 Oldham Metropolitan Borough Council (amongst others) has tackled this within its pilot[4] project by means of a Service Co-ordination Team. Previously, access to seven services (housing and building maintenance, refuse collection and environmental services, grounds maintenance, highways and street lighting) was obtained by contacting the appropriate section of the relevant Council Department. Naturally this:

'... led to some difficulty and confusion amongst members of the public who were often unaware of who to contact. Also members of the public who wished to contact more than one service e.g. to report a street light outage, a wheeled bin being missed and a housing repair, in the past involved contact with three separate departments'.[5]

---

1 See above.
2 *Brighton & Hove News* November 1999.
3 The February 2000 report of the Cabinet Office Perfomance and Innovation Unit, *Reaching Out: The Role of Central Government at Regional and Local Level* recommended (amongst other things) strengthened Government Offices for the Regions with clearer accountability for cross-cutting issues and 'Strengthened Ministerial and Whitehall co-ordination of policy initiatives and of Government Offices.' (See Executive Summary).
4 The best value pilot programme is referred to in Chapter 1.
5 This appeared on an earlier report on this initiative on Oldham MBC's Website. At the time of writing, an October 1999 'Progress Report on the Implementation of Best Value

With this initiative the public has a single access point for all seven services through the Service Co-ordination Team. Staff for the team:

> '... have been drawn from existing Departments' front office sections and in addition to handling service requests they are empowered to take them to a satisfactory conclusion. They will thus act as agents for local residents and ensure they receive an appropriate service. Initial staff training has been undertaken on the various pilot services and from the public launch date enquiries for the range of services have been able to be handled. A "can do" team working approach has been adopted which is supported by a real commitment to progressing customer requirements'.

Oldham MBC's 'Progress Report on the Implementation of Best Value Pilot Project'[1] is an honest report about best value in the real world, where staffing shortages and staff sickness are part of the environment to be addressed with practical solutions. The project is developing, with (amongst other things) a pilot 'call-centre' approach and customer survey and monitoring exercises. For example:

> 'A monthly customer follow up exercise ... where a randomly selected 5% sample of customers are contacted and asked their views on whether their request has been effectively resolved and their level of satisfaction is also being monitored'.

There are many more examples including the North Yorkshire Audit Partnership between Ryedale District Council, Scarborough Borough Council and Selby District Council. This provides for a consortium approach to the provision of internal audit services and involves 'joint arrangements for client services for the procurement, monitoring and performance measurement of the Internal Audit Services.'[2] The Partnership became operational on 1 February 1999.

4.8 The Law Society's *Gazette* on 20 October 1999 highlighted 'an ambitious scheme' being developed by the East Riding of Yorkshire Council's Community Advice and Legal Services Partnership. The idea is to bring legal advice services 'to the heart of remote rural communities' and the scheme covers 312,000 people over 1,000 square miles. According to the *Gazette* the partnership, which started up in 1997 and includes local Citizens' Advice Bureaux and the Humberside Police, 'already has council-funded drop-in "customer service centres" in ten urban centres, providing basic legal advice to residents'. These are (at the time of the report) receiving 390,000 enquiries from the public annually, which is a 30 per cent increase per year since the scheme commenced. The next step is 'to develop a network of electronic kiosks giving live access to trained advisers using video conferencing links. These would be booths similar in size to telephone boxes, possibly located in supermarkets'. This is just the sort of capacity-building community scheme which best value seeks to facilitate.

Pilot Project' prepared for the Authority's elected members can be found at: http://www.oldham.gov.uk/best_value/progress.htm.

1   At the time of writing, can be found at: http://www.oldham.gov.uk/best_value/progress.htm.

2   Geoffrey Filkin, *Achieving Best Value* (New Local Government Network, 1999).

4.9 Not surprisingly, therefore, the Guidance[1] provides that the review programme 'should be built around a mix of service specific and cross-cutting Reviews'. The Government acknowledges that service specific reviews 'can provide focus and clear accountability, and provided they are sufficiently ambitious and on a large enough scale, are likely to ensure that authorities make early improvements in efficiency and service quality'.[2] But on the other hand, 'cross-cutting Reviews, which are based on or around clear and recognisable themes or issues and which reflect strategic choices with other partners, are more likely to make a real and lasting difference locally'. Consequently, authorities which are proposing only a service specific review programme will have to 'explain why they have passed over the potential benefits of tackling at least one cross-cutting issue in each year of the Review cycle'.[3]

But in any event, 'it is important that Reviews are completed to a rigorous timetable, and structured and approached in a way that maximises the potential for innovation. For example, authorities might look at investment and service requirements together, and should recognise the importance of support services to effective front-line performance'.[4]

There will, however, be various other factors which authorities will need to take into account when structuring their review programme. These include:

- important legislative changes or national policy which 'could set a clear agenda for a particular service or group of services, as did legislation and policy on crime prevention';
- themed reviews, eg partnership, customer care, integrated service delivery or 'a particular social group such as the elderly';
- where appropriate, 'access to services in rural areas, or in specific neighbourhoods';
- in the need to release 'significant resources for specific new priorities'.[5]

In determining 'the appropriate mix of service and cross-cutting Reviews, authorities will need to balance the different resource implications and, regardless of the mix adopted, all Reviews can and should be demanding in terms of targets set for future performance'.[6]

4.10 Finally, *Joining it up locally – National Strategy for Neighbourhood Renewal* (Report of Policy Action Team 17[7]) is worth consideration. Hilary Armstrong, Local Government Minister, points out in her Foreword that this report sets out a 'useful analysis of wny local delivery has often not been joined up in the past; highlights how much is already going on to tackle social exclusion at local level,

---

1 At para 21.
2 Ibid.
3 Ibid.
4 Ibid. Whilst support services may not impact *directly* upon the public, they are often a vital component of front-line services and can consequently have a significant effect, in both cost and quality, on the public consumer of authority services and functions. Support services will therefore need to be reviewed, not only as a 'stand-alone' business unit, but also as part of the review programme for the substantive services.
5 DETR Circular 10/99, para 22.
6 Ibid.
7 DETR, April 2000.

that can be built on; and sets out the relevance of local government reform including community planning and best value.' She indicates that the report 'also rightly records some of the challenges that need to be met to join things up locally – involving communities properly; building real and lasting co-operation between levels of Government; setting targets but avoiding perverse effects; improving skills and changing cultures; and building owner-ship of the neighbourhood renewal vision throughout communities and service providers.' The Minister also refers to 'the key idea of "local strategic partnerships", bringing together local authorities and other service providers, business, voluntary sector and communities to develop more co-ordinated approaches to the challenges they all face.'[1]

LOCAL GOVERNMENT ACT 1999, s 5(4) AND THE 4Cs

4.11 As mentioned above[2] the 4Cs expect authorities to:

- **challenge** why, how and by whom a service is being provided;
- secure **comparison** with the performance of others across a range of relevant indicators, taking into account the views of both service users and potential suppliers;
- **consult** local taxpayers, service users, partners and the wider business community in the setting of new performance targets;
- use fair and open **competition** wherever practicable as a means of securing efficient and effective services.[3]

These principles will form an integral part of best value reviews, the contents of which (under s 5(4) of the 1999 Act) the Secretary of State has power to regulate closely.[4] The Guidance sensibly points out[5] that the experience of authorities which have already used the 4Cs in service reviews and other planning processes suggests that 'the 4Cs should be viewed not as a linear process but as interactive elements, each essential for a penetrating and comprehensive Review'. But, whatever the review focus, there will be common statutory considerations applying to the way in which the review process is to be conducted. These arise from s 5(4) of the LGA 1999[6] and also from the Local Government (Best Value) Performance Plans and Reviews Order 1999[7] referred to above.

4.12 Article 6(1) of the Plans and Reviews Order provides that in conducting a best value review, an authority must:

---

1   This document can be viewed on: http://www.local-regions.detr.gov.uk/pat17/pdf/ jiul17.pdf.
2   See, for example, Chapter 1.
3   See para 16 of DETR Circular 10/99.
4   As noted above and below in this chapter, the Secretary of State has power by order under s 5(4) of the LGA 1999 to 'specify matters which an authority must include in a review of a function under this section'. He has exercised these powers in the Local Government (Best Value) Performance Plans and Reviews Order 1999, SI 1999/3251.
5   At para 24.
6   See above.
7   SI 1999/3251 (the Plans and Reviews Order).

'(a)   consider whether it should be exercising the function;

(b)   consider the level at which, and the way in which, it should be exercising the function;

(c)   consider its objectives in relation to the exercise of the function;

(d)   assess its performance in exercising the function by reference to any best value performance indicator specified for the function;

(e)   assess the competitiveness of its performance in exercising the function by reference to the exercise of the same function, or similar functions, by other best value authorities and by commercial and other businesses, including organisations in the voluntary sector;

(f)   consult other best value authorities, commercial and other businesses, including organisations in the voluntary sector, about the exercise of the function;

(g)   assess its success in meeting any best value performance standard which applies in relation to the function;

(h)   assess its progress towards meeting any relevant best value performance standard which has been specified but which does not yet apply;

(i)   assess its progress towards meeting any relevant best value performance target'.

Section 5(4) of the LGA 1999 and art 6(1) of the Plans and Reviews Order make up the engine which drives the review process; and at its core are the 4Cs. Bearing in mind its importance, the requirements of art 6(1) will now be looked at more closely in relation to the 4Cs.

Challenge

4.13   *In conducting a best value review an authority shall consider: (a) whether it should be exercising the function; (b) the level at which, and the way in which, it should be exercising the function; (c) its objectives in relation to the exercise of the function.*[1]

These focus the attention of the authority, its members and managers upon present service practice and the changes that are necessary to achieve a best value outcome. As the first 'C' of the 4Cs (challenge) this is one of the most testing. Certainly it is difficult, if not impossible, for service managers to perform (or be perceived as performing) this objectively without the benefit of external input both from key stakeholder representatives and from sources outside the authority. A robust (yet constructive) review process involving external stakeholders should remove any unsafe assumptions.

At the heart of the challenge stage is the need for an earthquake in respect of complacent orthodoxy. Adherence to old ways against the requirements of reason and circumstance gives no licence for the present and no passport to the future. Practices which were once a dynamic reaction to a new environment can long have outlived their usefulness and have become empty rituals.

4.14   Sir John Harvey-Jones, the famous business guru and former chairman of ICI is a passionate advocate of change. Here are some of his thoughts in this area, which can open some long-locked doors[2]:

---

1   Article 6(1)(a), (b) and (c) of the Local Government (Best Value) Performance Plans and Reviews Order 1999, SI 1999/3251.

2   See Sir John Harvey-Jones, *Making it Happen; Reflections on Leadership* (1988), Chap 5, 'All Change'.

- 'Management is about change, and maintaining a high rate of change.'
- 'A feature of the Victorian era was a delight in the new and a willingness to see any amount of social upheaval based on economic change.'
- 'If we do not change the inexorable forces of economics and shifts in the external world will force change upon us.'
- 'The reality of life is that while staying put is without doubt the most comfortable for the short haul, it is in fact the highest risk strategy of all.'
- 'The task of leadership is really to make the status quo more dangerous than launching into the unknown.'

But for best value authorities, there is no choice. At strategic level, all activities and functions need to be rigorously reviewed with a view to establishing in consultation with relevant stakeholders what is likely to deliver a best value outcome.[1] It may be that some operations are no longer appropriate.

For example, a best value review in 1998 brought North Somerset District Council to the conclusion that it needed to sell off its substantial Contract Services Department after significant losses. In keeping with the staff-engagement principles of best value, LGCnet[2] reported[3] that the 'trade unions and staff are fully co-operating with the new arrangements in order to turn the situation around'.

In 1998 the London Borough Council of Newham was considering the feasibility of both a partnership with a private sector provider and the establishment of a trust to run the leisure management service. After Newham's in-house Leisure Service provider had been awarded the work through a CCT[4] process, Newham considered that it was worth 'exploring whether a more constructive partnership could be formed outside the restrictive CCT regime with a private sector provider to achieve improvements in both service quality and value for money'.[5]

4.15 As indicated above, it is vital to involve stakeholders[6] (external and internal) in the review. For they (together with representatives of private sector and other bodies from outside the authority) will be able to provide the necessary objective focus to inform the key decision as to whether the particular function should be exercised by the authority at all. As the Government points out:[7]

> 'Without the element of **challenge** there can be no effective Review: it is the key to significant improvements in performance and without it authorities are unlikely to reach the targets which the Government will set for authorities, and those which are set locally. Challenging why and how a service is provided requires a fundamental rethink, asking basic questions about the needs that each service is intended to address and the method of procurement that is used. Challenge is

---

1   Ie (amongst other things) one which will yield continuous improvement in the exercise of functions having regard to a combination of economy, efficiency and effectiveness per s 3 of the LGA 1999 and DETR Circular 10/99.
2   The internet service of the *Local Government Chronicle*.
3   On 18 June 1998.
4   Compulsory Competitive Tendering – see Chapter 1.
5   Reported on the website of the London Borough of Newham.
6   Those with a financial, consumer or other stake in a service.
7   In para 25 of DETR Circular 10/99.

therefore intrinsically tied up with the competition element as well as those of comparison and consultation'.

The Government will expect authorities to be able to produce 'evidence that they have considered the underlying rationale for the service(s) under review and the alternative ways in which it might be provided'.[1] The potential for 'new technology' in service provision should be explored and the Guidance also advises authorities to develop the ability to 'analyse the effects of demographic, social and economic changes on local service needs'.[2] And whilst the past 'can provide useful lessons as to what works and does not work it will usually point to incremental rather than fundamental change' and 'that may be insufficient to secure the step-change in performance that the Government expects from reviews and which local people may be seeking'.[3] Therefore, in the Government's view 'it is critical that authorities look forwards and outwards in reviewing their services: forwards to identify the significant changes in what local people want from their authority; outwards to identify the alternative ways in which those demands can be met and by whom'.[4] Success in identifying these factors results from 'a close engagement with the community – often through and driven by locally elected members – and with the market – principally through a capacity for market analysis and dialogue with the private and voluntary sectors, as well as with other local authorities'.[5]

4.16   The three elements of **challenge** in s 5(4)(a), (b) and (c) (and therefore in art 6(1)(a), (b) and (c)[6] – see above) will need to be conducted strategically in the authority in the light of performance data, stakeholder feedback and the Authority's strategic plan. For instance, a best value outcome may be very different from past service patterns and the review may point to the need for a joined-up solution. An example from the best value pilot[7] programme was given by the DETR in its 9 April 1999 letter to various chief executives of English local authorities:

> 'By developing one stop shops, one authority has improved service response times and staff have shown increased levels of job satisfaction. Integration of the authority's housing and building services cut repair and maintenance response times from 18 days to 3 days and street lighting response times for repairs have improved from 5 to 3 days. Whilst in the worst cases, before the pilots, street repairs were taking up to a year, the authority's new target for street repairs is now 2 weeks, with an average of 1 week'.

The Government considers that if reviews are to realise their potential to 'make a real difference on the ground' then they will need to:[8]

---

1   In para 25 of DETR Circular 10/99, para 26.
2   Ibid.
3   Ibid.
4   Ibid.
5   Ibid, para 27, which indicates that within DETR Circular 10/99, guidance 'on these matters is in paragraphs 33–35 on consultation and paragraphs 36–48 on competition'.
6   Local Government (Best Value) Performance Plans and Reviews Order 1999, SI 1999/3251.
7   See Chapter 1.
8   See DETR Circular 10/99, para 17.

'– **take a sufficiently long-term perspective**. Reviews will be unlikely to set targets that reflect best value unless they look far enough ahead to anticipate prospective changes in the demand for services and the means by which such services might be delivered. As far as possible, sufficient flexibility should be built into all delivery arrangements, particularly those with a term in excess of 3 years, to ensure that there are measures to secure continuous improvement and innovation and which can be adapted to meet changing local and national priorities. This flexibility must be balanced against a reasonable degree of certainty over the length of any contract to allow start-up costs, risk and investment to be managed at sensible cost.

– **involve elected members**. Elected members – whether with executive or non-executive roles once the provisions in the Local Government Bill 1999 are in force – have a key responsibility to ensure that Reviews reflect from the start the strategic objectives and corporate priorities of the authority and focus on the perspective of actual and potential service users, including those that are typically hard-to-reach. Elected members will also need to monitor action plans following the completion of Reviews.

– **seek advice from outside the authority**. Authorities with a track record of working with partners in the public, voluntary or private sectors recognise the benefits of involving them in the review process as an additional source of advice or as a sounding board for new ideas. Other external advice can be tapped by setting up expert panels or forums, perhaps involving service users (or potential service users). And the same principle can be applied through involving members and officers who are not directly involved in the particular service or group of services being reviewed.

– **involve those currently delivering services**. This applies to all employees, but particularly to frontline staff whose experience of face-to-face contact with the public and service users can bring an important perspective as to how a service is perceived and valued, and how it can be improved. Their support is critical to successful implementation.

– **question existing commitments**. Where authorities are committed to longer-term contracts, there are usually provisions that enable improvements to be made in agreement with the parties concerned. Where this is not the case, authorities should still consider the scope for changes – perhaps by measures complementing the contract – and where these are justified cost any such adjustments as part of their appraisal of service delivery options.

– **engage with users and potential users of services**. A customer focus to Reviews is essential. It is important that authorities seek out the views of all potential users, especially those who have traditionally been under-represented. Those that fail to engage local people fully from the outset – including hard-to-reach groups – will carry little conviction when it comes to explaining decisions on service targets and selected providers, and invariably overlook real opportunities to bring about lasting change.

– **address equity considerations**. Reviews should consider the way in which services impact on all sections of the community, including minority groups, and set targets to redress disparities in the provision of services to those that are socially, economically or geographically disadvantaged. Issues of social exclusion and isolation will be important ones for many authorities, and a service cannot be effective under best value unless it addresses equity considerations. Reviews should explicitly consider whether the authority complies with the relevant legislation.[1]

---

1   Local Agenda 21. This refers to the contents of Chapter 28 of Agenda 21 – a worldwide plan for sustainable development into the 21st Century which was produced by the United

– **give effect to the principles of sustainable development.** New performance targets generated by Reviews need to reflect the principles of sustainable development, set out in *A better quality of life – a strategy for sustainable development for the UK* (May 1999), and summarised in *The Government's sustainable development strategy: What does it mean for local authorities?* published in July [1999]. Where authorities have LA21[a] and any community strategies in place, Reviews will provide an opportunity to give such principles practical effect through the setting of consistent performance targets.

[a] Local authority service provision is covered by the Sex Discrimination Act 1975, the Race Relations Act 1976 and the Disability Discrimination Act 1995 which prohibit direct and indirect discrimination in the provision of services. Local authorities have a duty under section 71 of the Race Relations Act to make appropriate arrangements with a view to securing that their various functions are carried out with due regard to the need to eliminate unlawful racial discrimination and to promote equality of opportunity, and good relations, between persons of different racial groups.'[1]

4.17 Another example of the capacity of challenge to catalyse positive change was highlighted by Geoffrey Filkin in *Starting to Modernise, Achieving Best Value.*[2] An extract from the case study[3] indicates that:

'Hertfordshire County Council audited public contacts with the authority and found that most services had similar process characteristics – giving information, handling enquiries, managing cases, handling applications etc.

They found that a large number of contacts did not get through, or tied up a disproportionate amount of staff time or were passed round the system to find the right person.

Their MORI research found that the public wanted to access a single information point for all local services.

The Gateway will allow the public to contact the Council either by telephone on a single number or through the internet and a web site or in person through a variety of public access points including in libraries and supermarkets.'

4.18 With regard to sustainable development and the contribution of integrated waste management, in 1999 the Government issued *A Way with Waste*

Nations Conference on Environment and Development (*The Earth Summit*) which took place in Rio de Janeiro, Brazil in June 1992. Sustainable development is generally defined as 'economic and social development that meets the needs of the current generation without undermining the ability of future generations to meet their own needs'. This definition was formulated in 1987 by the World Commission on Environment and Development (known as the Brundtland Commission from its Chairperson, Gro Harlem Brundtland, then Norwegian Prime Minister). The Government's Sustainable Development Strategy, *A Better Quality of Life – A Strategy for Sustainable Development for the UK*, was launched by John Prescott, Deputy Prime Minister, on 17 May 1999. It indicated the four main aims of the Strategy, namely: social progress which meets the needs of everyone; effective protection of the environment; prudent use of natural resources; maintenance of high and stable levels of economic growth and employment. Chapter 28 of Agenda 21 indicated (at para 28.1) that: 'Because so many of the problems and solutions being addressed by Agenda 21 have their roots in local activities, the participation and cooperation of local authorities will be a determining factor in fulfilling its objectives.' And it recommended (at para 28.3) that 'Each local authority should enter into a dialogue with its citizens, local organizations and private enterprises and adopt "a local Agenda 21".' Tony Blair, speaking at the UN General Assembly on 23 June 1997, said that 'all local authorities in the United Kingdom must adopt local Agenda 21 strategies by the year 2000'.

1 DETR Circular, 10/99, para 17.
2 New Local Government Network, 1999.
3 At p 31.

– A draft waste strategy for England and Wales.[1] This (amongst other things) indicates that in addition to 'their statutory responsibilities for waste collection, waste disposal and waste planning … local authorities also have an important role to play in encouraging their local communities to practice sustainable waste management'.[2] And 'the Government is actively encouraging waste disposal and waste collection authorities to jointly prepare municipal waste management strategies' so as 'to develop a strategic framework for the management of municipal waste'.[3] Consequently, authorities will 'set out, particularly in relation to contract specification, policies and proposals for the various collection, treatment and disposal options (ie waste minimisation, reuse, recycling, composting, other forms of recovery and landfill), taking into account sustainability and local circumstances, with the aim of maximising environmental benefits, whilst at the same time minimising overall economic costs, and they will explain how these different practices can be developed in an integrated way'.[4] In preparing municipal waste management strategies, authorities should consult with those having a legitimate interest, including 'the waste management industry, other (tiers of) local authorities, voluntary groups' and 'other relevant waste-generating sectors'.[5]

4.19 Some pointers to **challenge** (with accompanying auditable evidence) might include consideration of the following.

– What is the service for and what are its key objectives?
– To what extent are these objectives met?
– How do the service objectives deliver service outputs and add corporate and community value?
– What other ways are there of meeting the Council's needs in the service areas in question?
– The importance of the service to the provision of other authority functions.
– Whether each aspect of the service is being provided at times and locations suitable to those who need them.
– The effectiveness of operational processes underpinning service delivery.
– Whether these processes are being properly complied with across the operation in question.
– Whether any aspect of the service could be delivered more economically.
– To what extent service quality can be improved in each of the key activities undertaken.
– Are there any parts of the service which attract general corporate and individual user esteem?
– The impact of equal opportunities in service delivery.
– The extent to which departmental practice and procedure add value to effective service outputs.
– The effectiveness of 'continuous improvement' processes and procedures.

---

1   DETR, 1999.
2   *A Way with Waste – A draft waste strategy for England and Wales*, Part Two, para 5.62.
3   Ibid, para 5.66.
4   Ibid.
5   Ibid, para 5.67.

Further ideas may be gained from the Best Value Healthcheck[1] which, although it focuses upon the legal function, can be adapted to be of wide applicability.

So the **challenge** stage will require authorities first to consider whether they should be exercising the function at all[2] and if the answer is affirmative the level at which and the way in which the function under review *should* be exercised.[3] This points to a radical and critical re-examination. As a further focus upon strategic direction to ensure that the carrying out of all functions is part of a coherent corporate strategy, art 6(1)(c) of the Plans and Reviews Order and s 5(4)(c) of the LGA 1999 require authorities to consider their *objectives* in relation to the exercise of the function in question. Challenge will therefore be a challenging process requiring disciplined analysis, cool and objective consideration and considerable courage to face up to conclusions which may not be palatable. Managing to fail can mean fitting management conclusions to personal predilections. Managing to succeed is more testing. This requires using the whole range of management skills to do what is necessary to achieve a successful outcome; and, for best value authorities, this means providing a best value service.

Consultation about Exercise of Functions

4.20 *(f) to consult other best value authorities, commercial and other businesses, including organisations in the voluntary sector,*[4] *about the exercise of the function*

In addition to the basic duty of consultation in s 3(2), (3) and (4) (considered in Chapter 2 above[5]), art 6(1)(f) of the Plans and Reviews Order[6] requires authorities to consult other best value authorities, commercial and other businesses including organisations in the voluntary sector, about the exercise of their functions. As to the interface between the duty in s 3 and the potential duty in s 5(4)(f), the Government regards these as 'complementary provisions which reflect the importance the Government attaches to the place of the citizen – as user and taxpayer – in best value, and to the role of the private and voluntary sectors in contributing to the overall health of the local community'.[7] This adds further conceptual layers to benchmarking comparisons and can, amongst other things, encompass:

–   consideration of new 'grass roots' or business ideas for achieving service outcomes;
–   discussions as to potential partnerships;

---

1   See below and Appendix 7. The Healthcheck was produced through Pinsent Curtis.
2   Article 6(1)(a) of the Plans and Reviews Order, SI 1999/3251 and s 5(4)(a) of the LGA 1999.
3   LGA 1999, s 5(4)(b) and art 6(1)(b) of the Plans and Reviews Order.
4   The words in bold appear in art 6(1)(f) of the Plans and Reviews Order but not in s 5(4)(f) of the LGA 1999. Section 5(4) of the 1999 Act details the matters in (a) to (i) indicatively since the Secretary of State is not restricted to these matters in specifying the factors to be included in a functional review.
5   The section on 'Consultation' in Chapter 2 should be read in conjunction with this section.
6   SI 1999/3251.
7   DETR Circular 10/99, para 33.

- adding value to comparison by involving external persons or organisations in the formal or informal service review;
- consideration of how the market operates (see below) as part of a search for new best value solutions.

4.21 The Audit Commission has indicated that:[1]

'– authorities need to get a cross-section of people involved, not just narrow, self-selecting groups
– consultees often disagree, so interpreting the results can be tricky
– what consultees say must be balanced with other factors that affect decisions, such as resources and statutory requirements
– direct community consultation must be squared with members' decision-making role
– a majority of authorities do not consistently use consultation results to inform decisions
– the quality of individual consultation exercises is patchy
– few authorities evaluate their consultation programmes.'

However, in the Commission's view, innovative authorities are responding to the challenge by:

'– linking consultation to the decisions that members need to take
– taking a strategic approach to planning consultation programmes, often jointly with partners
– designing and carrying out individual consultation exercises to high standards
– involving all sections of the community
– reporting the results to members so that consultation can directly inform policies and decisions
– letting consultees know how their contribution has influenced policies and services.'

The key is a receptive approach at both officer and member levels, 'putting the needs of service users uppermost' and 'adopting an open mind as to how a service might be provided and by whom, and by being prepared to seek out and listen to the views of others'.[2] Creative, strategic and joined-up interaction will add real value if approached in the right spirit.

Comparison and Competition

4.22 *(d) Authority to assess its performance in exercising the function by reference to any relevant performance indicator specified by the Secretary of State or set locally; (g) to assess its success in meeting any performance standard which applies in relation to the function; (h) to assess its progress towards meeting any relevant performance standard which has been specified but which does not yet apply; (i) to assess its progress towards meeting any relevant performance target set under subsection (6)(b);[3] (e) Authority to assess the competitiveness of its performance in exercising the function by reference to the exercise of*

---

1 *Listen up! Effective Community Consultation* – see Briefing Summary. The full Management Paper: of the same title (ISBN 1 86240 196 9) is available from Audit Commission Publications tel: 0800 502030.
2 DETR Circular 10/99, para 38.
3 Authority may be required 'to consider the level at which and the way in which it should be exercising the function': LGA 1999, s 5(4)(b).

the same function, or similar functions, by other best value authorities and by commercial and other businesses.

As indicated, this cluster encompasses the **comparison** and **competitiveness** stages of the 4Cs.

Comparison

4.23 The Government points out that 'Informed comparison is the basis of performance management, and is also critical to an effective Review'.[1] 'Informed comparison' presumably indicates that the process should have a clear objective rather than constituting a series of diffuse and potentially unstructured comparison exercises. Performance indicators, standards and targets have been considered in Chapter 3. As indicated, these are useful tools to enable managers to test the health of the operation in its various aspects and to underpin best value performance. They will also be the warning lights to show which parts of the operation are not functioning as they should against best value criteria. But in addition, national performance measures, bearing in mind their uniformity, will also provide a strong basis for comparison and 'will enable a rounded view to be taken'.[2] The Government advises that in the first year of best value 'in particular, authorities will need to take a sensible and realistic view as to ... [the comparative data] ... which is readily available, and **concentrate on putting in place the mechanisms that will build comparison into their normal performance management arrangements**'[3] (emphasis added).

Authorities 'should aim to compare their current and prospective performance against other public sector bodies, and those in the private and voluntary sectors'.[4] But this will 'rarely be a process of exact comparison, rather the intelligent exploration of how analogous services or elements of such services perform'.[5] This will need 'to be sufficient to enable authorities to identify the significant performance differences and the reasons for them, and thus the extent to which improvements are needed over the review period.'[6] In addition to the national performance measures published in December 1999 (and referred to above), authorities 'may also wish to use for comparative purposes any indicators which they have developed, for example with neighbouring authorities or similar types of authority'.[7]

'Comparison with other authorities will be necessary to set:

- quality targets that are, as a minimum, consistent with the performance of the top 25% of all authorities
- cost and efficiency targets over 5 years that, as a minimum, are consistent with the performance of the top 25% of authorities of the type to which they belong and which are consistent with the overall target of 2% p.a. efficiency improvement set for local government spending as a whole.'[8]

---

1   DETR Circular 10/99, para 28.
2   Ibid, para 29.
3   Ibid, para 28.
4   Ibid, para 29.
5   Ibid.
6   Ibid.
7   Ibid.
8   Ibid.

In this connection, 'benchmarking clubs' – meetings of representatives of a participating group of authorities – have become popular. Provided there is clarity of objectives and process, discipline and focus, these can be healthy in injecting and generating new ideas and challenging existing orthodoxies. They can also provide a basis for making resource/output comparisons. But inter-authority benchmarking will not be sufficient in itself. Focused networks with the private and voluntary sectors and best value partnerships are important to add strength and depth to the comparison process.

4.24 Significantly, in the nature of the outcome focus of best value, the Government advises that as 'far as possible comparisons should be made on the basis of outcomes'.[1] However, the Government acknowledges that a detailed input/output comparison will be necessary to 'assess the scope for greater efficiency consistent with the Government's overall target of 2% p.a. efficiency improvements for local government as a whole'.[2] It does not follow, however, that all reviews are to yield merely 2% improvement per annum. In some cases reviews will point to greater potential for improved efficiency and in others less so. There will be instances where 'improvements will be difficult to quantify precisely'.[3]

Positively for public local services, the Government indicates that it is not seeking through efficiency savings to reduce the overall cash available to local government since it is committed to ensuring 'that resources freed up through greater efficiency are made available to meet national and locally agreed priorities'.[4] Whilst the Government supports 'selective and informed' process benchmarking to assist in delivering 'better performance and outcomes' it will:

> '... look to evidence of a wider approach from authorities as part of the Review process, and will encourage other public sector bodies and those in the private and voluntary sectors to share and debate performance information more widely'.[5]

4.25 In this context recognised quality systems are acknowledged as having 'an important role to play through the contribution each can make to securing effective comparison and continuous service improvements'.[6] These are scheduled at Annex C to the Guidance[7] which indicates that whilst such schemes will be insufficient in themselves to deliver best value they can: 'support the necessary cultural changes required, ensure staff and members are fully involved, and create a commitment to quality and efficiency which fosters a determination to make a difference, which is the hallmark of best value'.[8]

There are, of course, other quality systems for specific types of service. A good example (for legal services) is the Law Society's Practice Management Standards Certification Scheme (LEXCEL) which (although at the time of

---

1   DETR Circular 10/99, para 30.
2   Ibid.
3   Ibid.
4   Ibid.
5   Ibid, para 31.
6   Ibid, para 32.
7   Ibid.
8   Ibid, para 32.

writing it is being revised and updated[1]) provides a comprehensive approach to the laying of 'quality foundations' upon which best value can be built. Local authority legal departments have led the way in this area.[2]

The Government indicates that although the quality schemes listed in Annex C 'serve different purposes, they should be considered as complementary'.[3]

> 'A report on how the different schemes can work together in the public sector to enhance their overall impact is to be issued by the end of the year by the Modernising Government Quality Schemes Task Force. The Government will at the same time publish a guide, following consultation with local government and the different scheme promoters, to help authorities assess how each scheme might assist in preparing for and achieving best value.'[4]

4.26 The Report and Guidance were issued in early 2000.[5] As the Cabinet Office Press Release[6] points out, in addition to giving practical advice on how such schemes can support best value, the guide also:

> 'spreads best practice through case studies such as:
>
> – The Property Management Services of Cambridge County Council found significant benefits from using the Excellence Model, Charter Mark and Investors in People during its early Best Value review. In particular, they achieved a 25% reduction in design costs and a 22% improvement in meeting target dates.
> – Portsmouth City Council have integrated the Excellence Model into its framework for Best Value performance reviews. In the initial reviews carried out so far, staff have been very enthusiastic about the process. The Council also use the Excellence Model to benchmark performance with similar local authorities.
> – Wycombe District Council, having brought together various quality initiatives (like Charter Mark) in its Quality Improvement Programme, found this greatly helped it to address Best Value. They see many benefits from the Programme, including a noticeable boost to staff morale and an independent view of their services from external assessors.'

The Quality Schemes Task Force in conjunction with the DETR and the Improvement and Development Agency also produced in February 2000 a *Guide to Quality Schemes and Best Value*.[7] The aim of the guide is set out in a box on its own page following the Ministerial Foreword.[8] It:

> 'describes the five main quality schemes used by local authorities (Charter Mark, the Excellence Model, Investors in People, ISO 9000 and the Local Government Improvement Programme), how they fit together and what and how you gain

---

1   The author is a member of the LEXCEL Revisions Task Force.
2   For example, amongst others, Sunderland City Council; Brighton and Hove Council; City and Council of Swansea; and Guildford Borough Council.
3   DETR Circular 10/99, para 32.
4   Ibid.
5   Quality Schemes Taskforce Report and Guidance, available from the Cabinet Office (Geoff Sadler, gsadler@cabinet-office.gov.uk).
6   17 February 2000 (see http://www.cabinet-office.gov.uk/index/news.htm).
7   This document can be viewed at: http://www.cabinet-office.gov.uk/servicefirst/2000/taskforce/bestvalue.pdf.
8   This is signed by Hilary Armstrong, Minister for Local Government and the Regions and Ian McCartney, Minister of State at the Cabinet Office.

benefit from them. But, above all, the guide explains **how they relate to Best Value; and what role they play in helping to achieve Best Value**.'

Figure 1 on page 12 of the document 'shows, in simplified form, the critical overlaps between the schemes', picturing 'the critical links between the enablers and results of the Excellence Model and the three other main schemes'.

Also useful in this area is the Best Practice Library on the Cabinet Office Website[1] which contains material on local authority services and quality schemes.

4.27 One approach which (amongst others) could be adopted at the comparison stage is a detailed examination of a key local authority corporate output. This might encompass a consideration of the entire actions and input needed to achieve the ultimate service 'product'. It could be considered on a quality, equality, process, people, customer interface, customer satisfaction, corporate and community value and cost basis against core Best Value principles. This analysis would in itself provide pointers to real improvements. However, it would also provide comparables for benchmarking against other public or private sector organisations. But as always, the key is that continuous improvement and other core objectives are kept firmly in view throughout all comparison processes and that the exercise is not merely activity to disguise inactivity.

An example of comparison was reported by LGCnet.[2] Surrey and Kent County Councils are engaging in a detailed 'peer review'. Both authorities have visited each other and will report on the other's strengths and weaknesses and opportunities for improvement. Peer review can be powerful in that it is constructive and non-threatening but gives ample scope for challenging existing orthodoxies and opening doors for improvement. It also assists with cultural change since influential existing staff (who will often be the keepers of the cultural tradition) are more likely to be swayed by external peer 'pressure' than prescription from Government or their own authority's management; and of course the 'peer group review' concept is at the heart of the Local Government Improvement and Development Agency approach (see below).

4.28 A flavour of things to come and the potential news power of comparative data was a feature in the *Independent on Sunday* on 11 July 1999[3] concerning the best area for elderly people to live. This considered data from Audit Commission performance indicators 1997/98 and pointed out that:

> 'Crucial indicators are council help for elderly people living at home, home help and meals on wheels provision, and the number and quality of residential places for those who can no longer look after themselves. And, for people looking after aged parents, the availability of council respite care. North Lincolnshire spends £83.30 for every resident aged over 65. Rutland, bottom of the league, managed £56.10.
>
> According to the survey, the Top 20 authorities are: North Lincolnshire; Newham; Salford; Sunderland; Rotherham; Bradford; North Tyneside; South Tyneside;

---

1   See http://www.cabinet-office.gov.uk/servicefirst/index/library.htm.
2   The internet service of the *Local Government Chronicle*, on 20 October 1999.
3   Page 8. The *Independent on Sunday* story was pointed out on LGCnet.

Rochdale, Durham (joint ninth); Knowsley; Calderdale Wigan; Wolverhampton; Camden; Gateshead; Dudley; Wandsworth; Luton; and Tameside ... and the Bottom 20, in descending order: Hampshire; Trafford; Bournemouth; York; Buckinghamshire; Havering; Bath and North East Somerset; Hillingdon; Poole; Surrey; Cambridgeshire; Berkshire; Hertfordshire; Harrow; Southampton; North Yorkshire; South Gloucestershire; Essex; Dorset; and Rutland.'[1]

Whatever individual authorities may say about the validity of popular conclusions to be drawn from such data, performance indicators are clearly a powerful force on public opinion. The suite of national indicators published in December 1999[2] will provide much more directly comparable data upon which the public will (no doubt assisted by the media) make their judgments. If the public, as market, wields devastating power over business, the power of awakened local democracy is likely to have a similar effect upon local government. And in an increasingly competitive public sector world, this may well impact upon the distribution of central government resources locally. This will be even more resonant in respect of locally specified indicators since they will represent performance measures set by authorities themselves. Failure or shortfall in these areas will echo loudly on the streets and in the local (and where sufficiently newsworthy, the national) press.

Competitiveness

4.29 This remains a sensitive subject. The first two Cs of CCT[3] (the *Compulsory Competitive* part of the Tendering) were fiercely unpopular, particularly with local authorities but also with many external contractors (see Chapter 1). A great number of local authorities bitterly resented what they perceived as unfair Government interference with their local democratic decisions, underpinned by draconian central powers. Moreover, many contractors were disenchanted at being caught in the cold war paper 'crossfire' between central and local government, the latter of which as a sector did not yield the expected commercial inroads. For its part the Government was increasingly irritated by what it saw as the recalcitrance of local government. It reacted by increasingly tightening the CCT rules as central–local relations became ever more cool.[4]

---

1   As reported in LGCnet, 12 July 1999 – see *Scunthorpe: The Best Place to Grow Old.*
2   *Best Value and Audit Commission Performance Indicators for 2000/2001.*
3   As indicated in Chapter 1, Compulsory Competitive Tendering (CCT) refers to previous obligations in Part III of the Local Government, Planning and Land Act 1980 (the 1980 Act) and Part I of the Local Government Act 1988 (the 1988 Act) which required local and certain other public authorities to subject certain work to competitive tender as prescribed before they undertook it in-house. These with related provisions were repealed on 2 January 2000: see LGA 1999, s 21.
4   As a general indicator of the tenor of central/local relations, Lord Hunt had chaired a House of Lords Ad Hoc Select Committee into relations between central and local government which had produced a report: *Rebuilding Trust.* The Government announced in its response to the report that it would not be accepting the Committee's recommendations to end routine capping, relax controls on self-financed expenditure and return business rates to local control. Speaking in Parliament on 18 November 1996, Lord Hunt said: 'Our recommendations may not be perfect, but I am bound to say it seems somewhat inconsistent, to say the least, to talk the language of rebuilding trust while refusing to make any concession at all on financial issues which are at the heart of the central/local relationship.' (LGCnet, 21 November 1996.)

The 30 July 1998 Local Government White Paper *Modern Local Government In Touch with the People* indicated the Government's essential approach on competition. This is that competition is viewed not as an end in itself 'but as a means of bringing about the continuous improvements that customers expect and best value demands'.[1] Competition will be designed 'to secure improvements in quality as well as in cost' and to be 'fair to all sides'.[2]

> 'The key strategic choice for authorities is whether to provide services directly themselves or to secure them through other means. The key test is which of the options is more likely to secure best value for local people. Services should not be delivered directly if other more efficient and effective means are available'.[3]

4.30   However, no doubt anxious to promote a more positive climate than that in cold war CCT, the Government in *Modern Local Government In Touch with the People*[4] presented competition options with a softer focus. It pointed out that the role of competition as an 'essential management tool' did not mean everything had to be subjected to tender. Competitiveness could be tested in various ways. For example, authorities could:[5]

– commission an independent benchmarking report so that it could restructure the in-house service to match the performance of the best private and public sector providers;
– provide a core service in-house and buy in top-up support from the private sector. This would enable comparisons to be made that could help improve in-house performance or result in more of the service being bought-in externally;
– contract out a service to the private sector after a competition between external bidders only;
– form a joint venture or partnership following a competition for an external partner;
– tender part of a service with an in-house team bidding against private sector and other local authority bidders, before deciding whether to provide the bulk of a service internally or externally;
– dispose or sell-off competitively a service and its assets to another provider.

The DETR Best Value Letter of 9 April 1999 indicated that 'best value will be achieved where authorities adopt an open mind as to how a service might be provided and by whom and actively seek to shape the form and type of competition that is needed to attain the standards of the best'.[6]

And earlier that year, on 23 January 1996, the House of Lords Committee heard from Scottish Office officials who said that, at their level, the relationship with the Convention of Scottish Local Authorities (COSLA) worked well. However, Lord Hunt, the Committee Chairman, said that COSLA had written saying that that partnership did not exist and that the two sides were like 'battleships firing at each other' (LGCnet, 24 January 1996, reporting from *The Herald*).

1   *Modern Local Government In Touch with the People*, para 7.23.
2   Ibid, para 7.27.
3   Ibid.
4   DETR, July 1998.
5   Ibid, para 7.29.
6   Paragraph 36 of the 9 April 1999 letter from DETR to various chief executives of English local authorities.

4.31   It is interesting that, whilst there is provision in Part I of the LGA 1999 to require authorities to assess the 'competitiveness' of their performance, there is no absolute statutory duty to subject services to competition.[1] Nevertheless, according to the Guidance,[2] the Government takes the view that 'fair and open **competition** will . . . most often be the best way of demonstrating that a function is being carried out competitively' and 'is expected to play an essential and enduring role in ensuring best value'. Consequently, 'Reviews will need to consider how this can best be achieved' which will not happen if 'authorities fail to approach competition positively, taking full account of the opportunities for innovation and genuine partnership which are available from working with others in the public, private and voluntary sectors'.[3]

The focus on competition has certainly hardened since the Local Government White Paper.[4] Whilst the Guidance has had some of its rougher edges sanded smooth, it still contains a strong current in favour of competition and a competitive approach to achieve a best value outcome. So the Government once again emphasises its view that 'the future for public service provision is one where there is real variety in the way services are delivered and genuine plurality among service providers'.[5] It opposes 'any single supplier dominating the provision of services either locally or nationally' since 'the public is not best served where this occurs'. Consequently, in the Government's view, 'local government, the trade unions and the private and voluntary sectors share a responsibility with Government itself' to bring about this variety and plurality.[6]

4.32   Bearing in mind the sensitivity of competition as an issue, the creation of the 'climate in which all parties can contribute to a discussion of the issues in a spirit of trust and co-operation'[7] will be demanding and evolutionary. Certainly what the Government describes as its 'fair employment agenda'[8] will help, and in particular reforms to the law surrounding transfers of undertakings (see Chapter 12 of this work); but the stigma which many in local government consider was attached to competition through CCT will take some time to disappear to enable rebranding of the concept in a positive context.

Local authorities are reminded that they 'have a key role to play by putting the needs of service users uppermost and by adopting an open mind as to how a service might be provided and by whom, and by being prepared to seek out and listen to the views of others'.[9] However, assistance can equally be given by the trades unions and the private and voluntary sectors in developing the conditions 'under which services are run for the benefit of those that require

---

1   This may result from productive discussions between the Government and the Local Government Association (with which the author was involved) in the gestation of the LGA 1999.
2   DETR Circular 10/99, para 36.
3   Ibid.
4   DETR, *Modern Local Government In Touch with the People* (July 1998).
5   DETR Circular 10/99, para 37.
6   Ibid.
7   Ibid, para 38.
8   Ibid, paras 84–94.
9   Ibid, para 38.

them, and where diversity can flourish'.[1] Clearly the Government believes that
Best Value cannot flourish without appropriate variety and plurality and it takes
the view that authorities that 'give insufficient weight to the merits of a healthy
and genuine partnership between public, private and voluntary sectors are
unlikely to achieve the sustained improvements that local people will rightly
expect under best value'.[2]

Consequently, authorities are advised to analyse the structure and development of supply markets for the various services 'and draw upon market
intelligence in carrying out their reviews'.[3] It is also suggested that authorities
consider in discussion with public, private and voluntary sector suppliers the
extent to which those suppliers might have the capacity to deliver the
improvements highlighted by consultation and also to identify the potential
benefits of introducing new providers into the market.[4] So, for instance,
services currently provided 'to a uniform standard ... could be restructured to
encourage variety and choice: alternatively, similar services which are currently
delivered by different authorities could be amalgamated to deliver economies
of scale'.[5]

4.33 A box following para 39 in the Guidance gives some guidance on
researching supply markets and engaging with markets as follows:

'In researching supply markets authorities should explore:

– the service developments that are anticipated in response to best practice,
   legislation or user views
– the current market for the provision of the service(s)
– new combinations of service which the marketplace suggests could deliver
   best value
– the alternative ways to procure the service(s).

This will require engagement with the markets, perhaps through:

– holding discussions with selected private and voluntary sector providers
– sending a questionnaire to suppliers to ask how they could add value
– discussing existing experience with other authorities who have contracted
   the service from an external provider
– holding a contractors' briefing day to explain the objectives of the authority
   and to elicit their views'.[6]

But (in some ways reminiscent of the approach of the former Conservative
administration[7] to CCT) authorities will also be expected to secure improved
performance from mature markets and also to 'create the conditions in which
new suppliers might take root where the current market is demonstrably weak,
poorly developed and offers no credible alternative to the current supplier'.[8]

---

1   DETR Circular 10/99, para 38.
2   Ibid.
3   Ibid, para 39.
4   Ibid.
5   Ibid.
6   Ibid at p 13.
7   1992–1997.
8   DETR Circular 10/99, para 40.

The object here is to 'encourage diversity, innovation and the competitiveness of the supply base' rather than 'to favour one supplier against another'.[1]

4.34 Some steps which authorities might take to achieve these objectives are set out in para 41 of the Guidance as follows:

'–   basing requirements on outcomes to allow for and encourage innovative methods of provision
–   grouping activities to reflect prospective market competencies. This too can help generate interest from innovative providers
–   packaging work appropriate to the market. In some areas of activity larger packages may generate more interest than smaller ones; in others authorities may wish to encourage small and medium-sized companies to bid
–   being clear about intentions. Authorities need to make clear where they want long-term relationships with potential suppliers, and demonstrate a genuine interest in using the best suppliers, regardless of the sector from which they come
–   developing an understanding of the potential sources of supply. Early discussions with prospective suppliers can help in shaping the optimum size, composition and length of contracts, whilst ensuring the fairness, openness and transparency required by EC procurement rules
–   being clear in advance whether there will be an in-house bid for the work.'

The Guidance indicates[2] that these 'developments will require authorities to develop new capacities, either alone or with others', to: 'analyse supply markets and identify what such markets can provide'; 'select the best suppliers' or 'to manage new forms of relationship designed to achieve whole life value for money, continuous improvement and the sharing of risks and rewards'.

4.35 Whilst there can be no argument about the need for authorities to procure and secure best value service provision, there will inevitably be some difference in view about the nature and extent of the role of the local authority as economic market manipulator. There is arguably some tension between the procurement of a best value service (where there may already exist an economic, efficient and effective in-house team, tested by a robust and audited or auditable review) and the diversion of valuable public resources into what some authorities will see as an exercise to improve private sector market opportunities. The primary focus must always be to obtain best value for the authority and its stakeholders. Whilst the Guidance in this area can assist authorities to a more mature and sophisticated understanding of service options and market context the primary aim must at all times be kept in mind if authorities are not to waste resources in economic development disguised as review.

Following the part of the Guidance which deals with market development and activation is likely to be time and labour intensive; councils are likely to require senior and informed (if not expert) input. Local authorities may therefore wish to 'join-up' in approaching this area to maximise existing expertise and experience and to achieve economies of scale. The Local Government Association (and the Improvement and Development Agency) may also be able to facilitate the process by supporting suitable research and

---

1   DETR Circular 10/99, para 40.
2   At para 42.

development and pilot programmes. No doubt the Government will similarly wish to underpin its advice in this area and the best value pilot (and other) Authorities may assist with 'road-testing' the approach. The Government does acknowledge the difficulties here by recognising that:

> '... moving towards a more plural and partnership based form of service provision may be challenging for many authorities and [it] is considering with the Local Government Association and others what further measures are needed to equip authorities for the new forms of procurement which best value demands'.[1]

And whilst some of the market defibrillation ideas are entirely consistent with a straightforward best value strategy – for example, clarity of intention and insight into potential supply sources – there still seems to be an underlying presumption that an in-house service is unlikely to be the best solution and that the market needs to be engineered to enable suitable private supply. This is not to say that there should not be close engagement with the private and voluntary sectors and a creative, innovative and challenging approach to service provision. It is also not to say that authorities should not actively and energetically be looking at different ways of doing things for the benefit of their stakeholders and that there is a real and positive role and need for appropriate private supply. It is the emphasis which still appears to be unhappily poised. Although an improvement upon the consultation document[2] the ghosts of CCT have not been entirely exorcised and their visitation will make hard-working in-house teams feel less than valued.

4.36 Contracts which are externalised are not in themselves a guarantee of best value[3] and neither (since best value is more holistic and radical than, for example, CCT) is the fact that work might have been placed in-house following a competition exercise. Paragraph 43 of the Guidance (amongst other things) acknowledges this issue and points out that the '... fact that a service is currently provided internally or externally following a competitive process is not in itself sufficient to demonstrate best value, particularly where the contract is of a long duration and has been in operation for several years'. Current and future needs must be considered (rather than assuming the continuing application of those needs at the time when the contract was initially let).

'Contracts with the private sector should be examined to see if they permit, and provide incentives for, innovation and continuous improvement. Where this is not the case, authorities need to discuss with providers how best to accommodate these improvements, taking into account the scope for agreeing or negotiating new contract arrangements, and their willingness to finance service improvements and share any risks and rewards'.[4] Whilst commercial contractors will understandably be conscious of the costs implications of any changes, many responsible private organisations will want to build up or maintain a trust relationship with their client authorities, and will therefore wish positively to embrace best value principles. Consequently they are likely to be amenable to reasonable changes in arrangements to accommodate these.

---

1   DETR Circular 10/99, para 48.
2   DETR, *Implementing Best Value – A Consultation Paper on Draft Guidance* (September 1999).
3   In Chapter 2 of this work there is consideration of some ways in which best value might be accommodated on contracting-out.
4   DETR Circular 10/99, at para 43.

4.37 Reviews giving full consideration to the 4Cs[1] are expected to set demanding targets for service improvement, and action plans to deliver these to a realistic timetable, including decisions on the best value option for future service delivery.[2] The main outcome options are expressed to include the:

- cessation of the service, in whole or in part;
- creation of a public/private partnership, through a strategic contract or a joint venture company, for example;
- transfer or externalisation of the service to another provider (with no in-house bid);
- market-testing of all or part of the service (where the in-house provider bids in open competition against the private or voluntary sector);
- restructuring or re-positioning of the in-house service;
- re-negotiation of existing arrangements with current providers where this is permissible;
- joint commissioning or delivery of the service.

The Guidance indicates that the chosen option will 'depend upon an objective analysis of what has emerged from the Review'.[3] This will emanate from 'a corporate perspective which embraces both a clear procurement strategy and a written policy on evaluation and appraisal'.[4] Also, for each review 'authorities will be expected to demonstrate that they have explored the full range of practical alternatives and selected the options most likely to deliver best value to the public. External auditors will expect a clear audit trail and proper justification for the preferred choice'.[5] This applies as much to internal as to externalised work. Furthermore:

> 'Retaining work in-house will therefore only be justified where the authority can show it is competitive with the best alternative. The way in which this is demonstrated is for an authority to determine in accordance with its procurement strategy and evaluation policy, but where there is a developed supply market this will most often be through fair and open competition'.[6]

Changes to accounting practice (see Chapter 11 below) 'should help ensure that the costs of work carried out in-house are fully transparent, so that in considering options for service delivery there is an improved basis for comparison, evaluation and auditing'.[7] Sensibly, authorities are advised to review their contract and procurement standing orders 'to ensure that they are consistent with the statutory provisions of the 1999 Act and the requirements of this guidance'.[8]

4.38 Whilst there are *always* improvements to be made in every service and a strong improvement action plan should also *always* emerge from a best value review, there will inevitably be occasions where the old proverb will apply: if it

---

1   See above: challenge, comparison, consultation and competition.
2   DETR Circular 10/99, para 44.
3   Ibid, para 45.
4   Ibid.
5   Ibid.
6   Ibid, para 46.
7   Ibid.
8   Ibid, para 47.

ain't broke, don't fix it. So if a review legitimately (and auditably upon
satisfactory evidence) concludes that the in-house solution is the most effective
(and 'competitive with the best alternative') but also that the current service
structuring is suitable to meet the present needs of the Council and those it
serves, a 'restructuring or re-positioning' (as envisaged in para 44 of the
Guidance) will not be necessary.

The Government points out that targets and action plans for delivering
service quality and efficiency improvements arising from the review process will
need to be within the range specified for the best value performance
indicators[1] and will also be supplemented by 'local improvement targets
developed through consultation with local people'. These targets and action
plans will underpin the continuing assessment which local people make of the
Authority's performance. Therefore, the Government considers it '... essential
that authorities put in place the necessary monitoring and scrutiny arrangements, involving elected members and officers, to provide a regular check on
performance' which will '... need to give an early warning of potential slippage
against targets or the emergence of unintended outcomes'.[2] Authorities 'will
recognise that these Reviews have the potential to demonstrate that best value is
owned by local government itself'; which is 'why inspection under best value
will as far as possible follow Reviews rather than precede them'.[3]

MEMBER INVOLVEMENT

4.39   The strong commitment of elected members and their proper strategic
involvement in best value is essential if the scheme is to have any chance of
working effectively. Members determine the culture and values of their
authority and (at executive level) have a responsibility to provide clear, strong
and positive political and policy direction. No matter what progress is made at
officer level aspirations will hit a ceiling unless there is active, positive
integrated and open-minded commitment from members. As the Government
points out:

> 'Elected members – whether with executive or non-executive roles once the
> provisions in the Local Government Bill 1999 are in force – have a key
> responsibility to ensure that Reviews reflect from the start the strategic objectives
> and corporate priorities of the authority and focus on the perspective of actual and
> potential service users, including those that are typically hard-to-reach. Elected
> members will also need to monitor action plans following the completion of
> Reviews.'[4]

Consequently, elected members will need to read carefully the DETR
publication *New Roles, New Opportunities The Role of Elected Members in Best Value.*[5]
This (amongst other things) gives a briefing on: best value and the role of
elected members (giving leadership, engaging with their communities, actively

---

1   See Chapter 3.
2   DETR Circular 10/99, para 49.
3   See paras 72–78 of Circular 10/99 and Chapter 7.
4   DETR Circular 10/99, para 17.
5   DETR, 24 November 1999. This can be viewed at: http://www.local-regions.detr.gov.uk/
    bestvalue/legislation/member.htm.

supporting the best value review and performance plan processes, decision-making and promoting excellence, innovation, partnership, performance management and strong neighbourhoods). The Paper also highlights member training and development needs for example in the areas of:

- '– consultation techiques
- – performance management
- – knowledge of service operations
- – negotiating
- – contracting and procurement
- – analysis of service and financial data'.

The Introduction sets the context:

'Elected members now face significant changes to the way they work and the way their councils work. These changes seek to modernise local government so that it can play a key role in leading their communities into the next century. They are about local government working constructively with others to deliver excellence in the service for which it is responsible. They are about local government engaging with local people in new ways. They are about the future of local government itself. Working together, central and local government can make a real difference to the quality of life in Britain today.'

And on the pain of change:

'Change is always difficult. And it affects elected members as much as anyone. Indeed it will not succeed if members do not lead from the front. Local people look to their elected members for a lead, and they are right to do so.

    Members also need to consider the options for change and to lead their councils through them, each making their own particular contribution to success. Even long standing members will need to learn new skills and acquire additional knowledge. That is why training and development for members is essential.'

4.40 *Best Value Performance Plans: Practice and Procedures*[1] (a report on a case study of eight authorities discussed below) also has some useful material on relevant aspects of member involvement. For instance, in box 5.3 participating authorities identified a number of roles for members in this context:

- '– Agreeing the authority's corporate priorities and developing their overall Best Value strategy;
- – Designing and agreeing the approach and timetable for consultation;
- – Agreeing the content of the BVPP;[2]
- – Determining the process, and agreeing the timetable, of Best Value reviews;
- – Scrutinising the authority's performance to ensure it meets performance targets and service standards set out in the BVPP'.

Members with different service responsibilities will play a key role in adding rigour to the 4Cs through their scrutiny role. As the elected representatives of local people, theirs can be a powerful voice for user-responsive change provided that this has a clear strategic focus. So as the changing roles for elected members emerge and settle – executive and scrutiny[3] – there is a real

---

1   DETR, 24 November 1999.
2   Best value performance plan.
3   See the Local Government Bill 1999 (introduced into Parliament in November 1999) following the Consultation Paper: *Local Leadership, Local Choice* and the accompanying draft Local Government (Organisation and Standards) Bill – DETR, March 1999. These

opportunity for members to react positively to the possibilities for improvement for their communities offered by best value.

INVOLVING STAFF

4.41   Paragraph 7.24 of *Modern Local Government In Touch with the People*[1] expressed the Government's view that:

> 'Well-motivated and well-trained employees are vital in the provision of best value services, whether they are working for local councils, the private sector, or the voluntary sector. The Government wants in future to see employees fully involved in improving the services that they provide to the community. The Government's best value framework aims to build mutual respect and trust, and to bolster confidence in local services. The task of local government will be to combine reassurance to employees with the necessary flexibility to allow transfer on a fair basis to other employers where this is in the public interest'.

This latter point on flexibility and transfer will be bolstered by the Government's proposals to amend the TUPE Regulations[2] to support a general presumption of the application of TUPE.

Paragraph 17 of the Guidance[3] indicates that in carrying out reviews authorities should:

> '**involve those currently delivering services.** This applies to all employees, but particularly to frontline staff whose experience of face-to-face contact with the public and service users can bring an important perspective as to how a service is perceived and valued, and how it can be improved. Their support is critical to successful implementation'.

One way of doing this effectively is to set up an individual, team and departmental improvement programme. This will feed into the Authority's corporate strategy. The idea is that each team will be asked to prepare a Team Improvement Plan (TIP) based upon their functions at the relevant time and linked to departmental strategy. As part of this, each team member will produce his or her own individual improvement plan containing real improvements on the ground which that individual can make. Then each team will take time out in a supportive environment to brainstorm overall team improvements with lateral thinking encouraged. Good and innovative ideas from the 'coal face' can therefore be actioned and the individuals are able to feel that they are playing an active and valued part in the organisation. Work motivation will often occur when people are able to unlock their personal talents and skills into their working life to make work what *they* want to do.

---

proposals have encountered some political turbulence in their passage through Parliament eg the Government's defeat in the House of Lords on 9 March 2000 and in the debate on Second Reading in the House of Commons on 11 April 2000. However, in the 11 April 2000 debate, Minister for Local Government, Hilary Armstrong, did indicate to Peter Pike MP that 'We are prepared to consider other ways of doing things' (see Hansard, Column 208).

1   DETR, 30 July 1998.
2   See Chapter 12.
3   DETR Circular 10/99.

If a best value approach can unlock some of the mental energy that staff reserve for their hobbies, public services will be transformed.

4.42 As a formal acknowledgment of the need to ensure that staff are fully engaged with the best value process, on 19 October 1999 the 'recognised' local government trade unions (GMB, TGWU and UNISON) entered into a 'Framework Agreement on Best Value'[1] with the 'National Employers' which set out 'joint views on the employee relations implications of Best Value'.

The Agreement (amongst other things) points out that:

> 'To succeed, Best Value needs the active support of the workforce. To gain this support, it is essential:
>
> – That employers and trade unions work together in co-operation, based on a clear commitment to high quality direct services to the communities we serve;
> – That employees and their unions are involved at the start and throughout the process of strategic review e.g. on review teams;
> – That employees and their trade unions are involved in the process of consulting the community;
> – That employees and their unions are involved in the process of implementation;
> – To ensure that employees are treated fairly and that Best Value is not used as a mechanism to drive down terms and conditions of Service'.

Also:

> 'Where it is proposed that a service is outsourced, the need to ensure that the workforce has a full understanding of, and involvement in, the process is crucial'.

Jack Dromey, Public Services National Organiser at the Transport and General Workers' Union is reported as saying:[2]

> 'We don't expect a veto, but we do insist on a voice. In too many councils workers are seen but not heard. The joint message now to all councils is that no vital decision with consequences for the workforce should be taken without that simple question to local government workers – tell us what you think'.

Clearly, without the active and enthusiastic support of staff, best value will be an empty system supporting a lame local government. Therefore, authorities which fail to engage staff in their best value planning do so at their peril.

4.43 Some practical experience of staff engagement can be found in Chapter 8 of *Best Value Performance Plans: Practice and Procedures*.[3] As indicated above, this Paper reports on research commissioned by the DETR into the performance planning process on the basis of a case study of eight local authorities[4] drawn from a matrix of variables to reflect: regional location, type of authority, best value pilot status and political control. It points out that many of the participating authorities 'saw their staff as a key asset' in the development of their best value agenda and formation of the best value performance plan

---

1   A full copy of the agreement is reproduced in Appendix 5.
2   LGCnet, 21 October 1999.
3   DETR, *A Review of Early Experiences within eight local authorities*, 24 November 1999.
4   Cambridgeshire County Council (non-pilot); Northamptonshire County Council (pilot); City of Bradford Metropolitan Council (pilot); London Borough of Hackney (non-pilot); Southampton City Council (pilot); Torfaen County Borough Council (pilot); Telford & Wrekin Council (non-pilot); Carrick District Council (pilot).

although it seems that none formally include a statement to that effect within their plan.[1]

The Document takes the view that 'consultation involves both an informing role about the requirements of Best Value and performance planning and how individuals effect its implementation, as well as a consulting role concerning how Best Value services might be delivered and performance measured'.[2] Leadership is identified as a key feature and this process 'has been strengthened by many of the authorities through the appointment (informally or formally) of "Best Value champions" – key members of staff across each service department who can persuade and "evangelise" about the process with their respective staff'.[3]

4.44   The Paper indicates that the authorities in question 'typically relied upon traditional communication methods' to consult with staff about best value and production of the performance plan, the responsibility typically falling upon corporate or strategic centre staff. Communication techniques included: 'staff briefings; meetings with Unit Heads, staff newsletters and Intranet, lunchtime seminars, employee surveys and induction and training programmes, many organised in conjunction with relevant Trade Unions'. Some authorities had produced information packs and toolkits dealing (amongst other things) with the conduct of service reviews, the development of performance indicators or how to address cross-cutting issues.

The pilot authorities participating in the Study had 'generally developed more extensive staff development and consultation programmes'. For instance, Southampton City Council had canvassed opinion from staff at all levels across the Authority in connection with their work on 'better life for older people' and many of the suggestions made were implemented.[4] Some authorities emphasised the importance of integrating staff involvement into management and planning processes (rather than bolting these on separately). For instance, Torfaen County Borough Council has (amongst other things) 'moved the focus' of its annual planning process to team level.[5]

Paragraph 86 of the Guidance makes clear that:

> 'Getting the best from staff and maximising the potential of the labour market generally involves more than compliance with minimum standards. It also depends on a positive and effective approach to **equal opportunities**. This applies throughout the process of delivering services, but authorities should consider corporately, and as part of their Performance Review programme, the extent to which their recruitment and management practices achieve the standards set out in the codes of practice on employment issued by the Commission for Racial Equality and the Equal Opportunities Commission, as well as guidance issued by DfEE in respect of the Disability Discrimination Act 1995. The Commission for Racial Equality's *Standard for Racial Equality for Local Government* and the Equal Opportunities Commission's *Mainstreaming gender equality in local authorities* will both assist authorities in securing an effective approach to equal opportunities.'

---

1   Paragraph 8.8.
2   Ibid.
3   Paragraph 8.9.
4   See generally para 8.10.
5   Paragraph 8.11.

BEST VALUE HEALTHCHECK

4.45 The author has developed a detailed Healthcheck and Performance Indicators primarily aimed at best value authority legal departments but readily adaptable to other services and functions, which appear in full at Appendix 6 and Appendix 7. The aim is to provide a focus for service managers in giving their service a thorough and testing pre-review (ie before the formal review takes place). The Healthcheck consists of a series of questions grouped under the following headings to enable a tailored improvement plan to be drawn up for the particular service:

Outcomes
Corporate value
Community value
Service outcomes

Enabling and Facilitating Outcomes
Operational systems
Client satisfaction
Financial systems
People issues
General management
Strategic planning

This should put services in a strong position for the formal review process.

BEST VALUE FOR LEGAL (OR OTHER SUPPORT) SERVICES[1]

4.46 For the majority of core local authority legal services, an efficient and effective in-house team will usually be the most economically advantageous option. However, particularly in a time of rapid and radical change for local government, demand for legal support can often outstrip the capacity to supply. Co-operation between local authority legal departments is widespread but generally limited in effect because of resource and operational pressures. A cross-cutting approach can provide synergy, economies of scale, improved staff development and a best value solution to the provision of legal services at regional level.

One solution might be to set up a joint committee (or if desired at any time a company limited by guarantee) to provide core legal services on a regional basis. This would take relevant existing staff from the participating constituent authorities and could be structured in any way considered appropriate by the parties to achieve a best value outcome. The regional service unit would have its own name (eg Blankshire Law) and would no doubt develop a branded identity consistent with public service principles. In addition, the participating authorities could retain a core staff and strategic legal adviser for high level

---

1   Whilst legal services is used as an example the concept is equally applicable to other support services. Although presumably different in operation, the North Yorkshire Audit Partnership (see above) is a practical example of a joined-up approach.

policy issues. Blankshire Law, whilst generally dealing with regular operational work could also in conjunction with the strategic in-house lawyers deal with regional strategic issues.

Some Possible Features of the Joint Committee

4.47   Some suggestions for features of a 'Blankshire Law' joint committee are given below.

- The Senior Management Team could consist of a chief executive (professionally qualified as a solicitor) together with a senior solicitor as 'lead partner' for each of the participating authorities. The Chief Executive would (for professional reasons) be the Solicitor responsible for Blankshire Law and would through his staff be acting for all the constituent authorities.
- The Chief Executive would ensure sound strategic service provision across the region and that resources were deployed to best advantage.
- The Chief Executive would also ensure sound working relationships with any in-house strategic solicitors (who could within Blankshire Law have status similar to non-executive directors).
- Staff could be transferred to a 'lead authority' which would be responsible for pay and conditions and which would be reimbursed by the other authority partners. The transfers could be effected as if TUPE[1] applied so as to preserve existing terms and conditions.
- As indicated, the relevant senior managers below the Chief Executive could each have a 'lead partner' responsibility for their allocated authority but would also provide support across the region.
- A detailed agreement would be needed between all participating authorities regulating precisely how the arrangement would work and covering such issues as:
  - service costs/budget issues;
  - equipment and assets;
  - manner of service provision;
  - responsibility for premises;
  - accountability arrangements;
  - professional responsibility;
  - professional indemnity;
  - liabilities;
  - dispute resolution;
  - staffing issues;
  - cessation and suspension;
  - discipline;
  - termination;
  - variation;

  together with a host of other matters.

---

1   See Chapter 12.

- There would presumably be no need for participation in the Law Society's professional indemnity arrangements since no clients' monies would be held. As is usually[1] the position with local authority legal departments monies would be held in the bank account of the relevant authority.
- If desired subsequently and subject to any additional legal powers needed (eg under s 16 of the LGA 1999) the operation could transfer to a special purpose vehicle (eg a private limited company).

Amongst the advantages would be:

- a substantial improvement of staffing resources;
- shared assets, resources and knowledge;
- radically improved development opportunities for legal staff;
- economies of scale;
- capacity to do work for other public bodies (as with the Yorkshire Purchasing Organisation[2]) and use the revenue to provide an enhanced service.

There are clearly many other ways of joining up legal and other services in innovative ways so as to benefit the end user rather than the provider staff. But strategic managers will also need to ensure that there are sufficient incentives for staff to keep them enthused and engaged.

THE IMPROVEMENT AND DEVELOPMENT AGENCY

4.48 This can offer a worthwhile best value consultancy resource to authorities in the review process. As the former Local Government Management Board disappeared, on 1 April 1999 the Improvement and Development Agency (IDA) rose phoenix-like from the ashes (hand-in-hand with its sister organisation, the Employers' Organisation for Local Government). It is divided into three arms, each headed by a Director:

- improvement and consultancy services;
- best practice and corporate services;
- learning and development services.

The Improvement and Consultancy arm is being set up as 'a medium-sized management consultancy' building on the 'peer group review' work of the former Local Government Improvement Project. The Project was set up in July 1998 as a team working with a group of pilot authorities to develop models for how a thorough healthcheck and improvement plan approach for best value authorities could work in practice.

The model consists of the following four elements:

'– a review of a local authority to asssess its current achievements (the diagnostic)

---

1   Although not inevitably.
2   See the decision of the Court of Appeal in *R v Yorkshire Purchasing Organisation, ex parte British Educational Suppliers Association* (1997) 95 LGR 727 (considered in Chapter 9), where substantial trading activities conducted across a wide authority client base were ruled lawful under the Local Authorities (Goods and Services) Act 1970.

- an analysis of its existing strengths and weaknesses to determine the gap between where the authority is currently and where it needs to be in order to be fully effective
- help in formulating an improvement plan in order to address areas of concern (weaknesses) and to bridge the gap
- practical support and advice on carrying through the improvements identified'.[1]

At that time, Len Duvall[2] said that:

> 'What is new and exciting about this project is that it will deliver a complete organisational assessment to a local authority, rather than a hit squad type approach to individual services.
>
> It will be local government taking on the challenge of improving itself, with the input of experts from throughout the public and private sector giving practical backing and support. Change from within rather than imposed from without will lead to the continuous improvement we seek, in a dual approach with external review.'

4.49 Work by the DETR, Local Government Association, the former Local Government Management Board,[3] Deloitte and Touche and 22 pilot councils participating in the Local Government Improvement Project has suggested the following competencies for a good council, namely that it should:

- be forward looking and innovative;
- recognise its community leadership role;
- have a clear vision;
- operate as a corporate entity and work in partnership with other public and private organisations and agencies;
- undertake rigorous performance review;
- ensure services are provided by well-trained and motivated people;
- be open and ethical;
- encourage participative democracy;
- have defined the roles and responsibilities of members and officers;
- deploy resources effectively;
- demonstrate positive trends in improvement of service delivery and achieving best value;
- be well regarded by the public.

The Improvement approach is by way of 'peer group review' and the review teams 'will be drawn from high quality local government practitioners and the private sector'.[4] Once reviews are complete 'the IDA will be able to offer advice and assistance on taking agreed action plans forward'. And 'Outside reviews this arm of the IDA will also be able to help on failing services and offer advice on continuous improvement programmes'. As the IDA points out:

---

1   Improvement and Development Agency.
2   Len Duvall is, at the time of writing, the Chair of the IDA.
3   As indicated above, as from 1 April 1999, the Local Government Management Board has been replaced by the IDA and the Employers' Organisation for Local Government.
4   The author is on the panel of private sector reviewers.

'This is local government's opportunity to show that it is the best placed to push forward improvement in the quality of services, management and representation at local level'.

The clear message here is for local government to take the opportunity to put its own house in order before central government does the job for it.

4.50 As to the other two arms (Best Practice and Corporate Services and Learning and Development Services), the 'key to all the work in the Best Practice arm is the creation of networks of experience, advice and information' and the 'main aim of Learning and Development will be to encourage local authorities to invest in effective and well targeted training'.

The Improvement and Development Agency has issued two useful publications in the 'Approaches to Best Value' series which will assist authorities in the Review process. These are: *Reviews in Best Value*[1] and *The Corporate Framework*.[2]

LATERAL THINKING

4.51 The best value review should give the opportunity for a mental clear-out, and some challenging lateral thinking. Those responsible for reviews will need to leave the tram-lines, change medium and take off. A good example appeared in *The Guardian* of 11 October 1999.[3] When East Sussex County Council was going to close a library because necessary building work was not affordable, the manager of the Marine Hotel agreed to lend the Council's books and the Council apparently co-operated. *The Guardian* reported on local reaction:

> ' "I think it's great," says a regular, Jay Stevenson, 27, an alarm engineer. "It's not like you could have a fag and a pint at a library. Here, we'll be able to relax and do a bit of reading. I don't get to do that very often." A fellow drinker, Gary Blackedge, 29, a pensions consultant, agrees. "You get all those olde worlde theme pubs with stacks of books that you can't read. Here at the Marine, the books are for real. I like that." '

The local libraries manager was reported as saying that this could be the way forward for libraries and, 'We're hoping this scheme means more people have access to the books. And with the money saved we've been able to invest £8,000 in new stock.'

4.52 Suffolk County Council is making innovative use of new technology. Its Website[4] (which amongst other things) enables public consultation, user comments on a 'graffiti wall' and the facility of being able to order or renew library books on line has won a variety of awards including the following:

---

1   Improvement and Development Agency for Local Government and the Local Government Association 1999 ISBN 1 84049 125 6 (£50 including postage: available from IDeA Publication Sales, Layden House, 76–86 Turnmill Street, London EC1M 5LG/Tel: 0207 296 6600).

2   Improvement and Development Agency for Local Government and the Local Government Association ISBN 1 84049 124 8 (£50 including postage: available from above address).

3   'Pub moves into book business as library closes', *The Guardian*, 11 October 1999.

4   Home page: http://www.suffolkcc.gov.uk./.

- the EARL Consortium of UK Public Libraries, special mention 'For breaking new ground in addressing the needs of the library user accessing the library service from a remote site. This site allows the user to join the library from home, check the catalogue, reserve and renew books, and suggest new books which the library might wish to consider purchasing. This is the way of the future and richly deserves the special mention';
- winner of the Local Government Association Website awards, 1999, in the Reinvigorating Local Democracy category;
- the Society of Public Information Networks annual award for excellence, 1998.

If information technology is assertively the present it is certainly and overwhelmingly the future. Suffolk's approach is in tune with the 'Information Age Government' commitment in the Cabinet Office's March 1999 *Modernising Government* White Paper.

4.53 Not all best value initiatives need to be equivalent to the Piccadilly Circus lights. Value can be added in quite modest but meaningful ways. For instance, Bolton MBC's Legal Services Division (which incidentally has an impressive range of awards and accreditations) has a duty solicitor and legal assistant on hand each working day to provide continuity of childcare service; and there is a 'Housing Helpdesk' operated by daily rota. This is good not only for service users but it also helps develop a range of different staff professionally, in use of initiative and in customer interface by giving them regular 'coal-face' experience in a supportive environment. It will no doubt also contribute to team-building.

THE PILOT EXPERIENCE

4.54 The background to the best value pilot programme was mentioned in Chapter 1. Some of the key messages which have emerged from the work of the pilot authorities to date were highlighted in the DETR's Best Value Update, Issue 4[1] as follows. It will be noticed that many of them have been addressed above:

- members have a key role in leading and managing the best value process;
- staff need to be involved and this takes training and a change of culture;
- the challenge element is the most difficult part of the best value process. Challenge should involve politicians and consumers;
- there should be a genuine decision-making process over whether to make or buy;
- reviews are a resource intensive and incremental process. They need clear objectives;
- consultation needs a strategic approach. This involves training partners and being clear about the purpose of the consultation;

---

1   Published 5 October 1999. See also DETR, *Good Practice, Best Value* (November 1999) which gives 'examples of good practices ... designed to illustrate the achievements of a selection of the pilots in the national Best Value Pilots Programme since April 1998'. This can be seen at http://www.local-regions.detr.gov.uk/bestvalue/pilot/pdf/bvpilot.pdf.

- local authorities need to compare themselves with different outside bodies;
- performance plans need to be co-ordinated with a range of other plans; and
- the inspectorates need to work together.[1]

In Best Value Update Issue 5 (under the title *The Warwick Evaluation*) Howard Davis of the Local Government Centre at Warwick Business School indicated that:

'A "culture challenge" needs to underpin all elements of the Best Value framework. This often requires cultural change. The most effective Best Value reviews have been:

- informed by corporate, strategic priorities;
- properly scoped and resourced at the outset;
- undertaken within a clearly defined timetable;
- performed by a team with an appropriate balance of seniority, skills and personality types;
- informed by the views of elected members and front line staff;
- robust, challenging and focused on achieving 'step changes' as opposed to incremental improvements; and
- linked into mainstream service planning and budgetary processes.'

In addition:

'Consultation has also been an important influence. The most effective approaches to date have involved continuous, authority-wide, engagement with a wide range of customers, citizens and communities, plus more narrowly-focused consultation about specific services or issues. A number of authorities have identified scope for major improvements and/or cost savings through tendering exercises and, as time has progressed there has been an increasing awareness of the need to develop more sophisticated corporate approaches to market analysis and procurement. Most pilots have also reported a need to improve corporate performance management systems.'[2]

4.55 It is rarely worthwhile to expend creative energy in reinventing the already invented. Therefore, in seeking inspiration, it is well worth looking at what the pilot authorities[3] are doing. Of course, this is not with a view to taking the existing approaches 'off the peg'; but looking at these authorities can assist with the generation of ideas so that best value can be fitted appropriately into the local context. For instance, Newham LBC has produced a very useful best value toolkit,[4] not as an end in itself, but to help realise the Council's vision that by '2010 Newham will be a major business location where people will choose to

---

1   Inspection is dealt with in Chapter 6.
2   DETR February 2000, see http://www.local-regions.detr.gov.uk/bestvalue/ implementation/bvup5.htm#improving.
3   A list of the best value pilot authorities is available in Annex A to DETR Circular 10/99 and at http://www.local.detr.gov.uk/research/bvsummar/preface.htm#List. See also DETR, *Good Practice, Best Value* (November 1999) which can be seen at http://www.local-regions. detr.gov.uk/bestvalue/pilot/pdf/bvpilot.pdf.
4   This can be viewed at http://www.newham.gov.uk/bestvalue/year2toolkit/ bvsectionA.htm#thematic.

live and work'. Former Chief Executive Wendy Thomson[1] said in a Foreword to the toolkit:

> 'We hope the review process will enable you better to put yourselves in the shoes of your customers. The aim is that we will provide the services our customers want at a price they wish to pay. No ideas or suggestions that help us achieve this goal will be rejected.'

Significantly (and this can be the key to success) Ms Thomson described the first year of best value as being 'very challenging but also exciting and fun'. If the process is to take wings this is essential. Nevertheless, best value is becoming airborne despite the weighty ballast of indicator and statutory process.

4.56   Brighton and Hove Council (another pilot) has involved the public through the Council newspaper in choosing the areas to be reviewed with the aid of a prize draw incentive: 'Give us your Best Value priorities – and win a computer'.[2] The Council divided its functions and activities into twenty-five categories with the intention of reviewing five per year over a five-year cycle.
  The categories are as follows.

- **Safety** (the effectiveness of strategies to reduce crime and the fear of crime);
- **Democracy** ('improving citizen involvement in decision making');
- **Legal** (ensuring Council actions are within the law);
- **Involvement** ('how we engage with the community to ensure everyone has a voice');
- **Workforce** (policies and training for staff 'to promote a motivated and well trained workforce');
- **Recycling** ('Managing waste and promoting a sustainable future through increased recycling and waste reduction');
- **Life events** ('Births, deaths, marriages and all points in between' with related advice and support);
- **Regeneration** ('Creating jobs and improving the local economy through an effective regeneration strategy between the council and its partners');
- **Homes 1** ('Ensuring that council housing meets the needs of the next decade');
- **Homes 2** ('How we enable people to gain access to the type of housing they need');
- **Tax and benefits** ('Ensuring local taxes and benefits are efficiently collected and paid out and contribute to reducing local poverty');
- **Time off** (ensuring leisure and cultural pursuits are 'affordable and accessible to all');
- **Schools** (Council advice and support to schools);
- **Appearance** (management of the City's physical appearance);
- **Travel** (transport policy);

---

1   Wendy Thomson is at the time of writing Director of Inspection at the Audit Commission, responsible for: the Best Value Inspectorate, the Housing Inspectorate, LEA inspectors, Joint Reviews, Liaison and co-ordination with other inspectorates and the DETR. See also Chapter 7.
2   *Brighton & Hove News*, November 1999.

- **Education** (maximising opportunities for lifelong learning);
- **Safety first** (ways in which the Council works to create a safe and healthy local environment);
- **Contracts** (how the Council purchases services to ensure 'they are cost effective and lead to better partnership working');
- **Investment** ('encouraging tourism and supporting the local economy through investing in key projects');
- **Heritage** ('Planning the built environment and promoting responsible ownership to make sure we maintain our unique heritage');
- **Finance** (ensuring the Council's financial systems are 'efficient, effective and meet all legal requirements');
- **Assets** (ensuring all the Council's assets 'are well managed to maximise the benefit to the community');
- **Care and support** ('Providing support for vulnerable people, balancing their need for independence with the level of risk to themselves or others');
- **Contact** (improving public communication with the Council 'through phones, new technology and at reception desks');
- **Improvements** ('The ways in which we strive for year on year improvements and "joined-up working" across council departments').

4.57 Whilst not everyone would agree with this taxonomy it does illustrate a strategic and participative approach. The public was consulted in November 1999 concerning which five of the above services were to be examined in the first review year. As the Council indicated:

'The Council intends to leave no stone unturned in its Best Value reviews. The aim is for reviews to **MAKE A DIFFERENCE** to the services you receive. We already have some excellent services but we need to learn from other organisations how to improve our performance in some service areas . . . If there is something we are not doing well we intend to review it first. We want to know where you think it is most important that we improve our performance by carrying out a review'.

In the course of Brighton and Hove Council's pilot programme, the Council has been 'carrying out best value reviews for the last 18 months':

'All of these reviews have consulted with their customers to find out what they need and expect from council services. In some cases, the reviews have also asked people who do not use the services, why they do not use them. This information is also important in finding new ways to make sure you get the services you need. As a result of these reviews improvements have been made to local libraries, refuse and street cleaning services, planning and building control, meals in the community and many more services'.[1]

Governance is of course more than mere adherence to the views of the majority. The process of government should add value by making informed choices and decisions on behalf of those governed. Brighton and Hove do not therefore undertake to accept a majority verdict but indicate that 'We will take your views into account when we finally agree the five year programme.'[2]

---

1 *Brighton & Hove News*, November 1999.
2 Ibid.

4.58 Southampton City Council has a sound and comprehensive methodology for reviews and has issued corporate guidance emphasising that 'reviews
may take a variety of different sizes and be undertaken at different intervals;
they may be cross-service departments or as small as one particular performance indicator'.[1] They can encompass:

'– **Service Reviews:** Undertaken by each Service Head for the activities for which
they are responsible, to ensure that they are delivered at the right price to
sufficiently high standard. Each department has adopted different
approaches, but the corporate centre (the Executive Director) ensures that
robust planning and review frameworks are followed;

– **Policy Reviews:** Led by Policy Managers (on behalf of relevant Committee
Chairs), to review selected areas of a committee's policies. They explore the
availability of better or more cost-effective alternatives to current ways of
securing broad thematic outcomes sought by committees;

– **Thematic Reviews:** Lead and co-ordinated by the Executive Director with
strategic responsibility for a specific area, for example, 'a better life for older
people', it involves a programme of reviews and initiatives across each of the
Council's departments which address the issue;

– **Service Improvement Reviews:** These seek to secure accelerated improvements in areas of apparent under-performance, and with a view to securing
improvements.'[2]

4.59 Finally, the DETR Publication, *Achieving Best Value through Performance
Review*[3] whilst recognising that best value was continually evolving provisionally
highlighted

'some of the themes around which key issues are emerging, relating to the
requirement for review processes to be:

– feasible and sustainable – developing processes which are feasible, "practical"
and sustainable

– challenging and critical – overcoming "defensiveness" and ensuring the
required skills, competencies and "cultural" attributes are developed

– objective and rigorous – "quality assuring" the process

– inclusive and consensual – involving all stakeholders and ensuring that their
views are taken fully into account

– embedded and useful – ensuring review processes develop as an integral part
of core planning, management and budgetary processes and result in
effective action to improve

– appropriate and adaptable – tailoring approach, methods and depth of
review to circumstances, service context and to area- and issue-based foci.'

4.60 The same document pointed to some issues for performance review
identified by Bristol City Council, Manchester City Council, the City of
Bradford Metropolitan Council, and Newham and Camden London Borough
Councils.
Bristol highlighted:

---

1   DETR, *Best Value Performance Plans: Practice and Procedures* (24 November 1999), para 7.6.
2   Ibid, Box 7.2.
3   Published 12 February 1999 – see Warwick/DETR Best Value Series, Paper No. 5 by Ian
     Sanderson, Policy Research Institute, Leeds Metropolitan University.

'– the need to allow flexibility in approach according to different service contexts and circumstances while ensuring an appropriate degree of "rigour" and consistency

– the need to ensure a mix of staff in review teams and leaders from a different service area; but this has implications for staff time (cf. limited resources) and training needs

– the need to promote ownership of reviews by services yet provide necessary audit and "quality control" arrangements to ensure a thorough and objective approach is pursued

– the need to ensure full involvement of all stakeholders (service users, wider community, service providers, TUs); in particular, develop appropriate approaches for involving users and non-users and obtaining the views of the wider community

– the need to develop approaches to testing competitiveness which take account of specific circumstances (nature of service, nature of market, appropriateness of comparators); the development of benchmarking appropriate to particular circumstances will represent a particular challenge

– the need to ensure co-ordination with "external" reviews and inspections taking place simultaneously (eg SSI/Audit Commission Joint Review of Social Services coincides with first year of pilot).'

4.61 Bradford identified 'certain issues which will need to be resolved, for example, assimilating issue-based and service-based review, promoting "ownership" of review findings by services, ensuring appropriate levels of "rigour" and objectivity, ensuring that directorates are prepared to allow staff time to be available for review teams'. Manchester highlighted 'key issues which need to be resolved around, for example, assimilating area-based and authority-wide review processes, the depth and intensity of the review, "ownership" of the process, reconciling periodic review with the need for continuous improvement'.

Finally, Newham and Camden 'reviewed experience with the first round of FPRs and have identified issues relating to "defensiveness" on the part of service departments, the need to "quality assure" the process and the need to develop processes which are sustainable in resource terms'.

THE GOVERNMENT VIEW

4.62 Mixed messages appeared to come from Government in late 1999 about the outcomes from the pilot process. Hilary Armstrong, Minister for Local Government and the Regions, spoke at the Best Value National Conference in London on 22 November 1999. However, reports of how pleased she was with the progress of best value on the ground have differed in emphasis. For example, *Municipal Journal*[1] reported her as indicating that whilst councils were 'performing well' in their preparations for best value, the pilots had found best value 'more challenging than anticipated' and initiatives had been 'bogged down in processes'. The journal went on to quote her as saying 'Some reviews have failed to engage and to be innovative, some authorities have not recognised the need to fully involve elected members and front-line staff, and

---

1   26 November–2 December 1999.

some have not had the skills to complete their tasks.' The Minister was, however, reported as indicating that three-quarters of local authorities were performing 'reasonably well' on: agreeing a corporate approach; agreeing service selection methodology; and conducting trial reviews. She was also reported as praising councils for their progress on partnership.

However (perhaps with a whiff of spin doctor's ether), in a DETR Press Release of 22 November 1999 initially entitled: 'Armstrong Praises Early Best Value Success – Correction' the tone was slightly more positive:

> 'Ms Armstrong urged councils to learn from these experiences in their prep-arations for the introduction of Best Value – just over four months away. Paying tribute to the pioneering work of the Best Value Pilots she said:
>
> "The pilots have shown extraordinary commitment to making Best Value work. The interim evaluation by the Warwick Business School shows that most pilots have found Best Value a greater challenge than expected.
>
> "But what is a considerable challenge has also proved to be a major opportunity. Even at this early stage we are beginning to see real change. From Southampton to Sunderland, from Liverpool to Lincolnshire, Best Value Pilots are bringing solid benefits to their local communities." '

4.63   Prime Minister, Tony Blair, in a 'letter of support' to delegates at the same Best Value Conference (22 November 1999) said that:

> 'Best Value drives up standards, encourages innovation and promotes compe-tition. It strengthens partnership by recognising the contribution made by the private and voluntary sector. Above all, it ensures local people and local communities are put first.'

The Prime Minister was also reported to have written that:[1]

> 'I value local government. I know that in some cases councils are already providing excellent services to local people. But even where services are good this of course does not mean there is no room for further improvement'.

In Best Value Update 5[2] Local Government Minister, Hilary Armstrong, has indicated that the message she is getting is that:

> 'Best Value through partnership is working now and working well. Councils understand and accept what modernisation really means: higher quality services driven by what local people want and need, at a price they are prepared to pay. We must never forget this is the central purpose of Best Value. Public expectations must – and will – drive change in public service delivery. The public are less deferential, more demanding and more knowledgeable. They do not want public services as a form of welfare, but as a right. They expect high quality services. And they expect to get more choice in the form and delivery of those services and quick redress if things go wrong. Government, local authorities, trade unions, private and voluntary sectors must work together in the spirit of true partnership to make Best Value a reality. Let's all grasp this opportunity to improve the quality of people's lives.'

---

1   *Municipal Journal*, 26 November–2 December 1999.
2   DETR, April 2000 (see http://www.local-regions.detr.gov.uk/bestvalue/implementation/bvup5.htm#speech).

So whilst the general message seems to be positive, there is a need constantly to move forward and there is no room at all for complacency.

Change is an integral part of human affairs. A robust but realistic and practical approach to the best value review, responding positively to the innovations of time, should help authorities be fit for, and fit well into, the future.

Chapter 5

PERFORMANCE PLANS

INTRODUCTION

5.1   The purpose of the best value performance plan is to provide 'authorities with the opportunity to engage with local people, and with others with an interest, around their record of delivering local services and their plans to improve upon them'.[1] Performance plans are 'intended as the principal means by which an authority is held to account for the efficiency and effectiveness of its services, and for its plans for the future.'[2]

> 'Performance Plans should reflect the strategic objectives and corporate priorities of the authority, and act as a bridge between these and the service specific and financial plans which are required for resource allocation and other purposes. They will bring together performance information of corporate relevance from these different sources in a form which is accessible to local people. Such plans are therefore more than summaries of information provided elsewhere: they offer the potential to add real value by bringing together information on authorities' performance and budgeting across all services. This will facilitate a genuine dialogue with local people on local priorities, and also influence the response local authorities receive from the private and voluntary sectors, who will be looking to Performance Plans to provide an indication of service delivery opportunities and of an authority's commitment to engage in constructive partnership.'[3]

STATUTORY MATERIAL

5.2   The statutory duty is in s 6(1)[4] of the LGA 1999 which requires best value authorities to 'prepare a best value performance plan for each financial year in accordance with any order made or guidance issued under' s 6. As to 'any order', on 7 December 1999, the Local Government (Best Value) Performance

---

1   DETR Circular 10/99, para 51.
2   Ibid.
3   Ibid, para 52.
4   Section 6 of the Local Government Act 1999 came into force fully in England (and in Wales in relation to police and fire authorities) on 27 September 1999 by virtue of the Local Government Act 1999 (Commencement No 1) Order 1999, SI 1999/2169, which is reproduced in Appendix 2. In respect of Wales, on 23 September 1999, the National Assembly for Wales approved the Local Government Act 1999 (Commencement) (Wales) Order 1999, SI 1999/2815, which was made on 28 September 1999 and which brought the general duty of best value into force in relation to Wales from 1 April 2000 and commenced a number of provisions from 1 October 1999 and others from 1 April 2000 (see Chapter 2 of this work: 'Commencement Issues in Wales'). The Wales Commencement Order is reproduced in Appendix 3.

Plans and Reviews Order 1999[1] was made, which came into force on 4 January 2000. Concerning 'guidance', paragraphs 51 to 60 of the Guidance[2] specifically deal with this area. Relevant provisions of the Plans and Reviews Order and the Guidance will be referred to below in coverage of this area.

By s 6(3), an authority must publish its plan for the financial year either before 31 March of the previous financial year or on such other date as the Secretary of State may by order specify. First performance plans will be expected by no later than 31 March 2000 and thereafter by 31 March annually.[3] Section 6(4) enables the Secretary of State to 'issue guidance on the form and content of plans and the manner in which they should be published'. As indicated, this Guidance has been issued.[4]

5.3 Section 6(2) contains a comprehensive list of matters which (amongst others) the Secretary of State is empowered by order to require an authority to include in its performance plan. These are:

'(a) to summarise the authority's objectives in relation to the exercise of its functions;

(b) to summarise any assessment made by the authority of the level at which and the way in which it exercises its functions;

(c) to state any period within which the authority is required to review its functions under section 5;

(d) to state the timetable the authority proposes to follow in conducting a review;

(e) to state any performance indicators, standards and targets specified or set in relation to the authority's functions;

(f) to summarise the authority's assessment of its performance in the previous financial year with regard to performance indicators;

(g) to compare that performance with the authority's performance in previous financial years or with the performance of other best value authorities;

---

1   SI 1999/3251 (the Plans and Reviews Order). On 28 January 2000 the DETR published 'Clarifications on Statutory Instrument 1999 No. 3251'. This can be viewed at: http://www.local-regions.detr.gov.uk/bestvalue/indicators/clarification.htm. The DETR indicates that since '[t]here have been a number of questions raised about the interpretation of this SI ... this document seeks to make clear what is needed in Best Value Performance Plans (BVPPs) particularly the ones that have to be prepared by March 31 2000'. Authorities will wish to satisfy themselves that their approach is properly meeting the requirements of SI 1999/3251 having regard to the 'Clarifications' issued by the DETR.

2   DETR Circular 10/99.

3   DETR Circular 10/99, at para 55. However, in respect of Wales, on 8 March 2000 a Paper before the Local Government and Environment Committee of the National Assembly for Wales referred to concerns that '31 March was too early to publish final performance plans' and that 'authorities were uncomfortable at being audited on figures that would change soon after the plan was published'. The Paper consequently indicated (at para 18) that: 'The discussion at the Local Government and Environment Committee on 16 February led to a new proposal for a compromise that met both sets of concerns. This proposal was for the final plan to be published by 30 June, with a consequent change to the audit date, but for draft plans to be published by 31 March. This proposal has been welcomed, and we therefore propose to include in the performance plans Order a provision to change the statutory publication deadline to 30 June. The guidance issued to authorities will make clear that they are required to publish a draft plan by 31 March, if they have not already published their final plan by that date as they are free to do. The draft Order and guidance attached to this paper reflect that change.' See Best Value: The Way Forward: http://www.wales.gov.uk/show.dbs.

4   DETR Circular 10/99, December 1999.

(h) to summarise its assessment of its success in meeting any performance standard which applied at any time in the previous financial year;

(i) to summarise its assessment of its progress towards meeting any performance standard which has been specified but which does not yet apply;

(j) to summarise its assessment of its progress towards meeting any performance target;

(k) to summarise any plan of action to be taken in the financial year to which the plan relates for the purposes of meeting a performance target;

(l) to summarise the basis on which any performance target was set, and any plan of action was determined, in relation to a function reviewed under section 5 in the previous financial year'.[1]

Performance Plans 2000

5.4 As indicated, the Secretary of State has exercised his powers under s 6(2) of the LGA 1999 by means of the Plans and Reviews Order.[2] Article 3 specifies (as follows) the content of best value performance plans 'for the financial year 2000' which reflects in updated format s 6(2)(a) to (g) of the LGA 1999. It also seems implicitly to acknowledge that the year in question is the first formal year of best value:

'(a) a summary of the authority's objectives in relation to the exercise of its functions;

(b) a summary of any assessment made by the authority of the level at which, and the way in which, it exercises its functions;

(c) a statement specifying any period within which the authority is required to review its functions under section 5 of the Act and articles 5 and 6 of this Order;[3]

(d) a statement indicating the timetable the authority proposes to follow in conducting a best value review;

(e) a statement specifying any best value performance indicators, best value performance standards and best value performance targets specified or set in relation to the authority's functions;[4]

(f) a summary of the authority's assessment of its performance in the previous financial year with regard to the relevant Audit Commission indicators, where applicable;[5]

(g) a comparison of that performance with the authority's performance in previous financial years.'

Performance Plans 2001 and Thereafter

5.5 For 'the financial year 2001 and each financial year thereafter', pursuant to art 4 of the Plans and Reviews Order, best value authorities must include in their performance plans all the matters in (a) to (e) of art 3 above and *in addition* the following:

---

1 LGA 1999, s 6(2).
2 SI 1999/3251.
3 See Chapter 4.
4 See Chapter 3.
5 See Sch 1 to the Local Government (Best Value) Performance Plans and Reviews Order 1999, SI 1999/3251.

'(a) a summary of the authority's assessment of its performance in the previous financial year with regard to best value performance indicators, where applicable;

(b) a comparison of that performance with the authority's performance in previous financial years;

(c) a comparison of the authority's performance as summarised in accordance with paragraph (a) above, with the performance of other best value authorities in previous financial years;

(d) a summary of its assessment of its success in meeting any best value performance standard[1] which applied at any time in the previous financial year;

(e) a summary of its assessment of its progress towards meeting any best value performance standard which has been specified but which does not yet apply;

(f) a summary of its assessment of its progress towards meeting any best value performance target;

(g) a summary of any plan of action to be taken in the financial year to which the plan relates for the purposes of meeting a best value performance target;

(h) a summary of the basis on which any best value performance target was set, and any plan of action was determined, in relation to a function reviewed under section 5 of the Act and articles 5 and 6 of this Order, in the previous financial year.'[2]

As to Wales, the National Assembly for Wales 'acknowledges the concerns of best value authorities that a 31 March publication date would result in some data needing to be of a provisional nature, and also that it does not, in all cases, fit well with other planning cycles. On the other hand there is value in linking the production of the Best Value Performance Plan to the financial year cycle.' Consequently, the Local Government (Best Value) (Reviews and Performance Plans) (Wales) Order 'sets the date by which performance plans must be published formally as 30 June. This will allow authorities extra time to finalise (as far as is possible) the data included in the plans and to take into account budget and policy decisions taken at the end of the financial year. As a consequence the date for the submission of the auditor's report will be changed to 31 October.'[3]

Performance Pressure

5.6 Clearly, the provisions in the 1999 Act, the Plans and Reviews Order and the Guidance, are designed to put best value authorities under performance pressure and to provide transparent comparative and other information about authorities' progress in achieving continuous improvement. As the Guidance indicates, s 6 of the LGA 1999 and the Plans and Reviews Order[4]

'amount to a clear statement about:

– what services an authority will deliver to local people

---

1   As indicated in Chapter 3, the Government does not intend to specify standards for the first year of best value but the issue will be reconsidered for later years (see *Best Value and Audit Commission Performance Indicators for 2000/2001*, Vol 1, para 15.4).

2   Local Government (Best Value) Performance Plans and Reviews Order 1999, SI 1999/3251, art 4.

3   National Assembly for Wales Circular 14/2000, para 19.

4   At para 53.

–   how it will deliver them
–   to what levels services are currently delivered
–   what levels of service the public should expect in the future
–   what action it will take to deliver those standards and over what timescale'.

As with other parts of the best value regime, the matters in s 6(2) demand a clear and strong strategic focus at both corporate and departmental levels. The performance plan affords no opportunity for the late creative ad lib. There needs to have been in place a coherent vision and strategy from which the objectives, indicators, standards and targets can flow. Given that authorities' external auditors will have a duty under s 7 of the LGA 1999 to audit best value performance plans,[1] it may often be desirable to involve the auditor as appropriate in the production process. This will aid mutual understanding and facilitate the handling of difficult issues co-operatively to avoid entrenched positions. It will therefore be more likely to assist a positive outcome.

KEY INGREDIENTS OF THE PERFORMANCE PLAN

5.7   This section will consider in turn the key factors in s 6(2) with reference as appropriate to the Plans and Reviews Order and the Guidance.

(a) To summarise the authority's objectives in relation to the exercise of its functions

5.8   Objectives will also need to be (or to have been) considered under the best value review.[2] This underlines the importance of authorities conducting a strategic review at the earliest possible opportunity and where necessary in advance of the formal review process in relevant areas. For corporate objectives constitute the authority's purpose and direction – why it is in business. These should permeate throughout the whole organisation. As the Guidance notes,[3] the functional objectives 'will derive from the authority's overall vision and community strategy, and from any corporate planning processes which give effect to that vision'. The performance plan summary 'will also reflect nationally set objectives, any medium term financial strategy, and identify service priorities'.[4]
   It will also be helpful to consider the following.

–   How have the operations of the authority and its constituent parts made a 'real difference' to the community?
–   How have support services contributed to corporate outputs?
–   What improvements have there been across the authority and how can they be demonstrated to have been continuous?
–   How can economy, efficiency and effectiveness be demonstrated in each key output?

1   See Chapter 6.
2   LGA 1999, s 5 – see Chapter 4.
3   At para 54.
4   DETR Circular 10/99, para 54.

– What combination of these 3 'E's was adopted? What was the weighting and how was this justified?
– How has the authority approached consultation? Has consultation been integral to strategic planning and actions?
– What 'joined-up' initiatives have been pursued and what value have they added?

It will clearly be important to ensure that the authority knows where it is going, why it is going there and how, that the passengers are happy with the destination and the different means of transport available and that the whole operation is economically, efficiently and effectively conducted.

(b) To summarise any assessment made by the authority of the level at which and the way in which it exercises its functions

5.9 Section 6(2)(b) links in with the *challenge* stage of the 4Cs considered in Chapter 4.[1] Even though the provision refers to 'any assessment', authorities will in practice need to have made such an assessment even if this is on an interim basis. Clearly the more fundamental and comprehensive the assessment, the greater credibility it will have within the published performance plan. The fact that this assessment is made in the 'shop window' of the plan will obviously concentrate minds. It will be helpful if authorities can in connection with s 6(2)(b) of the LGA 1999 and art 3(1)(b) of the Plans and Reviews Order point to a strategic and detailed review programme (linking up with s 6(2)(c) and (d) of the LGA 1999 and art 3(1)(c) and (d) of the Plans and Reviews Order – see below) to signal the way in which they will be taking a completely fresh look at how they discharge their functions in the light of the duty of best value and a consideration of 'joined-up' solutions.

Paragraph 54 of the Guidance[2] states that in 'summarising the level at which it exercises its functions and to assist local people in understanding how well it has performed, an authority should provide suitable financial information that places cost indicators in a wider context'.

Whilst the status quo (with a robust improvement action plan) may turn out to be the most satisfactory solution in certain cases, this will require detailed justification with an audit trail of thought processes leading to a reasoned conclusion.

(c) To state any period within which the authority is required to review its functions under section 5
(d) To state the timetable the authority proposes to follow in conducting a review

5.10 These provisions in s 6(2) of the LGA 1999[3] require authorities to specify the period for reviewing their functions and the proposed timetable for so

---

1   See, for example, s 5(4)(b) of the 1999 Act and art 6(1)(b) of the Plans and Reviews Order, SI 1999/3251.
2   DETR Circular 10/99.
3   Together with consequential reflective provisions in art 3(1)(c) and (d) of the Plans and Reviews Order, SI 1999/3251.

doing.[1] There will be no discretion for the former since this has been specified under s 5(2) by means of art 5 of the Plans and Reviews Order.[2] As to the timetable, authorities are likely to have discretion since as 'a general rule, the Government does not intend to prescribe a common Review timetable'.[3] However, as noted in Chapter 4, the Guidance expects that this will be 'practical and realistic'[4] in the light of available authority resources, the opportunity for tackling cross-cutting issues and the demands of other statutory, financial and contractual requirements. The review programme will need to flow from any community strategy and corporate vision and from a 'clear analysis of current performance – based on a comparison using the best value and other indicators as well as from consultation with local people, business and employees'. There will be a general expectation that 'poorly performing services' should be reviewed early in the five-year cycle in the absence of good reasons; and authorities will need to demonstrate a 'clear audit trail' as to how the review programme was formulated.[5]

5.11   Paragraph 54 of the Guidance[6] indicates that:

> 'Authorities will need to explain and justify their Review programme, together with the commencement and completion dates for the early Reviews and the resources they intend to devote to them. Where there are critical areas of uncertainty that might affect a Review's timetable then these should be identified clearly. Otherwise, authorities should explain variations to previous Review programmes, and highlight where the Secretary of State or an Inspectorate has required a Review to be carried out at their request'.

And although this will not be relevant for all authorities in the first year of best value:[7]

> 'All Reviews that have been completed in the previous year should be reported on in summary form, and the Plan should include where possible information from those that are in train. The results of consultation, the alternatives considered, an explanation of the agreed outcome and a plan of action to achieve the new targets should be summarised clearly and, where necessary, should include a cross-reference to the source material'.

The key is to have a clear and justifiable strategy which makes sense and has public credibility in a local context and which is likely to deliver best value outcomes. Clearly this has to be within a context of valuing employees; creating demotivation and recrimination within any organisation is obviously not productive.

---

1   Section 6(2)(c) and (d) respectively of the LGA 1999.
2   See Chapter 4.
3   DETR Circular 10/99, para 18.
4   Ibid.
5   Ibid, para 19.
6   DETR Circular 10/99.
7   Ibid, para 54.

(e) To state any performance indicators, standards and targets specified or set in relation to the authority's functions

5.12 Article 3(1)(e) of the Plans and Reviews Order amplifies this (in the light of the *Best Value and Audit Commission Performance Indicators for 2000/2001*) to the requirement that best value authorities include in their performance plans for the financial year 2000 'a statement specifying any best value performance indicators, best value performance standards and best value performance targets specified or set in relation to the authority's functions'.

As indicated in Chapter 3 (which deals substantively with performance indicators and related issues), *Best Value and Audit Commission Performance Indicators for 2000/2001*,[1] gives some indicative definitions of these terms:

'–   Performance indicator: means the measure of a best value authority's performance in exercising a function.
–   Performance standard: means the minimum acceptable level of service provision which must be met by a best value authority in the exercise of a function and measured by reference to a performance indicator for that function. A failure to meet a performance standard will be judged as failing the test of best value for that service or function.
–   Performance target: means the level of performance in the exercise of a function that a best value authority is expected to achieve, as measured by reference to the performance indicator in relation to that function.'

Issues of performance against these measures and otherwise are now considered.

Review of Performance

5.13 In the LGA 1999, this area is covered by s 6(2)(f) to (l) (as follows) which underpin the relevant provisions in arts 3 and 4 of the Plans and Reviews Order (see above):

'(f)   to summarise the authority's assessment of its performance in the previous financial year with regard to performance indicators;
(g)   to compare that performance with the authority's performance in previous financial years or with the performance of other best value authorities;
(h)   to summarise its assessment of its success in meeting any performance standard which applied at any time in the previous financial year;
(i)   to summarise its assessment of its progress towards meeting any performance standard which has been specified but which does not yet apply;
(j)   to summarise its assessment of its progress towards meeting any performance target;
(k)   to summarise any plan of action to be taken in the financial year to which the plan relates for the purposes of meeting a performance target;
(l)   to summarise the basis on which any performance target was set, and any plan of action was determined, in relation to a function reviewed under section 5 in the previous financial year'.

These factors and the relevant provisions in the Plans and Reviews Order focus on the assessment, comparison and planning of performance. Although it will clearly be easier to report on a historic basis since otherwise outcome data is

---

1   Vol 1, para 4.4.

likely to be immature or non-existent, nevertheless, for the financial year 2001 and thereafter, art 4(1)(g) of the Plans and Reviews Order requires performance plans to contain 'a summary of any plan of action to be taken in the financial year to which the plan relates for the purposes of meeting a best value performance target'.

5.14 Paragraph 54 of the Guidance supports this requirement by indicating that performance plans should include 'a summary of current performance'. The current performance summary will therefore:

> '... need to include performance against the national best value indicators, and might usefully draw upon any indicators that are identified by the Audit Commission or required by Government for planning or programme purposes. It should also include performance against local sustainable development[1] indicators and especially those developed locally to reflect community preferences. The summary should also include any commentary that authorities might wish to make which would help place their performance in context. For example, comparative information can be presented in the form of a schematic diagram showing performance against the average nationally or by type of authority.'

More straightforward in reporting terms is the requirement for an authority in the performance plan to assess its performance in the previous financial year. Paragraph 54 of the Guidance[2] indicates that:

> 'Authorities will need to provide an historic context for local people to understand the performance data for the year in question. Fully audited indicators from the preceding financial year and, where practicable, a consideration of comparative information from other best value authorities, should be included. Discrepancies that occur between estimated outturn and actual audited figures for each performance indicator should be highlighted.'

5.15 For 'the financial year 2000' the Plans and Reviews Order requires the performance plan to contain 'a summary of the authority's assessment of its performance in the previous financial year with regard to the relevant Audit Commission indicators, where applicable'.[3] The comparison with Audit Commission indicators is presumably because the best value performance indicators and related performance measures were not available in the previous financial year. In addition, art 3(1)(g) requires performance plans for 2000 to contain a comparison of the performance just referred to[4] with the authority's performance in previous financial years.

For 2001 (and beyond) when both best value and Audit Commission performance indicators will be available for comparison, art 4(2) of the Plans and Reviews Order prescribes a range of performance information to be included in performance plans. This includes:

– a summary of the authority's assessment of its performance in the previous financial year with regard to best value performance indicators, where applicable;

1   See footnote 1 at p 66.
2   DETR Circular 10/99.
3   Article 3(1)(f) of the Plans and Reviews Order, SI 1999/3251.
4   Ibid.

–   a comparison of that performance with the authority's performance in previous financial years;

–   a comparison of the authority's performance, as summarised, with the performance of other best value authorities in previous financial years;

–   a summary of its assessment of its success in meeting any best value performance standard which applied at any time in the previous financial year;

–   a summary of the basis on which any best value performance target was set, and any plan of action was determined, in relation to a function reviewed under s 5 of the LGA 1999 and arts 5 and 6 of the Plans and Reviews Order, in the previous financial year.

FINANCIAL ISSUES

5.16   In the summary of financial performance for the past year to be included in performance plans, authorities should also 'include the budgeted income of the authority with an analysis of budgeted expenditure for the year ahead'. In addition other relevant financial information should be included 'such as details of major capital projects and investments' and 'changes to purchasing proposals'.[1]

5.17   The Chartered Institute of Public Finance and Accountancy (CIPFA) on 22 February 2000 published a *Best Value Accounting – Code of Practice* to provide guidance and 'enhance the comparability of local authority financial information'.[2] This document[3] will assist authorities to comply with the statutory requirements surrounding performance plans and reviews and will be 'recognized as proper practice for all best value authorities'.[4] Paragraph 71 of the Guidance indicated that following publication of the Code, the Secretary of State would decide whether to exercise his powers in s 23 of the LGA 1999 to make regulations about the keeping of accounts by best value authorities. However, Hilary Armstrong, Minister for Local Government and the Regions, announced following publication of the *Best Value Accounting – Code of Practice* that:

> '... given the positive approach to trading accounts the Code promotes we will not need to exercise these powers at this time. We will monitor its introduction to ensure that it achieves its objectives and will review this decision following CIPFA's own review of the Code later in the year.'[5]

Before publication of the CIPFA Code of Practice and for the first performance plan 'the Government recommends that authorities include a summary disclosure note listing the nature, turnover and profit/loss of any significant trading operations engaged in by the authority for which separate accounts are maintained';[6] and 'where balances on trading accounts are significant such that

1   DETR Circular 10/99, para 54.
2   Ibid, para 68.
3   CIPFA's *Best Value Accounting – Code of Practice*.
4   DETR Circular 10/99, para 68.
5   CIPFA Press Release, 23 February 2000.
6   DETR Circular 10/99, para 69.

relevant performance indicators would be materially misstated, the balances should be re-apportioned to services. The apportionments should be disclosed as part of the summary disclosure note'.[1] Further guidance appears in the Code of Practice.

5.18 Provisional accounting returns will be necessary where any such information is to be included in the performance plan, drawing wherever possible upon 'regular monthly or quarterly returns to enhance its credibility'.[2] Accounting and budgeting systems will need to be developed in-house 'to ensure the accuracy of any financial information required for inclusion in Plans in subsequent years'.[3]

Finally, performance plans must contain recommendations from the previous year's audit report. Any changes made or expected following audit or inspection reports or because of directions given by the Secretary of State must also be highlighted.[4]

Efficiency Improvement

5.19 The Government indicates in para 54 of the Guidance that performance plans should contain a summary of the authority's approach to efficiency improvement:

> 'Authorities need to take a corporate approach to improving efficiency, as well as to improving quality and effectiveness. The Performance Plan should set out how authorities have assessed the scope for improvements in efficiency, both in individual services and in the way the authority manages itself and its assets; how they propose to deliver better performance; and the level of efficiency improvement that they expect to achieve.'

But whilst the 'Government accepts that the scope for efficiency improvements will vary year-on-year and between authorities and services ... authorities should ensure that over time their proposed aggregate efficiency gains are consistent with the 2% per annum target currently set for local authority expenditure as a whole.'[5]

Action Planning

5.20 Article 4(2)(g) and (h) of the Plans and Reviews Order (underpinned by s6(2)(k) and (l) of the LGA 1999) refer to action planning. The former requires a summary of any plan of action to be taken in the financial year to which the Plan relates for the purposes of meeting a best value performance target. The latter requires a summary of the basis on which any best value performance target was set, and any action plan determined in relation to a function subject to statutory review in the previous financial year.

Wherever appropriate a 'SMART' (Specific, Measurable, Accountable, Realistic and Time based) action plan having the confidence and commitment of all those who have to implement it should be considered in relation to

---

1   DETR Circular 10/99, para 69.
2   Ibid, para 70.
3   Ibid.
4   Ibid, para 54.
5   Ibid.

targets. This provides the requisite discipline and also facilitates the allocation of time and physical resources to assist achievement of the target. In this connection, the Government indicates that all 'action plans should include measurable milestones against which progress can be monitored'[1] and:

> 'Targets which involve a substantial departure from previous targets or performance, or which are set following a Review in the last year, should be accompanied by an action plan explaining how they are to be met. Similarly, when authorities have had to respond to an auditor or inspector's report, then there should be a clear response from the authority as to the steps it has taken or intends to take to address the issues raised.'[2]

Performance Targets for Future Years

5.21 As for future years, the Government indicates[3] that the service targets set for previous years in respect of both local and national indicators will usually 'roll forward' to future years 'adjusted as necessary in the light of the resources available and the authority's priorities'. If there are variations in targets (and particularly if these were set following earlier reviews) full justification for the variations will need to be included together with assurance that the new targets will comply with best value. New targets derived from reviews with any implications for other service targets should be highlighted.[4] This is rightly stated to be particularly important following reviews which have identified cross-cutting themes. It is equally relevant for support services which may not directly impact upon community outputs but will clearly be enabling services and functions which do. Also:

> 'In the first Performance Plan authorities will need to set targets against those BVPIs[5] which mirror existing Audit Commission indicators. Authorities will not be expected to set targets against new indicators for 2000/01, given the lack of historic data, but will need to do so in their subsequent Performance Plans. Authorities will also wish to set other targets which reflect local priorities and build wherever possible on relevant historic data, such as recorded crime.'[6]

5.22 As will be seen below, an authority's auditor must by s 7(4) of the LGA 1999 annually report upon the authority's performance plan. The Guidance requires that recommendations from 'the previous year's audit report must be included' and authorities should also 'highlight any changes that have been made, or are expected to be made, following audit or inspection reports, or because of directions given by the Secretary of State'.[7]

Consultation

5.23 The performance plan must include a brief statement explaining how the authority has complied with its statutory duties to consult under ss 3 and 5 of

---

1   DETR Circular 10/99, para 54.
2   Ibid.
3   Ibid.
4   Ibid.
5   Best value performance indicators.
6   DETR Circular 10/99, para 54.
7   Ibid. See below.

the LGA 1999. This 'could usefully comment on the forms and types of consultation carried out over the previous year, the numbers or types of groups, bodies and individuals involved and an analysis of the results'.[1] In addition,

> 'The statement could refer to previous consultations that have informed the Performance Plan, include contact details for those who wish to make representations, and provide information on how or where local people can remain involved or provide feedback. Any changes planned over the coming year to secure improved results from consultation should be highlighted.'[2]

SUMMARY OF WHAT THE PERFORMANCE PLAN MUST INCLUDE

5.24 It is useful to summarise those issues which the Guidance[3] indicates must be contained in performance plans and which have been considered above in the course of examining the statutory requirements. These are:

- a summary of the authority's objectives in respect of its functions;
- a summary of current performance;
- a comparison with performance in previous financial years;
- a summary of the authority's approach to efficiency improvement;
- a statement describing the review programme;
- the key results of completed reviews;
- the performance targets set for future years;
- a plan of action;
- a response to audit and inspection reports;
- a consultation statement; and
- financial information.

OTHER ISSUES ON THE CONTENT OF PERFORMANCE PLANS

5.25 Performance plans will in their nature look both forwards and backwards. The backwards look is at 'the performance of the authority for the financial year just ending'.[4] Provisional data will be necessary for this, possibly including estimates and projections. The plan will also contain the audited information for the preceding year. Whilst the quality of performance information is expected to improve in robustness and breadth as 'authorities establish better performance management procedures', nevertheless, 'local people will rightly look for information of the highest possible standard and authorities are responsible for its accuracy'.[5] As to the forward projection, the plan will identify targets set by authorities for themselves 'for the next and

---

1   DETR Circular 10/99, para 54. See below.
2   Ibid.
3   Ibid.
4   Ibid, para 56.
5   Ibid.

future years, and a concise course of action for achieving these targets'.[1] As indicated in Chapter 3, guidance on Performance Targets and Top Quartile Values appears in *Best Value and Audit Commission Performance Indicators for 2000/2001*.[2]

FORM OF THE PERFORMANCE PLAN

5.26 Since performance plans are public documents, it is obviously important that they are clear, accessible, jargon-free and with 'an attractive design'.[3] The Government points out that it is working with the Audit Commission, the Local Government Association and the Improvement and Development Agency 'to identify good practice in presenting auditable Performance Plans to a wider audience and will discuss its proposals with those representing service customers, providers and employees'.[4]

The published plan 'will enable authorities to demonstrate to a wider audience the effectiveness of the authority itself and its relations with the community of which it is a part'.[5] But there is a balance to be struck between overwhelming the community with explanation of all the other 'plans, processes and initiatives in which the authority is involved, and providing local people with sufficient information to reach a rounded view on the perform-ance and aims of the authority'.[6] A 'clear summary' of individual service plans, inspectors' reports and reviews 'focusing on the key outcomes and targets – is necessary, together with an audit trail of supporting information.'[7]

5.27 The Government does not intend to prescribe the format of perform-ance plans and accepts that the information can be presented in many different ways depending upon an authority's corporate approach. For instance an authority might choose:

> '... to present the relevant details within service specific chapters, or list all the performance information targets within a separate section, with another section explaining the service strategy and review work of the authority. Alternatively, some authorities may take as a starting point the results of the year's Reviews and provide information in later sections. Other authorities might adopt an approach focusing on particular neighbourhoods, urban or rural areas, sections of the community, or based on cross-cutting themes'.[8]

Although as indicated there is a variety of legal requirements surrounding performance plans the mode of presentation in published plans will need to balance these against 'the general requirements of transparency and accessi-bility'.[9] Whilst both are 'consistent with real accountability to local people'[10] for

---

1   DETR Circular 10/99, para 56.
2   Vol 1, Chap 15.
3   DETR Circular 10/99, para 59.
4   Ibid.
5   Ibid, para 57.
6   Ibid.
7   Ibid.
8   Ibid, para 58.
9   Ibid, para 60.
10   Ibid.

full and effective engagement of local people and interests, authorities will need to 'supplement these Plans by providing summarised information to local households and other places of residence, and to service users and local business and voluntary interests'.[1] Such summaries:

> '... should offer a fair and accurate reflection of information within the Plans themselves. Authorities will be free to select which indicators and targets they might highlight alongside other information, but should have regard to key national and local priorities and any action which they have in hand to tackle performance weaknesses. Summaries should also include a guide as to how the complete documentation might be viewed or accessed (in libraries or on the Internet, for example), and what arrangements are in place to handle queries and comments. Both Plans and summaries should be available by 31 March each year in as many forms as necessary to ensure fair access for the whole local community.'[2]

AUDIT OF PERFORMANCE PLANS

5.28 Plans will be subject to audit under s 7 of the LGA 1999[3] 'normally by the same team auditing the previous year's financial accounts'.[4] As indicated above, first performance plans were to be published by 31 March 2000 and thereafter by 31 March annually. The first performance plan 'will report on performance and preparations made prior to the statutory introduction of the duty of best value'.[5] Therefore, auditors will take this into account in their audit assessment (to be completed by 30 June 2000). As noted, the Plans and Reviews Order requires 'for the first Performance Plan, the inclusion of information for 1999/2000 as specified in the Audit Commission's Direction of 1998'.[6]

The Government makes it clear that:

> '[t]he auditor will look to establish that the necessary statutory requirements have been complied with as well as at actual and planned performance. Information contained within the Plan will be scrutinised to ensure it is reasonable and robust. The first Performance Plan is likely to provide clear evidence of an authority's approach to the introduction of best value and the steps it has taken to embrace the challenge of the years ahead. Auditors may refer Plans to the Secretary of State where they are not persuaded that an authority has made a serious attempt to address the issues in such a way as to ensure best value for local people.'[7]

---

1   DETR Circular 10/99, para 60.
2   Ibid.
3   See Chapter 6.
4   DETR Circular 10/99, para 55.
5   Ibid.
6   Ibid.
7   Ibid.

PILOT PERFORMANCE PLANS

(1) Some Material Available Before Best Value Performance Plans: Practice and Procedures[1]

5.29   On 24 November 1999 the DETR published a detailed research paper on best value performance plans. This gave a detailed critique of the approach of eight sample local authorities. However, before considering this, it is worth looking at the experience of the best value pilot authorities[2] to see how authorities have grappled in practice with some of the performance planning principles from the early days of best value. It should nevertheless be borne in mind that the pilots have been in operation since the conception of best value and before the principles evolved into their present statutory form.[3]

Newark and Sherwood District Council produced its first local performance plan in October 1998 covering in respect of 19 service areas: service aim; key objectives; a range of performance indicators; budget and staffing levels; comparisons with other authorities; links with other plans; key partners; consultation techniques; and areas for improvement. The plan was to be monitored and reviewed by customer panels.

Newark and Sherwood's second plan for 1999/2000[4] covers the best value pilot services of: revenues and benefits, information systems, environmental services, housing services and legal services. The local performance plans for individual services aim to review the Council's performance in 1998/99 and specify service objectives, performance targets and areas for improvement for 1999/2000.

5.30   Taking legal services as an example, the 1999/2000 plan 'emphasises the aim of the section to provide a service which is efficient and effective and which is responsive to customer needs and requirements'. The purpose of the Service is to 'meet the ever changing needs and expectations of our clients in an efficient and professional manner'. There are then sections dealing with:

–   **Achievements in 1998/99. Did we meet our key objectives?** (with outcomes reported into categories of yes, no or partially).

–   **How did we perform (in 1998/99)?** The percentage target set and percentage achievement is reported against indicators covering: strategic objectives, effectiveness, quality, cost and efficiency, and fair access.

–   **Did we address our areas for improvement (1998/99)?** (with the outcome reported into categories of yes, no or partially).

–   **Key objectives for 1999/2000** (given as: (1) to continue to develop a service which is responsive to customer needs and requirements (2) to develop and review service standards (3) to continue to develop a Benchmarking Club to compare our performance against other Notting-

---

1   DETR, *A Review of Early Experiences within eight local authorities* (24 November 1999) – see below.
2   See Chapter 1.
3   As mentioned above, the pilot authorities are listed in Annex A to DETR Circular 10/99 and also (at the time of writing) on the DETR's internet site: http:// www.local.detr.gov.uk/research/bvsummar/preface.htm#List.
4   This can be viewed at http://www.newark-sherwooddc.gov.uk/bestvalue/bvintro.htm.

hamshire authorities (4) to evaluate and introduce new technology where appropriate and where funding permits.

- **Performance Indicators for 1999/2000** These are all local indicators and again cover: strategic objectives, effectiveness, quality, cost and efficiency and fair access.
- **Key resource information with comparisons with similar local authorities/organisations.**
- **Consultation techniques used** These are reported as: Customer panels, Workshops, Customer surveys with internal client departments, Benchmarking Club.
- **Key links and partners** (none yet identified).
- **Areas for improvement in 1999/2000** (given as (1) More effective case management performance review (2) More efficient use of information technology).

The other services follow a similar methodology appropriate to their particular services. In the light of the statutory duty of best value, all the non-pilot services will be included in the first statutory local performance plan which (as has been noted) had to be in place by 31 March 2000. Newark and Sherwood Council point out that:

'It is important to see this local performance plan within the context of our overall Council priorities, demonstrating Best Value underpins the Council's corporate activities and its main priorities. This 1999/2000 local performance plan will be monitored and reviewed during the financial year and the results will be fed into the 2000/2001 plan.'

5.31 The DETR Publication, *Achieving Best Value through Performance Review*[1] indicates that:

'Manchester [City Council] is testing approaches to producing Local Performance Plans which will be delivered to all residents and other stakeholders in the three pilot areas. The first plans are planned to be produced in December 1999 informed by surveys of residents' views on current services, and the outputs of FPRs[2] on current performance and improvement targets. The second plans will follow surveys of resident's views on how services have improved and will show the extent of improvement against targets and additional targets deriving from further FPRs.'

Also:

'Braintree produced a first Local Performance Plan in September 1998 – "Our Plans and Performance Levels for 1998/99". It comprises 147 pages bringing together all service plans but it is intended to convert it into a series of consultation documents for distribution to residents.'

A suggested individual, team and departmental team improvement plan model has been suggested above. Provided that this is 'wired-up' to corporate

1 Published 12 February 1999 – see Warwick/DETR Best Value Series, Paper No 5 by Ian Sanderson, Policy Research Institute, Leeds Metropolitan University.
2 Fundamental performance review – the original title for the best value review – see, for example, DETR, *Modern Local Government In Touch with the People* (July 1998), paras 7.16–7.18.

objectives, this could form the basis of a departmental or directorate service delivery plan which could 'cascade-up' to play a part in the overall performance plan.

The contents of performance plans will be more tightly focused and comparable with other authorities following the publication in December 1999 of the *Best Value and Audit Commission Performance Indicators for 2000/2001.*

(2) Best Value Performance Plans: Practice and Procedures[1]

5.32 As mentioned above, this Paper (which can be seen at the DETR's website at http://www.local-regions.detr.gov.uk/bestvalue/performance/ppindex.htm) reports on research undertaken by the DETR into the performance planning process on the basis of a case study of eight local authorities[2] 'drawn from a matrix of variables to reflect: regional location, type of authority, Best Value pilot status and political control'.[3] It contains a wealth of practical and useful guidance and information including case study summaries for four of the authorities examined.[4] The fieldwork for the study took place during Summer 1999 and the conclusions and observations include the following:[5]

–   Performance plans 'are both the public statements and summaries of a local authority's Best Value position as well as a reporting and accountability mechanism'.[6] They should provide (as per the DETR's July 1998 White Paper[7]) '... *a clear practical expression of an authority's performance in delivering local services and its proposals to improve*'. The aim of the plan is 'more than a service delivery plan writ large. It is about delivering existing services more efficiently, but it also seeks to promote a process and framework for wider engagement and debate in the process of local governance'.[8]

–   There is no universal performance plan model being adopted by the authorities[9] studied. Most followed a 'broadly similar "hierarchical" template' setting down the corporate vision supported by 'increasingly specific priorities for its realization' accompanied by some performance information (targets and achievements). This was 'underpinned by the service-specific plans, which provide detailed action plans and the basis for performance review'. However, no individual authority studied had all of these elements in their entirety.[10]

---

1   DETR, 24 November 1999.
2   Cambridgeshire County Council (non-pilot); Northamptonshire County Council (pilot); City of Bradford Metropolitan Council (pilot); London Borough of Hackney (non-pilot); Southampton City Council (pilot); Torfaen County Borough Council (pilot); Telford & Wrekin Council (non-pilot); Carrick District Council (pilot).
3   *Best Value Performance Plans: Practice and Procedures*, Executive Summary, para 1c.
4   Northamptonshire County Council; Southampton City Council; Telford & Wrekin Council; Torfaen County Borough Council.
5   References are to the Executive Summary unless otherwise stated.
6   Paragraph 1.1.
7   *Modern Local Government In Touch with the People*, para 7.31.
8   *Best Value Performance Plans: Practice and Procedures*, para 1.3.
9   Paragraph 1d.
10   Ibid.

– Whilst most of the authorities identified their corporate priorities most failed to 'include any detail of the choice or source of these priorities' which were 'generally presented as a *fait accompli*'.

– Many action plans for 'realizing the vision' remain 'insufficiently explicit' and 'there remains the danger that plans become "corporate wishlists" '.[1]

– The participating authorities had 'yet to make significant progress in developing performance frameworks'.[2] The Paper expressed the view that performance information relates to a number of potential measures relating to 'different *elements* of service activity, (inputs, outputs, outcomes), and the *purpose for which* that information is sought, (measure or baseline of current performance; target for future performance; comparator with previous performance or other service delivery bodies). Taken as a whole, they need to provide information, which relates to performance in achieving corporate priorities'. It also noted that 'Comparator informations, and benchmarking of performance, are notable by their absence'.[3]

– Most authorities studied included no details of the services to be reviewed or the timetable for review.[4]

– The majority of the participating authorities emphasised that they experienced difficulty in reconciling the requirements of the different statutory planning systems with those of the performance plan regime. With the exception of Hackney LBC (which included all of its nine service plans within the overall 'Hackney Plan'), most referred to these in an annex to the main plan.[5]

– As to consultation and public engagement, most 'plans contained general exhortations of the importance of responding to the needs of the public, though few include details of any consultation strategy'. However, a number included 'ways in which the public can express opinions, (giving addresses or names of contacts)' and both Hackney LBC and City of Bradford included freepost questionnaires within their plans.[6]

– Regarding format, since there is no accepted model authorities are being 'creative (or otherwise) in their approaches'.[7] The focus to date appears to have been on content rather than presentation although participating authorities realised the need to 'tailor different publications for different groups'. Currently most 'take the form of "internal" reports, of between 30–60 pages, with little, or no, illustrative material'.[8] Few of the participating authorities have explored 'producing summaries or extracts from the plan in more accessible formats' and none had yet placed its plan on its council 'website, produced audio versions nor editions in foreign languages'.[9]

---

1   Paragraph 1f.
2   Paragraph 1g.
3   Paragraph 1h.
4   Paragraph 1i.
5   Paragraph 1j.
6   Paragraph 1k.
7   Paragraph 1l.
8   Ibid.
9   Paragraph 4.29.

–   Whilst the authorities in question felt that best value should not, of itself, dictate specific changes in organisational arrangements (to avoid being considered as a project separate from mainstream authority activities) nevertheless they had generally organised their departmental structures 'into broader directorates or teams in order to prevent "silo" working'. In addition, there was a move to strengthen corporate capacity 'to develop a strategic approach to planning and performance'.[1]

–   Concerning committee (or other democratic) structures, there was a move away from traditional service committees towards the development of 'cross-department committees utilising different modes of working'.[2] Whilst several authorities had in place or in train member structures to take responsibility for best value initiatives, there was some concern that separate member frameworks may 'exacerbate the perception' that best value is a separate 'project' and not 'integral to all of the Council's activities'.[3]

–   The Paper expressed the view that the purpose of the best value performance plan is to 'bring together the outcomes from different planning systems to illustrate an authority's integrated corporate strategy and performance'. However, most of the participating authorities were seeking ways of co-ordinating different planning frameworks. There was also an identified gap between corporate vision and service-specific plans which could be 'brokered' by the best value performance plan.[4]

–   Most authorities were 'still in the process of defining the parameters of change required'. They emphasised the need for 'guidance and leadership within the authority, to lend both drive and rigour to the process'. Nevertheless, the Paper made the point that the best value 'process is an iterative one, requiring information exchange and learning between service departments and the corporate centre' and 'Time is an essential ingredient in this process'.[5]

–   Few authorities had any formal system for selecting the performance review areas but most were 'wary of adopting a "worst first" basis in exclusion of other factors'. The importance of seeing the reviews as 'continual rather than episodic' was stressed, as was the 'need for better coordination and exchange of learning between the many different reviews which may be operating at any one point in time'.[6] Most of the authorities saw reviews in terms of a whole service examination every five years. This was considered to be restrictive. Southampton City Council, by contrast, 'had issued corporate guidance which stresses that reviews may take a variety of different sizes and be undertaken at different intervals; they may be cross-service departments or as small as one particular performance indicator. Furthermore, systems for monitoring performance need to be continual rather than episodic.'[7]

---

1   Paragraph 1n and paras 5.2–5.6.
2   Paragraph 1o.
3   Paragraph 5.10.
4   Paragraph 1p and paras 6.4 and 6.5.
5   Paragraph 1r.
6   Paragraph 1s.
7   Paragraph 7.6.

– The problems concerning development of a performance framework centred around:

  '• Lack of information: Authorities found that performance reviews were impeded by a lack of current available performance data within service areas and a lack of objectives upon which to base assessment of performance and establish targets;

  • Lack of guidance: Many felt that central government could, and should, provide more information and guidance about the processes which underpin performance review and how authorities can respond to them;

  • The strategic-service gap: Different levels of understanding, knowledge and support for performance review between those within the corporate centre and those within departments under review. Many found the process threatening and unrepresentative, and breaking down barriers is time consuming, (and never complete);

  • Member involvement: Effective performance review requires that members adopt different roles. There is not scope for them to be "defensive" about service areas; rather they need to ensure that reviews are rigorous and effective, and that the performance information within the BVPP[1] is accurate. Again, this requires communication and skill development.

  • Identification of boundaries: Few, if any, areas of an authority's work were seen as being completely independent. Indeed, many felt that development of the BVPP encouraged them to see their work in relation to much wider aims. Most authorities experienced enormous difficulties in delineating between service areas and defining those service areas which are material to the delivery of a service and those which are incidental.'[2]

– Authority-wide processes for 'the collation and monitoring of performance data are very much embryonic' within the authorities studied.[3]

– Most authorities considered that the requirement to publish the performance plan by 31 March each year was problematic. This was essentially because: (a) the data was provisional and 'the extent to which incomplete or inaccurate information would help or impede accountability was an issue of concern'; and (b) the political implications of siting the date so near to the local elections where there would be political pressure for the performance plan to report good news. This was felt likely to impair the cross-party working which best value has encouraged. The approach of the National Assembly for Wales is interesting in this context (see above).

– Regarding consultation processes, the authorities had 'adopted a variety of different techniques for consulting with the public, including news-letters, surveys, panels and meetings' although most had not done so specifically for the performance plan. It was also recognised that 'a variety of different techniques would be necessary to reach the many different "publics", and that authorities had to be creative in order to counter indifference or suspicion of the Council'. A co-ordinated approach was

---

1   Best value performance plan.
2   Paragraph 7.7.
3   Paragraph 1u.

desirable not only in itself, but also to avoid 'consultation fatigue' by both public and officers.

–   Staff engagement was recognised by the authorities to be pivotal, and 'adequate consultation involves both informing and consulting'. Some authorities had developed 'champions' within departments to function as both 'liaison points and evangelists about the reforms'. As for staff communication methods, while most authorities used traditional communication methods, some had distributed best value handbooks or toolkits amongst staff. Some had specific sessions with staff to consider cross-cutting work and others used quality initiatives as a means of engaging staff and forging the link between individual and organisational performance.

–   The authorities considered that there was an important role for elected members as the bridge between the community and the authority. However, some members felt that best value threatened their representative role.

5.33   The Paper[1] pointed to the following lessons emerging from this research 'which distinguish the more comprehensive and effective plans, from those which are less so':

'–   All authorities need to develop an overall vision and link it to corporate objectives and methods of delivery and performance planning;

–   The development of service- and policy-specific planning and performance arrangements provides the foundation for the BVPP, as a basis from which to deliver, monitor and evaluate performance. It is important to place the BVPP within the context of the corporate planning process;

–   Consultation needs to be an integral part of the process of developing the BVPP, and the plan needs to demonstrate the extent to which such consultation has been effective and continuous. Authorities need to consider a range of media for publication;

–   There needs to be a clear link between corporate priorities and action plans, and the performance measurement framework. The outcomes of policy are those which ultimately affect citizens and measures which reflect these should be sought;

–   BVPPs can provide an important education role about the role of the authority. The relationship between the BVPP and other planning arrangements within the Council, as well as the activities and responsibilities of other agencies might usefully be included;

–   The role of organisational structures and leadership (amongst both members and officers) in the process of developing a BVPP is vital, in terms of developing a proactive "culture". A number of authorities have found changed committee or departmental structures a useful step to developing work on cross-cutting issues. However, there is not a need for a wholly new "Best Value infrastructure".'

---

1   At para 9.2.

THE DETR VIEW[1]

5.34   On 28 January 2000 the DETR published *Notebook – Issue 1.*[2] This is 'an occasional publication of practical ideas that might help authorities in their search for best value' and can be found 'on the DETR website at http:// www.detr.gov.uk'. Whilst it is produced by the DETR, it is 'based on the experience of local authorities and others who are already involved in developing best value projects'. The first issue highlights some key issues from *Best Value Performance Plans: Practice and Procedures*[3] considered above, and also gives up-to-date Performance Plan information from Manchester City and Stockton-on-Tees Councils.

5.35   Amongst the key points made by the DETR on the performance plan process are:

- The best value performance plan is closely linked to the authority's management framework. And 'all eight authorities had undergone some form of organisational or management change as a result. This had helped them to build a performance culture and to develop a more holistic approach to service planning and review'. In addition, all authorities recognised that both officers and members needed leadership and guidance, to give the process drive and rigour.
- Very different approaches had been taken by authorities to the content and presentation of plans. 'They were aware that they serve some very different audiences, and each audience may need a different approach if consultation is to work.'
- Most plans followed broadly a pyramidal structure with the authority's vision at the top and 'levels of increasingly specific priorities to show how the vision will be achieved'. A model pyramid was presented as follows (see figure 2) but 'no one plan contained every element of the pyramid'.
- As noted above, the research[4] did not find much evidence 'for how the vision or priorities had been arrived at'. Greater accountability comes from explaining the prioritisation process in the light of the 'three central elements' underpinning priorities, namely 'an authority's understanding of local needs; its political priorities; and views from the consultation processes'.
- Although action plans are an essential part of the performance plan showing an authority's means for realising its vision, some authorities 'did not relate their objectives and action plans to the other parts of their plans very clearly'. Also, the reason behind action plans and targets 'and how they relate to service-specific objectives and action plans could ... have been made clearer'.

---

1   All quotations and diagrammatic reproductions in the section are taken from the DETR
    Notebook – Issue 1, January 2000.
2   See http://www.local-regions.detr.gov.uk/bestvalue/nbook/nbk1.htm.
3   DETR, 24 November 1999.
4   DETR, *Best Value Performance Plans: Practice and Procedures. A Review of Early experiences within eight local authorities* (24 November 1999).

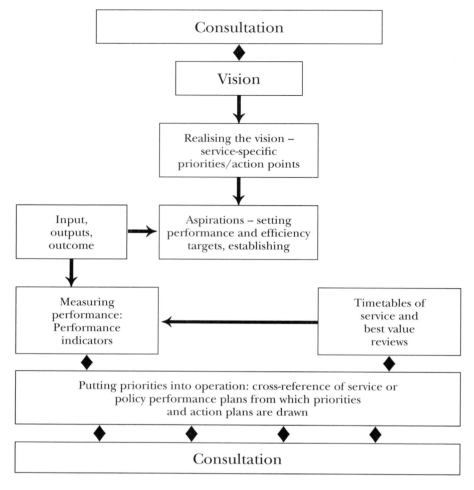

Figure 2: The Best Value Performance Planning Process[1]

- There was some difficulty in establishing local indicators and most performance plans omitted information on the best value review agenda.

Other points are also made by the DETR in the light of the research study *Best Value Performance Plans: Practice and Procedures,* considered above.

Example Performance Plans

5.36 It is certainly worth looking at the material on the performance plans of both Manchester City and Stockton-on-Tees Councils in the DETR *Notebook*[2] and obtaining copies of these and other plans. This is clearly not with a view to replicating the precise approach but rather to appreciate the scope of different ways of presenting performance information. But if there are techniques which

---

1   Crown copyright, reproduced with the permission of the Controller of HMSO.
2   Referred to above. The DETR points out that their material on the plans 'is not intended as a critical assessment'.

suit the local context then they may well be worth adapting. For the wheel, whilst at the hub of civilisation, needs no reinvention.

Manchester's plan[1] (as a prototype with limited distribution) is in two parts – the performance plan and the performance plan companion. The former is 'a 16 page, full colour document with photographs, simple diagrams and illustrations.' It 'comes across as lively, drawing attention to itself with bold colours, straightforward text with numerous bullet-points, and coloured headings. On the back page are contact details in eight languages for those who want the plan in translation, in larger print or on tape.' Its writing style is 'personal and direct' using 'phrases like "*your City*", "*our schools*", "*you told us*", "*our corporate objectives*", which complement the liveliness of the mostly column-based layout.' The 'companion' contains (amongst other things) detailed statistical and performance data. The plan itself contains the following:

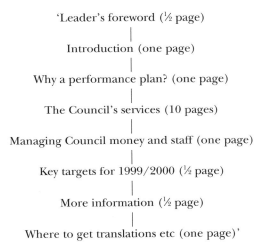

'Leader's foreword (½ page)

Introduction (one page)

Why a performance plan? (one page)

The Council's services (10 pages)

Managing Council money and staff (one page)

Key targets for 1999/2000 (½ page)

More information (½ page)

Where to get translations etc (one page)'

5.37 Stockton-on-Tees[2] published its 60-page 1999/2000 performance plan in August 1999, which aims to 'cover all aspects of performance'.

> 'With a glossy photo montage cover and printed in varying shades of blue throughout, Stockton has used the same design for all its best value publications. Stockton is also publishing leaflets for each key service, which will be available from housing offices, libraries and other outlets. It will print a summary of the plan in Stockton News, which it distributes to all households and major businesses in the borough (a total of 75,000 copies). Stockton is also revising its customer contracts to include targets for medium term improvement, in line with the plan.'

---

1   The DETR indicates that further information is available from Beverley Taylor at: Beverley_Taylor/Chief.Executives/MCC@note.manchester.gov.uk or tel: 0161 234 3910.

2   The DETR indicates that further information is available from David Coulson, the Council's best value adviser, at: dave.coulson@stockton-bc.gov.uk or tel: 01642 393011.

The plan (which also includes detailed performance information) contains:

'Best value (one page)

Corporate objectives (½ page)

Contents (one page)

Overall aims and objectives (policy platform – one page)

Overall performance (three pages)

Performance in eight service areas (13 pages)

District Auditor's role and comment (one page)

Appendices of performance against indicators (40 pages)

Reply card (one page)'

MAKE BEST VALUE FUN

5.38 Whatever the nature of fun, it will often be found where it is least expected. The challenge is to make best value continually fun, inspiring and empowering for unless it is it will be in danger of creating box ticking, form filling automata. The evidence from the Pilots is that best value has inspired the imaginations of those taking part and has given rise to some innovative and ground-breaking means of providing services. Maintaining this momentum under the unremitting prescriptive weight of the statutory best value regime will require inspirational management and considerable energy and resilience.

Chapter 6

BEST VALUE AUDIT

INTRODUCTION

6.1 The last chapter concluded on a note of fun. However, if A P Herbert[1] was right when he asserted that 'there is no reference to fun in any Act of Parliament',[2] his comment would be particularly appropriate to audit matters. No one likes to be subject to a high level of potentially threatening scrutiny. However, inspection is a necessary function of public accountability and it is clearly important to understand the nature and legal basis of the scrutiny in question in order to deal positively and effectively with it.

Audit[3] encompasses notions such as an official examination of the accounts of an organisation, a systematic inspection by reference to specified criteria or a general calling to account. The concept is well known to local authorities, the District Audit Service having been established in 1846 'to examine the accounts for districts of the Poor Law Unions, the forerunners of the present system of local government in England and Wales'.[4] There have been audit arrangements in place for local authorities and similar bodies since.

6.2 The redoubtable, late Lord Denning MR in *Asher v Secretary of State for the Environment*[5] (re the once celebrated Clay Cross councillors) gave an indication of how the courts saw the duty of district auditors:

> 'The district auditor holds a position of much responsibility. In some respects he is like a company auditor. He is a watchdog to see that the accounts are properly kept and that no one is making off with the funds. He is not bound to be of a suspicious turn of mind: see *In re Kingston Cotton Mill Co. (No. 2)* [1896] 2 Ch. 279; but, if anything suspicious does turn up, it is his duty to take care to follow it up: see *In re Thomas Gerrard & Son Ltd* [1968] Ch. 455. In other respects, however, the duties of a district auditor go far beyond those of a company auditor. He must see whether, on the financial side, the councillors and their officers have discharged their duties according to law. He must listen to any elector who makes objection to the accounts. He must make his own investigation also. If he finds that the councillors or the officers, or any of them, have expended money improperly, or unreasonably, or allowed it to be so expended, it is his duty to surcharge them: see *Roberts v. Hopwood* [1925] A.C. 578 and *Pooley v. District Auditor No. 8 Audit District* (1965) 63

---

1 1890–1971, English novelist, playwright, poet, and politician.

2 *Uncommon Law* (1935).

3 Derived from the Latin *auditus* a hearing, from *audire* to hear. The auditor may still choose to consider objections to the accounts under s 16 of the Audit Commission Act 1998 by way of an oral hearing – see the *Code of Audit Practice* referred to below. An example was the Auditor's hearing in the Westminster 'Homes for Votes' issue which gave rise to subsequent appeals to the Divisional Court and the Court of Appeal – *Porter v Magill; Weeks v Magill* [1999] 1 LGLR 523, CA.

4 Source: The Audit Commission.

5 [1974] Ch 208.

L.G.R. 60 and in the Court of Appeal, (1965) 63 L.G.R. 236. If he finds that they have failed to get in money which they ought to have done, and thus brought about a loss or deficiency – owing to their negligence or misconduct – it is his duty to surcharge them so as to make it good …'.

6.3   The Government indicates that:

'The independent audit of Performance Plans is designed to reassure local people first and foremost that their authority's account of its own performance and its targets for the future are reasonable and robust. It is not intended as a commentary on the policies of the authority as such, and neither does it purport to cover the ground principally envisaged for an inspection under best value. It is an important check on an authority's capacity to achieve best value, and will complement the financial audit and the inspection process.'[1]

THE AUDIT COMMISSION

6.4   The modern District Audit system known to local government today originated in the Local Government Finance Act 1982 which set up the Audit Commission for Local Authorities and the National Health Service in England and Wales (known generally as the Audit Commission).[2] This body started life on 21 January 1983. The Audit Commission is now regulated by Part I of the Audit Commission Act 1998 and consists of 'not less than 15 nor more than 20 members appointed by the Secretary of State'.[3] The Secretary of State must appoint one of the members to be chairman and another to be deputy chairman.[4] Appointments to the Commission 'shall be made after consultation with such organisations and other bodies as appear to the Secretary of State to be appropriate'.[5]

The Commission must appoint (with the approval of the Secretary of State) a chief officer to be known as the Controller of Audit[6] and 'shall appoint such other officers and servants as it considers necessary for the discharge of its functions'.[7] At the time of writing the officers and directorates are:

- Controller – Andrew Foster
- Director of Audit Policy and Appointments – Martin Evans
- Director – Public Services Research Directorate – Terry Hannafin
- Director of Inspection – Wendy Thomson
- Director of Corporate Resources – Peter Wilkinson
- Director of People Development – Trish Longdon
- Director of Performance Development – Joanne Shaw

---

1   DETR Circular 10/99, para 61.
2   Audit Commission Headquarters: 1 Vincent Square, London SW1P 2PN; tel: 0207 828 1212; fax: 0207 976 6187.
3   Audit Commission Act 1998, s 1(2).
4   Ibid, s 1(3).
5   Ibid, s 1(4).
6   Ibid, Sch 1, para 7(1).
7   Ibid, Sch 1, para 7(2).

• Chief Executive – District Audit[1] – David Prince.

6.5 By s 5 of the 1998 Act, an auditor's general duties in conducting the statutory audit of accounts are by examination of those accounts and otherwise to satisfy himself:

– that they are prepared in accordance with statutory regulations;[2]
– that they comply with the requirements of all other statutory provisions applicable to the accounts;
– that proper practices have been observed in the compilation of the accounts;
– that the body whose accounts are being audited has made proper arrangements for *securing economy, efficiency and effectiveness in its use of resources*;[3]
– that the body has made any necessary arrangements for collecting, recording and publishing performance information if so required under s 44 of the 1998 Act.

Until recently this was the Code (Circular 14/95) which came into effect on 21 July 1995. However, 14/95 has now been replaced by a new Code of Audit Practice following approval by the House of Lords on 23 March 2000 (see Hansard Columns 486–488). The revised Code came into effect on 29 March 2000. Transitional provisions are set out in the Annex to the Code which apply to audit work relating to financial years ending on or before 31 March 2000. These 'comprise the provisions of the *Code of Audit Practice* that came into effect on 21 July 1995, and which has now been replaced, updated to include references to the Audit Commission Act 1998 and to the National Assembly for Wales.' These provisions lapse with effect from 1 January 2001. (See Annex to the Code – 'Transitional Provisions').

6.6 By s 22(1) of the LGA 1999, a reference within the 1999 Act to the Audit Commission is a reference to the Audit Commission for Local Authorities and the National Health Service in England and Wales. The Audit Commission is empowered[4] to delegate any of its best value functions (under Part I of the 1999 Act) to 'a committee or sub-committee established by the Commission (including a committee or sub-committee including persons who are not members of the Commission), or . . . an officer or servant of the Commission'. Section 22(3) to (6) make various amendments and additions to the Audit Commission Act 1998 to take account of best value and the Commission's best value functions under Part I of the 1999 Act; and s 22(7) and (8) make amendments to the Housing Associations Act 1985 (amongst other things) to enable the Housing Corporation (or the Secretary of State: general functions in relation to Wales) to provide 'advice and assistance' 'on request' to the Audit Commission in respect of the Commission's best value functions[5] and for the

---

1   This operates as an arm's length agency of the Commission, carrying out the audit of local government and NHS bodies throughout England and Wales. Headed by its own chief executive, it is organised geographically in five regions – Source: Audit Commission.
2   At the time of writing these are the Accounts and Audit Regulations 1996, SI 1996/590.
3   See Chapter 2 and also below.
4   See s 22(2) of the LGA 1999.
5   Section 22(7).

Audit Commission to make payments to the Housing Corporation or Secretary of State in respect of such advice and assistance.[1]

6.7   As will be seen, there is a clear linkage between the general duty of best value in s 3(1) of the LGA 1999 (best value authorities to make arrangements to secure continuous improvement in the way in which their functions are exercised having regard to a combination of economy, efficiency and effectiveness) and the duty of the auditor under s 5 of the Audit Commission Act 1998 to satisfy himself that the body whose accounts are being audited has made proper arrangements for securing economy, efficiency and effectiveness in its use of resources. As has been seen, best value has developed the 3Es, taking on board new notions of democratic empowerment and stakeholder responsiveness.

AUDIT OF BEST VALUE PERFORMANCE PLANS

6.8   These provisions are contained in s 7[2] of the LGA 1999. Section 7(1) provides that a 'performance plan published by a best value authority for a financial year under section 6 shall be audited by the authority's auditor'. Section 7 requires the auditor to issue a report annually by 30 June of the financial year to which the relevant performance plan relates or by such other date as the Secretary of State may specify by order.[3] By s 7(5) this is to be sent:

-   to the authority;
-   to the Audit Commission; and
-   if the report recommends that the Secretary of State give a direction under s 15 (see below – powers of Secretary of State where he is satisfied that a best value authority is failing to comply with its duties in Part I of the LGA 1999) to the Secretary of State.[4]

In accordance with s 7(4) the auditor's report must:

-   certify that he has audited the plan;
-   state whether he believes that it was prepared and published in accordance with s 6[5] and any order or guidance under that section;
-   if appropriate, recommend how it should be amended so as to accord with s 6 and any order or guidance under that section;

---

1   Section 22(8).
2   Section 7 came into force fully in England (and in Wales in relation to police and fire authorities) on 1 April 2000 under the Local Government Act 1999 (Commencement No 1) Order 1999, SI 1999/2169 which is reproduced in Appendix 2. In respect of Wales, on 23 September 1999, the National Assembly for Wales approved the Local Government Act 1999 (Commencement) (Wales) Order 1999, SI 1999/2815 which was made on 28 September 1999 and which brought the general duty of best value into force in relation to Wales from 1 April 2000 and commenced a number of provisions from 1 October 1999 and others from 1 April 2000 (see Chapter 2: 'Commencement Issues in Wales'). The Wales Commencement Order is reproduced in Appendix 3.
3   Section 7(4) and (6).
4   At the time of writing this is the Secretary of State for the Environment, Transport and the Regions.
5   Section 6 of the LGA 1999 deals with best value performance plans: see Chapter 5.

- if appropriate, recommend procedures to be followed by the authority in relation to the plan;
- recommend whether the Audit Commission should carry out a best value inspection of the authority under s 10[1]; and
- recommend whether the Secretary of State should give a direction under s 15.[2]

It will be seen that this provides a tightly circumscribed scrutiny of and encouragement to the authority's whole approach to best value (in terms of management, procedure and output) as evidenced in the performance plan.

6.9 The Government indicates that:

'In completing the report, the auditor will seek to ensure that the Performance Plan has been prepared and published in accordance with the statutory requirements and guidance. This will include an assessment of whether the Plan includes all the required information, whether the authority has in place proper arrangements to ensure that the Plan presents a fair and accurate reflection of its performance for that year and the targets set are realistic and achievable. The Government recommends that authorities include a "statement of responsibility" in the Performance Plan. Such a statement might take the following form:

"The Authority is responsible for the preparation of the Performance Plan and for the information and assessments set out within it, and the assumptions and estimates on which they are based. The Authority is also responsible for setting in place appropriate performance management and internal control systems from which the information and assessments in the Performance Plan have been derived. The Authority is satisfied that the information and assessments included in the plan are in all material respects accurate and complete and that the plan is realistic and achievable." '[3]

6.10 Auditors will also, before reaching a view, be expected to consult the relevant inspectorates.[4] Where appropriate they will make recommendations as to:

- the way in which the plan should be amended;
- any procedures to be followed by the authority in relation to the plan;
- whether or not there should be a special inspection of the authority; and
- whether or not the Secretary of State should give a direction.[5]

In addition, auditors will be expected to:

- adopt an open-minded and supportive approach to innovation;
- support well thought through risk-taking and experimentation;
- provide advice and encouragement to authorities by promoting good practice and shared experience.[6]

---

1   See Chapter 7.
2   See Chapter 8.
3   DETR Circular 10/99, para 63. The 'statement of responsibility' was added following consultation.
4   See Chapter 7.
5   DETR Circular 10/99, para 64.
6   Ibid, para 65.

The Audit Commission is expected in 2000 to publish guidance to auditors on the audit of performance plans 'with a view to securing consistency in the interpretation of legislation and the advice' in the Guidance.[1]

6.11   All reports produced by the external auditor must be published by the local authority as quickly as possible following receipt.[2] Furthermore:

> 'Where the auditor's report contains a recommendation for action, the authority must prepare a statement explaining the action that it intends to take as a result of the report and its proposed timetable for doing so. This statement should be prepared within 30 working days of receipt of the report, or within any shorter period specified by the auditor, and sent to the Secretary of State where required. The auditor will assess whether the action taken is appropriate and make further recommendations where necessary. The finalised statement and relevant explanations must be incorporated within the following year's Performance Plan.'[3]

Auditors are likely to be alert to any 'significant differences between projected and annual returns'[4] and where these happen 'they should be explained and corrected in the following year's Performance Plan'.[5] The Guidance highlights the 'key role' that *internal* auditors play in every aspect of best value and guidance is expected from the Audit Commission 'as to how that role might be enhanced'.[6] A constructive but robust partnership relationship between internal and external auditors will be healthy in this context.

6.12   The auditor, in preparing his report, has[7] relevant rights to documents and information conferred by s 6 of the Audit Commission Act 1998 (with the exception of s 6(3) which applies to recognised fund-holding practices within the National Health Service). These are:

–   a right of access at all reasonable times to every document relating to a body subject to audit which appears to the auditor necessary for the purposes of his statutory functions;[8]
–   a right to require a person holding or accountable for any such document to give the auditor such information and explanation as he thinks necessary for the purposes of his statutory functions[9] and a right if the auditor thinks it necessary to require the person to attend before him in person to give the information or explanation or to produce the document;[10]
–   without prejudice to the provisions above, a right to require any officer or member of a body subject to audit to give the auditor such information or explanation as he thinks necessary for the purposes of his statutory

---

1   DETR Circular 10/99, para 65.
2   Ibid, para 66.
3   Ibid.
4   Ibid, para 67.
5   Ibid.
6   Ibid. This was published by the Audit Commission in March 2000: *An Inside Job?: Internal Audit and Best Value* Management Paper, ISBN 1 86240 211 6.
7   See s 7(3) of the LGA 1999.
8   Audit Commission Act 1998, s 6(1).
9   Ibid, s 6(2)(a).
10 Ibid, s 6(2)(b).

functions[1] and, if the auditor thinks it necessary, require the officer or member to attend before him in person to give the information or explanation;[2]

– without prejudice to the above provisions, a right to be provided with every facility and all information which he may reasonably require for the purposes of his statutory functions by every body subject to audit.[3]

In addition, it is a summary criminal offence without reasonable excuse to fail to comply with any requirement of an auditor under the provisions summarised in (1), (2) and (3) above. Those convicted are liable to a fine not exceeding level 3 on the standard scale[4] and to an additional fine (at the time of writing) not exceeding £20 for each day on which the offence continues after conviction for that offence.[5]

6.13 The Guidance[6] indicates[7] that those auditing performance plans will normally be 'the same team auditing the previous year's financial accounts'. 'The first Plan will report on performance and preparations made prior to the statutory introduction of the duty of best value' and 'auditors will take this into account in their assessment which is to be completed by 30 June 2000'.[8]

Financial and accounting issues concerning the performance plan have been touched on in Chapter 5 and will also be covered in Chapter 11.

Authorities will clearly need an energetic and challenging approach but they should also foster a constructive and co-operative partnership relationship with their external auditor. If the relationship between authority and auditor is positive and productive and he or she is involved from the outset, there is greater likelihood of a beneficial outcome to the s 7 audit.

CODE OF PRACTICE AND FEES

6.14 By s 8(2)[9] of the LGA 1999, the Audit Commission must 'prepare, and keep under review, a code of practice prescribing the way in which auditors are to carry out their functions under section 7'. However, before 'preparing or

---

1 Audit Commission Act 1998, s 6(4)(a).
2 Ibid, s 6(4)(b).
3 Ibid, s 6(5).
4 See s 37(2) of the Criminal Justice Act 1982. At the time of writing level 3 is set at £1000.
5 Audit Commission Act 1998, s 6(6).
6 DETR Circular 10/99.
7 Ibid, para 55.
8 Ibid.
9 Section 8(2)–(7) came into force fully in England (and in Wales in relation to police and fire authorities) on 27 September 1999 and s 8(1) came into force fully in England (and in Wales in relation to police and fire authorities) on 1 April 2000 under the Local Government Act 1999 (Commencement No 1) Order 1999, SI 1999/2169, which is reproduced in Appendix 2. In respect of Wales, on 23 September 1999, the National Assembly for Wales approved the Local Government Act 1999 (Commencement) (Wales) Order 1999, SI 1999/2815, which was made on 28 September 1999 and which brought the general duty of best value into force in relation to Wales from 1 April 2000 and commenced a number of provisions from 1 October 1999 and others from 1 April 2000 (see Chapter 2: 'Commencement Issues in Wales'). The Wales Commencement Order is reproduced in Appendix 3.

altering' such a code the Commission must consult both the Secretary of State and persons who appear to it to represent best value authorities.[1] Auditors (by virtue of s 8(1)) carrying out a s 7 audit must have regard to any such code of practice which[2] is to be governed by the following provisions in s 4(3) to (6) of the Audit Commission Act 1998:

> '(3) A code prepared under this section shall embody what appears to the Commission to be the best professional practice with respect to the standards, procedures and techniques to be adopted by auditors.
>
> (4) A code does not come into force until approved by a resolution of each House of Parliament, and its continuation in force is subject to its being so approved at intervals of not more than five years.
>
> (5) Subsection (4) does not preclude alterations to a code being made by the Commission in the intervals between its being approved in accordance with that subsection.
>
> (6) The Commission shall send copies of any code prepared under this section, and of any alterations made to such a code, to the Secretary of State who shall lay them before Parliament; and the Commission shall from time to time publish any such code as for the time being in force'.

As to fees, the Audit Commission is to prescribe 'a scale or scales of fees'[3] in respect of the performance plan audit[4] and, by s 8(5) of the LGA 1999, the relevant fee provisions in the Audit Commission Act 1998[5] apply to such fees. These include the power under s 7(8) of the Audit Commission Act 1998 for the Secretary of State, if he 'considers it necessary or desirable to do so', to prescribe by regulations a scale or scales of fees 'to have effect, for such period as is specified in the regulations, in place of any scale or scales prescribed by the Commission'. However, before the Secretary of State makes any such regulations, he must consult the Commission and persons appearing to him to represent best value authorities.[6]

---

1   LGA 1999, s 8(6).
2   See s 8(3) of the LGA 1999.
3   Having first consulted the Secretary of State and persons appearing to the Commission to represent best value authorities; LGA 1999, s 8(6).
4   LGA 1999, s 8(4).
5   Section 7(3)–(8) of the Audit Commission Act 1998 read with s 52(1) and (3) of that Act.
6   LGA 1999, s 8(7).

DUTIES OF BEST VALUE AUTHORITY FOLLOWING AUDIT

6.15 Section 9[1] of the LGA 1999 contains the Authority's duties in response to the annual performance plan audit. The first duty (under s 9(1)) is to publish the auditor's report. If, however, the report recommends:

– how the plan should be amended to comply with the statutory requirements;
– procedures which the authority must follow in connection with the plan;
– that the Audit Commission should carry out a best value inspection under s 10 of the LGA 1999 Act (see below);
– that the Secretary of State should issue a direction under s 15 of the LGA 1999 Act (see below),

then the authority will be under a duty to prepare a statement of the action it proposes to take as a result of the report, with a proposed timetable.[2] This must be done 'before the end of the period of 30 working days, starting with the day on which the authority receives the report'[3] or if the report specifies a shorter period starting with that day, before the end of that period.[4] The authority must then incorporate the statement in its next best value performance plan.[5]

However, if the statement relates to a report recommending that the Secretary of State gives a direction under s 15 of the LGA 1999 (sanction powers of the Secretary of State – see Chapter 8) then the authority must supply a copy of that statement to the Secretary of State. This must also be done 'before the end of a period of 30 working days starting with the day on which the authority receives the report'[6] or if the report specifies a shorter period starting with that day, before the end of that period.[7]

In reckoning time under this section, a working day is a day other than a Saturday or Sunday, Christmas Day or Good Friday or 'a day which is a bank holiday under the Banking and Financial Dealings Act 1971 in England and Wales'.[8]

---

1   Section 9 came into force fully in England (and in Wales in relation to police and fire authorities) on 1 April 2000 under the Local Government Act 1999 (Commencement No 1) Order 1999, SI 1999/2169, which is reproduced in Appendix 2. In respect of Wales, on 23 September 1999, the National Assembly for Wales approved the Local Government Act 1999 (Commencement) (Wales) Order 1999, SI 1999/2815, which was made on 28 September 1999 and which brought the general duty of best value into force in relation to Wales from 1 April 2000 and commenced a number of provisions from 1 October 1999 and others from 1 April 2000 (see Chapter 2: 'Commencement Issues in Wales'). The Wales Commencement Order is reproduced in Appendix 3.
2   LGA 1999, s 9(3).
3   Ibid, s 9(4)(a).
4   Ibid, s 9(4)(b).
5   Ibid, s 9(5).
6   Ibid, s 9(6)(a).
7   Ibid, s 9(6)(b).
8   Ibid, s 9(7)(a), (b) and (c).

AUDIT COMMISSION APPROACH

6.16   How the Audit Commission sees its role in best value is clearly set out in
the Commission's *Best Assured* paper ('the Paper') published in December
1999. The Paper, in its Introduction, makes the point that it is 'important that
the key players in best value should share an understanding of their respective
roles: these players include best value authorities themselves, the Government,
the local government associations and their agencies, existing inspectorates,
and the Audit Commission and its appointed auditors'. *Best Assured* 'addresses
that uncertainty by setting out the way in which the Commission intends to
carry out the roles that it has been asked to play in best value, and the ways in
which it is changing to take on the challenges of these new roles'. References to
paragraphs in this section will be to those in *Best Assured*.

Form of Plan

6.17   The Paper notes[1] that s 7 of the LGA 1999 'requires the appointed
auditor to audit and report on the best value performance plan (BVPP) that
each best value authority will be publishing'. Whilst authorities might have 'a
number of different documents that they refer to as their "best value
performance plan"' ranging from 'a substantial document that contains
corporate plans and service plans for all of the authority's functions, to a
shorter leaflet to be distributed to every household in the authority's area',
nevertheless, 'auditors will expect to see a BVPP that contains all of the
information specified in the Local Government Act 1999 and any statutory
guidance'.[2] Therefore, since it is unlikely that the requisite information will be
containable in the shorter versions of the plan designed for widespread
distribution auditors will be auditing and reporting on the full versions of
authorities' BVPPs and not the shorter documents.[3]

Audit Methodology

6.18   To assist auditors with their duty under s 7(4) of the 1999 Act to issue a
report on the audit of a best value performance plan, the Audit Commission
has 'developed an audit methodology' which was 'field tested at 14 authorities
across England and Wales during 1999'.[4] This is structured around reviews of:

–   the extent to which an authority's best value performance plan has been
    prepared and published in compliance with the legislation and statutory
    guidance;
–   the systems set in place by the authority for collecting and recording
    specified performance information; and
–   the extent to which the authority's corporate performance management
    framework in relation to best value complies with the legislation and
    statutory guidance.[5]

---

1   At para 21.
2   See DETR Circular 10/99 which contains statutory guidance on performance plans.
3   Paragraph 23.
4   Paragraph 25.
5   Paragraph 26.

The Paper usefully advises[1] that relevant authority staff should consult external auditors at an early stage in performance plan preparation to ensure that the plan contains all the requisite information since this 'may help authorities to avoid failing to comply with statutory requirements simply as a result of oversight'.

Performance Information

6.19 Bearing in mind that best value authorities are to include current performance information in plans to be published by 31 March this will mean that authorities will have data available for only 'nine or ten months of that year'. Consequently, authorities will 'need to project this data forward to the year-end'.[2]

Since authorities are responsible for 'setting in place appropriate performance management and internal control systems to generate the information and assessments' in the performance plan,[3] auditors will review 'whether the authority has adequate arrangements for collecting, recording and publishing the required performance information'.[4]

Corporate Management Processes

6.20 The Audit Commission will be assessing authorities' corporate management processes to ensure they have the necessary infrastructure in place to achieve continuous improvement. The arrangements should encompass:

– performance management arrangements;
– corporate approaches to the 4Cs;
– a corporate best value review;
– developing and managing the review programme; and
– dealing with internal and external challenge.[5]

Reviewing these processes will be 'an important element of the audit'[6] and will 'involve liaison between the auditors and best value inspectors, who will need to work together in an appropriate way'.

What the Auditor will be Asking

6.21 An important guide to what authorities should expect appears in para 38 of the Paper which indicates that the following are among 'the sorts of question that the auditor will be seeking to answer'.

– Does the authority operate a recognised performance management system aimed at delivering continuous service improvement?
– Has the authority approved and adopted a corporate approach to the 'challenge' element of the 4Cs in accordance with statutory guidance?

---

1 At para 29.
2 Paragraph 31.
3 Paragraph 32.
4 Paragraph 33.
5 Presumably in the sense of the 4Cs (see, for example, Chapter 3).
6 Paragraph 37.

–   Has the authority approved and adopted a corporate approach to comparison in accordance with statutory guidance?
–   Has the authority approved and adopted a formal consultation strategy in accordance with statutory guidance?
–   Has the authority approved and adopted a corporate procurement strategy in accordance with statutory guidance?
–   Has the authority approved and adopted a methodology for defining and selecting its functions for review in accordance with statutory guidance?
–   Does the authority have a formal process for reporting and implementing the recommendations from internal and external challenge?

It will clearly be crucial for authorities to ensure that they have all of these strategies in place before the first audit.

All Evolving with Best Value

6.22   Clearly best value itself will evolve as it finds universal and various practical expression. The audit approach will also need to tailor itself to its particular environment. So in the first year of best value issues 'of particular interest' to the auditor will include 'the phasing of the best value review … programme and the development of a corporate approach to the 4Cs'.[1] However, in 'year two, and in subsequent years, the emphasis is likely to shift and audit work will be directed more towards reviewing and assessing published performance information – for example, comparisons against performance indicators, and trends in performance'.[2] So (as the Paper puts it) 'The audit approach will … evolve alongside the development of best value'.[3]

Pragmatic Audit Approach (But Not Too Pragmatic)

6.23   If justice will not necessarily be tempered with mercy auditors will nevertheless 'recognize that authorities are new to the process in the first year and will take a common sense approach, consistent with their statutory and professional responsibilities'.[4] Nevertheless, the quality of any mercy does seem rather strained since the performance plan audit will 'still be rigorous and challenging'.[5] For pilot authorities, whilst their best value reviews conducted on or before 31 March 2000 will 'not necessarily be subject to the inspection process', nevertheless the 'learning and action plans arising from those early reviews will be taken into account in those authorities' BVPPs'.[6]

Audit Report

6.24   The statutory report (to be issued under s 7(4) of the LGA 1999 – see above) will comprise:

---

1   Paragraph 39.
2   Ibid.
3   Ibid.
4   Paragraph 40.
5   Paragraph 40.
6   Paragraph 41.

'–   a certificate that the audit of the BVPP has been completed in accordance with the legislation and relevant regulations;

–   an opinion on the extent to which the plan complies with the requirements of the legislation and statutory guidance, together with recommendations as to any amendments that may be required;

–   recommendations on matters of substance or significant issues arising from the auditor's review of the performance information systems and of the authority's corporate performance management framework in relation to best value, and on procedures to be followed in relation to the plan; and

–   recommendations on whether or not the Audit Commission should carry out a best value inspection of the authority or the Secretary of State or National Assembly for Wales should issue a direction.'[1]

Instances where the Audit Commission may make a recommendation to the Secretary of State include: a failure to put in place adequate systems to measure performance or to meet national standards and targets; or, in terms of corporate processes, a failure to manage and develop the whole best value process.[2]

In addition to the statutory audit report, auditors will also prepare 'a longer form of report, or a properly evidenced presentation, for members and officers' setting out 'the extent and nature of the work' carried out by the auditor 'and the basis of his or her recommendations'.[3] Authorities will be encouraged to make these reports publicly available.

Local Indicators

6.25   As to performance indicators, the Audit Commission will also be encouraging authorities 'to develop and use local performance indicators[4] and local performance targets'. This is because local indicators 'will be an important measure of local performance and of the authority's responsiveness to meeting local needs'; and they 'will also allow local authorities to reflect local priorities and strategies'.[5]

CONCLUSION

6.26   The auditor in best value has a complex set of roles to play. In one manifestation the auditor will be a supportive family doctor, knowing the patient and all its health foibles and giving friendly and constructive advice about healthy living. In another, the auditor will be the police; sometimes the local bobby, sometimes the 'heavy mob'. But authorities with a positive and dynamic approach and which are taking active steps to embrace the spirit as well as the letter of best value should not have too much to fear. Nevertheless, it will be essential to forge a constructive partnership with the audit team from

---

1   Paragraph 44.
2   Paragraph 46.
3   Paragraph 48.
4   As indicated in Chapter 3, some suggested local indicators for legal services appear in Appendix 7.
5   Paragraph 52.

the outset and involve them in all key best value developments. For although, as Henry Kissinger once pointed out, 'Even a paranoid can have enemies',[1] the wise select their enemies with care; and when assembling such a list, the sensible authority will leave its auditor off.[2]

---

1   United States politician and diplomat, *The Times*, 24 January 1977.
2   This is, of course, a light-hearted comment since no authority could ever be lawfully vindictive – all decisions must be made lawfully, reasonably and for proper statutory purposes (see the principles in *Associated Provincial Picture Houses Ltd v Wednesbury Corporation* [1948] 1 KB 223 and *Council of Civil Service Unions v Minister for Civil Service* [1985] AC 374, below). Also, in *R v Derbyshire County Council, ex parte The Times Supplements Ltd* [1991] COD 129, the Divisional Court quashed a decision of Derbyshire County Council to remove its advertising from newspapers owned by Rupert Murdoch. On the evidence the Court was satisfied that there was no educational ground for the decision and that the ruling Labour Group had been driven by bad faith or vindictiveness. The principles from the European Convention on Human Rights will enhance this when the Human Rights Act 1998 comes fully into effect on 2 October 2000.

Chapter 7

BEST VALUE INSPECTION

INTRODUCTION

7.1   The Government gave notice in its July 1998 White Paper, *Modern Local Government in Touch with the People* that an inspector would call upon local government, when it indicated in para 7.35 that:

> 'New audit and inspection arrangements will be needed to give a clear view of whether best value is being obtained. There will be a rigorous external check on the information provided by authorities in local performance plans, and on the management systems that underpin them. There will be regular external inspections of performance analogous to those currently being carried out by the separately constituted Inspectorates, such as OFSTED and the Social Services Inspectorate. These arrangements will be consistent with the Government's determination to establish high standards of probity in local government and to restore local accountability. They will be the foundation upon which decisive action will be taken should authorities fail to act when performance falls short.'

In para 7.39, the Government charted the creation of 'a new Best Value Inspectorate' which 'will be given powers, in common with the specialist inspectorates, to trigger swift and energetic action where an authority's performance falls short of reasonable expectations'.[1]

In the Guidance[2] the Government made clear that every best value authority function will be subject to inspection. It pointed out that:

> 'All functions will be subject to inspection under best value. Many are already scrutinized by the existing specialist Inspectorates: the Benefit Fraud Inspectorate; HM Fire Services Inspectorate; HM Inspectorate of Constabulary; the Social Services Inspectorate; and the Office for Standards in Education (OFSTED). The Audit Commission has been given the scrutiny role for those areas not previously subject to inspection, and will work in partnership with the existing specialist Inspectorates where it is sensible to do so.'

7.2   The Government has consequently set up the new Best Value Inspectorate (incorporating a Housing Inspectorate) under the auspices of the Audit Commission. This commenced operations on 1 April 2000.

The Government considers that the new inspection arrangements are to play a pivotal role in the delivery of best value.

> 'Inspection reports will:
>
> – enable the public to see whether best value is being delivered
> – enable the inspected body to see how well it is doing
> – enable the Government to see how well its policies are working on the ground

---

1   *Modern Local Government In Touch with the People*, para 7.41.
2   DETR Circular 10/99, at para 72.

    –   identify failing services where remedial action may be necessary
    –   identify and disseminate best practice.'[1]

We shall now look at the statutory mechanics for making this happen.

THE STATUTORY POSITION

7.3   The concepts of inspection have become incarnate in ss 10 to 14 and s 25 of the LGA 1999. Section $10(1)$[2] enables the Audit Commission of its own volition to 'carry out an inspection' of a best value authority's compliance with its statutory best value duties. But s 10(2) *requires* the Audit Commission (if so directed by the Secretary of State following consultation by him[3]) to 'carry out an inspection of a specified best value authority's compliance' with the statutory requirements of best value 'in relation to specified functions'. In carrying out the inspection (and in deciding whether to do so[4]), the Commission must have regard to any recommendation in the auditor's report on the performance plan[5] that the Audit Commission 'should carry out a best value inspection' and 'any guidance issued by the Secretary of State'.

    An inspector is defined by s 11(7) as 'an officer, servant or agent of the Audit Commission carrying out an inspection under section 10'. To help the inspector with his or her inquiries, s 11[6] confers investigatory powers underpinned by criminal sanction as with the primary best value audit under s 7. An inspector is by s 11(1) given a right of access at all reasonable times to any premises of the best value authority concerned[7] and also to 'any document

---

1   DETR Circular 10/99, para 74.
2   Section 10(1)–(4) came into force fully in England (and in Wales in relation to police and fire authorities) on 1 April 2000, although s 10(4) came into force fully in England (and in Wales in relation to police and fire authorities) on 27 September 1999 for the purposes of the issue of guidance by the Secretary of State – see the Local Government Act 1999 (Commencement No 1) Order 1999, SI 1999/2169, which is reproduced in Appendix 2. In respect of Wales, on 23 September 1999, the National Assembly for Wales approved the Local Government Act 1999 (Commencement) (Wales) Order 1999, SI 1999/2815, which was made on 28 September 1999 and which brought the general duty of Best Value into force in relation to Wales from 1 April 2000 and commenced a number of provisions from 1 October 1999 and others from 1 April 2000 (see Chapter 2: 'Commencement Issues in Wales'). The Wales Commencement Order is reproduced in Appendix 3.
3   LGA 1999, s 10(3).
4   This presumably relates to the Commission's discretionary power to inspect in s 10(1) since, as indicated, if the Secretary of State directs the Commission to inspect it will be obliged to do so. However, as noted, the Secretary of State is bound under s 10(3) to consult the Commission before making a direction. DETR Circular 10/99 (at para 76) points out that whilst the 'frequency of best value inspections is at the discretion of the Inspectorates carrying them out ...', nevertheless the expectation of the Audit Commission is that 'as with the Reviews themselves, inspections of all functions will take place at least once within any five year period' (see also below).
5   See LGA 1999, s 7(4)(e).
6   Section 11 came into force fully in England (and in Wales in relation to police and fire authorities) on 1 April 2000 by virtue of the Local Government Act 1999 (Commencement No 1) Order 1999, SI 1999/2169 which is reproduced in Appendix 2. In respect of Wales, see fn 2 above.
7   LGA 1999, s 11(1)(a).

relating to the authority which appears to him to be necessary for the purposes of the inspection'.[1] Any person 'holding or accountable for any such document' may be required by an inspector to provide the inspector with 'such information and explanation as he thinks necessary'.[2] The inspector may also require such person to attend before him in person to 'give the information or explanation or to produce the document'.[3]

7.4 Authorities must actively co-operate in facilitating inspections. Section 11(3) requires best value authorities to provide 'an inspector with every facility and all information which he may reasonably require for the purposes of the inspection'. But inspectors are obliged to give three clear days'[4] notice of any requirement under s 11[5] and must, if so required, produce identification documents.[6] Just in case anyone acting on behalf of an authority fails to be impressed by a statutory duty, s 11(5) renders anyone who without reasonable excuse fails to comply with an inspector's requirement under s 11 liable on summary conviction to 'a fine not exceeding level 3 on the standard scale[7]'. Any expenses incurred by an inspector in connection with such an offence 'alleged to have been committed in relation to an inspection of a best value authority are, so far as not recovered from any other source, recoverable from the authority'.[8]

In an exception to the proverb 'He who pays the piper calls the tune', best value authorities will have to pay for their inspections. Shelley advised us that 'The rich have become richer, and the poor have become poorer'.[9] This may also turn out to be true of best value authorities. For not only is life increasingly competitive, with fortune more likely to favour the effective, economic and efficient, but, as will be seen, poor performing authorities may receive more inspection attention.

7.5 Whilst the 'frequency of best value inspections is at the discretion of the Inspectorates carrying them out', nevertheless the expectation of the Audit Commission is that 'as with the Reviews themselves, inspections of all functions will take place at least once within any five year period'.[10] In addition, as

---

1   LGA 1999, s 11(1)(b).
2   Ibid, s 11(2)(a).
3   Ibid, s 11(2)(b).
4   The term 'three clear days' is not defined in the 1999 Act. However, by analogy with (for example) s 100B of the Local Government Act 1972 (copies of agenda and reports for principal council meeting to be open to public inspection for at least three clear days before the meeting, subject to statutory provisions) this would presumably mean that three clear days must elapse *after* the giving of the notice before the inspector's requirement complies with the statute (see *Elitestone's Application for Judicial Review* (1993) P&CR 422; affirming 90 LGR 604 – the phrase 'three clear days' is a term of art which refers to days other than publication and of the meeting). So, on this basis, if notice were given on a Monday, it could not be executed until the Friday. In practice, it is hoped that relations between authorities and inspectors will not at this stage be sustained by the minutiae of forensic consideration. Certainly that would be inconsistent with the style of the present Audit Commission Director of Inspection, Wendy Thomson.
5   LGA 1999, s 11(4)(a).
6   Ibid, s 11(4)(b).
7   See s 37(2) of the Criminal Justice Act 1982. At the time of writing, level 3 is set at £1000.
8   LGA 1999, s 11(6).
9   Percy Bysshe Shelley (1792–1822), *A Defence of Poetry* (1821).
10 DETR Circular 10/99, para 76.

indicated above, the Secretary of State may at any time 'direct that an inspection should be carried out wherever there is a cause for concern about the performance of the authority, following an annual audit report for example'.[1] Such inspections 'may necessarily take place ahead of an authority's own Review and will typically be more fundamental and searching in order to reach a proper diagnosis of the problems.'[2] Of course, the Audit Commission may also of its own volition decide to carry out an inspection outside the inspection timetable (using its s 10(1) powers), for example, if there is an auditor's recommendation for inspection under s 7(4)(e) of the LGA 1999. So those with a sound approach to the duty of best value will presumably avoid a preponderance of inspections and thus a further charge upon scarce resources. Whilst the DETR has indicated that 'Cost for the new Best Value Inspectorate will be met by a combination of grants and fees charged to best value local authorities, for whom the additional resource will be made available through central government grant',[3] it is unlikely that the Government will be generous with defaulting authorities.

FEES

7.6 Section 12(1)[4] of the LGA 1999 requires the Audit Commission to 'prescribe a scale or scales of fees in respect of inspections carried out under section 10' and an authority inspected under s 10 must 'pay to the Commission the fee applicable to the inspection in accordance with the appropriate scale'.[5] However, there is some flexibility (at least from the Commission's point of view). For if 'it appears to the Commission that the work involved in a particular inspection [is] substantially more or less than that envisaged by the appropriate scale, the Commission may charge a fee' larger or smaller than that in the appropriate scale.[6] Before prescribing a scale of fees the Commission must consult both the Secretary of State and those 'appearing to the Commission to represent best value authorities'.[7]

---

1   DETR Circular 10/99, para 76.
2   Ibid.
3   DETR, *Best Value Inspectorate Forum for England* (15 September 1999).
4   Section 12(1) came into force fully in England (and in Wales in relation to police and fire authorities) on 27 September 1999, s 12(4) came into force fully in England (and in Wales in relation to police and fire authorities) on 10 August 1999 and s 12(2) and (3) came into force fully in England (and in Wales in relation to police and fire authorities) on 1 April 2000 – see the Local Government Act 1999 (Commencement No 1) Order 1999, SI 1999/ 2169, which is reproduced in Appendix 2. In respect of Wales, on 23 September 1999, the National Assembly for Wales approved the Local Government Act 1999 (Commencement) (Wales) Order 1999, SI 1999/2815, which was made on 28 September 1999 and which brought the general duty of best value into force in relation to Wales from 1 April 2000 and commenced a number of provisions from 1 October 1999 (see Chapter 2: 'Commencement Issues in Wales'). The Wales Commencement Order is reproduced in Appendix 3.
5   LGA 1999, s 12(2).
6   Ibid, s 12(3).
7   Ibid, s 12(4).

REPORTS

7.7   Once a s 10 inspection has taken place, the Audit Commission must issue a report.[1] This must mention anything where, as a result of the inspection, the Commission believes that the authority is failing to comply with its statutory best value duties.[2] If it does so, the Commission may recommend that the Secretary of State gives a s 15 direction (see below – sanction powers of Secretary of State for default in best value duties).[3] The Commission must send a copy of any report to the authority in question and may publish it and 'any information in respect of a report'.[4] Furthermore, if an inspection report recommends that the Secretary of State issue a s 15 direction then 'as soon as reasonably practicable' the Commission must arrange for that recommendation to be published and also send a copy of the report to the Secretary of State.[5]

Bearing in mind the pragmatic reality that the local press (which thrives on the real, imaginary or hoped-for misdoings of public bodies and their servants) is a key instrument of public accountability, the publication of statutory defaults in respect of a duty so democratically sensitive as best value will not enhance the careers of the politicians or officers concerned. So, to the extent that the key people in authorities are not sufficiently motivated by the positive aspects of best value, this 'sword of Damocles' should be a continuous reminder of the precariousness of executive fortune.

Should the report express the Commission's view as a result of an inspection that an authority is failing to comply with its statutory best value duties, then the next performance plan prepared by that authority under s 6 of the LGA 1999 must record this fact together with any action taken by the authority as a result of the report.[6]

THE AUDIT COMMISSION APPROACH

7.8   The way the Audit Commission envisaged approaching its statutory inspection responsibilities was helpfully indicated in broad terms in Chapter 3 of *Best Assured*,[7] although the Commission at that stage indicated that it 'will be publishing a substantial paper early in 2000 with further details of the way in which it will fulfil its inspection role'. This paper, published in February 2000, contains the detail and is entitled *Seeing is Believing – how the Audit Commission will carry out best value inspections in England* and will be considered briefly below. However, to gain some perspective of the issue relevant material from *Best*

---

1   LGA 1999, s 13(1). Section 13 came into force fully in England (and in Wales in relation to police and fire authorities) on 1 April 2000 under the Local Government Act 1999 (Commencement No 1) Order 1999, SI 1999/2169 which is reproduced in Appendix 2. For the position in Wales, see the Local Government Act 1999 (Commencement) (Wales) Order 1999, SI 1999/2815, referred to above.
2   LGA 1999, s 13(2)(a).
3   Ibid, s 13(2)(b).
4   Ibid, s 13(3).
5   Ibid, s 13(4).
6   Ibid, s 13(5).
7   Audit Commission, December 1999. This publication covers the role of the Audit Commission in best value generally and not merely the inspection function.

Assured will first be considered. Consequently, until consideration of *Seeing is Believing*, references to paragraphs will be to those in *Best Assured* unless otherwise indicated. Chapter 3 of *Best Assured* is entitled 'Inspection: acting as a catalyst for improvement'. This identifies as follows the 'existing inspectorates with responsibility for best value in England and Wales':

'**England**
- The Office for Standards in Education (OFSTED)
- The Social Services Inspectorate (SSI)
- The Benefit Fraud Inspectorate (BFI)
- Her Majesty's Fire Service Inspectorate (HMFSI)
- Her Majesty's Inspectorate of Constabulary (HMIC)

Wales
- The Social Services Inspectorate in Wales (SSIW)
- Estyn (for education services)
- The Benefit Fraud Inspectorate (BFI)
- Her Majesty's Fire Service Inspectorate (HMFSI)
- Her Majesty's Inspectorate of Constabulary (HMIC)

Source: Audit Commission'.[1]

These inspectorates will continue to inspect under existing powers. However, they will in addition be considering the extent to which authorities are 'complying with best value principles in their specialist areas'.[2] As from 1 April 2000, the Audit Commission will be examining authority functions which are not covered by existing inspectorates 'such as housing, environmental services, libraries and refuse collection'.[3] In addition, the Commission will continue joint inspections of local education authorities with OFSTED and Estyn together with reviews of social services departments in conjunction with SSI and SSIW (see above). The Commission will 'build on the experience of its current inspections when conducting best value inspections'.[4]

The Inspection Service

7.9 This will join together the Commission's current and new inspectorate functions. The Service 'will be managed through four regions in England and an office in Wales'. At local level 'every authority will have a single "lead inspector" who will agree the annual programme of inspections and co-ordinate inspection teams'. There will also be 'dedicated teams for SSI Joint Reviews, LEA inspections, and housing inspections'.[5] As mentioned below, the Government has set up a Best Value Inspectorate Forum for England (amongst other things) to co-ordinate the various inspection regimes.

The Commission's Approach to Inspection

7.10 This is summarised in the following eight 'principles for public inspection', namely that inspection should:

---

1   *Best Assured*, Box B, Chap 3.
2   Paragraph 57.
3   Paragraph 58.
4   Paragraph 59.
5   Paragraph 60 and Exhibit 3.

- be based on what works – including what works in inspection;
- speak without fear or favour;
- be proportionate to risk;
- inform national policy and local practice;
- be a catalyst for improvement – securing local ownership of findings;
- provide user focus;
- take account of use of money, people, assets;
- inform the public.[1]

Since a 'basic principle of best value is that authorities are *themselves* responsible for securing continuous improvement in everything that they do' (emphasis added) and, in line with DETR Guidance Audit Commission inspections will not generally take place until an authority has completed a best value review.[2]

7.11 Inspectors will start with the authority's own assessment of its current performance and the action planned for future improvement as contained in the best value review. Inspectors will then independently assess:

- the validity of the authority's review processes;
- the quality of the service that the authority is providing; and
- the likelihood that the service will improve in future.[3]

The Commission points out that the programming of inspections (generally following best value reviews) gives authorities 'considerable influence over the timing and nature of their inspections', and in particular 'it will be for authorities to decide whether their reviews should be service-based, or whether they should aim to be customer – or thematically focused'.[4] A proper balance should be struck between individual service and cross-cutting reviews across 'traditional service boundaries'.[5] The Government has indicated that cross-cutting[6] reviews 'which are based on or around clear and recognisable themes or issues and which reflect strategic choices with other partners, are more likely to make a real and lasting difference locally'.[7] On occasion, inspections will occur when there has been no best value review – for instance, if the Secretary of State so directs or if an auditor has concerns about a particular service.[8]

---

1   *Best Assured*, Exhibit 4.
2   Paragraph 66.
3   Paragraph 67.
4   Paragraph 68.
5   Ibid.
6   Cross-cutting services may be described as those which, focusing on outputs, now provide a more economic, efficient and effective unified service by way of a partnership or other joint working arrangements between two or more organisations who had previously provided their services separately. On 2 February 2000, the DETR published a report entitled *Cross-cutting Issues in Public Policy and Public Service* which was 'prepared and written by a team of six from the University of Birmingham's School of Public Policy'. This (amongst other things) concluded that 'Cross-boundary working will be a characteristic feature of the new paradigm or system, since no one structural solution can solve all the problems. It will have a tight-loose framework – tight on outcomes, loose on the means of achieving them in particular circumstances. The new system will have direction setting at the centre, local judgment and planning on how best to deliver the outcomes, audit of the results, with help and assistance to do better made available for service providers.' (See Executive Summary.)
7   DETR Circular 10/99, para 21.
8   Paragraph 69.

Key Stages of an Audit Commission Best Value Inspection[1]

7.12   Stage 1 – Context
           Stage 2 – Performance Review
           Stage 3 – Reality Check
           Stage 4 – Interim Challenge
           Stage 5 – Trade off Evaluation
           Stage 6 – Synthesis and Reporting.

Seeing is Believing

7.13   As indicated above, for the detail it will be necessary to consult the Audit Commission's publication *Seeing is Believing: How the Audit Commission will carry out best value inspections in England*[2] (*Audit Commission Briefing*).[3] Authorities will need to peruse this document carefully for it details developments in thinking as to the purpose and practice of inspections. However, some of the salient points are highlighted here (references to pages and paragraphs will be to those in *Seeing is Believing* unless otherwise indicated):

- Best value inspections 'will normally take as their starting point an authority's inspections' which will give authorities 'a key role in determining the timing and scope of their reviews and inspections'.[4] Inspections will 'look at the service being provided as well as checking whether the authority's review complies with the requirements of best value'.[5]

- Inspectors will (in the light of a customer focus) 'look at the quality of a service, regardless of whether it is provided directly by the authority or through a private contractor or a partner voluntary organization'.[6] 'An authority's partners and contractors are key to whether or not it can achieve best value ...'.[7]

- Inspection will also examine 'how community strategies and cross-cutting themes fit with the authority's corporate aims, its political agenda and its capacity to manage change'.[8]

- Authorities will have influence over the 'length and cost of inspections'[9] for the 'intensity of inspections will vary depending upon the nature of the services being reviewed and, more importantly, on the quality of an authority's own best value review'.[10]

---

1   *Best Assured*, Exhibit 5, where the stages are presented as steps upward from 1 to 6.
2   It is pointed out in the Introduction to *Seeing is Believing* that 'A separate report explaining how inspection will be carried out in Wales will be published following discussions and consultation with the National Assembly for Wales, the Best Value Inspectorate Forum for Wales, and the Welsh Best Value Project Group.'
3   Audit Commission, February 2000. This can be ordered free of charge from the Audit Commission: Communications Department, The Audit Commission, 1 Vincent Square, London SW1P 2PN (tel: 0207 396 1494).
4   Paragraph 15.
5   Ibid.
6   Paragraph 16.
7   Ibid.
8   Paragraph 17.
9   Paragraph 18.
10 Ibid.

- Consequently, when an 'authority has carried out a comprehensive review and can prove this to the inspection team, the inspection is likely to be a 'light touch'. As a minimum, this might mean that the lead inspector reviews the best value review and produces a short report with recommendations'. However 'many inspections will lead to a full report showing how the inspectors' judgements were reached, and providing recommendations for improvement. Therefore, the length of inspections might vary from as little as one day at the authority to as many as twenty'.[1]

- Since improvement of local services is the purpose of best value 'the overriding purpose of inspection is to act as a catalyst for improvement'.[2] Further 'the nature and range of improvements that result' from best value reviews will be expected 'to reflect the diversity of authorities' local political agendas and the communities that they serve'.[3]

- 'Clear communication of purpose and outcomes is one of the elements that distinguishes a modern service culture from more traditional ones'.[4] An effective inspection service will be characterised by views which are challenging but impartial 'based on reliable evidence and ... conveyed clearly by credible inspectors in a constructive way'.[5]

- 'Whether the inspection is more supportive and encouraging, or more challenging, will depend on the performance, attitudes and capability of both the authority and the services being inspected'.[6]

- 'Inspection reports will offer practical recommendations for improvement, drawing on inspectors' knowledge of best practice and what works in other authorities'.[7]

- Good practice will be identified and promoted and inspections will seek out 'examples of good practice and innovation, and for creative ways to overcome barriers and resistance to change or make better use of resources'.[8] These good practice examples 'will be fed into a national "information warehouse"' which, linking with databases of the Improvement and Development Agency, will be made available to authorities through: best practice publications; workshops and conferences; web-based comparative information and self-improvement tools.[9]

- 'Inspection will take full account of local priorities and targets' and whether the best value review 'has a service or cross-cutting focus'.[10]

- Inspection will utilise 'a range of "reality checks"' to provide other sources of evidence about the reliability of an authority's' best value review. Amongst other things, these will 'provide an important means of

---

1   Paragraph 19.
2   Paragraph 24.
3   Paragraph 25.
4   Paragraph 27.
5   Ibid.
6   Paragraph 30.
7   Paragraph 33.
8   Paragraph 35.
9   Ibid.
10   Paragraph 39.

connecting inspectors with local people's experience of a service, without which the inspection judgment will have little local credibility'.[1]

- The Inspection Service recognises that the 'arguments for evidence-based, continual improvement are as true for ... [it] ... as for the authorities it inspects'. So to achieve *fitness for purpose* 'the Inspection Service will focus on the results of inspection and what works best to help authorities to improve'.[2]

- Paragraph 62 indicates that at the end of each inspection inspectors will have two judgments to make, namely '(1) How good are the services that they have inspected? – rated from 3 stars (excellent) to 0 stars (poor); and (2) Will they improve in the way that best value requires? – rated on a scale that runs from "yes", to "probably", to "unlikely", to "no".'

- The key questions leading to these two judgments will be:
  - Does the service meet the aims?
  - Are the authority's aims clear and challenging?
  - Will the authority deliver the improvements?
  - How does its performance compare?
  - Does the best value review drive improvement?
  - How good is the improvement plan?[3]

- The questions underpinning each judgment will be drawn from 'a core set of criteria and supporting guidance ... for each of the six questions and the main issues that underpin them'.[4] However, an indicative flavour is given in Exhibit 4 (which starts on p 11).

- The stages of inspection have been refined as follows:[5]
  - **Preparation** (four weeks before the inspection): understanding the context; reviewing performance; briefing the authority
  - **Inspection** (one to four weeks on site): carrying out reality checks; presenting interim challenge
  - **Publishing the report** (one to two weeks afterwards): publishing final report; carrying out follow-up inspection.

- Best value inspections will usually follow a best value review so 'authorities themselves will determine when most inspections take place, except for directed inspections or referrals'.[6]

- The three broad sets of circumstances that may lead to referral to the Secretary of State by the Commission are:
  - Serious service failures in an authority that could result in danger or harm to the public;
  - Persistent failure by an authority to address recommendations made by inspectors; and

---

1   Paragraph 45. See Case Study 2 on p 19 of *Seeing is Believing* for a street cleansing best value review reality check.
2   Paragraph 57.
3   Exhibit 3 on p 10.
4   Paragraph 65.
5   See Exhibit 5 on p 15.
6   Paragraph 116.

– Failures in a number of services in an authority, that reveal serious weaknesses in an authority's corporate capacity to manage services and make improvements.[1]

Finally, on the Audit Commission approach to inspection, Dr Wendy Thomson, the Director of Inspection at the Audit Commission – in an interview with the *Local Government Chronicle* on 4 February 2000 – gave an indication of her approach which will not be 'just about value for money, we will be looking at the whole range of social issues. Social exclusion is very much the context in which we will be working – is the local authority intervening to make it a better place?' And as to the difference between inspectors and auditors: 'We are into services, they are into systems.'

HOUSING BENEFIT AND COUNCIL TAX BENEFIT ADMINISTRATION

7.14 Section 14 of the LGA 1999[2] deals with inspection of Housing Benefit and Council Tax Benefit Administration. The section operates by inserting substituted provisions into s 139A(1) and (2) of the Social Security Administration Act 1992 (which deal with reports on the administration of housing benefit and council tax benefit). The Secretary of State may thereby 'authorise persons to consider and report to him on the administration by authorities of housing benefit and council tax benefit'.[3] Persons so authorised may be asked by the Secretary of State in particular to consider authorities' performance in the prevention and detection of housing benefit and council tax benefit fraud and their compliance with their statutory best value duties.[4] The Secretary of State has wide discretion in such appointments. He may authorise such persons on such terms and for such period as he thinks fit, to act generally or in relation to a specified authority or authorities and to report on administration generally or on specified matters.[5] Section 14(2) of the LGA 1999 makes substitutions in respect of reporting requirements in s 139C(1) of the 1992 Act (which deals with reports) to encompass the prevention and detection of benefit fraud and compliance with the statutory best value duties.

INSPECTION – THE GOVERNMENT VIEW

7.15 Paragraph 75 of the Guidance points out that inspection 'will not remove the responsibility for delivering best value from local authorities', which is why 'best value inspections will, as far as possible, and where legal and resource considerations permit, follow authorities' own Reviews'. Also:

1 Paragraph 134.
2 Section 14 of the 1999 Act came into effect in England and Wales on 1 April 2000 – see the Local Government Act 1999 (Commencement No 1) Order 1999, SI 1999/2169, which is reproduced in Appendix 2. See Part I of the LGA 1999 reproduced in Appendix 1.
3 LGA 1999, s 14(1).
4 Ibid, s 14(1).
5 Ibid, s 14(1).

'Authorities can make a significant difference to the inspection process by ensuring that their Reviews show clearly how the statutory guidance has been followed and how outcomes have been and will be secured. This will avoid duplication of effort between the Review and the inspection processes, and in turn minimise pressure on the inspected body.'[1]

But authorities should be clear that 'inspection is not limited to the information generated by a Review: it will also probe the current state of service provision, particularly from the viewpoint of users'.[2] This approach was echoed by Audit Commission Director of Inspection, Wendy Thomson, when in the interview referred to above (published in the *Local Government Chronicle* on 4 February 2000) she was quoted as saying: 'Councils should put more effort into getting performance management, and services up to scratch, not gearing up to pass inspections. We will spot that and we will see through it.'

7.16 An important principle highlighted in the Guidance is that the inspection and review processes should so far as possible be organically related and not distinct. This is sensible since otherwise the valuable resources of authorities would be continually absorbed in potentially competing account-ability procedures. So, para 75 of the Guidance indicates that details 'of the Review programme provided in annual Performance Plans will increasingly be taken into account in the programming of inspections'; but, as a transitional arrangement for the first year of best value, authorities have been asked 'to provide such information to their external auditors ahead of completing their first Performance Plans'.[3]

   The Audit Commission has 'consulted on a set of principles for public inspection which received widespread endorsement'.[4] These included confir-mation that 'inspection should inform the public and focus on services as users experience them, and that the scale of inspection should be proportionate to risk'.[5] It is intended that:

   'authorities will have an opportunity to own the findings of inspection – because inspections will build upon Reviews and share an interim view with the authority, for example – and that the relevant report will be clear and simple, and addressed to all the key audiences, including local people.'[6]

BEST VALUE INSPECTORATE FORUM

7.17 Many in local government were rightly concerned that a preponderance of different inspection regimes each responsible for different aspects of local authority functions would create administrative chaos. The Government recognised this and promised in its July 1998 White Paper[7] that '[t]he Government will ensure that the different inspectorates work together to

---

1   DETR Circular 10/99, para 75.
2   Ibid.
3   Ibid.
4   Ibid, para 77.
5   Ibid.
6   Ibid.
7   *Modern Local Government in Touch with the People*, para 7.44.

ensure a consistent perspective and approach, and avoid timetabling difficulties'. This has now been done. A *Best Value Inspectorate Forum for England*[1] was launched in July 1999 and consists of the heads of the following inspectorates (the relevant incumbents at the time of writing are given for each organisation):

- The Best Value Inspectorate (set up by the Audit Commission) – Wendy Thomson
- The Office for Standards in Education (OFSTED) – Mike Tomlinson
- The Social Services Inspectorate – Denise Platt
- HM Inspectorate of Constabulary – Sir David O'Dowd
- HM Fire Services Inspectorate – Graham Meldrum
- The Benefit Fraud Inspectorate – Chris Bull

7.18 The Terms of Reference[2] for the English Forum indicate that it will meet:

> 'to consider strategic issues relating to the inspection of best value authorities in England. It will be an effective channel of communication for inspectorates: with central government, with best value authorities and other interested parties. The Forum will act to increase the effectiveness of inspection on behalf of service users while minimising the demands on inspected bodies'.

It will:

- consider the scope for co-ordinating programmes of audit and inspection;
- develop arrangements to inspect across organisational boundaries including the identification of thematic issues for cross cutting inspection;
- ensure a consistent approach to best value arrangements by different inspectorates and auditors and that they do not provide conflicting evaluations of the same arrangements;
- build on and develop joint inspection methodologies and develop protocols and similar agreements to facilitate working together and information sharing;
- consider the scope for involving users more in the inspection process;
- consider ways of targeting resources on those areas where the risks involved are the greatest;
- identify and promote best practice in best value inspection.[3]

7.19 The Forum is to meet at least twice a year and 'will consider how lessons learnt during inspections can be disseminated effectively and efficiently'. It 'will from time to time publish reports and papers for discussion and will welcome views and comments from those with an interest in improving public services'.[4] Its first meeting was held on 13 September 1999. It was then scheduled to meet again in February and Summer 2000. Following its first

---

1 The DETR points out at footnote 2 to para 78 in DETR Circular 10/99 that: 'A separate Inspectorate Forum, with broadly similar Terms of Reference, exists for Wales. HM Inspectorate of Constabulary and HM Fire Service Inspectorate are also members of that Forum in order to ensure consistency between inspection arrangements for the police and fire services in England and Wales.'
2 DETR, 15 September 1999.
3 Ibid.
4 Ibid.

meeting, the Forum issued a Newsletter (No 1) in September 1999. This can be found on the DETR's Best Value Website (in the Newsletter Index).[1] Newsletter No 2 (dealing with the Best Value Inspectorate Forum Meeting of 10 February 2000) was published on the same site on 17 April 2000. This indicates that:

> 'The Forum reached agreement on three key documents, which will ensure better co-ordination, and help to minimise the burden on authorities.
>
> The first, Memorandum of Understanding between Auditors and Inspectors, provides for co-ordination before, during and after both audit and inspection. This will lead to better informed judgements from both auditors and inspectors, and lesser burdens on authorities.
>
> The second, The "4Cs" of Best Value: Key Questions for Inspection, sets out the essential questions which each best value inspection should ask.
>
> The third, Key Practical Inspection Issues, is a set of agreed principles on which Inspectorates will base their inspection principles and working arrangements, such as agreement to co-ordinate inspection programming at the local level, and features of a good inspection.
>
> These three agreed statements are included with this Newsletter. Please circulate them widely.'[2]

The Forum was scheduled to meet again on 4 April 2000.

In the Guidance[3] the Government indicates that the Forum will 'provide a channel of communication between local authorities, Inspectorates and central government, and be an important vehicle for sharing best practice.' The Forum's priorities for the year 2000 are:

- to consider the scope for co-ordinating programmes of audit and inspection;
- to develop and enhance arrangements for working together'.[4]

The Government expects the inspection process to 'evolve in line with the experience gained by both the Inspectorates and the inspected bodies'. The Forum will periodically publish reports and papers for discussion and will welcome views from those with an interest in improving public services.[5]

STATUTORY CO-ORDINATION

7.20 Section 25(1) of the LGA 1999 provides that in arranging for or carrying out inspections of best value authorities or inquiries or investigations in relation to such authorities, statutory inspectors[6] must have regard to any 'guidance issued by the Secretary of State for the purposes of securing the coordination of different kinds of inspection, inquiry and investigation'.

The 'statutory inspectors' are set out as follows in s 25(2) of the LGA 1999:

---

1   http://www.local-regions.detr.gov.uk/bestvalue/inspection/news/index.htm.
2   See the Inspection and Intervention Index on the DETR's Best Value Website: http://www.local-regions.detr.gov.uk/bestvalue/inspection/inspectionindex.htm.
3   See DETR Circular 10/99, September 1999, at para 78.
4   Ibid.
5   Ibid.
6   These are any 'person or body to whom' s 25 of the LGA 1999 applies and are specified in s 25(2) of the LGA 1999.

'(a)   the Audit Commission;

(b)   an inspector, assistant inspector or other officer appointed under section 24(1) of the Fire Services Act 1947 (inspectors of fire brigades);

(c)   Her Majesty's Chief Inspector of Schools in England;

(d)   Her Majesty's Chief Inspector of Schools in Wales;

(e)   a person carrying out an inquiry under section 7C of the Local Authority Social Services Act 1970 (inquiries);

(f)   a person carrying out an inspection under section 48 of the National Health Service and Community Care Act 1990 (inspection of premises used for provision of community care services);

(g)   a person conducting an inspection under section 80 of the Children Act 1989 (inspection of children's homes, &c.) or an inquiry under section 81 of that Act (inquiries in relation to children);

(h)   a person authorised under section 139A(1) of the Social Security Administration Act 1992 (reports on administration of housing benefit and council tax benefit);

(i)   an inspector appointed under section 54 of the Police Act 1996 (inspectors of constabulary).'

By s 25(3) the Secretary of State may by order make provision for the section to apply to any 'person or body specified in the order'.

POSITIVE INSPECTION

7.21   Happily for local government, Audit Commission Head of Inspection, Wendy Thomson views her role positively. *Municipal Journal*[1] reported her as indicating that the Best Value Inspectorate would be 'engaging hearts and minds' rather than issuing edicts and persuading and inspiring rather than shouting; and she apparently considered that some regulation is old-fashioned on the basis that 'people change if they're told to'. Ms Thomson was reported as indicating that although there were national standards, the new Inspectorate would be 'supporting councils in their aspirations'; and perciviently: 'We have to keep re-inventing [best value] and not get into a routine and hang onto the idea that there is always something new'.

However, as indicated above, in an interview reported in *Local Government Chronicle* on 4 February 2000, her approach is also likely to be dynamic and firm: 'We will need to be much more independent than the IdeA. We will have a view which is very evidence based ... I am not into taking the long run in local government with an eight-year development plan. If [changes] take more than eight to nine months you won't be on the ball any more.' It is equally clear that the Best Value Inspectorate will be robust in promoting improvement. For (as indicated above) whether 'the inspection is more supportive and encouraging, or more challenging, will depend on the performance, attitudes and capability of both the authority and the services being inspected'.[2]

So, the audit and inspection regime will be testing and especially so for those who are reluctant to test themselves. The key is to have a consistently positive but robustly self-critical approach and wherever possible to work in partnership

---

1   12–18 November 1999.

2   *Seeing is Believing*, para 30.

with the external auditor from the outset to achieve the 'real and positive difference'[1] for local people which best value was created to deliver.

---

1   *Implementing Best Value,* para 9.

Chapter 8

STATUTORY INTERVENTION

INTRODUCTION

8.1   Many in local government may feel that no sooner has the 'Berlin Wall' of CCT[1] been destroyed[2] than another, apparently more kindly, but actually more challenging, structure has been constructed with its own new array of instruments of statutory correction.

Section 15 of the LGA 1999[3] contains the sanction powers of the Secretary of State where he is satisfied that there is default in discharging the duty of best value. The Government points out that it 'is committed to working with best value authorities and others to ensure that the incidence of such failure is minimised'. Nevertheless, 'it will not hesitate to act where necessary to protect the interests of local people and the users of services'.[4]

PROTOCOL ON INTERVENTION POWERS

8.2   However, in para V of the *Protocol on Intervention Powers*[5] agreed between the Government and the Local Government Association it appears that the Government would prefer local government to put its own house in order to direct central intervention:

> 'Where evidence and experience show that a local authority is at risk of failing in that duty in respect of a service or services, there are several ways of achieving improvements. Councillors, officials and contractors have the prime responsibility for delivering quality services and addressing the shortcomings and failings. The LGA and the Improvement and Development Agency are committed to work with local authorities to support improvement where problems exist and the LGA encourages its member authorities to give early warning of potential problems

---

1   See Chapter 1.
2   See s 21 of the LGA 1999, below, which repealed CCT on 2 January 2000.
3   Section 15 (except subs (7) and (8)) came into force fully in England (and in Wales in relation to police and fire authorities) on 1 April 2000. Section 15(7) and (8) came into force fully in England (and in Wales in relation to police and fire authorities) on 27 September 1999 – see the Local Government Act 1999 (Commencement No 1) Order 1999, SI 1999/2169 which is reproduced in Appendix 2. In respect of Wales, on 23 September 1999, the National Assembly for Wales approved the Local Government Act 1999 (Commencement) (Wales) Order 1999, SI 1999/2815, which was made on 28 September 1999 and which brought the general duty of best value into force in relation to Wales from 1 April 2000 and commenced a number of provisions from 1 October 1999 and others from 1 April 2000 (see Chapter 2 above: 'Commencement Issues in Wales'). The Wales Commencement Order is reproduced in Appendix 3.
4   DETR Circular 10/99, para 79.
5   DETR, September 1999. This is contained in Annex D to DETR Circular 10/99, which is reproduced in Appendix 5.

emerging from inspections, draft reports, complaints, reviews or other sources so that advice and support can be offered. Support may be offered by other authorities through networks, or the authority may be helped to identify and procure other external advice and assistance.'

8.3   At paras VI to XI the *Protocol* sets out the following Principles governing intervention by the Secretary of State:

'VI. The Secretary of State will exercise intervention powers under section 15 of the Local Government Act 1999 only when there is clear evidence that an authority is failing either to discharge its functions adequately or failing to meet its statutory obligations.

VII. The Secretary of State will inform the authority of the reasons for intervention whenever using his powers under this legislation.

VIII. The form and extent of intervention will reflect the type and seriousness of failure and the need for effective improvement.

IX.   Except in cases of serious service failure or unless there is a need for urgent intervention, the authority will normally be given the opportunity to make the necessary improvements itself.

X.   Best value authorities will provide accurate and timely responses to requests for information and co-operate with such action as the Secretary of State may direct in accordance with his powers and this protocol.

XI.   In cases where a function is exercised by the Secretary of State or a person acting on his behalf, both the Secretary of State and his nominee will be subject to the statutory duties that the authority would normally be subject to in respect of that function.'

The *Protocol* indicates[1] that 'Intervention powers will be invoked on the basis of clear evidence' which indicatively could emerge from:

'–   annual audits of financial accounts
–   audit of local performance plans
–   Audit Commission inspections of fundamental reviews
–   inspection reports
–   public interest reports
–   reports of inquiries, Ombudsman investigations or judicial findings
–   concerns raised about serious danger or harm to the public.'

NATURE OF DEFAULT

8.4   In Chapter 5 of its 3 March 1998 Consultation Paper, *Modern Local Government Improving Local Services through Best Value*, the Government categorised default in delivering best value into failure of substance and failures of process. At this stage these were as follows:

'5.17 Failures of substance might be defined as including:

–   unit costs which are persistently high in relation to other councils in similar circumstances, which cannot be explained in terms of higher quality or greater local need;
–   deterioration in service standards against specified targets;
–   failure to improve in relation to the performance of other councils;

---

1   See para XII.

- failure to achieve set local targets of performance (or a second failure);
- failure to meet specified national performance standards.

5.18 Failure of process might be defined as including:

- failure to consult, or to respond to consultation;
- failure to review an area of under-performance;
- failure to complete a review of all service provision over a five year cycle;
- unreasonable neglect of alternative options for provision when services are reviewed;
- failure to set sufficiently demanding standards.'

8.5 These have now been refined in the light of experience and the development of the LGA 1999 and other material. Whilst they do not appear in the LGA 1999, they are included as follows in Appendix A to the *Protocol on Intervention Powers* referred to above:

'Failure of process

- a failure to consult or to consult adequately as identified by the external auditor
- a failure to produce a best value performance plan, or a failure to include any of the prescribed elements within it
- a failure to agree, publish, or carry out a programme of fundamental performance reviews in compliance with the statutory framework
- unreasonable neglect of alternative options for service provision when conducting performance reviews
- a failure to set performance targets or publish details of performance against them
- a failure to set performance targets, which, in the opinion of the external auditor, are sufficiently challenging
- a failure to publish details of how performance compares with that of others
- a failure to publish performance information as prescribed (in respect of content, form or timing)
- a failure to make adequate information available to local people about the comparative performance of other bodies

Failure of substance

- failure to meet any single nationally prescribed standard of performance
- persistently high unit costs (by comparison with other councils or, where appropriate, with private and voluntary sector providers) which are not satisfactorily accounted for by higher quality service or greater level of need
- failure to improve service standards or a deterioration in standards
- failure to draw up and implement an action plan following a critical inspection report.'

Whilst the opening para I of Appendix A to the *Protocol* makes clear that the Secretary of State reserves the right to exercise his sanction powers in any of the circumstances mentioned 'his intention is to intervene proportionately to the seriousness of the failure. A single failure of process, for example, is unlikely to trigger intervention by the Secretary of State, whereas a failure of substance is more likely to attract intervention'.

It will therefore be important to ensure that both the letter and the spirit of the best value requirements are being fully, properly and positively followed. It will also be beneficial to work in partnership with the external auditor (as well as appropriate other persons and bodies) and to keep an open mind as to what is the most effective way to achieve best value in respect of all the different outputs required.

INTERVENTION POWERS

8.6   Section 15(1) is expressed to apply 'in relation to a best value authority if the Secretary of State is satisfied that it is failing to comply with the requirements of' Part I of the LGA 1999 (best value default). Where the Secretary of State is so satisfied he may direct the authority to:

'(a)   to prepare or amend a performance plan;
 (b)   to follow specified procedures in relation to a performance plan;
 (c)   to carry out a review of its exercise of specified functions'.[1]

Whilst these gradated measures on their face appear relatively anodyne, nevertheless they will give a clear signal that, in the Government's view, and to a greater or lesser extent, the authority is off course with its approach to best value. This is more than a warning light on the instrument panel; it means parking on the hard shoulder and identifying and remedying the problem. In those circumstances the authority will need as soon as possible to agree appropriate and practical remedial action with the external auditor and the Secretary of State. Paragraph XIV of the *Protocol* points out the process:

'XIV. Once the Secretary of State decides that the facts of the case mean that intervention is likely to be necessary, he will formally notify the authority and the LGA. The usual sequence of action would be as follows:

–   the authority will be notified in writing of the improvements the Secretary of State judged necessary;
–   the authority will be given until a specified deadline to produce and publish a statement of action for making such improvements;
–   the statement of action will need to set out clearly the actions to be carried out, the people responsible, the costs involved, the intended outcomes, the dates by which they are to be achieved and the authority's own proposals for monitoring and implementing the statement of action;
–   if the statement of action is acceptable to the Secretary of State, the authority will be notified, informed how implementation will be monitored and given a deadline by which specific improvements must be completed;
–   if the statement is unacceptable, the Secretary of State will notify the authority and the LGA of his decision to direct the authority under the powers contained in section 15 of the Local Government Act 1999;
–   the authority will be given the opportunity to make representations about the direction proposed.'

8.7   If the 'statement of action' monitoring process indicates that this is not being carried out effectively or in a timely manner as to outcomes the Secretary

---

1   LGA 1999, s 15(2).

of State will notify the authority and intervene as necessary to secure improvements.[1] If it 'emerges that the authority is failing adequately to discharge one or more of its other functions' the authority will be notified as to how the Secretary of State intends to proceed.[2]

The Secretary of State also reserves power under the *Protocol* to take emergency intervention action when, although the measured, interactive response mentioned above will be the norm:

> 'there may be exceptional cases where the severity of persistence of failure, or the continuing risk of harm or financial loss, show that urgent intervention is necessary. If these circumstances prevail and an authority could be reasonably expected to be aware of these problems and has failed to take adequate action to address them, then the Secretary of State retains the discretion to abbreviate the procedures outlined above as he sees necessary. When exercising his powers in this way, the Secretary of State will notify the authority and the LGA[3] of the intervention that is necessary and the reasons for intervention, and will provide a full explanation of his reasons for curtailing the procedures.'[4]

Local Inquiry

8.8 Where there is best value default the Secretary of State may also (under s 15(3)) 'direct a local inquiry to be held into the exercise by the authority' of the functions specified.[5] Section 250(2) to (5) of the Local Government Act 1972 is expressed to apply to any such local inquiry.[6]

Section 250(2) provides that

> 'the person appointed to hold the inquiry may by summons require any person to attend, at a time and place stated in the summons, to give evidence or to produce any documents in his custody or under his control which relate to any matter in question at the inquiry, and may take evidence on oath ... Every person who refuses or deliberately fails to attend in obedience to a summons issued under this section, or to give evidence, or who deliberately alters, suppresses, conceals, destroys, or refuses to produce any book or other document which he is required or is liable to be required to produce for the purposes of this section, shall be liable on summary conviction to a fine not exceeding level 3 on the standard scale or to imprisonment for a term not exceeding six months, or to both.'[7]

Section 250(4) provides (amongst other things and accommodating contextual changes) that the costs incurred by the Secretary of State in relation to the inquiry are to be paid by such local authority or party to the inquiry as he may direct.

For the authority in general and its members, the chief executive and managers in particular, a local inquiry in these circumstances will not be good news. For even if there are positive aspects and valuable outcomes the local media are likely to transmit a message of poor stewardship of public resources.

---

1   *Protocol on Intervention Powers*, para XV.
2   Ibid, para XVI.
3   Local Government Association.
4   *Protocol* at para XVII.
5   LGA 1999, s 15(3).
6   Ibid, s 15(4).
7   Local Government Act 1972, s 250(3).

Necessary or Expedient Action

8.9   Section 15(5) also enables the Secretary of State where there is best value default to 'direct the authority to take any action which he considers necessary or expedient to secure its compliance with the requirements of' Part I of the LGA 1999.

The power given in s 15(5) is very wide and would seem to be limited only by:

–   whether the Secretary of State has material before him on which he can reasonably make the judgment that he is satisfied that the authority is failing to comply with its best value duties in Part I of the Local Government Act 1999 (see below)
–   whether his 'consideration' that the action is 'necessary or expedient' is soundly and reasonably based having regard to the relevant statutory purposes of the 1999 Act ('An Act to make provision imposing on local and certain other authorities requirements relating to economy, efficiency and effectiveness ...')
–   the existence and terms of other specific statutory powers in s 15: ie if the Secretary of State wishes to transfer a function to a nominee he should proceed in accordance with s 15(6) (see immediately below).

However, as will be seen below, the courts have generally been slow to construe legislation giving power to central government to regulate local government against central government. Whilst the *Protocol* will be relevant in any litigation this (as well as s 15 itself) does give the Secretary of State sufficient flexibility to act quickly if he deems it appropriate.

Transfer of Function to Nominee of Secretary of State

8.10   Section 15(6) enables the Secretary of State in the event of a best value default to direct that a specified authority function will be exercised by himself or his nominee for a period specified in the direction or for so long as the Secretary of State considers appropriate.[1] This will be referred to as an outsourcing direction. The Secretary of State may also direct that the authority must comply with any instructions from him or his nominee 'in relation to the exercise of that function and shall provide such assistance as the Secretary of State or his nominee may require for the purpose of exercising the function.[2]

Forms of Intervention

8.11   Appendix B to the *Protocol on Intervention Powers* referred to above indicates that in addition to the holding of a local inquiry (see above) intervention might include a direction by the Secretary of State to:

–   prepare or amend a performance plan;
–   follow specified procedures in relation to a performance plan;
–   carry out a review of its exercise of specified functions;

---

1   LGA 1999, s 15(6)(a).
2   Ibid, s 15(6)(b).

- take such other action as in the Secretary of State's opinion is necessary or expedient to secure compliance with the requirements of Part I of the LGA 1999;
- make sure a function is carried out so as to achieve specified objectives;
- secure advice/consultancy on the performance of that function;
- secure the function from a specified provider or put the function out to tender to expose a particular service or work of a particular description to competition (with or without an in-house bid to carry out the work);
- accept external advice from a specified source relating to the performance of a management function;
- obtain a function from a specified provider;
- transfer responsibility to another authority or third party.

Power to Make Regulations

8.12 Section 15(7)[1] empowers the Secretary of State to make regulations relating to any enactment conferring functions on him in respect of a best value authority function and which he considers 'necessary or expedient' for when he makes an outsourcing direction. The regulations may for the purposes of cases in which he makes an outsourcing direction under s 15(6)(a), disapply or modify any such enactment as confers a function on the Secretary of State 'in respect of a function of a best value authority' or have an effect similar to such enactment.[2] These are no doubt designed to deal with the situation of a private sector contractor taking over statutory functions which were always envisaged to be carried out by a relevant authority and to ensure that the statutory and functional regime works smoothly.

Section 15(9) to (13) give statutory underpinning to the *Protocol* processes. Subject to the power in s 15(11) to take urgent and summary action, before he gives a direction the Secretary of State must give the authority in question an opportunity to make representations about any report which has resulted in the proposed direction and the proposed direction itself.[3] Also subject to s 15(11), before giving a direction following a recommendation to do so in an auditor's report under s 7(4)(f) (see above), the Secretary of State must have regard to any statement by the authority of any timetabled action which it proposes to take as a result of the report[4] which the authority has sent to him within one month (or as otherwise specified) of the date of receipt by the authority of the report.[5]

---

1   By s 29(4) of the LGA 1999, s 15(7)(a) (which empowers the Secretary of State by regulations to make provision which relates to an enactment which confers a function on him in respect of a function of a best value authority) 'shall apply to Wales as if the reference to a function conferred on the Secretary of State were a reference to a function conferred on the National Assembly for Wales or the Secretary of State; but the Assembly may not make regulations under section 15(7) which relate to a function conferred on the Secretary of State without his approval.'
2   LGA 1999, s 15(8).
3   Ibid, s 15(9).
4   See ibid, s 9(2) to (4) above.
5   Ibid, s 15(10).

8.13 However, as indicated, the Secretary of State may (by virtue of s 15(11)) give a direction without complying with the above two duties (s 15(9) representations and s 15(10) statement) if 'he considers the direction sufficiently urgent'. However, if he does so he must (under s 15(12)) inform both the authority concerned and 'such persons appearing to him to represent best value authorities as he considers appropriate' of the direction and why it was given without complying with s 15(9) and (10).

A s 15 direction is enforceable by an order of *mandamus* on the application of the Secretary of State.[1] *Mandamus* is an order of the High Court in judicial review proceedings requiring the performance of a specified duty.

POWERS OF THE SECRETARY OF STATE – LEGAL ISSUES

CCT Case-law

8.14 Authorities will clearly wish, if at all possible, to avoid being in the position where they are considering a legal confrontation with the Secretary of State. For such a course will be time-consuming, expensive and (provided the Secretary of State has in all the circumstances behaved properly in accordance with his legal discretion) unlikely to yield a positive outcome in the English courts. As Andrew Arden QC[2] has put it[3] 'the courts afford to central government a greater respect and tolerance than local government'.

The cases on compulsory competitive tendering (CCT) may give an indication of the likely judicial approach. Under CCT, authorities were required, in reaching the decision that they should undertake the work and in doing anything else in connection with the work before reaching the decision, not to have acted in a manner having the effect or intended or likely to have the effect of restricting, distorting or preventing competition (see, for example, s 7(7) of the Local Government Act 1988 and s 9(4)(aaaa) of the Local Government, Planning and Land Act 1980).[4]

8.15 Under the CCT regime, the sanction provisions available to the Secretary of State in respect of anti-competitive behaviour were contained in ss 13 and 14 of the 1988 Act (and similarly in ss 19A and 19B of the 1980 Act). Section 13 of the 1988 Act enabled the Secretary of State to serve a notice upon an authority which appeared to him to have acted anti-competitively or otherwise in breach of the statutory requirements. The notice would inform the authority of this (with particulars and reasons) and require the authority to respond in writing within a specified time either demonstrating that it had not acted as alleged or admitting it had but giving reasons why a direction should not follow.

---

1   Section 15(13).
2   With Jonathan Manning and Scott Collins.
3   See Andrew Arden QC, Jonathan Manning and Scott Collins, *Local Government Constitutional and Administrative Law* (Sweet & Maxwell, 1999), para 8.5.67.
4   Repealed by s 21 of the LGA 1999 on 2 January 2000.

If, following an expired s 13 notice (whether or not there had been a written response) it still appeared to the Secretary of State that the authority had acted as alleged, the Secretary of State was empowered to issue a direction under s 14. This (amongst other things) could remove an authority's entitlement to carry out any or all relevant work or allow it to carry out such work upon specified conditions.

So under CCT, the question is whether it '*appears to the Secretary of State*' that an authority is in default, and under best value, it is whether the Secretary of State is '*satisfied*' that an authority is in default. The best value test is (on the face of it) more stringent since for a reasonable Secretary of State to be 'satisfied' that an authority 'is failing to comply' with its statutory duties would seem to require more cogent evidence of default than merely for it to *appear* to him that an authority is in breach.

8.16   However, the following three cases are noted which (amongst other things) illustrate the restrictive approach which the courts have taken to authorities that have challenged the regulatory discretion of the Secretary of State under the CCT regime. Under present circumstances the approach is unlikely in practice to be more liberal under best value.

R v Secretary of State for the Environment, ex parte Knowsley Metropolitan Borough Council and Others[1]

8.17   In this case, the local authorities at Knowsley, York and Leicester unsuccessfully challenged s 14 directions issued by the Secretary of State. However, Ralph Gibson LJ in the Court of Appeal did indicate that the Secretary of State must have before him 'if the section 13 powers are to arise, material upon which he could reasonably conclude that the local authority were in breach'.

R v Secretary of State for the Environment, ex parte Haringey London Borough Council[2]

8.18   Here, the Court of Appeal overturned a decision of the High Court that the Secretary of State was wrong to have issued a 'barring order' (ie preventing the Authority from carrying out the work) without first having considered the appropriateness of a conditions order. Haringey had awarded refuse collection work to its Direct Service Organization which had submitted the highest of three bids. Ralph Gibson LJ noted that a statutory sanction at the disposal of the Secretary of State for authorities who have acted anti-competitively is to make a barring order and:

> 'An intention to demonstrate to the country at large, and to those entrusted with the making of decisions on behalf of authorities in the tendering process under the 1988 Act, that action by the authority which is clearly in favour of the authority's DSO and is in breach of [the anti-competitive behaviour provision] may be met with the imposition of a barring order, seems to me to be an intention to promote the policy and the objects of the Act.'

---

1   (1991) *The Independent*, 25 September, CA.
2   92 LGR 538, CA.

R v Secretary of State for the Environment ex parte Bury Metropolitan Borough Council[1]

8.19   More recently, the Court of Appeal (Schiemann LJ, Millett LJ and Auld LJ) upheld the decision of Potts J in the High Court that the Secretary of State had acted lawfully in issuing the Council with a direction under s 14 of the 1988 Act. The Council had failed to provide to tenderers sufficient information concerning relevant assets (vehicles and depots) and this (according to the High Court) had 'caused the Secretary of State to conclude that [the Council's] conduct was likely to have the effect of distorting etc competition'. Potts J (whose reasoning was approved by the Court) had said that 'In my judgment there was material on which the [Secretary of State] could reasonably conclude that [the Council] had failed to comply with the relevant conditions.'

A submission for the Council based on community law (the Public Service Contracts Directive 92/50/EEC) failed (amongst other things) because: (per Schiemann LJ) in-house arrangements are not contractual and the Directive regulates contracts, the 'Circular in question did not infringe any relevant right given to the Council by the Directive because none such was given' and (per Millett LJ) Art 36 of Directive 92/50/EEC 'does not confer rights on contracting authorities but on the contrary circumscribes their freedom of action and ... accordingly the direction of the Secretary of State was not a derogation of any rights of the Council guaranteed by Community law'.

Some Administrative Law Considerations

8.20   Whilst a discussion of all the aspects and requirements of English administrative law surrounding decisions of the Secretary of State in this context is beyond the scope of this book, it is worth charting some of the key relevant milestones in this area:

- Discretion must be exercised properly and reasonably in the sense outlined in *Associated Provincial Picture Houses Ltd v Wednesbury Corporation*.[2] In that case (which involved the exercise of local authority discretion concerning the grant of a cinema performance licence for Sundays) Lord Greene, MR said:

  '... the court, whenever it is alleged that the local authority have contravened the law, must not substitute itself for that authority ... When an executive discretion is entrusted by Parliament to a body such as the local authority in this case, what appears to be an exercise of that discretion can only be challenged in the courts in a strictly limited class of case. As I have said, it must always be remembered that the court is not a court of appeal. When discretion of this kind is granted the law recognizes certain principles upon which that discretion must be exercised, but within the four corners of those principles the discretion, in my opinion, is an absolute one and cannot be questioned in any court of law ... The exercise of such a discretion must be a real exercise of the discretion. If, in the statute conferring the discretion, there is to be found expressly or by implication matters which the authority exercising the discretion ought to have regard to, then in exercising the

---

1   (1998) 26 February (unreported), CA.
2   [1948] 1 KB 223.

discretion it must have regard to those matters. Conversely, if the nature of the subject-matter and the general interpretation of the Act make it clear that certain matters would not be germane to the matter in question, the authority must disregard those irrelevant collateral matters.'

And:

'The court is entitled to investigate the action of the local authority with a view to seeing whether they have taken into account matters which they ought not to take into account, or, conversely, have refused to take into account or neglected to take into account matters which they ought to take into account. Once that question is answered in favour of the local authority, it may still be possible to say that, although the local authority have kept within the four corners of the matters which they ought to consider, they have nevertheless come to a conclusion so unreasonable that no reasonable authority could ever have come to it. In such a case ... I think the court can interfere. The power of the court to interfere in each case is not as an appellate authority to override a decision of the local authority, but as a judicial authority which is concerned, and concerned only, to see whether the local authority have contravened the law by acting in excess of the powers which Parliament has confided in them.'

• In 1985, the House of Lords restated the principles of administrative law in *Council of Civil Service Unions v Minister for Civil Service*[1] where Lord Diplock put forward as follows the following classification into illegality, irrationality and procedural impropriety:

'Judicial review has I think developed to a stage today when without reiterating any analysis of the steps by which the development has come about, one can conveniently classify under three heads the grounds upon which administrative action is subject to control by judicial review. The first ground I would call "illegality", the second "irrationality" and the third "procedural impropriety". That is not to say that further development on a case by case basis may not in course of time add further grounds. I have in mind particularly the possible adoption in the future of the principle of "proportionality" which is recognised in the administrative law of several of our fellow members of the European Economic Community; but to dispose of the instant case the three already well-established heads that I have mentioned will suffice.

By "illegality" as a ground of judicial review I mean that the decision-maker must understand correctly the law that regulates his decision-making power and must give effect to it. Whether he has or not is *par excellence* a justiciable question to be decided, in the event of dispute, by those persons, the judges, by whom the judicial power of the state is exercisable.

By "irrationality" I mean what can by now be succinctly referred to as "*Wednesbury* unreasonableness"[2] ... It applies to a decision which is so outrageous in its defiance of logic or of accepted moral standards that no sensible person who had applied his mind to the question to be decided could have arrived at it. Whether a decision falls within this category is a question that judges by their training and experience should be well equipped to answer, or else there would be something badly wrong with our judicial system. . . .

---

1   [1985] AC 374.
2   See, above, *Associated Provincial Picture Houses Ltd v Wednesbury Corporation* [1948] 1 KB 223.

I have described the third head as "procedural impropriety" rather than failure to observe basic rules of natural justice or failure to act with procedural fairness towards the person who will be affected by the decision. This is because susceptibility to judicial review under this head covers also failure by an administrative tribunal to observe procedural rules that are expressly laid down in the legislative instrument by which its jurisdiction is conferred, even where such failure does not involve any denial of natural justice.'

- Following *Padfield v Minister of Agriculture, Fisheries and Food,*[1] public purpose powers must be exercised consistently with the policy and objects of the enabling statute. In the case (which concerned ministerial refusal to refer a complaint to a committee of investigation (amongst other things) since the Minister would be expected to give effect to the committee's recommendations if the complaint were upheld) Lord Reid said that:

    'Parliament must have conferred the discretion with the intention that it should be used to promote the policy and objects of the Act; the policy and objects of the Act must be determined by construing the Act as a whole and construction is always a matter of law for the court. In a matter of this kind it is not possible to draw a hard and fast line, but if the Minister, by reason of his having misconstrued the Act or for any other reason, so uses his discretion so as to thwart or run counter to the policy and objects of the Act, then our law would be very defective if persons aggrieved were not entitled to the protection of the court.'

- It follows that no authority can lawfully act maliciously or vindictively. For example, in *R v Derbyshire County Council, ex parte The Times Supplements Ltd*[2] the Divisional Court quashed a decision of Derbyshire County Council to remove its advertising from newspapers owned by Rupert Murdoch. On the evidence the Court was satisfied that there was no educational ground for the decision and that the ruling Labour Group had been driven by bad faith or vindictiveness.

- Before exercising discretion to issue a direction in such circumstances the Secretary of State must have before him material upon which he could reasonably conclude that the local authority were in breach (see *R v Secretary of State for the Environment, ex parte Knowsley MBC and Others,* above).

8.21 So it would seem that before the Secretary of State can issue a s 15 direction in respect of a best value authority are at least two essential criteria to be fulfilled:

– he must be *satisfied* that the authority 'is failing to comply' with the requirements of Part 1 of the LGA 1999 (best value);

– there must be before the Secretary of State material upon which he could reasonably conclude that the local authority was 'failing to comply' with the statutory best value requirements so as properly to base satisfaction; and whether or not this is so is a matter of law for the court.[3]

---

1   [1968] AC 997.
2   (1990) *The Times,* 19 July.
3   In *R v Secretary of State for the Environment, ex parte Knowsley MBC and Others* (see above), Ralph Gibson LJ indicated that as with *Secretary of State for Education and Science v Tameside Metropolitan Borough Council* [1977] AC 1014 'it is not open to the Secretary of State to say: "It appears to me that the authority has acted in a manner having the effect of distorting

New Jurisprudential Influences

8.22 Administrative law will undoubtedly change with the advent of the Human Rights Act 1998 which becomes fully effective on 2 October 2000; and (even if a decision of the Secretary of State does not breach any of the Convention Rights identified in the Human Rights Act) the principles of interpretation adopted by (amongst others) the European Court of Human Rights and the European Commission on Human Rights will inevitably become part of mainstream UK jurisprudence.[1] Therefore, considerations of illegality, irrationality and procedural impropriety[2] are likely (even in respect of cases where a breach of Convention rights is not alleged) to absorb new concepts and considerations such as whether the aim of a statutory restriction is legitimate and whether it is necessary in a democratic society. 'Necessary in a democratic society' 'implies the existence of a "pressing social need"', whether the restriction or interference in question is 'proportionate to the legitimate aim pursued' and 'whether the reasons adduced by the national authorities to justify it are "relevant and sufficient"'.[3]

8.23 Particularly potentially relevant here will be whether (if best value default is established) the decision of the Secretary of State is a proportionate response. In this connection Art 8, para 3 of the European Charter of Local Self Government[4] provides that:

> 'Administrative supervision of local authorities shall be exercised in such a way as to ensure that the intervention of the controlling authority is kept in proportion to the importance of the interests which it is intended to protect.'

The Convention is not substantive law since it is not incorporated into UK legislation. Nevertheless, in a Cabinet Office Explanatory Memorandum[5] the Government indicated[6] that 'By subscribing to the Charter, the United Kingdom is bound to apply the standards prescribed in the Charter to its own system of local government'. Further:

> 'in relation to the existing compatibility of the United Kingdom system of local government with the principles of the Charter, the United Kingdom proposes to undertake in subscribing to the Charter to be bound by all of its provisions, without

---

competition" unless that which appears to him to have been the relevant act of the local authority is capable of being regarded as distorting etc. competition, and whether it is so capable is a matter of law for the court'. The best value regime is structured so as to provide a Secretary of State with sufficient potential material (eg audit and inspection reports with relevant recommendations). However, it will be important to consider whether a decision on such material is soundly based.

1 By s 3(1) of the Human Rights Act 1998 'So far as it is possible to do so, primary legislation and subordinate legislation must be read and given effect in a way which is compatible with the Convention rights.'

2 See *Council of Civil Service Unions v Minister for Civil Service*, above.

3 See, for example, *Vogt v Germany* (1995) 21 EHRR 205 restated in *Ahmed and Others v United Kingdom* [1999] 1 LGLR 94. For a percipient analysis of this area see *Judicial Review after the Human Rights Act* by Michael Supperstone QC and Jason Coppel, barristers, 11 King's Bench Walk Chambers, London (European Human Rights Law Review Issue 3, 1999).

4 Opened for signature as a Convention on 15 October 1985 and signed on behalf of the United Kingdom Government on 3 June 1997.

5 Cm 3884, March 1998.

6 See ibid, para 11.

recourse to the provision in Article 12 for subscribing only to certain of its provisions.'[1]

Consequently, it is strongly arguable that principles of proportionality would be applicable in a judicial review. This is particularly so given the Principles governing intervention by the Secretary of State contained in the *Protocol on Intervention Powers* (see above) including: 'The form and extent of intervention will reflect the type and seriousness of failure and the need for effective improvement'.[2]

8.24 Authorities will clearly wish to represent their interests resolutely if they consider that the application (or potential application) of s 15 sanction powers is unfair or improper in any particular aspect or instance. They will also have in mind the legal principles which surround the proper exercise of s 15 power in discussions and correspondence which may take place with the Secretary of State in this area. However, the spirit of the times is somewhat different from the 'cold war' atmosphere of CCT. Whilst there will always be a tension between superior central power and substantially autonomous (but inferior) local power there is now a firm expectation that both sides will work in partnership for the public good. Although many local government commentators still worry that there is an essential absence of trust displayed by central to local government, the central–local partnership[3] has certainly charted a more positive approach to central–local relations than existed under the previous administration. The public[4] is less likely to be impressed by gung-ho litigation at their expense in the absence of justifiable cause.

Strategy

8.25 Prevention is always better than cure. Consequently, the key is to have a rigorous, robust and auditable approach to best value at all levels in the organisation in the light of clear and effective strategic direction which is linked to the needs of the community. Whilst this is clearly a matter for the authority, nevertheless, it is obviously beneficial to seek to agree strategy and approach with the external auditor and to keep him/her on board so far as possible throughout the whole process. It goes without saying that the statutory requirements of Part I of the LGA 1999 should be properly complied with and attention given to avoiding the failures of process and substance identified in the *Protocol on Intervention Powers* and set out above. It will therefore be necessary to make and retain throughout the organisation proper records of all key actions and processes within the implementation of the continuing best value strategy.

8.26 If there is correspondence with the DETR which seems to signal impending intervention, it will clearly be important to seek to persuade the Secretary of State as compellingly as possible that intervention is both

---

1   Cm 3884, March 1998, para 13.
2   Ibid, para 8.
3   This first met on 16 July 1997 (shortly after the present Government came into power) and
     has been meeting since.
4   The public would in any event expect to be kept closely in touch with what is happening
     under best value consultation duties.

inappropriate and unnecessary. This must be done using sound arguments rooted in the duty to provide best value to the public.

As noted above, before making a direction the Secretary of State will normally give authorities the chance to make representations about any report as a result of which a direction is proposed and also upon the direction proposed.[1] This should be seized positively and (in the light of an energetic and effective approach) the DETR should be clearly, coolly, logically but compellingly encouraged not to pursue intervention.

As mentioned, if the Secretary of State considers that intervention is necessary, the authority will be notified in writing of the improvements which the Secretary of State deems necessary. Under those circumstances, the authority will be given until a specified deadline to produce and publish a statement of action for making such improvements. This statement should clearly and cogently set out 'the actions to be carried out, the people responsible, the costs involved, the intended outcomes, the dates by which they are to be achieved and the authority's own proposals for monitoring and implementing the statement of action'.[2] The document should (so far as possible) be drafted (with identifiable and auditable action and systems in place to underpin it) so that no reasonable Secretary of State could fail to accept it.

8.27 If, however, the Secretary of State does decide to proceed with action then the authority will need to consider carefully whether:

– intervention action is objectively justifiable[3] in legal terms having regard to the considerations noted above;
– the Secretary of State has before him material upon which he could reasonably conclude that the authority has failed in its statutory duty;
– the proposed statutory action is proportionate in that the form and extent of intervention reflects the type and seriousness of failure and the need for effective improvement.

There may well be scope for negotiation on any of these matters. Ultimately, if the Secretary of State does decide to proceed very careful consideration will need to be given before any legal action is taken having regard to (amongst others):

– the likelihood of success in the light of all the factual and legal circumstances;
– how the action would benefit the authority and the community it has been set up to serve;
– costs considerations.

Generally, it is important to react promptly, credibly and powerfully to all correspondence from the DETR or other challenging organisation. But when personal propulsion intensifies (or, as the popular saying goes, when push

---

1   LGA 1999, s 15(9).
2   *Protocol on Intervention Powers*, at para XIV.
3   In considering this, it is suggested that those concerned try to see the matter in the way the courts are likely to, rather than through the eyes of those within the authority who may not be entirely disinterested.

comes to shove) the authority may be faced with some tough decisions. However, as mentioned, the zeitgeist (that most fickle of creatures embodied in public opinion and the national and local press) is unlikely at present to support legal action against the Government unless there is good reason; and that will be a rounded and sensitive judgment for the authority upon which sound professional advice will be needed.

Chapter 9

SMOOTHING THE PATH TO BEST VALUE – LEGAL POWERS

INTRODUCTION

9.1   The Book of Common Prayer (dating from 1660) required that:[1] 'If any of you know cause, or just impediment, why these two persons should not be joined together in holy Matrimony, ye are to declare it.' Whilst this chapter, happily, will venture no wisdom on such matters, in a rather different context, the Secretary of State will no doubt be equally keen to hear about enactments which give cause or just impediment why an authority and best value cannot live together in lawful wedded (or otherwise cohabitant) bliss.

LOCAL GOVERNMENT ACT 1999, ss 16 AND 17

9.2   Section 16 of the LGA 1999[2] gives the Secretary of State power to modify enactments and confer new powers. Where existing legislative measures are blocking the path to best value, s 16(1) is on hand to help. This enables the Secretary of State if he 'thinks that an enactment prevents or obstructs compliance by best value authorities with the requirements of' Part I of the LGA 1999 (best value) by order to 'make provision modifying or excluding the application of the enactment in relation to those authorities'.

If existing legal powers are insufficient for authorities to achieve the best value solutions they wish, s 16(2) allows the Secretary of State by order to 'make provision conferring on best value authorities any power which he considers necessary or expedient to permit or facilitate compliance with the require-ments' of Part I of the LGA 1999.

Section 16(3) gives the Government some flexibility in the management of this power by providing that an order under the section may:

'(a)   impose conditions on the exercise of any power conferred by the order (including conditions about consultation or approval);
(b)   amend an enactment;
(c)   include consequential, incidental and transitional provision;
(d)   make different provision for different cases'.

---

1   *Solemnization of Matrimony*, The Banns.
2   Section 16 of the 1999 Act came into effect in England and Wales on 27 September 1999 – see the Local Government Act 1999 (Commencement No 1) Order 1999, SI 1999/2169, which is reproduced in Appendix 2. By s 29(3) of the LGA 1999, in exercising a power under s 16, the Secretary of State 'shall not make any provision which has effect in relation to Wales unless he has consulted the National Assembly for Wales and shall not amend, or modify or exclude the application of, legislation made by the National Assembly for Wales, unless the Assembly consents'.

Orders made under this section are subject to the 'affirmative resolution' procedure. This affords much closer parliamentary scrutiny than the negative resolution procedure (under which the provision will come into force on the relevant date but subject to nullification if either House of Parliament (or, with instruments dealing with financial matters, the House of Commons only)) passes a Motion calling for their annulment within a certain time.[1] The affirmative resolution procedure in this case means that (as s 16(4) puts it): 'No order shall be made under this section unless a draft has been laid before, and approved by resolution of, each House of Parliament.'

9.3 In respect of any power conferred under s 16(2) a best value authority must have regard to any guidance issued by the Secretary of State.[2] At the time of writing, no such guidance has been issued for consultation or otherwise.

In constitutional terms this power is interesting and perhaps can be seen as the legislative equivalent of the cordless telephone. This is because it affords the Government flexibility within limits. Although it is right to be wary of liberalising legislative checks on the exercise of executive power, it is suggested that in this particular case (and provided the powers are properly and reasonably exercised) this is justifiable. As will be noted below, local authorities have long considered themselves to be constrained by inadequate legal powers. Section 16 can provide a valuable solution for authorities that have identified an innovative way of achieving a best value solution but which may not be lawful under the existing legislative regime.

9.4 In any event, s 17[3] contains important safeguards in respect of the exercise of these powers of the Secretary of State. First, before the Secretary of State makes a s 16 order he must first 'consult such authorities or persons as appear to him to be representative of interests affected by his proposals'.[4] If, following such consultation, the Secretary of State does decide to make a s 16 order he must (under s 17(2)) 'lay before each House of Parliament a document explaining his proposals and, in particular – (a) setting them out in the form of a draft order, and (b) giving details of' the consultation carried out under s 17(1).

The Secretary of State must not (by s 17(3)) place a draft order before Parliament 'to give effect to the proposals (with or without modification)' until 60 days after the document referred to in s 17(2) has been laid before Parliament, 'beginning with the day on which the document was laid'. In calculating the 60-day period, no account is to be taken of any time during which Parliament is dissolved or prorogued[5] or either House of Parliament is adjourned for more than four days'.

---

1   By s 28(2) 'An order under section 4, 5, 6, 7 or 25, and regulations under section 15 or 23, shall be subject to annulment in pursuance of a resolution of either House of Parliament'. See generally http://www.parliament.uk/parliament/index.htm.
2   LGA 1999, s 16(5).
3   Section 17 of the LGA 1999 Act came into effect in England and Wales on 10 August 1999 – see the Local Government Act 1999 (Commencement No 1) Order 1999, SI 1999/2169, which is reproduced in Appendix 2.
4   LGA 1999, s 17(1).
5   Prorogation is the ending of a session of Parliament by the exercise of the Royal prerogative. According to A V Dicey, the famous constitutional lawyer (1835–1922), the

In preparing a draft order to be laid before each House of Parliament under s 16(4), the Secretary of State must consider any representations made during the 60-day period referred to in s 16(3). Such draft order must be accompanied by a statement of the Secretary of State detailing any such representations considered and any changes made to the proposals contained in the document laid before Parliament under s 16(2).[1]

A QUESTION OF POWER

9.5   Why does the Secretary of State potentially need to jump through such hoops? The answer lies in the legal constitution of local government and the essential tenet that local authorities must act only within the bounds of their legal powers. Any other actions are unlawful as *ultra vires* (beyond their powers). Whilst it would exceed the scope of this book to deal in any detail with the complexities of local authority legal powers it is useful to identify some of the key issues. A good modern starting point is the restatement by Lord Templeman in the celebrated interest rates swaps case, *Hazell v Hammersmith and Fulham London Borough Council*,[2] that:

> 'A local authority, although democratically elected and representative of the area, is not a sovereign body and can only do such things as are expressly or impliedly authorised by Parliament.'

This means that a legal power has to be identified for every action taken by a local authority. Clearly (as Lord Templeman seems to acknowledge) there cannot be a specific Act of Parliament to cover every type of local authority activity. Therefore, the courts have long accepted that statutory corporations (such as local authorities) have implied powers to do what is incidental to the primary enabling statute. An example is *Attorney-General v Great Eastern Railway*[3] where Lord Selborne said of *ultra vires* that:

> 'this doctrine ought to be reasonably, and not unreasonably, understood and applied, and that whatever may fairly be regarded as incidental to, or consequential upon, those things which the legislature has authorised ought not (unless expressly prohibited) to be held by judicial construction, to be *ultra vires*.'

9.6   The current statutory embodiment of the incidental power is s 111 of the Local Government Act 1972. This provides as follows:

> '(1)   Without prejudice to any powers exercisable apart from this section but subject to the provisions of this Act and any other enactment passed before or after this Act, a local authority shall have power to do anything (whether or not involving the expenditure, borrowing or lending of money or the acquisition or disposal of any property or rights) which is calculated to facilitate, or is conducive or incidental to, the discharge of any of their functions.

Royal prerogative is 'The residue of discretionary or arbitrary authority which at any given time is legally left in the hands of the Crown'.
1   LGA 1999, s 16(6).
2   [1992] 2 AC 1.
3   (1880) 5 App Cas 473, HL.

(2) For the purposes of this section, transacting the business of a parish or community meeting or any other parish or community business shall be treated as a function of the parish or community council.

(3) A local authority shall not by virtue of this section raise money, whether by means of rates, precepts or borrowing, or lend money except in accordance with the enactments relating to those matters respectively.

(4) In this section "local authority" includes the Common Council.'

9.7 As to 'functions', Lord Templeman in *Hazell*[1] agreed with the Court of Appeal that 'in s 111 the word "functions" embraces all the duties and powers of a local authority; the sum total of the activities Parliament has entrusted to it'. An incidental power to do 'anything' looks wide on the face of it. However, in recent years the courts have construed the section restrictively. To look at a few examples:

- In *Allsop v Council of the Metropolitan Borough of North Tyneside*[2] (partially in reliance upon s 111) the authority's enhanced voluntary severance scheme provided for payments in excess of those authorised by the Employment Protection (Consolidation) Act 1978 and under statutory regulations dealing with superannuation, compensation for premature retirement and compensation for redundancy and premature retirement. The Court of Appeal upheld the decision of the Divisional Court that s 111(1) was expressly subject to the provisions of any other enactment, which included delegated legislation. To do otherwise would (in the view of Parker LJ) 'involve ignoring the restriction or limitation imposed by the opening words of section 111 of the Local Government Act 1972 and the plain intention of Parliament that the Secretary of State, subject to Parliamentary power to annul regulations in accordance with the Act, should be in complete charge of what is to be or may be paid on redundancy in addition to the payments provided for by the 1978 Act.'

- In *R v Richmond-upon-Thames London Borough Council, ex parte McCarthy & Stone (Developments) Ltd*[3] the House of Lords (reversing decisions of the Divisional Court and the Court of Appeal) held that whilst there was an incidental (but not a primary functional) power for authorities to give pre-application planning advice there was no power to charge for this since this would be 'incidental to the incidental' which was too remote to be authorised by s 111(1).[4]

- The decisions which registered dangerously high on the local authority and City Richter scales were those of the Court of Appeal on 8 May 1996 in *Credit Suisse v Borough Council of Allerdale*[5] and *Credit Suisse v Waltham Forest*

---

1   Noted above: [1992] 2 AC 1.

2   (1992) 90 LGR 462.

3   [1992] 2 AC 48.

4   However, on the facts of particular cases, what might be perceived as incidental could in fact be integral to the performance and discharge of the primary power. Andrew Arden QC, Jonathan Manning and Scott Collins indicate that it would be 'dangerous to elevate the term "incidental to the incidental" to an independent proposition of law. What is incidental in a particular case, as distinct from what is merely an implied power, are questions in respect of which different people may come to different answers'. (See paragraph 1.6.125 of *Local Government Constitutional and Administrative Law* (Sweet & Maxwell, 1999).)

5   [1997] QB 306.

London Borough Council.[1] In simple terms *Allerdale* concerned a scheme by the Council to provide a leisure pool financed by a time-share development. To avoid restrictive statutory borrowing controls this was to be done through a new company acquired for the purpose. The Company borrowed £6 million from Credit Suisse for 'Construction of time-share and leisure pool complex' and this was guaranteed by the Council 'on a full and unqualified indemnity basis'. But the time-share sales were unsatisfactory and the Company was unable to service the loan. Consequently the Bank called in its guarantee, which resulted in the proceedings. On 6 May 1994 the High Court rejected the Bank's claim since it had accepted Allerdale's argument that it had had no statutory power to give the guarantee. The Court of Appeal agreed. Neill LJ, who gave the leading judgment, agreed with the conclusion of the High Court judge that he had failed 'to see how there could be any implication empowering a local authority to acquire the use of borrowed money [to discharge a particular function] by any other means than by borrowing the required funds itself and doing so conformably with' the relevant statutory regime. Neill LJ said that: 'The establishment of the company and the giving of the guarantee were part of an ingenious scheme designed to circumvent the no doubt irksome controls imposed by central government. The council, however, could only do what it was empowered to do by statute. Neither the establishment of a company nor the giving of a guarantee fell within the express or implied powers of the council'. 'The implied powers in section 111 do not provide an escape route from the statutory controls. In my view that is clear not only as a matter of principle but also on the construction of section 111 itself. Section 111(3) ensures that the powers exerciseable under section 111(1) have to be used in conformity with the other statutory provisions.'

- In *Credit Suisse v Waltham Forest London Borough Council* a council guarantee for a loan facility of up to £11 million to a company set up by the Council for housing purposes which (amongst other things) avoided capital expenditure and other restrictions was also held by the Court of Appeal to be unlawful. As Neill LJ said: 'I am afraid that I have come to the conclusion, as I did in the *Allerdale* case, that where Parliament has made detailed provisions as to how certain statutory functions are to be carried out there is not scope for implying the existence of additional powers which lie wholly outside the statutory code. Section 111(3) makes it clear that the power to enter into financial obligations is subject to any statutory controls which may be imposed.'

LOCAL GOVERNMENT (CONTRACTS) ACT 1997

9.8   The *Credit Suisse* decisions caused so much nervousness amongst financial institutions (and disquiet about the likely sedative effect of the judgments upon the Private Finance Initiative) that the Labour Government following election in May 1997 enacted the Local Government (Contracts) Act 1997 which made

---

1   [1996] 4 All ER 176.

provision (amongst other things) for contracts certified in accordance with the Act to be deemed *intra vires* (within local authority powers) for private law purposes subject to judicial and audit review and specific provision for compensation. In summary, the Local Government (Contracts) Act 1997 (which was intended to clarify rather than extend local authority powers):

– makes clear that local authorities when exercising their statutory functions have power to contract with others for the provision or availability of assets and/or services for the purposes of or in connection with those functions;[1]
– enables authorities to enter into related contracts with third party financiers;[2]
– enables authorities to certify such contracts which (except for judicial review and audit proceedings) will then be presumed lawful between the parties;[3]
– provides that an authority which has issued a statutory certificate will be presumed to have had power to do so despite any inaccuracy or untruthfulness in the certificate;[4] and
– provides that any compensation provisions agreed between the parties ('relevant discharge terms') will survive any order (eg nullifying the contract) in judicial or audit review proceedings[5] and in the absence of such provisions gives contractors a right to monies to which they would have been entitled to at the time of the order on an accepted repudiatory breach of the contract.[6]

However, whilst the 1997 Act does provide some assistance within its particular purview, it will not assist authorities that wish to introduce imaginative schemes as part of the realisation of best value for their communities. Consequently, the s 16 power can afford significant flexibility (depending upon how the Government chooses to exercise it). Any statutory guidance issued under s 16(5) may give some indication of this. However, authorities for whom potential best value solutions are currently roadblocked by existing legislative restrictions or absence of legal powers should notify the Secretary of State and invite him to make the requisite order. Full details (with supporting evidence) of how best value is being prevented or obstructed or would be permitted or facilitated by a new power will no doubt be necessary together with a comprehensive explanation of why existing powers are inadequate. Clause 2(1) of the Local Government Bill 1999 will also be helpful in this context.

---

1   Local Government (Contracts) Act 1997, s 1(1).
2   Ibid, s 1(2).
3   Ibid, ss 2–5.
4   Ibid, s 4.
5   Ibid, s 6.
6   Ibid, s 7.

LOCAL GOVERNMENT ACT 1972, s 137

9.9 It is worth giving brief mention to this power[1] which, whilst quite limited in its application, has occasionally had its uses.[2] Section 137 of the Local Government Act 1972 enables local authorities to incur expenditure for certain purposes not otherwise authorised. Like a ramshackle array of extensions to the original building, s 137 currently contains an unwieldy series of restrictions upon the original power which those interested will need to peruse carefully.

The core power is now (per s 137(1)) that 'a local authority may, subject to the provisions of this section, incur expenditure which in their opinion is in the interests of, and will bring direct benefit to, their area or any part of it or all or some of its inhabitants'. By s 137(2), the power in s 137(1) to incur expenditure 'includes power to do so by contributing towards the defraying of expenditure by another local authority in or in connection with the exercise of that other authority's functions.' However, a local authority must not under s 137(1) incur any expenditure:

> '(a) for a purpose for which they are, either unconditionally or subject to any limitation or to the satisfaction of any condition, authorised or required to make any payment by or by virtue of any other enactment; nor (b) unless the direct benefit accruing to their area or any part of it or to all or some of the inhabitants of their area will be commensurate with the expenditure to be incurred.'

9.10 Expenditure under s 137 is to be limited[3] to the amount produced by multiplying a sum specified in s 137(4AA) or by order of the Secretary of State by the 'relevant population of the authority's area'.[4] By s 137(7) all expenditure under s 137 is to be accounted for separately in the authority's accounts. This includes the requisite proportion of pay and expenses referable to officer time which would not have been incurred if s 137 had not authorised the expenditure in question.[5]

Section 137A(1) requires authorities providing financial assistance above a specified amount to voluntary bodies or charitable or related bodies under

---

1 However (as will be seen below), it is to be substantially disabled for principal councils if Clause 7 of the Local Government Bill 1999 is enacted in the form in which it was introduced into Parliament on 25 November 1999.

2 An example is *Manchester City Council v Greater Manchester Metropolitan County Council* (1980) 78 LGR 560, where the House of Lords held that payments made by the former County Council (which was not an education authority) to a trust set up by the County Council for the provision of free or assisted independent school places for children of resident parents were lawful. The monies were lawfully disbursed to the trustees by the Council as expenditure under s 137(1) and the creation of the trust was 'purely incidental' to the exercise of the GMC's power to expend the monies in question 'as they desired to do'. See Lord Keith of Kinkel.

3 See s 137(4).

4 See the Local Authorities (Discretionary Expenditure) (Relevant Population) Regulations 1993, SI 1993/40.

5 See *R v District Auditor for Leicester, ex parte Leicester City Council* (1985) 25 RVR 191.

s 137(3) of the 1972 Act to require the recipient as a condition of assistance within 12 months to supply the authority with a written statement of the use to which the monies have been put. The written statement can if required consist of an annual report or accounts containing the information in question[1] and must in any event be deposited with the authority's proper officer.[2]

LOCAL AUTHORITIES (GOODS AND SERVICES) ACT 1970

9.11 The Local Authorities (Goods and Services) Act 1970 has been the traditional cornerstone of local authority powers to 'trade'. For it enables local authorities[3] and designated public bodies to enter into agreements containing 'such terms as to payment or otherwise as the parties consider appropriate'[4] for (amongst other things) the supply by the authority to the body of any goods or materials[5] or the provision by the authority to the body of any administrative, professional or technical services.[6] The Act also enables public bodies to use authority vehicle, plant or apparatus together with 'the services of any person employed in connection with the vehicle or other property in question'[7] and empowers an authority to carry out maintenance work[8] over land or buildings for which the public body is responsible.[9] Also, an authority may 'purchase and store any goods or materials which in their opinion they may require for the purposes of' supplying goods and materials under the Act.[10]

However, s 1(1)(a) to (c) of the 1970 Act does not authorise local authorities to 'construct any buildings or works; or ... to be supplied with any property or provided with any service except for the purposes of functions conferred on the authority otherwise than by this Act'. But it seems that the powers conferred by the 1970 Act are self-contained since nothing in s 1 'shall be construed as derogating from any powers exercisable by any public body apart from that section'.[11] Any agreements made under the 1970 Act must be accounted for separately in the accounts of the authority.[12]

9.12 In addition to local authorities, public bodies include (by s 1(4) of the 1970 Act) police authorities, the Service Authority for the National Crime Squad, the Service Authority for the National Criminal Intelligence Service, housing action trusts established under Part III of the Housing Act 1988 and

---

1   Local Government Act 1972, s 137A(4).
2   Ibid, s 137A(5).
3   By s 1(4) of the Local Authorities (Goods and Services) Act 1970 this includes county, district and London borough councils together with the Broads Authority, the Common Council of the City of London, the Council of the Isles of Scilly and any joint board, joint committee and joint authority established by Part IV of the Local Government Act 1985.
4   Local Authorities (Goods and Services) Act 1970, s 1(3).
5   Ibid, s 1(1)(a).
6   Ibid, s 1(1)(b).
7   Ibid, s 1(1)(c).
8   Including (by s 1(4) of the 1970 Act) renewals, minor improvements and minor extensions.
9   Ibid, s 1(1)(d).
10   Ibid, s 1(1).
11   Ibid, s 2(1).
12   Ibid, s 2(2).

parish councils and representative bodies of rural parishes in England and Wales.[1] However, most significantly, public bodies are also those persons designated as such by the relevant Secretary of State.[2] These bodies are very numerous and (as indicated) are those which have been so designated as appearing to the Secretary of State to be exercising functions of a public nature.

Many local authority lawyers (including the writer) have long been urging the government to dispense with the rather cumbersome power to designate public bodies in favour of a generic definition detailing the type of body which will be deemed to be 'public' for the purposes of the 1970 Act. A consultation paper concerning, amongst others, s 16 powers is expected from the DETR in 2000. It is hoped that this might encompass such proposals to define rather than to designate public bodies. It is also understood that a review of the 1970 Act is being considered.

9.13 It is possible for 1970 Act trading activity to be substantial and extensive. In *R v Yorkshire Purchasing Organisation, ex parte British Educational Suppliers' Association*[3] the appellant trade association which represented the interests of private sector suppliers in competition with the Yorkshire Purchasing Organisation (YPO) failed in its contention that YPO's activities were outside the powers conferred by the 1970 Act. Simon Brown LJ rejected as 'an impossible argument' the Association's submission that 'a local authority proposing to supply goods or materials to a public body under s. 1(1)(a) of the 1970 Act cannot themselves acquire and store such goods unless and until they have a firm contractual commitment for their onward supply to the public body'. The primary intention of s 1(1)(a) is 'to enable local authorities and other public bodies to benefit from bulk buying and resultant economies of scale'. Simon Brown LJ considered that that would be 'obviously best achieved if the purchasing authority is free to go out into the market place to buy in such quantities and at such times as sound business sense dictates, unconstrained by the limitations which would be imposed if it could buy only to satisfy already established requirements.'

YPO's operation was considerable. For instance (amongst other things):

> 'In 1994 it was holding over 12,000 product lines in stock; it was employing the equivalent of 373 full-time staff; it operated in 37 local authority areas apart from those of its own members; it spent £267,940 on the production of catalogues advertising goods for sale; it engaged widely in marketing campaigns, attending trade fairs, making promotional visits, entertaining potential customers and the like; it employed a fleet of 52 vehicles to make deliveries of goods sold. Its 1994 turnover was £161 million ...'.[4]

Whilst 'those enacting this legislation[5] would have been surprised, perhaps even shocked, to see the limits to which YPO has taken it ... I can see no basis whatever for construing this legislation restrictively so as to prevent it.'[6]

---

1   Local Authorities (Goods and Services) Act 1970, s 1(4).
2   Ibid, s 1(5). The designation is by order by statutory instrument and is subject to the negative resolution procedure. It is in respect of persons or descriptions of persons appearing to the Secretary of State 'to be exercising functions of a public nature'.
3   (1997) 95 LGR 727, CA.
4   Simon Brown LJ.
5   Ie the 1970 Act.
6   Simon Brown LJ.

LOCAL GOVERNMENT BILL 1999

9.14   Section 16 of the 1999 Act is one part of a new legal backdrop for local government of which Part I of the Local Government Bill 1999[1] introduced into Parliament following the Queen's Speech on 17 November 1999 is another. Clause 2(1) of the 1999 Bill gives every local authority power to do anything which they consider is likely to achieve any one or more of the following objects:

'(a)   the promotion or improvement of the economic well-being of their area,

 (b)   the promotion or improvement of the social well-being of their area, and

 (c)   the promotion or improvement of the environmental well-being of their area.'

By clause 2(2) this power may be exercised 'in relation to or for the benefit of the whole or any part of a local authority's area or all or any persons resident or present in a local authority's area'.

9.15   Environmental considerations are accommodated by clause 2(3), which requires authorities in determining 'whether or how to' exercise the power to promote or improve economic, social and environmental well-being (ESEW) to 'have regard to the effect which the proposed exercise of the power would have on the achievement of sustainable development[2] in the United Kingdom'. This helps to fulfil the Government's commitment in paragraph 8.10 of the July 1998 White Paper[3] 'to put sustainable development at the heart of council decision making' as well as providing an 'overall framework within which councils must perform all their existing functions'.

By clause 2(4), the ESEW power includes power for authorities to: incur expenditure; give financial assistance to any person; enter into arrangements or agreements with any person; co-operate with, or facilitate or co-ordinate the activities of, any person; exercise on behalf of any person any functions of that person; and provide staff, goods, services or accommodation to any person.

Consistent with the Government's aim for 'joined-up' service provision[4] 'cross-boundary' activity is permitted consistent with the essential power. This is

---

1   The Local Government Bill, its provisions and clause numbers now referred to are as passed by the House of Lords and introduced into the House of Commons on 13 March 2000. Clearly subsequent changes in numeration and substance will occur.

2   See footnote 1 at p 66.

3   DETR, *Modern Local Government In Touch with the People* (30 July 1998), para 8.10.

4   Joined-up or cross-cutting services may be described as those which, focusing on outputs, now provide a more economic, efficient and effective unified service by way of a partnership or other joint working arrangements between two or more organizations who had previously provided their services separately. On 2 February 2000 the DETR published a report entitled *Cross-cutting Issues in Public Policy and Public Service* which was 'prepared and written by a team of six from the University of Birmingham's School of Public Policy'. This (amongst other things) concluded that 'Cross-boundary working will be a characteristic feature of the new paradigm or system, since no one structural solution can solve all the problems. It will have a tight-loose framework – tight on outcomes, loose on the means of achieving them in particular circumstances. The new system will have direction setting at the centre, local judgment and planning on how best to deliver the outcomes, audit of the results, with help and assistance to do better made available for service providers.' (See Executive Summary.) The February 2000 report of the Cabinet Office Performance and Innovation Unit: *Reaching Out: The Role of Central Government at Regional and Local Level* recommended (amongst other things) strengthened Government

because clause 2(5) provides that the ESEW power 'includes power for a local authority to do anything in relation to, or for the benefit of, any person or area situated outside their area if they consider that it is likely to achieve any one or more of the objects in that subsection'; and, helpfully, clause 2(6) makes explicit what in any event was arguably implicit, that the instances mentioned of how the power might be exercised do not affect its general application. So, if authorities wish to exercise the power in ways not specified under clause 2(4) or (5) (all other legalities, proprieties and procedures permitting) they may do so.

9.16 Since local authorities are stewards of public monies some conditions and restrictions on the exercise of the power are to be expected. These include guidance, in particular on the exercise of the ESEW power (clause 3(5)) but also on the preparation of any strategy for promoting or improving ESEW (clause 4(2)(b) – see below). The contents of this statutory guidance will clearly be of significance to the practical application of the power. It is therefore encouraging that (per clause 3(6)) before issuing any guidance under clause 3(5) the Secretary of State will be obliged to 'consult such representatives of local government and such other persons (if any) as he considers appropriate'. It is hoped that local government (and other key stakeholders) will be closely involved with the drafting of the Guidance since practitioners (by definition) understand closely the practicalities of delivering the services that people need within their communities.

'Limits' on the power to promote well-being are contained in clause 3. Under clause 3(1), the ESEW power does not enable local authorities to do anything 'which they are unable to do by virtue of any prohibition, restriction or limitation on their powers which is contained in any enactment (whenever passed or made)'. So the Bill is subject to any previous or future statute or subordinate legislation. The restrictions in clause 3(1) do therefore result in something of a clawback from the powers in clause 2. In addition, the restrictions may well create uncertainty in the formation of partnerships. A certification process (as in the Local Government (Contracts) Act 1997)[1] might have been useful to provide a solid basis for any actions taken under this power.

9.17 Nevertheless, on the more positive side, there is a useful provision in clause 5 (analogous to the power in s 16 of the LGA 1999 discussed above[2] and subject to consultation and special parliamentary procedure) which enables the Secretary of State, if he thinks that any legislative measure 'prevents or obstructs local authorities from exercising' their ESEW power, by order to 'amend, repeal or revoke that enactment'. This is a helpful provision which provides a benign shadow to clause 3(3) (which, as will be seen, empowers the Secretary of State to *prevent* certain local authority actions by order). Again it would be helpful if the Government could give an indication of its policy towards use of this provision and its interaction with s 16 of the 1999 Act.

9.18 Clause 3(2) maintains control on public sector spending by making clear that the ESEW power 'does not enable a local authority to raise money

---

Offices for the Regions with clearer accountability for cross-cutting issues and 'Strengthened Ministerial and Whitehall co-ordination of policy initiatives and of Government Offices.' (See Executive Summary.)

1   See above.
2   To modify enactments and confer new powers.

(whether by precepts, borrowing or otherwise)'. This also prevents legalisation of 'cunning wheezes' to get around local authority financial controls.[1]

As mentioned, the Secretary of State has also reserved power in clause 3(3) to make an order preventing authorities from exercising the ESEW power to do anything specified or described in the order. This is perhaps a function of the residual nervousness still felt by central government towards local government and enables fast action against any local authority activity under the ESEW power of which the Government disapproves. No doubt the Government will be giving an indication of the circumstances in which it envisages using this power.

9.19 Clause 4 empowers (but does not compel) authorities to prepare a 'strategy for promoting or improving the economic, social and environmental well-being of their area'. If they do so, authorities may consult or seek the participation of anyone they consider appropriate[2] and must (as indicated above) have regard to any relevant guidance from the Secretary of State.[3]

Clause 6(1) (which relates to clause 4) enables the Secretary of State by order to 'amend, repeal or disapply any enactment which requires a local authority to prepare, produce or publish any plan or strategy relating to any particular matter'. This will clearly facilitate meaningful strategic provision to promote ESEW and may be exercised only if the Secretary of State considers that it is inappropriate for the enactment in question to apply to the authority or that the enactment should be amended to make it operate more effectively in relation to that authority.[4]

9.20 As indicated above, for principal councils the well-known (and significantly restricted) power in s 137 of the Local Government Act 1972[5] has had most of its vital organs removed. English county councils, district councils, London Boroughs (amongst others) and Welsh county or county borough councils will, following enactment of the Bill, be able to incur s 137 expenditure only on certain charitable and related purposes. Parish and community councils will be able to use s 137 to its limited full.[6]

DEREGULATION AND CONTRACTING OUT ACT 1994

9.21 Section 101(1) of the Local Government Act 1972 enables local authorities to arrange for the discharge of any of their functions by a committee, a sub-committee or an officer of the authority or by any other local authority. By s 101(5) of the 1972 Act, two or more local authorities may discharge any of their functions jointly and, where arrangements are in force

---

1   As noted, the Court of Appeal in the *Credit Suisse* cases discussed above ruled two such schemes to be unlawful.
2   Clause 4(2)(a).
3   Clause 4(2)(b).
4   Clause 6(3).
5   Power for local authorities to incur expenditure for certain purposes not otherwise authorised subject to restrictions and a financial limit.
6   See clause 7 of the Local Government Bill 1999.

for them to do so, they may also arrange for the discharge of those functions by a joint committee of theirs or by an officer of one of them.[1]

Therefore, whilst an authority may contract out the performance of certain activities on an agency basis (ie where the authority retains executive discretion for the function in question), it may not delegate responsibility for the discharge of a function otherwise than under s 101 of the 1972 Act.[2] This point was recognised by (amongst others) Hobhouse LJ in *Credit Suisse v Borough Council of Allerdale*,[3] where he said that s 101(1):

> 'authorises a local authority to arrange for the discharge of any of its functions by a committee, sub-committee or an officer of the authority or by any other authority. Save for immaterial exceptions this delimits how a local authority may discharge its functions. Any delegation beyond those prescribed limits is unlawful. Thus a local authority may not delegate the discharge of its functions to members of the council.[4] Still less may it delegate them to the directors of a company'.

9.22 Consequently, to enable some careful flexibility, s 70 of the Deregulation and Contracting Out Act 1994 enables a Government Minister by order to provide that any statutory function specified in the order and which may be exercised by an authority officer (except one which is excluded by s 71 of the 1994 Act) may be contracted out to another person or the employees of that person if the authority so chooses. Before making such an order, the Minister must first consult such representatives of English or Welsh local government and, in the case of an authority in Scotland, such associations of Scottish authorities as he considers appropriate.[5] Section 71(1) (subject to specified exceptions in s 71(2) and (3)) excludes a function from contracting out if:

> '(a) its exercise would constitute the exercise of jurisdiction of any court or of any tribunal which exercises the judicial power of the State; or
> (b) its exercise, or a failure to exercise it, would necessarily interfere with or otherwise affect the liberty of any individual; or
> (c) it is a power or right of entry, search or seizure into or of any property; or
> (d) it is a power or duty to make subordinate legislation'.

An authorisation in a Ministerial order made under the 1994 Act may be for a specified period not exceeding 10 years, is revocable at any time by the Minister and will not prevent the authority from conducting the function in question itself.[6] An order may authorise the exercise of a function:

> '(a) either wholly or to such extent as may be specified in the order or authorisation;

---

1   Other arrangements will be permitted under Part II of the Local Government Bill 1999 if it becomes law. Details of how this is envisaged to operate were set out by the DETR in 'Consultative Drafts of Proposed Guidance and Regulations on New Constitutions for Councils' which was issued on 21 January 2000.

2   Or pursuant to Part II of the Local Government Bill 1999 – 'Arrangements with Respect to Executives' – assuming it becomes law in substantially the form it was introduced into Parliament on 25 November 1999.

3   See above: [1997] QB 306.

4   Ie individual members of a council. However, if the Local Government Bill 1999 is enacted in the form in which it was introduced into Parliament, it will be possible for authorities to delegate certain functions to individual executive members.

5   Deregulation and Contracting Out Act 1994, s 70(3).

6   Ibid, s 69(5).

(b)   either generally or in such cases or areas as may be so specified; and

(c)   either unconditionally or subject to the fulfilment of such conditions as may be so specified'.[1]

9.23   Section 18(1) of the LGA 1999[2] effectively extends s 70 of the Deregulation and Contracting Out Act 1994 so that it 'shall apply in relation to functions of any best value authority (other than excluded functions within the meaning of section 71) as it applies in relation to certain functions of local authorities'. By s 18(2) of the 1999 Act, in these circumstances an order under s 70 of the 1994 Act may be made only by the Secretary of State and 'if he considers the order necessary or expedient for the purpose of permitting or facilitating compliance with the requirements' of Part I of the LGA 1999 (best value).

So although (as indicated) local authority legal powers have been a rather frugal and uncertain feast, s 16 of the 1999 Act and the proposals in Part I of the Local Government Bill 1999 should bring to the table more generous fare for best value depending upon how beneficent the restaurant management and serving staff are prepared to be. If (as Francis Bacon[3] indicated) 'Knowledge itself is power',[4] then the knowledge that sufficient powers exist to support creative best value initiatives should be as motivating for authorities as the *ancien* powers *régime* was frustrating.

---

1   Deregulation and Contracting Out Act 1994, s 69(4).

2   Section 18 of the LGA 1999 came into effect in England and Wales on 27 September 1999 – see the Local Government Act 1999 (Commencement No 1) Order 1999, SI 1999/2169, which is reproduced in Appendix 2.

3   1561–1626.

4   *Religious Meditations.* Of Heresies.

Chapter 10

NON-COMMERCIAL CONSIDERATIONS

INTRODUCTION

10.1 The 1980s saw increasing tensions between local and central government. As local authorities struggled to assert their somewhat illusory independence, central government hit back with more and more restrictions. Compulsory competitive tendering (CCT) which escalated during the 1980s and 1990s was finally laid to rest on 2 January 2000 by s 21 of the Local Government Act 1999. However, the Local Government Act 1988 (LGA 1988) was not entirely revoked. Part II remains. This deals with the exclusion of non-commercial matters in local and other public authority contracts.

The Conservative Government which was in power when Part II of the LGA 1988 was introduced was unhappy with the increasing tendency of some local authorities to use their procurement power to achieve policy objectives irrelevant to the contract sought. This was known as 'contract compliance'. As the Bill was debated on second reading, the Secretary of State for the Environment said that 'political discrimination in the award of contracts is an offensive and growing practice; increasing numbers of councils subjugate the interests of their ratepayers and business men to futile political gesturing. All that is required of local authorities is to provide good local services at minimum cost to their ratepayers.'[1] 'Too many councillors seem to find it more fun to play at national politics at their ratepayers' expense than to deal with the real local challenges and problems'.[2]

10.2 However, Dr John Cunningham, for the opposition, felt that there should be legislation for contract compliance. He cited as an illustration that contract compliance was not 'some awful Left-wing radical idea which can only harm our economy', that in the United States of America 'the home of the market economy and free enterprise ... 80 per cent. of all jobs in manufacturing and 83 per cent. of all jobs in transportation, public utilities and communications are now governed by contract compliance legislation.' His view was that contract compliance was a 'positive and innovative development in the best traditions of British local government ... in the forefront of social and economic progress.'[3] Alastair Darling MP (in the course of his maiden speech) asked: 'Where is the local authorities' right to choose? Coming from a Government who support the right to choose and freedom of choice, this part

---

1   Mr Nicholas Ridley MP, Secretary of State for the Environment, *Hansard*, 6 July 1987, Col 83.
2   Ibid, Col 84.
3   Dr John Cunningham MP (Jack Cunningham) – ibid, Col 91.

of the Bill is ill-founded. It strikes at the very right of local authorities to make choices, not just on cost but on matters of straightforward decency.'[1]

However, Part II came into the world on 7 April 1988. Since it is still alive and thriving (albeit with a slight makeover) it will be necessary to consider it before looking at s 19 of the LGA 1999, which empowers the Secretary of State to disapply certain of its provisions.

LOCAL GOVERNMENT ACT 1988, PART II

Non-Commercial Considerations

10.3   Section 17(1) of the LGA 1988 imposes a duty upon local and certain other public authorities to exercise specified functions in relation to their existing or proposed public supply or works contracts without reference to certain matters which are designated as 'non-commercial'. The authorities regulated by s 17 are specified in Sch 2 to the LGA 1988[2] and include (amongst others):

–   county, district, London borough, parish and community councils (including the Common Council of the city of London in its capacity as local authority or police authority);
–   police authorities;
–   fire authorities constituted by a combination scheme and metropolitan county fire and civil defence authorities;
–   the London Fire and Civil Defence Authority;
–   metropolitan county passenger transport authorities;
–   waste disposal authorities;
–   National Park authorities;
–   joint planning boards constituted under s 2(1B) of the Town and Country Planning Act 1990;
–   Passenger Transport Executives;
–   probation committees;
–   any joint committee discharging under s 101 of the Local Government Act 1972 functions of local authorities (within the meaning of that section).

Public supply or works contracts are those 'for the supply of goods or materials, for the supply of services or for the execution of works'.[3] However, the section does not apply to contracts entered into before its commencement on 7 April 1988.[4]

The functions specified as regulated by s 17 are set out in s 17(4) and are:

'(a)   the inclusion of persons in or the exclusion of persons from—
        (i)   any list of persons approved for the purposes of public supply or works contracts with the authority, or

---

1   *Hansard*, 6 July 1987, Col 108.
2   Pursuant to s 17(2) of the LGA 1988.
3   Section 17(3).
4   By s 23, ss 17–22 of the LGA 1988 came into force at the end of the period of 14 days beginning with the day on which the Act was passed. Since the Act was passed on 24 March 1988, Part II of the Act came into force on 7 April 1988.

(ii)   any list of persons from whom tenders for such contracts may be invited;

(b)   in relation to a proposed public supply or works contract with the authority—

   (i)   the inclusion of persons in or the exclusion of persons from the group of persons from whom tenders are invited,

   (ii)   the accepting or not accepting the submission of tenders for the contract,

   (iii) the selecting the person with whom to enter into the contract, or

   (iv)   the giving or withholding approval for, or the selecting or nominating, persons to be sub-contractors for the purposes of the contract; and

(c)   in relation to a subsisting public supply or works contract with the authority—

   (i)   the giving or withholding approval for, or the selecting or nominating, persons to be sub-contractors for the purposes of the contract, or

   (ii)   the termination of the contract.'

10.4   But what are the famous (or perhaps in some cases notorious) 'non-commercial matters'? These are set out as follows in s 17(5) of the LGA 1988 and relate to the public supply or works contracts of a public authority or, as the case may be, any proposed or any subsisting such contract:

'(a)   the terms and conditions of employment by contractors of their workers or the composition of, the arrangements for the promotion, transfer or training of or the other opportunities afforded to, their workforces;

(b)   whether the terms on which contractors contract with their sub-contractors constitute, in the case of contracts with individuals, contracts for the provision by them as self-employed persons of their services only;

(c)   any involvement of the business activities or interests of contractors with irrelevant fields of Government policy;

(d)   the conduct of contractors or workers in industrial disputes between them or any involvement of the business activities of contractors in industrial disputes between other persons;

(e)   the country or territory of origin of supplies to, or the location in any country or territory of the business activities or interests of, contractors;

(f)   any political, industrial or sectarian affiliations or interests of contractors or their directors, partners or employees;

(g)   financial support or lack of financial support by contractors for any institution to or from which the authority gives or withholds support;

(h)   use or non-use by contractors of technical or professional services provided by the authority under the Building Act 1984 or the Building (Scotland) Act 1959.'

By s 17(6) the matters in question include those 'which have occurred in the past as well as matters which subsist when the function in question falls to be exercised'; and in a quiet efflorescence of distrust s 17(7) (presumably by way of anti-avoidance) makes the exercise of any non-commercial matter in relation to any of the following referable to the contractor as a non-commercial matter for the purposes of the section:

'(a)   a supplier or customer of the contractor;

(b)   a sub-contractor of the contractor or his supplier or customer;

(c)   an associated body of the contractor or his supplier or customer; or

(d)   a sub-contractor of an associated body of the contractor or his supplier or customer'.

There is an extensive definitions section in s 17(8) which defines all the terms used in that section.

Race Relations

10.5   As to race relations matters, s 18(1) of the LGA 1988 provides that, except as permitted by s 18(2), 'section 71 of the Race Relations Act 1976 (local authorities to have regard to need to eliminate unlawful racial discrimination and promote equality of opportunity, and good relations, between persons of different racial groups) shall not require or authorise a local authority to exercise any function regulated by section 17 ... by reference to a non-commercial matter'.

Subject to an exception in s 18(3), s 18(2) permits local authorities to ask approved questions seeking information or undertakings relating to workforce matters and to consider the responses to them or to include in a draft contract or draft tender for a contract terms or provisions relating to workforce matters and to consider the responses to them 'if, as the case may be, consideration of the information, the giving of the undertaking or the inclusion of the term is reasonably necessary to secure compliance with' s 71 of the Race Relations Act 1976. By s 18(4) of the LGA 1988, authorities may also make an approved written request for evidence to support answers to permitted questions. The exception (in s 18(3)) is that the permission in s 18(2) does not cover the termination of existing contracts and, in relation to approved lists or proposed contracts, 'does not authorise questions in other than written form'.

10.6   The Secretary of State is authorised under s 18(5) to specify in writing approved questions and 'descriptions of evidence' concerning such questions[1] and has done so in Annex B to Department of the Environment Circular No 8/88 of 6 April 1988. The wording is as follows:

'*Specification of questions and descriptions of evidence*

The Secretary of State for the Environment, as respects England, and the Secretary of State for Wales, as respects Wales, in exercise of the powers conferred on them by s.18(5) of the Local Government Act 1988 hereby specify the following questions and description of evidence—

> 1. Is it your policy as an employer to comply with your statutory obligations under the Race Relations Act 1976 and, accordingly, your practice not to treat one group of people less favourably than others because of their colour, race, nationality or ethnic origin in relation to decisions to recruit, train or promote employees?
>
> 2. In the last three years, has any finding of unlawful racial discrimination been made against your organisation by any court or industrial tribunal?
>
> 3. In the last three years, has your organisation been the subject of formal investigation by the Commission for Racial Equality on grounds of alleged unlawful discrimination?
>   If the answer to question 2 is in the affirmative or, in relation to question 3, the Commission made a finding adverse to your organisation.
>
> 4. What steps did you take in consequence of that finding?
>
> 5. Is your policy on race relations set out—

---

1   The Secretary of State may (by s 18(6)) also 'include such consequential or transitional provisions as appear to the Secretary of State to be necessary or expedient'.

(a) in instructions to those concerned with recruitment, training and promotion;

(b) in documents available to employees, recognised trade unions or other representative groups of employees;

(c) in recruitment advertisements or other literature?

6. Do you observe as far as possible the Commission for Racial Equality's Code of Practice for Employment, as approved by Parliament in 1983, which gives practical guidance to employers and others on the elimination of racial discrimination and the promotion of equality of opportunity in employment, including the steps that can be taken to encourage members of the ethnic minorities to apply for jobs or take up training opportunities?

Description of evidence

In relation to question 5: examples of the instructions, documents, recruitment advertisements or other literature.'

Other Provisions

10.7 Section 19 of the LGA 1988 (amongst other things) enables the Secretary of State by order[1] to specify additional matters as non-commercial which appear to him to be 'irrelevant to the commercial purposes of public supply or works contracts of any description'[2] and also to amend any of the s 17 definitions.[3] However, the section does *not* empower him to remove any non-commercial matter.[4] Section 17 of the LGA 1988 will also apply[5] to functions delegated to other authorities under s 101 of the Local Government Act 1972 (see above).

Although breach of s 17(1) (duty to exercise the relevant function without reference to designated non-commercial matters) is not a criminal offence, it does create civil liability actionable by anyone who suffers loss or damage in consequence.[6] In respect of judicial review proceedings, the following will be deemed to have sufficient interest: any potential contractor or, when a contract has been concluded, a former potential contractor (or, in any case, any body representing contractors).[7] Tenderers claiming for breach of s 17(1) will be 'limited to damages in respect of expenditure reasonably incurred ... for the purpose of submitting the tender.'[8] Section 17 is not, of course, a complete statement of civil and administrative law obligations. Authorities will still be expected to comply with the substantial body of legal principles in question

---

1 Such orders are to be made under the affirmative resolution procedure. By s 19(3) no order is to be made 'unless a draft of it has been laid before and approved by a resolution of each House of Parliament'. This affords much closer parliamentary scrutiny than the negative resolution procedure, under which the provision will come into force on the relevant date but subject to nullification if either House of Parliament (or, with instruments dealing with financial matters, the House of Commons only) passes a Motion calling for their annulment within a certain time.

2 LGA 1998, s 19(1).

3 Ibid, s 19(2).

4 This is why s 19 of the LGA 1999 is needed – see below.

5 See s 19(6) of the LGA 1988.

6 LGA 1988, s 19(7)(b).

7 Ibid, s 19(7)(a).

8 Ibid, s 19(8).

including (as noted above) the duties to act lawfully, reasonably and with procedural propriety.[1] Section 19(9) makes this clear by providing that:

'Nothing in section 17 above or subsection (1) above implies that the exercise of any function regulated by that section may not be impugned; in proceedings for judicial review, on the ground that it was exercised by reference to other matters than those which are non-commercial matters for the purposes of that section'.

Duty on Public Authorities to Give Reasons for Certain s 17 Decisions

10.8 When an authority makes a relevant decision concerning 'any person' in respect of a matter regulated by s 17(1) of the LGA 1988, the authority must 'forthwith' notify that person of the decision and if so requested in writing within 15 days of the notification, supply the person with written reasons for the decision,[2] also within 15 days of the request.[3] This applies to the following decisions:[4]

'(a) in relation to an approved list, a decision to exclude him from the list,
(b) in relation to a proposed public supply or works contract—
   (i)   where he asked to be invited to tender for the contract, a decision not to invite him to tender,
   (ii) a decision not to accept the submission by him of a tender for the contract,
   (iii) where he has submitted a tender for the contract, a decision not to enter into the contract with him, or
   (iv) a decision to withhold approval for, or to select or nominate, persons to be sub-contractors for the purposes of the contract, or
(c) in relation to a subsisting public supply or works contract with him—
   (i)   a decision to withhold approval for, or to select or nominate, persons to be sub-contractors for the purposes of the contract, or
   (ii) a decision to terminate the contract'.

The Secretary of State may (by s 20(4)) amend the 15-day period by order[5] to substitute 'such other period as he thinks fit' and 'such an order may make different amendments of' s 20(1) and (3).

10.9 Section 21 of the LGA 1988 deals with the 'transitional duty of public authorities' concerning 'approved lists' (ie 'any list of persons approved for the purposes of public supply or works contracts with the authority or any list of persons from whom tenders for such contracts may be invited'[6]) maintained when the section commences on 7 April 1988. Since this is unlikely now to be relevant for most authorities no further consideration will be given to it.

---

1   See *Council of Civil Service Unions v Minister for Civil Service* [1985] AC 374, referred to above.
2   LGA 1988, s 20(1).
3   Ibid, s 20(3).
4   Ibid, s 20(2).
5   By s 20(5) of the LGA 1988, the order-making power in this case is exerciseable by statutory instrument and is subject to annulment in pursuance of a resolution of either House of Parliament.
6   See s 17(4)(a) through s 17(8) and s 21(9) of the LGA 1988.

IMPETUS FOR REFORM OF THE LOCAL GOVERNMENT ACT 1988, PART II

10.10 In 1997, Oona King, a Labour MP, introduced the Local Authorities Tenders Bill (as a private Member's measure) with a view to reforming Part II of the LGA 1988. The Bill received its second reading in July 1998. Ms King said of her Bill that 'Councils will now be able to insist that companies to whom they give contracts have an equal opportunities policy. This isn't too much to ask, but the worst employers have tried to avoid it.'[1] The Bill would have enabled the Secretary of State to have provided that any matters specified by order would cease to be non-commercial matters under s 17 of the LGA 1988. This power would have been subject to any guidance and provided that the Secretary of State considered the matters in question 'irrelevant to the commercial purposes of public supply or works contracts of any description'.

10.11 However, following an objection from former Environment Minister, Sir Paul Beresford, the Bill effectively fell at its third reading in early July 1998. Ms King was reported as saying:

> 'I couldn't believe it when Sir Paul Beresford strolled into the Chamber only seconds before the title was read, objected to my bill and then walked straight back out again. Thousands of council workers now face redundancy or wage cuts.
>
> The bill had cross party support, with the backing of the CBI and TUC. It would have made a real difference to both council workers and the quality of service provided by local authorities. Cowboy operators will be thanking their lucky stars for having someone like Sir Paul on their side.'[2]

LOCAL GOVERNMENT ACT 1999, s 19

10.12 The Government supported Oona King's Bill. Section 19 of the LGA 1999[3] achieves substantially the same result.[4] In the course of Parliamentary Debate in Standing Committee on this provision,[5] Hilary Armstrong, Minister for Local Government said that whilst Part II of the LGA 1988 (which contains s 17 and other provisions relevant to the exclusion of non-commercial considerations for local and other public authority contracts) had advantages

---

1 LGCnet, 15 January 1998.
2 LGCnet, 20 July 1998.
3 Section 19 of the LGA 1999 came into force fully in England (and in Wales in relation to police and fire authorities) on 27 September 1999 – the Local Government Act 1999 (Commencement No 1) Order 1999, SI 1999/2169, which is reproduced in Appendix 2. In respect of Wales, on 23 September 1999, the National Assembly for Wales approved the Local Government Act 1999 (Commencement) (Wales) Order 1999, SI 1999/2815, which was made on 28 September 1999 and commenced a number of provisions from 1 October 1999 and others from 1 April 2000 (see Chapter 2: 'Commencement Issues in Wales'). The Wales Commencement Order is reproduced in Appendix 3.
4 In the House of Commons Standing Committee B on 16 February 1999, Local Government Minister, Hilary Armstrong, pointed out that the clause (as it then was) reflected Oona King's Bill 'which had a smooth passage through this House until the final stage when it was blocked by an hon. Member who was not content to allow any private Member's Bill through'.
5 The House of Commons Standing Committee B on 16 February 1999.

in that 'it prevents authorities from pursuing ideological idiosyncrasies at the expense of value for money', which is 'why we do not propose to repeal the measure', nevertheless it:

> '... also has manifest disadvantages, because it prevents local authorities from making a thorough and reasonable assessment of the quality and capability of tenderers. Important considerations, such as a company's training policy, have been off-limits simply because of how non-commercial matters have been defined ... The fact is that good procurement practice has moved on in recent years, especially since the Local Government Bill 1988 was enacted. It is therefore high time that the legislative framework was amended to reflect that. That is not just the Government's view: it is shared by local authorities and the private sector.'[1]

Further, the Minister said that:

> 'We must move away from the position in which short-term gain is more important than long-term capabilities. Authorities must have confidence in their private sector partners, and private companies must be able to demonstrate that they are well run organisations, capable of fulfilling contracts and annually improving the level of service in a way that delivers efficiencies. The provisions of the 1988 Act are an obstacle to that.'

Therefore, the clause (which was to become s 19 of the LGA 1999):

> '... gives the Secretary of State the power to remove categories of non-commercial matters so as to bring the framework into step with good procurement practice and with best value. Such power will balance the provision in the 1988 Act which allows for additional non-commercial matters to be specified'.[2]

10.13   Section 19(1) consequently enables the Secretary of State to provide by order[3] in relation to best value authorities:

> 'for a specified matter to cease to be a non-commercial matter for the purposes of section 17 of the Local Government Act 1988 (local and other public authority contracts: exclusion of non-commercial considerations)'.

Such an order may:[4]

> '(a)   provide for a matter to cease to be a non-commercial matter for specified purposes or to a specified extent;
> (b)   apply in relation to specified authorities, functions or contracts;
> (c)   make different provision for different cases;
> (d)   include consequential or transitional provision (including provision amending an enactment)'.

It will be seen that this gives the Secretary of State considerable latitude. For instance he may maintain any of the existing 'non-commercial matters' but may alter the extent of any or the circumstances in which they will apply. An order may apply in respect of 'specified authorities, functions or contracts'.

By s 19(4) of the LGA 1999, where a best value authority is discharging a function regulated by s 17 of the LGA 1988 with reference to a matter which is

---

1   The House of Commons Standing Committee B on 16 February 1999.
2   Ibid.
3   Using the affirmative resolution procedure, by s 19(3) of the LGA 1999: 'No order shall be made under this section unless a draft has been laid before, and approved by resolution of, each House of Parliament.'
4   See s 19(2) of the LGA 1999.

the subject of an order under s 19(1) of the LGA 1999, the authority must have regard to any guidance issued by the Secretary of State.

10.14 Paragraph 88 of the Guidance[1] indicates as follows that some reform of Part II of the LGA 1988 lies ahead:

> 'Both employers and employees need to have confidence in the fairness of the competitive process. The Government will amend Part II of the Local Government Act 1988 in such a way as to enable local authorities to take into account appropriate workforce matters in the selection of tenderers and the award of contracts, consistent with its EC obligations and the achievement of value for money. A consultation paper will be issued shortly and the Government expects to make the necessary Regulations ahead of 1 April 2000.'

It had been expected that, amongst others, s 17(5)(a) ('the terms and conditions of employment by contractors of their workers or the composition of, the arrangements for the promotion, transfer or training of or the other opportunities afforded to, their workforces') would be given early consideration by the Government for an order and related Guidance under s 19 of the LGA 1999. This is because (amongst other reasons):

- The January 2000 Cabinet Office publication, *Staff Transfers in the Public Sector – Statement of Practice*[2] (subject to genuinely exceptional circumstances and the duty of best value) expects that TUPE[3] principles will generally apply in respect of public sector organisations on 'contracting exercises with the private sector and voluntary organisations and transfers between different parts of the public sector'. However, s 17(5)(a) as presently framed could well prevent an authority from procuring on the basis that TUPE principles apply in line with the *Statement of Practice*. This inhibits best value since, for example, should an authority decide (on a Review or otherwise) that outsourcing is the most economic, efficient and effective way of providing a particular service, if the authority is unable to provide in the tender documents for the application of TUPE principles, uncertainties surrounding TUPE and related issues of staff motivation may make outsourcing a less attractive and commercially viable option. Conversely, a transfer on TUPE principles will provide certainty and also secure the continued employment (and therefore the likely well-being and motivation) of the affected staff in the business unit (or undertaking) in question.[4]

---

1 DETR Circular 10/99.
2 This is dealt with in Chapter 12.
3 TUPE refers to the Transfer of Undertakings (Protection of Employment) Regulations 1981, SI 1981/1794, and the underlying Council Directive 77/187/EEC (amended by Council Directive 98/50/EC on 29 June 1998) – see Chapter 12. TUPE (in brief summary) provides (on a transfer of a business or economic entity as a going concern) for the employees to transfer to the transferee business on their existing terms and conditions of employment. Whilst currently, as a matter of law, pensions are excepted from TUPE, there are developments in this area which are mentioned in the footnote below and in Chapter 12.
4 The Government intends to revise the TUPE Regulations under powers in s 2(2) of the European Communities Act 1972 and s 38 of the Employment Relations Act 1999. Section 38 enables the Secretary of State to make regulations achieving a similar effect to the TUPE Regulations in circumstances where TUPE would not otherwise apply. This is intended to

- Staffing costs and issues underpinning them go to the sustainability of a bid which is clearly a commercial matter.
- The fact that the terms and conditions of employment by contractors of their workers is clearly a commercial matter is supported by the facts in the decision of the European Court of Justice (ECJ) in *Allen and Others v Amalgamated Construction Co Ltd*.[1] This case concerned whether there could be a relevant transfer of an undertaking between two companies in the same group. Relevant to the facts surrounding the transfer was that the private sector client (RJB Mining (UK) Ltd) had, on the transfer of employees from one group subsidiary to another, 'expressed concern about the terms and conditions of employment being provided ... believing that they were the reason for lack of motivation of employees of those undertakings'. Whilst the ECJ concluded that the Directive underlying TUPE[2] 'can apply to a transfer between two companies in the same group which have the same ownership, management and premises and which are engaged in the same works', the essential point here is that the terms and conditions of workers were considered to be a commercial consideration in an entirely private sector context.

Also a potentially commercially relevant factor is that contained in s 17(5)(d) ('the conduct of contractors or workers in industrial disputes between them ... '). If a contractor has a poor industrial relations record this must surely be a relevant matter to be taken into account when deciding whether to purchase from such a person.

10.15 Consequently, the Consultation Paper on Draft Guidance *Best Value and Procurement Handling of Workforce Matters in Contracting*[3] issued on April 11 2000 which (amongst other things) charts the Government's intention to remove these two workforce matters (s 17(5)(a) and (d)) is extremely welcome. This refers to a proposed statutory instrument to be made under s 19 of the LGA 1999 which provides 'in respect of best value authorities' for these workforce matters 'to cease to be defined as non-commercial matters for the purposes of Part II of the Local Government Act 1988 to the extent that they are relevant to the achievement of best value, and in circumstances where they are relevant for the purposes of a TUPE transfer.'[4]

Paragraph 4 of the Draft Guidance sets out as follows the scope of the proposed statutory guidance issued under s 19 of the LGA 1999 which:

---

be used to support a general presumption that TUPE applies, subject (as mentioned in the January 2000 Cabinet Office publication, *Staff Transfers in the Public Sector – Statement of Practice*) to necessary exceptions to accommodate, for instance, genuine Best Value innovations. The Government is also examining options for the continuation of pension provision after transfer. Also, on 22 December 1999, the Local Government Pension Scheme (Amendment) Regulations 1999 were issued which (amongst other things) enable employees of organisations which provide services or assets to local authority or other best value authorities under specified circumstances to be members of the Local Government Pension Scheme. These Regulations came into force on 13 January 2000. A consultation exercise on proposed revisions to the TUPE Regulations is expected in 2000.

1   (Case C-234/98) [2000] IRLR 119, ECJ.
2   77/187/EEC (amended by Council Directive 98/50/EC on 29 June 1998) – see above and Chapter 12.
3   DETR April 2000. Consultation closed 26 May 2000.
4   See para 3.

'... sets out how workforce matters may be handled in contractual and other partnering arrangements under best value. It clarifies the extent to which workforce matters can be taken into account by a best value authority in the contracting process consistent with the achievement of value for money, the principles of good public procurement and EU public procurement law. Section 19(4) of the Local Government Act 1999 requires best value authorities to have regard to this guidance in exercising a function regulated by section 17 of the 1988 Act which is also the subject of an order made under the 1999 Act.'

However, the proposed Statutory Instrument 'does not relax the restriction on those matters that can be said to be truly non-commercial. Workforce matters that are not directly relevant to the delivery of the service in question should not be taken into account (eg local labour). Also, the other non-commercial matters specified at s 17 of the LGA 1988, which do not relate to workforce matters, will continue to be excluded from the contractual process.'[1]

In taking account of workforce issues arising in best value procurement, local authorities will need to recognise:

'–   the connection between service quality and handling of workforce issues. Good quality services depend on appropriately skilled and motivated workforces. Neglecting workforce matters in order to drive down costs can have adverse effects on the desired quality and value for money of the service being provided;

–   the necessity of achieving the appropriate balance between considerations of cost and quality. This will depend on the nature of the service to be provided and the requirements of the service users. It is unlikely that either a purely cost-driven or an unjustifiably expensive service will represent best value;

–   that a transparent, open and fair procurement process is essential to attracting bids that provide the optimum combination of whole-life cost and quality. All decisions should be based on objective measures that are justifiable in terms of the performance of the service specified under the contract. Authorities should therefore have clear procurement strategies, procedures and written policies for evaluating tenders (see paragraph 45 of DETR Circular 10/99);

–   the emphasis on continuous improvement within best value and the implications for how strategic contracts in particular are structured;

–   the relevance of equal opportunities to the delivery of contracts;

–   the importance of handling TUPE well, so as to allay workforce reservations about transferring to new employers.'[2]

CONCLUSION

10.16 Clearly local government and the wider world has changed substantially from what it was when Part II of the LGA 1988 was born. If authorities are to give best value in the broadest sense of the word then they need appropriate flexibility to do so; for it will be the responsibility of authorities 'to secure' best value, even if the work in question is carried out externally. Given that the purpose of best value (and its social, economic and environmental context) is different from the narrow statutory considerations in Part I of the LGA 1988,

---

1   Paragraph 4.
2   Paragraph 7.

authorities clearly need tools to do the job which are fit for their current purpose. So a recast (within proper and responsible limits) for Part II is welcome to enable it to enhance rather than constrain best value as local government and the public it serves move forward to meet the challenges of the third millennium.

Chapter 11

ACCOUNTING ISSUES

INTRODUCTION

11.1   If authorities will have to give a comprehensive account of their actions and proposals in the annual performance plan, best value review programme and the inspection regime, they will also have to account for their financial stewardship within best value. For as the public might say, 'Tell us what you've done with our money.'

STATUTORY MATERIAL

11.2   Unlike with compulsory competitive tendering (CCT) (where detailed accounts requirements appeared in the primary statutes,[1] supported by subordinate legislation), s 23 of the LGA 1999[2] (which deals with 'the keeping of accounts by best value authorities') continues the modern trend and confers regulation-making power upon the Secretary of State as well as dealing with related issues.

Section 23(1) provides that the 'Secretary of State may make regulations about the keeping of accounts by best value authorities' and these (by s 23(2)) may:

> '(a)   require accounts and statements of accounts to be prepared, kept and certified in such form or manner as the regulations may specify;
> (b)   require accounts to be deposited at such places as the regulations may specify;
> (c)   require the publication of information about accounts and of statements of accounts;
> (d)   make provision (which may include provision requiring the payment of fees) entitling specified classes of person to inspect and to make or receive copies of specified documents'.

In keeping with a prevailing theme of legislative flexibility for the Secretary of State throughout the LGA 1999, the Regulations may also 'make provision in

---

1   For example, s 10 of the Local Government, Planning and Land Act 1980 and s 9 of the LGA 1988.

2   Section 23(4) (consultation) came into force fully in England (and in Wales in relation to police and fire authorities) on 10 August 1999. The remainder of s 23 came into force fully in England (and in Wales in relation to police and fire authorities) on 27 September 1999 – see the Local Government Act 1999 (Commencement No 1) Order 1999, SI 1999/2169, which is reproduced in Appendix 2. In respect of Wales, on 23 September 1999, the National Assembly for Wales approved the Local Government Act 1999 (Commencement) (Wales) Order 1999, SI 1999/2815, which was made on 28 September 1999 and which brought the general duty of best value into force in relation to Wales from 1 April 2000 and commenced a number of provisions from 1 October 1999 and others from 1 April 2000 (see Chapter 2: 'Commencement Issues in Wales'). The Wales Commencement Order is reproduced in Appendix 3.

relation to best value authorities generally or in relation to one or more particular authorities ... [and] ... make different provision for different cases'.[1] This, of course, enables a tailored approach to address what the Secretary of State considers to be the particular requirements of individual authorities.

11.3   Consistent with the spirit of best value, by virtue of s 23(4) there is a duty on the Secretary of State before making s 23(1) regulations to consult the Audit Commission, the authorities in question (or persons appearing to the Secretary of State to represent them) and 'such bodies of accountants as appear to him to be appropriate'. CIPFA[2] will no doubt be a key consultee here.

11.4   There is a glimpse of the dock in s 23(5) for anyone who without reasonable excuse contravenes any regulations made under s 23(1) where 'the regulations declare that contravention of the provision is an offence'. On summary conviction a person in default is liable to a fine 'not exceeding level 3 on the standard scale'.[3] The external auditor is not to be out of pocket as a result of any such 'monkey business'. Section 23(6) provides that if such an auditor incurs any expenses in connection with proceedings for an offence of contravening the best value accounting regulations 'which is alleged to have been committed in relation to the accounts of an authority' then these expenses 'are recoverable from the authority so far as they are not recovered from any other source'. Those who have any dealings with best value accounting (whether as manager, accountant or in any other capacity) will clearly want to be sure they are at no time 'any other source'. Since (as mentioned above) prevention is always better than cure, it will be wise to ensure that any contribution to any best value accounting regime is completely proper, lawful and reasonable. If in doubt, professional advice should be sought.

11.5   The Guidance[4] indicates that the Secretary of State will decide whether he should exercise these regulation-making powers following publication by CIPFA of the *Best Value Accounting – Code of Practice* (see below). However, in light of the publication of this document on 22 February 2000, Hilary Armstrong, Minister for Local Government and the Regions announced that the powers would not be exercised at this stage:

> 'It is essential that best value is underpinned by a modern, effective accounting framework which promotes transparency, comparability and financial discipline. I fully endorse the Best Value Accounting – Code of Practice developed by CIPFA. This Code will be the recognised standard for all local authorities and will be crucial in demonstrating whether an authority is achieving best value.'[5]

> 'Under the Local Government Act 1999 the Secretary of State has powers to regulate the keeping of accounts by best value authorities. However, given the positive approach to trading accounts the Code promotes we will not need to exercise these powers at this time. We will monitor its introduction to ensure that it

---

1   See s 23(3).
2   The Chartered Institute of Public Finance and Accountancy, 3 Robert Street, London
     WC2N 6BH; Tel: 0207 543 5600, fax: 0207 543 5700. Website: http://www.cipfa.org.uk.
3   See s 37(2) of the Criminal Justice Act 1982. At the time of writing level 3 is set at £1000.
4   DETR Circular 10/99, para 71.
5   CIPFA Press Release, 23 February 2000.

achieves its objectives and will review this decision following CIPFA's own review of the Code later in the year.'[1]

CIPFA'S APPROACH

11.6 CIPFA is the professional body for best value authority accountants and finance officers. Therefore, its views, recommendations and guidance are highly significant for best value authorities in respect of their financial and accounting arrangements. Paragraph 68 of the Guidance that:

> 'CIPFA's Best Value Accounting – Code of Practice is being prepared to provide local authorities with accounting guidance which will enhance the comparability of local authority financial information. The Code will help authorities comply with the provisions of Sections 5 and 6 of the 1999 Act and the order made under these sections, and be recognised as proper practice for all best value authorities. The Code, upon which there has already been wide consultation, will be published in early 2000 and will apply to the accounting arrangements supporting March 2001 Best Value Performance Plans.'

The *Best Value Accounting – Code of Practice* (the Code) (which CIPFA indicates is designed to complement the existing Code of Practice on Local Authority Accounting in Great Britain) was (as indicated above) published on 22 February 2000. References in this section to paragraphs and pages will be to those in the Code unless otherwise indicated.

11.7 CIPFA indicates that the Code 'modernises the system of local authority accounting and reporting to ensure that it meets the changed and changing needs of modern local government; particularly the duty to secure and demonstrate best value in the provision of services to the community'.[2] Amongst others, it deals with the following key issues:

'– The Definition of Total Cost
– Partnerships and Joint Working Arrangements
– Trading Accounts
– Service Expenditure Analysis.'

CIPFA has indicated that the above are 'inextricably linked to the key objective to establish a wide range of financial reporting requirements in order that data consistency and comparability is achieved.'[3] The Code 'applies to all Best Value reporting requirements for accounting periods beginning on or after 1 April 2000'.[4] 'This means that the requirements of the *Best Value Accounting – Code of Practice* apply to 2000/01 statements of accounts and March 2001 Best Value Performance Plans'.[5] Detailed treatment of this area is beyond the scope of this book. It is therefore proposed merely to summarise the above four issues as follows.

---

1   CIPFA Press Release, 23 February 2000.
2   Paragraph 1.1.
3   CIPFA Policy and Technical.
4   Paragraph 1.14.
5   Paragraph 1.15.

Total Cost[1]

11.8 'Total cost' is to be used for reporting service costs in the consolidated revenue account.[2] CIPFA also intends 'that information requirements for public performance reports and Best Value Performance Plans, for performance indicators and for statistical returns will be harmonised to use total cost'. Clearly also the use of 'total cost' as a common methodology for 'less formal purposes, such as unpublished local performance indicators, activity based costing ... and cost benchmarking ... will ... enhance the reliability and comparability of such information'.[3] 'Total cost' will encompass (amongst others) the following elements:

- The total cost of a service or activity includes all costs which relate to the provision of the service (directly or bought in) or to the undertaking of the activity.[4] This includes all costs 'associated with that service/activity, wherever in the management structure they arise'.[5]
- Gross total cost includes all expenditure relating to the service/activity, including employee costs, expenditure relating to premises and transport, supplies and services, third party payments, transfer payments, support services and capital charges.[6]
- Gross total cost also 'includes an appropriate share of all support services and overheads, which need to be apportioned'.[7]

'Net total cost' is gross total cost less income.[8]

'Corporate and Democratic Core'[9] should be 'split into Corporate Management, Democratic Management and Representation, with clear and explicit guidance on the scope of these activities'.[10] 'The latter should include all councillor-based activities. Consideration needs to be given to determining a contribution from the HRA[11] and other principal non-general fund activities (eg pension funds) to these costs'.[12]

Partnership Arrangements

11.9 Local authorities are increasingly 'working in partnerships to secure best value',[13] and CIPFA indicated in October 1999 that 'the ability to assess performance in accordance with best value will require the reassessment of the way these arrangements are accounted for. This applies equally for formal external reporting, through annual audited accounts and the Best Value

---

1   See section 2 of the Code.
2   Paragraph 2.1.
3   Paragraphs 2.1 and 2.2.
4   Paragraph 2.6.
5   Ibid.
6   Paragraph 2.10.
7   Paragraph 2.12.
8   Paragraph 2.15.
9   See section 3 of the Code for detail in this area and in particular the service expenditure analysis for Central Services.
10 Principle 3, Appendix 1 – Statement of Principles.
11 Housing Revenue Account – see the Local Government and Housing Act 1989.
12 Principle 3, Appendix 1 – Statement of Principles.
13 Annex C – C1.

Performance Plan, and internal reporting, including management accounting'.[1]

At that stage CIPFA addressed the relevant issues under the following heads:[2]

– the fundamental accounting concepts for accounting for partnerships, as contained in ASB[3] Statements of Standard Accounting Practice (SSAPs) and Financial Reporting Standards (FRSs), and the underlying statutory framework for the private sector which is encapsulated in the requirements of the Companies Acts – this will provide guidance as to GAAP[4] in respect of accounting for partnerships in the private sector;

– consideration of the types of partnership that currently are used by authorities and the developments that might be expected in the future;

– how these partnerships can be mapped to the types of partnership recognised by private sector GAAP;

– a review of the current accounting rules and how best value affects these;

– the proposals for revising the accounting treatment for partnerships in local authority accounts; and

– other considerations, including the implications for management accounting in local authorities, and practical issues for collecting the required information.

All these issues were considered in some detail in CIPFA's *Best Value Accounting – Accounting for Partnerships*.[5] That document also contains (at paras 301 to 334 and amongst other things) a helpful summary of some of the different types of partnerships found within local authorities.

11.10 In the Code[6] it is indicated that the 'total cost of a service includes those costs attributable to an authority's proportion of a relevant partnership'.[7] For those accounting periods which begin on 1 April 2000, 'relevant partnerships are those governed by statute, agency arrangements, contractual relationships or understandings that are in substance dealt with as if there is a formal relationship'.[8] Where 'the authority is the accountable body for a relevant partnership, the gross total cost of the service(s) concerned includes all the authority's expenditure, whether by way of contribution of otherwise, which relates to that partnership. Contributions received from other parties will be included as income'. There will be a phased introduction of the Code in relation to partnerships.[9]

Trading Accounts

11.11 The Code indicates that a trading account is:

'a method of matching income and expenditure for a particular activity or group

1   CIPFA, *Best Value Accounting – Accounting for Partnerships*, October 1999.
2   Ibid.
3   Accounting Standards Board.
4   Generally accepted accounting principles.
5   CIPFA Policy and Technical, October 1999.
6   See paragraph 2.17.
7   Ibid.
8   Ibid.
9   See para 2.19 of the Code.

of activities. It is not a performance measurement tool. Trading accounts may be kept for a wide variety of different purposes. Each account can provide for the different needs of different stakeholders. CIPFA recommends the maintenance of trading accounts where activities are provided on a cost plus basis or at a quoted price.'[1]

The disclosure requirements for Trading Accounts under best value will be 'linked to the environment within which these activities operate'.[2] So where 'an activity is provided in a competitive environment and where there is a competitive process, the income and expenditure of the activity must be maintained within a trading account and disclosed appropriately'.[3]

11.12   The main types of trading accounts which authorities may maintain are listed as follows in Annex D to the Code:

'a)   Accounts of the income and expenditure of services which involve trading with the public or with other third parties. Trading services include catering undertakings, cemeteries & crematoria, trade refuse and building control accounts.

b)   The accounts of ExTOs (external trading organisations) which have won contracts from other public bodies, for example under the Goods & Services Act 1970.

c)   DSO revenue accounts until 31 March 2000.

d)   Continuing trading accounts for ex-CCT contracts. These are contracts for work previously won by DSOs, to which CCT no longer applies, but which is still being done within the original contract specifications and period.

e)   Trading accounts for contracts won by InTOs (internal trading organisations) in VCT (voluntary competitive tendering).

f)   Trading accounts for support services which have won work in a free internal market ie from schools, or from other budget holders who have been given freedom to buy externally if they wish.

g)   Trading accounts for support services which have won work in a limited internal market e.g. where budget holders are free to decide the quantity and type of work to be done, on the basis of the prices quoted to them; but not to buy externally.

h)   Trading accounts kept to enable managers to compare total charges with total costs, for support services which are charged for at unit rates (eg £ per tonne-km for transport) and for which budget holders are responsible for deciding what quantity of work to order.

i)   Holding accounts kept (to enable managers to compare total charges with total costs) when standard charges (for example £ per productive hour) are made for service inputs such as the productive time of specified types of staff.'

CIPFA points out that '[t]rading account information is currently disclosed within the statement of accounts through the following notes to the Consolidated Revenue Account: "(g) The nature, turnover and profits/losses of any significant trading operation (l) Income from bodies under the Local Authorities (Goods and Services) Act 1970[4] and the related expenditure".'[5]

---

1   Paragraph 2.21.
2   Paragraph 2.22.
3   Ibid.
4   See Chapter 9.
5   The Code, Annex D, para D3.

11.13   Paragraph D8 of Annex D to the Code indicates that the disclosure requirements for trading accounts will be as follows:

–   accounts falling within (a) above (trading with the public or other third parties) 'are not disclosed as trading accounts because the standard classification already provides for the separate identification of both the income and the expenditure in general accounts';

–   trading accounts falling within (b) to (f) above may be aggregated into a single trading account. CIPFA indicates that unsuccessful 'tenderers can see from an aggregate trading account whether DSO, ExTO and InTO tenders for all contracts as a whole have covered costs'; and they 'will know that auditors will have access to the necessary detail'. The accounting Statement of Recommended Practice (SORP) 'does not require analysis of types b to f, although it does require significant trading activities to be referred to in notes to the accounts';

–   as to types (g) to (i), these 'do not need to be included in published statements of account at all'.

In respect of England, the DETR has 'recommended that trading accounts of type d (ex-CCT contracts) should be kept until 31 March 2000, except where the work covered is reorganised or re-specified'. 'Extended DSO revenue accounts can be included in the aggregate trading accounts mentioned above'.[1]

11.14   The Government, in para 69 of the Guidance states that:

'For the first Performance Plan, and prior to the introduction of the Best Value Accounting – Code of Practice, the Government recommends that authorities include a summary disclosure note listing the nature, turnover and profit/loss of any significant trading operations engaged in by the authority for which separate accounts are maintained. For this, where balances on trading accounts are significant such that relevant performance indicators would be materially mis-stated, the balances should be re-apportioned to services. The apportionments should be disclosed as part of the summary disclosure note. The forthcoming Code will provide further guidance on this.'

Also:

'Any such information included in the Performance Plan will require the use of provisional accounting returns and wherever possible authorities should aim to draw upon regular monthly or quarterly returns to enhance its credibility.'[2]

Authorities 'will need in any case to develop in-house accounting and budgeting systems to ensure the accuracy of any financial information required for inclusion in Plans in subsequent years'.[3]

Service Expenditure Analysis/Segmental Reporting

11.15   Section 3 of the Code contains 'a revised Service Expenditure Analysis of local authority . . . expenditure' bearing in mind that the duty of best value:

---

1   The Code, Annex D, para D9.
2   Guidance, para 70.
3   Ibid.

'will increase expectations about:

- – The level of detail that will be available from local authority accounts;
- – The degree to which the accounts of Best Value authorities can be compared; and
- – The extent to which a single set of financial records should be compatible with the diverse reporting requirements placed upon local authorities.'

Appendix 1 to the Code (Statement of Principles) indicates that 'Segments of service should be defined at the lowest practical level possible, with the objective of making them flexible enough to support multiple uses, including focusing on service outcomes on a cross-cutting basis'.[1]

The Service Expenditure Analysis for each service[2] 'has been analysed across a number of mandatory service divisions' and in turn 'most service divisions are split into several discretionary subdivisions.'[3] Paragraph 3.6 points out that the 'aim of the hierarchy within the new Service Expenditure Analysis is to promote consistency between local authorities in terms of the format and comparability of financial performance reporting'. Consequently, 'a common format of service divisions and subdivisions is recommended'.[4]

CONCLUSION

11.16   Clear and transparent accounting information is important not only to underpin sound and effective management but also to provide transparency and accountability for stewardship of public monies to those who have provided the funds and to all other stakeholders, internal and external. As indicated, this chapter has merely sought to give a broad overview of some of the principles of this area. Those needing deeper coverage will need to look closely at the *Best Value Accounting – Code of Practice* together with related documentation and other specialised material and commentary.

---

1   See para 4.
2   These are: Central Services; Court Services (yet to be issued); Cultural, Environmental and Planning Services; Education Services; Fire Services; Highways, Roads and Transport Services; Housing Services; Police Services; Probation Services (yet to be issued) and Social Services (England and Wales)/Social Work (Scotland).
3   Paragraph 3.5.
4   See para 3.6.

Chapter 12

TUPE

INTRODUCTION

12.1   When a business transfers, the existing staff should, if at all possible, be safely escorted to the transferee. For certain types of transfers,[1] TUPE (the Transfer of Undertakings (Protection of Employment) Regulations 1981[2]) will provide a recovery service. The trouble is that this service has been unreliable and unpredictable. If the rescue company is unhelpful and points sanctimoniously to the fine print in its contract to avoid turning out, these considerations will not be much comfort to those left behind.

BEST VALUE AND STAFF TRANSFERS

12.2   As we have seen in previous chapters, best value requires authorities to take a radical and fresh look at their services with an emphasis on outcomes where making 'a real and positive difference to the services which local people receive from their authority ... matters far more than who is providing the service or indeed how it is provided'.[3] So, if '[w]hat matters is what works',[4] authorities are likely to find that in some circumstances the best value solution for a service or function is to arrange for it to be provided by an organisation external to the authority – outsourcing. However, the Government has accepted that '[w]ell-motivated and well-trained employees are vital in the provision of best value services';[5] and this is so whether the staff are 'working for local councils, the private sector, or the voluntary sector'.[6] So the 'task of local government will be to combine reassurance to employees with the necessary flexibility to allow transfer on a fair basis to other employers where this is in the public interest'.[7] In the Cabinet Office Document, *Staff Transfers in the Public Sector – Statement of Practice*,[8] the Government continued this theme by expressing its commitment to 'ensuring that staff involved in all such transfers are treated fairly and consistently and their rights respected'.

---

1   There must be a transfer to another employer – a mere share transfer to the same employer will be insufficient for TUPE (see below) to apply. See *Brookes and Others v Borough Care Services* [1998] IRLR 636, where the EAT noted that it is 'widely recognized that a transfer of shares, as distinct from a transfer of business, is outside the scope of TUPE and, indeed, the ARD' (the Directive).

2   SI 1981/1794.

3   DETR Circular 10/99 (14 December 1999), paras 9 and 10.

4   Ibid, para 10.

5   DETR, *Modern Local Government In Touch with the People* (July 1998), para 7.24.

6   Ibid.

7   Ibid.

8   January 2000. See *Guiding Principles* at the beginning of the document.

BASIC PRINCIPLES OF TUPE

Nature of TUPE

12.3   This chapter aims to give a brief overview of some of the basic principles surrounding TUPE and the underlying Directive 77/187/EEC[1] since the issue of transfers to outside bodies is very likely to arise under best value. The coverage cannot in the circumstances be detailed. For those requiring detail, reference to a more specialist text is recommended.[2]

TUPE was introduced in 1982[3] to implement Council Directive 77/187 of 14 February 1977 'on the approximation of the laws of the Member States relating to the safeguarding of employees' rights in the event of transfers of undertakings, businesses or parts of businesses'.[4] The preamble to the Directive notes that 'it is necessary to provide for the *protection of employees* in the event of a change of employer, in particular, to ensure that their rights are safeguarded' (emphasis added). This is an essential purpose of the Directive which has underpinned decisions of both the European Court of Justice (ECJ) and UK courts and tribunals. Article 1(1) of the Directive[5] provided: 'This Directive shall apply to the transfer of an undertaking, business or part of a business to another employer as a result of a legal transfer or merger'. Article 3(1) (amongst other things) provided:[6] 'The transferor's rights and obligations arising from a contract of employment or from an employment relationship existing on the date of a transfer ... shall, by reason of such transfer, be transferred to the transferee'.

12.4   The essential function of TUPE is therefore to ensure that if an employer transfers its business to another employer then (at the time of writing, with the exception of pension rights[7]) the employees affected will transfer to the new employer upon their existing terms and conditions of employment. Regulation 3(1) of TUPE provides: 'Subject to the provisions of these Regulations', TUPE

---

1   In this chapter, the Transfer of Undertakings (Protection of Employment) Regulations 1981 (SI 1981/1794) will be referred to as 'TUPE' and Council Directive 77/187/EEC (amended by Council Directive 98/50/EC on 29 June 1998) as 'the Directive'.

2   For instance, see John McMullen, *Business Transfers and Employee Rights* (Butterworths, 1998) or Nicholas Dobson, *TUPE, Contracting-Out and Best Value* (Sweet & Maxwell, 1998).

3   The Transfer of Undertakings (Protection of Employment) Regulations 1981 (by reg 1(2)) came into effect on 1 February 1982, except for regs 4–9 and 14 which came into operation on 1 May 1982.

4   This was part of the original title of the Directive which has (pursuant to Council Directive 98/50/EC) since 29 June 1998 been amended to '... on the approximation of the laws of the Member States relating to the safeguarding of employees' rights in the event of transfers of undertakings, businesses or parts of undertakings or businesses'.

5   Before amendment. The Article now has three subparagraphs. Article 1(a) now reads: 'This Directive shall apply to any transfer of an undertaking, business, or part of an undertaking or business to another employer as a result of a legal transfer or merger.'

6   Before amendment. The first paragraph of Art 3(1) has not been materially amended.

7   The traditional position is now settled: see *Adams v BET Catering Services Limited* [1997] IRLR 436, CA. However, pursuant to Art 3 of the Directive 77/187/EEC (as amended by Council Directive 98/50/EC) Member States may now make provision for the transfer of pension rights and, as mentioned below, the Government is giving some consideration to the whole area of pension rights on transfers of undertakings.

applies to 'a transfer from one person to another of an undertaking situated immediately before the transfer in the United Kingdom or part of one which is so situated'.

When TUPE applies (by reg 5(1) and subject to what had been thought to be a rather forlorn right of employee objection in reg 5(4A) and (4B)[1]), a relevant transfer:

> 'shall not operate so as to terminate the contract of employment of any person employed by the transferor in the undertaking or part transferred but any such contract which would otherwise have been terminated by the transfer shall have effect after the transfer as if originally made between the person so employed and the transferee'.

And by reg 5(2) (without prejudice to reg 5(1) and again subject to employee objection) on completion of a relevant transfer:

> '(a) all the transferor's rights, powers, duties and liabilities under or in connection with any such contract shall be transferred by virtue of this Regulation to the transferee; and
>
> (b) anything done before the transfer is completed by or in relation to the transferor in respect of that contract or a person employed in that undertaking or part shall be deemed to have been done by or in relation to the transferee.'

A transferee employer will therefore be liable and responsible for all matters relating to the contract of employment of the transferred employee and also for anything done by the transferor before transfer in respect of a transferred employee.

---

1 Following the decision of the ECJ in *Katsikas and Others v Konstantinidis* [1993] IRLR 179, reg 5(4A) provides (in respect of an employee) that paras (1) and (2) of reg 5 (which provide for the transfer of contractual and other rights and liabilities) 'shall not operate to transfer his contract of employment and the rights, powers, duties and liabilities under or in connection with it if the employee informs the transferor or the transferee that he objects to becoming employed by the transferee'. And per (4B): 'Where an employee so objects the transfer of the undertaking or part in which he is employed shall operate so as to terminate his contract of employment with the transferor but he shall not be treated, for any purpose, as having been dismissed by the transferor'. So, on the face of it, whilst TUPE does give an employee the right to object, this is hollow since, if it is exercised, the employee's contract will terminate without employment law rights. However, in *Oxford University v Humphreys* [2000] IRLR 183, the Court of Appeal (on 20 December 1999) noted the provisions of reg 5(5) of the TUPE Regulations: 'Paragraphs (1) and (4A) above are without prejudice to any right of an employee arising apart from these regulations to terminate his contract of employment without notice if a substantial change is made in his working conditions to his detriment; but no such right shall arise by reason only that, under that paragraph, the identity of his employer changes unless the employee shows that, in all the circumstances, the change is a significant change to his detriment.' And so where a constructive dismissal had been claimed by an employee against a transferor employer in circumstances where the employee had exercised his statutory right to object to a proposed transfer, and where the transfer would involve a substantial and detrimental change in the employee's contract of employment, bearing in mind the purpose of the Directive, the employee was in the circumstances entitled to treat his contract of employment as terminated by his employer and to pursue a claim for wrongful dismissal as against the transferor.

Application of TUPE

12.5 To understand the application of TUPE on a service or functional outsourcing, it is first necessary to consider the root authority on the application of the Directive which underlies TUPE: *Spijkers v Gebroeders Benedik Abbatoir CV.*[1] In that case, the activities of the transferor (owning and operating a slaughterhouse) had ceased and there was no longer any goodwill in the business. The premises, land and specified goods were transferred. The transferee commenced a new slaughterhouse business with none of the transferor's customers but all the employees except Mr Spijkers. The ECJ considered that:

> 'it is necessary to consider, in a case such as the present, whether the business was disposed of as a going concern, as would be indicated, inter alia, by the fact that its operation was actually continued or resumed by the new employer, with the same or similar activities.
>
> In order to determine whether those conditions are met, it is necessary to consider all the facts characterizing the transaction in question, including the type of undertaking or business, whether or not the business's tangible assets, such as buildings and movable property, are transferred, the value of its intangible assets at the time of the transfer, whether or not the majority of its employees are taken over by the new employer, whether or not its customers are transferred and the degree of similarity between the activities carried on before and after the transfer and the period, if any, for which those activities were suspended.[2] It should be noted, however, that all those circumstances are merely single factors in the overall assessment which must be made and cannot therefore be considered in isolation.
>
> It is for the national court to make the necessary factual appraisal, in the light of the criteria for interpretation set out above, in order to establish whether or not there is a transfer in the sense indicated above.'

12.6 These principles and this approach were applied in the later ECJ case of *Dr Sophie Redmond Stichting v Bartol and Others.*[3] There the Directive was held to apply where a local authority decided to terminate its subsidy to the Redmond Foundation which provided assistance to drug addicts and to transfer the subsidy to the Sigma foundation which had similar aims. In the course of its judgment the Court noted that in previous case-law[4] the ECJ had given a sufficiently broad interpretation to the concept of 'legal transfer' 'to give effect to the purpose of the Directive which is to ensure that the rights of employees are protected in the event of a transfer of their undertaking and held that that Directive was applicable wherever, in the context of contractual relations, there is a change in the legal or natural person who is responsible for carrying on the business and who incurs the obligations of an employer towards employees of the undertaking'. The ECJ referred to *Spijkers* (see above) and pointed out that:

---

1   [1986] ECR 1119, ECJ.
2   These considerations have been recited in a multiplicity of cases since and have become known as the *Spijkers* factors.
3   (Case C-29/91) [1992] IRLR 366, ECJ.
4   See, for example, *P Bork International A/S v Foreningen af Arbejdsledere i Danmark* No 101/87 [1990] 3 CMLR 701.

'the decisive criterion for establishing whether there is a transfer within the meaning of the Directive is whether the business in question retains its identity as would be indicated, in particular, by the fact that its operation was actually continued or resumed'.

Following this case and with the increasingly noticeable effects of Compulsory Competitive Tendering (CCT[1]) on the services of local authorities and similar bodies, there was a growing body of opinion that TUPE would apply where services were outsourced by CCT or otherwise. The Government (albeit somewhat grudgingly) moved with what was to become the legal zeitgeist into an acceptance that TUPE could (depending upon a factual analysis of the circumstances) apply.[2]

12.7   Following *Sophie Redmond*[3] there was a succession of cases which found the application of TUPE in a variety of different situations which would once have been considered unusual. These include: *Rask and Christensen v ISS Kantineservice A/S*[4] (contracting-out the operation of a staff canteen for a fee); *Kenny and Others v South Manchester College*[5] (outsourcing of prison education contract) and, significantly, *Dines and Others v Initial Health Care Services Ltd and Pall Mall Services Group Ltd*[6] (expiry of one hospital cleaning contract and the awarding of another to a different contractor).

However, the high point of the liberal approach to the application of TUPE came with the decision of the ECJ in *Schmidt v Spar-und Leihkasse der früheren Ämter Bordesholm, Kiel und Cronshagen*, Case C-392/92.[7] Here Mrs Schmidt was employed as a cleaner by a savings bank branch office in Germany. She was dismissed when the Bank entrusted the cleaning to an outside contractor. The contractor offered to employ Mrs Schmidt on a higher monthly wage. However, she declined since she considered that her hourly wage would be lower since the surface area to be cleaned would increase. The Court considered relevant caselaw and held that the Directive covers a situation 'in which an undertaking entrusts by contract to another undertaking the responsibility for carrying out cleaning operations which it previously performed itself, even though, prior to the transfer, such work was carried out by a single employee'.

---

1   Compulsory Competitive Tendering (CCT) refers to previous obligations in Part III of the Local Government, Planning and Land Act 1980 and Part I of the LGA 1988 which required local and certain other public authorities to subject certain work to competitive tender as prescribed before they might undertake it in-house. These, with related provisions, were repealed on 2 January 2000 by s 21 of the LGA 1999.

2   On 20 November 1992 the Department of the Environment (DOE – which on 16 June 1997 changed its name to the Department of the Environment, Transport and the Regions (DETR)) stated that: 'DOE takes the view that as a general rule ... [TUPE] ... will not apply where in-house services are to be contracted out'. On 11 March 1993, the Secretary of State for the Environment made a statement to Parliament which contained a quotation from a statement to the House of Commons on 21 January 1993 from the Attorney-General including: 'The contracting out of a service is not a transfer of an undertaking unless it involves enough of the elements of the original operation such as premises, staff, goodwill or customer base to constitute the transfer of a going concern.'

3   See above.

4   (Case C-209/91) [1993] IRLR 133, ECJ.

5   [1993] IRLR 265, QBD.

6   [1994] IRLR 36, CA.

7   [1994] IRLR 302, ECJ.

What made this case celebrated was the ECJ's approval of the concept that there could be a transfer of an undertaking of a single person. As the ECJ pointed out, the application of the Directive:

> 'does not depend on the number of employees assigned to the part of the undertaking which is the subject of the transfer. It should be noted that one of the objectives of the directive, as clearly stated in the second recital in the preamble thereto, is to protect employees in the event of a change of employer, in particular to ensure that their rights are safeguarded. That protection extends to all staff and must therefore be guaranteed even where only one employee is affected by the transfer'.

Therefore, although there was no transfer of tangible assets (since the 'safeguarding of employees' rights, which constitutes the subject-matter of the directive ... cannot depend exclusively on consideration of a factor which the Court has in any event already held not to be decisive on its own'[1]):

> 'the similarity in the cleaning work performed before and after the transfer, which is reflected ... in the offer to re-engage the employee in question, is typical of an operation which comes within the scope of the directive'.

12.8   After *Schmidt* was a sequence of cases which found that TUPE applied when the same or similar activities were identifiable in the hands of the transferee.[2] However, but for a couple of small ripples in the form of *Rygaard* and *Henke*,[3] the TUPE millpond remained relatively calm until the perceived cataclysm of the decision of the ECJ on 11 March 1997 in *Süzen v Zehnacker Gebaudereinigung GmbH Krankenhausservice, Lefarth GmbH.*[4]

This case (as with *Schmidt*)[5] concerned a building cleaning function. Mrs Süzen and her colleagues were employed by a school cleaning contractor. They were dismissed when the school terminated the contractor's contract and placed the work with another contractor. Whilst noting (without disapproval) key ECJ case-law (including *Spijkers, Sophie Redmond* and *Schmidt*[6]), there was now a focus on the nature of the undertaking, or economic entity itself since an 'entity cannot be reduced to the activity entrusted to it'. Therefore (and distinct from earlier apparent approaches of the UK tribunals) 'the mere fact that the service provided by the old and the new awards of a contract is similar

---

1   See *Spijkers v Gebroeders Benedik Abbatoir CV*, above.
2   For example, *Birch v Nuneaton and Bedworth Borough Council* [1995] IRLR 518, EAT and *BSG Property Services v Tuck and Others* [1996] IRLR 134, EAT.
3   In (Case C-48/94), *Rygaard, Ledernes Hovedorganisation, acting for Rygaard v Dansk Arbejdsgiverforening, acting for Strø Mølle Akustik a/s* [1996] IRLR 51, the ECJ indicated that its previous caselaw had presupposed that the transfers related 'to a stable economic entity whose activity is not limited to performing one specific works contract'; and that was 'not the case of an undertaking which transfers to another undertaking one of its building works with a view to the completion of that work'. In (Case C-298/94) *Henke v Gemeinde Schierke* [1997] 2 All ER (EC) 173, the ECJ found that 'the reorganisation of structures of the public administration or the transfer of administrative functions between public administrative authorities does not constitute a "transfer of an undertaking" within the meaning of the Directive'.
4   Case C-13/95 [1997] All ER (EC) 281.
5   See above.
6   See above.

does not ... support the conclusion that an economic entity has been transferred'. The ECJ considered that the 'term entity ... refers to an organised grouping of persons and assets facilitating the exercise of an economic activity which pursues a specific objective'.[1] Therefore (although 'it must be recognized that such an entity is capable of maintaining its identity after it has been transferred where the new employer does not merely pursue the activity in question but also takes over a major part, in terms of their numbers and skills, of the employees specially assigned by his predecessor to that task'[2]) in the circumstances referred to the Court, the Directive would not apply in the absence of a:

> 'concomitant transfer from one undertaking to the other of significant tangible or intangible assets *or* taking over by the new employer of a major part of the workforce, in terms of their numbers and skills, assigned by his predecessor to the performance of the contract' (emphasis added).

It is for the national court to determine in the light of the ECJ's 'interpretative guidance' whether a transfer has occurred in the particular case.

12.9 *Süzen* was followed closely (in both time and approach) by the decision of the Court of Appeal in *Betts and Others v Brintel Helicopters Ltd and KLM ERA Helicopters (UK) Ltd.*[3] In the case, where Brintel Helicopters lost one of three oil rig helicopter services contracts to KLM, whilst the Court found that there was an undertaking, on the facts it did not consider that there was a transfer of that undertaking so that it retained its identity in the hands of KLM. The decision of the High Court (noted above) that there was a TUPE transfer since (amongst other things) 'there is no change in the basic activity, although some of the details as to how it is provided have changed ...' was overturned. In so doing, Kennedy LJ accepted 'that the decision in *Süzen* does represent a shift of emphasis, or at least a clarification of the law, and that some of the reasoning of earlier decisions, if not the decisions themselves, may have to be reconsidered.'

12.10 Both *Süzen* and *Betts* were the storm after the calm. Whilst *Süzen* gave interpretative guidance on the facts before it and it was for the national court to determine in the light of that guidance whether there was a transfer in the particular circumstances, many were regarding *Süzen* as universally binding declaration of the state of TUPE. This caused instability in the market place in respect of all types of contracting-out arrangements. However, *Süzen* did restate the *Spijkers* factors and pointed out that 'the degree of importance to be attached to each criterion for determining whether or not there has been a transfer ... will necessarily vary according to the activity'. Consequently, a careful analysis of whether there is an undertaking in the sense of an 'organized grouping of persons and assets facilitating the exercise of an economic activity which pursues a specific objective'[4] and whether this undertaking is properly

---

1   This underpinned the revised definition of 'an economic entity which retains its identity': see Art 1(b) of Council Directive 77/187/EEC (as amended by 98/50/EC – 29 June 1998).
2   *Süzen* decision, para 21, ECJ.
3   [1997] IRLR 361, CA.
4   See *Süzen* and the amendments to Council Directive 77/187/EEC incorporated by Council Directive 98/50/EC, and in particular those in Art 1(b) which apparently draws on this wording.

identifiable in the hands of the transferee (bearing in mind that (per *Süzen*) 'An entity cannot be reduced to the activity entrusted to it') will often be productive, particularly bearing in mind that if there are no tangible assets there may be intangible assets transferring (eg goodwill).

In decisions on five cases issued by the ECJ in December 1998[1] there was a helpful focus upon whether there was an economic entity which transferred. So, for example, in the *Francisco Hernández Vidal SA* cases which involved the absorption back into the client organisation of cleaning work which had previously been contracted-out, the ECJ concluded (amongst other things) that:

> 'Article 1(1) of Directive 77/187 is to be interpreted as meaning that the directive applies to a situation in which an undertaking which used to entrust the cleaning of its premises to another undertaking decides to terminate its contract with that other undertaking and in future to carry out that cleaning work itself, *provided that the operation is accompanied by the transfer of an economic entity between the two undertakings*. The term "economic entity" refers to an organised grouping of persons and assets enabling an economic activity which pursues a specific objective to be exercised.' (Emphasis added.)

However, the 'mere fact that the maintenance work carried out first by the cleaning firm and then by the undertaking owning the premises is similar does not justify the conclusion that a transfer of such an entity has occurred.'

12.11 In the United Kingdom, the judiciary seem to have honed their navigation skills sufficiently to enable a skilful negotiation of the tricky TUPE straits. For example, in *ECM (Vehicle Delivery Service) Ltd v Cox and Others*[2] (which concerned the employees of Axial Limited, which lost a VAG vehicle delivery contract to ECM) the Court of Appeal (in finding that there was a relevant transfer even though the transferee had refused to engage the staff in question) considered that the importance of *Süzen* has 'been overstated' and 'should be seen in its proper context'. This is that the key ECJ case-law decisions in cases such as *Spijkers* and *Schmidt* (the latter of which in particular had founded the earlier more liberal approach to TUPE) had not been overruled by *Süzen*. It is still for the national court to make the 'necessary factual appraisal' to determine whether or not a transfer has taken place in the light of 'all the facts characterising the transaction in question' referred to in *Spijkers*. *Süzen* was important in that the ECJ had 'identified limits to the application of the Directive' – for example, 'the mere fact that the service provided by the old and the new awardees of a contract is similar does not ... support the conclusion that an economic entity has been transferred'.

---

1   (Case C-127/96) *Francisco Hernández Vidal SA v Prudencia Gómez Pérez, María Gómez Pérez, Contratas y Limpiezas SL*; (Case C-229/96) *Friedrich Santner v Hoechst AG*; (Case C-74/97) *Mercedes Gómez Montaña v Claro Sol SA and Red Nacional de Ferrocarriles Españoles (Renfe)* [1999] IRLR 132; and (Case C-173/96) *Francisca Sánchez Hidalgo ea v Asociación de Servicios Aser and Sociedad Cooperativa Minerva*; (Case C-247/96) *Horst Ziemann v Ziemann Sicherheit GmbH and Horst Bohn Sicherheitsdienst* [1999] IRLR 136.
2   [1999] IRLR 559, CA. It is understood that there will be no appeal to the House of Lords. So the Court of Appeal decision is the final word within this jurisdiction.

Further, bearing in mind that ECM had refused to employ any ex-Axial workers because they were claiming that TUPE applied and were threatening unfair dismissal proceedings if not appointed:

> 'The tribunal was entitled to have regard, as a relevant circumstance, to the reason why those employees were not appointed by ECM. The [ECJ] has not decided in *Süzen* or in any other case that this is an irrelevant circumstance or that the failure of the transferee to appoint any of the former employees of the transferor points conclusively against a transfer.'

Who is Assigned to the Undertaking?

12.12 If a transferring undertaking is identified it is important to establish which employees were assigned to the undertaking at the time of transfer. The leading case in this area is *Botzen v Rotterdamsche Droogdok Maatschappij BV* No 186/83,[1] which was a decision of the ECJ on 7 February 1985. This concerned staff and assets who transferred to a new company which had been formed just before the liquidation of the old. Out of a total workforce of 3,184, 1,478 employees were transferred. Mr Botzen and his seven colleague plaintiffs worked in divisions of the old company which were not transferred; they had provided support services. They were not taken on by the new company but instead were dismissed and consequently brought proceedings to the national court, seeking a ruling that their dismissals were null and void. The court referred (amongst others) the following question to the ECJ:

> 'Does the scope of the directive also extend to the rights conferred upon and the obligations imposed upon the transferor by contracts of employment which exist at the time of transfer and which are made with employees who are employed in a staff department of the undertaking (for example, general management services, personnel matters, etc.), where that staff department carried out duties for the benefit of the transferred part of the undertaking but has not itself been transferred?'

12.13 The ECJ adopted the view of the Commission that 'the only decisive criterion regarding the transfer of employees' rights and obligations is whether or not a transfer takes place of the department to which they were assigned and which formed the organisational framework within which their employment relationship took effect'.

The court continued by indicating that:

> 'An employment relationship is essentially characterised by the link existing between the employee and the part of the undertaking or business to which he is assigned to carry out his duties. In order to decide whether the rights and obligations under an employment relationship are transferred under [the Directive] by reason of a [relevant] transfer ... it is therefore sufficient to establish to which part of the undertaking or business the employee was assigned.'

Therefore, the ECJ held that Art 3(1) of the Directive (which prescribes the transfer of the transferor's rights and obligations arising from an employment contract or employment relationship):

---

1   [1986] 2 CMLR 50, ECJ.

'must be interpreted as not covering the transferor's rights and obligations arising from a contract of employment or an employment relationship existing on the date of the transfer and entered into with employees who, although not employed in the transferred part of the undertaking, performed certain duties which involved the use of assets assigned to the part transferred or who, whilst being employed in an administrative department of the undertaking which has not itself been transferred, carried out certain duties for the benefit of the part transferred.'

12.14 There has been a succession of cases in this area. For example: *Northern General Hospital NHS Trust v Gale*[1] (contractual provisions can be relevant); *Duncan Web Offset (Maidstone) Ltd v Cooper*[2] (where the employees were assigned to a company even though they worked also for other companies within a group); *Securicor Guarding Ltd v Fraser Security Services Ltd*[3] (employees assigned to habitual rather than contractual site). However, there is no universal formula and it will always be necessary to consider all the surrounding facts and circumstances when coming to a conclusion as to whether a particular employee can reasonably be said to have been assigned to the undertaking in question.

GOVERNMENT DEVELOPMENTS

12.15 In the light of the long history of uncertainty surrounding TUPE, the Government had taken advantage of the UK presidency of the European Union (between 1 January and 30 June 1998) to update and improve the Directive which underlies the TUPE Regulations. Amongst other things, the amendments to Directive 77/187/EEC (by Council Directive 98/50/EC, implemented on 29 June 1998):

– effectively codified ECJ decisions in *Süzen, Henke* and *Rask*;
– enabled Member States to provide for the transfer of continuing pension rights.

Building on this, to bolster its pragmatic approach to modernising public services 'based on finding the best supplier who can deliver quality services and value for money for the taxpayer',[4] the Government intends to amend the TUPE Regulations to support a general presumption that TUPE applies, subject to necessary exceptions to accommodate, for instance, genuine best value innovations. So, as para 89 of the Guidance indicates:

'The Government will also act to bring greater certainty to the processes involved in transferring staff to new employers. It will amend the *Transfer of Undertakings (Protection of Employment) Regulations 1981* (TUPE) in order to implement the revised *Acquired Rights Directive* and to improve their operation. The intention is that TUPE will apply to all staff transfers under best value, and will protect employees during the life of a contract. This will build upon the definition of a

1   [1994] IRLR 292, CA.
2   [1995] IRLR 633, EAT.
3   [1996] IRLR 552, EAT.
4   *Staff Transfers in the Public Sector – Statement of Practice* (January 2000), Introductory *Guiding Principles*.

transfer secured in the revised Directive, adopted during the UK Presidency in 1998, in order to achieve as great a degree of certainty and clarity as possible in the Regulations' application (including the reassignment of contracts)'.

12.16 Therefore, the policy approach that the Government considers 'should be adopted for the transfer of staff from the public sector to a private sector employer or a voluntary sector body'[1] should, 'except in genuinely exceptional circumstances'[2] (but subject to the duty of best value and any subsisting statutory duties), be based on the following principles:

'– contracting exercises with the private sector and voluntary organisations and transfers between different parts of the public sector, will be conducted on the basis that staff will transfer and TUPE should apply, unless there are genuinely exceptional reasons not to do so;

– this includes second and subsequent round contracts that result in a new contractor, and where a function is brought back into a public sector organisation, where, in both cases, when the contract was first awarded staff transferred from the public sector;

– in circumstances where TUPE does not apply in strict legal terms to certain types of transfer between different parts of the public sector, the principles of TUPE should be followed (where possible using legislation to effect the transfer) and the staff involved should be treated no less favourably than had the Regulations applied; and

– there should be appropriate arrangements to protect occupational pensions, redundancy and severance terms of staff in all these types of transfer'.[3]

The 'genuinely exceptional' circumstances which may qualify are, broadly:

'• where a contract is for the provision of both goods and services, but the provision of services is ancillary in purpose to the provision of the goods; or

• where the activity for which the public sector organisation is contracting is essentially new or a one off project; or

• where services or goods are essentially a commodity bought "off the shelf" and no grouping of staff are specifically and permanently assigned to a common task; or

• where the features of the service or function subject to the contracting exercise are significantly different from the features of the function previously performed within the public sector, or by an existing contractor e.g. a function to be delivered electronically and in such a way that it requires radically different skills, experience and equipment.'[4]

Where 'a public sector organisation believes such genuinely exceptional circumstances exist then it should be prepared to justify this, and the departure from the Government's policy ... publicly, if challenged'.[5]

Consequently, new TUPE Regulations under powers in s 2(2) of the European Communities Act 1972 and s 38 of the Employment Relations Act 1999 (which enables the Secretary of State to make regulations achieving a similar effect to the TUPE Regulations in circumstances where TUPE would

1   *Staff Transfers in the Public Sector – Statement of Practice, para 10.*
2   These are noted below.
3   *Staff Transfers in the Public Sector – Statement of Practice,* para 5.
4   Ibid, para 14.
5   Ibid, para 15.

not otherwise apply) are expected (following consultation) in 2000 with a view to addressing the types of TUPE difficulty which have been experienced to date.

12.17   As to pensions, Annex A to *Staff Transfers in the Public Sector – Statement of Practice* indicates[1] that '[t]he guiding principle should be that the new employer offers transferring staff membership of a pension scheme which though not identical is "**broadly comparable**" to the public service pension scheme which they are leaving'. Whilst this was drafted 'with specific reference to staff transfers from central Government Departments and Agencies, on whom it was binding immediately ... Ministers said at the time that they also wanted other public sector contracting authorities to make arrangements to meet the standards of protection for staff pensions which it set out, consistent with the law and good procurement practice'.[2] Consequently:

> 'As set out in the guidance,[3] there are two separate but related aspects to protection of pensions in a staff transfer. First, to ensure continuity of pension accrual where the transferred staff leave the public pension scheme they should be offered membership of an alternative scheme by the new employer which is actuarially certified as being "broadly comparable" with the public service scheme. This certification should be by reference to the criteria for "broad comparability" set out by the Government Actuary, meaning that no identifiable employees should suffer material detriment overall in terms of future pensions accrual. Secondly, there should be a "bulk transfer" agreement with the new employer's pension scheme providing that staff will be able to transfer their accrued service credits into that scheme on a day-for-day, or equivalent, basis.'[4]

On 22 December 1999, the Local Government Pension Scheme (Amendment) Regulations 1999[5] were issued which (amongst other things) enable employees of organisations which provide services or assets to local or other best value authorities under specified circumstances to be members of the Local Government Pension Scheme. These Regulations came into force on 13 January 2000 and are the proposed regulations referred to in para 93 of the Guidance, which states that:

> 'In the case of employees who are members of the Local Government Pension Scheme (LGPS), there will be an alternative to the requirement to the broadly comparable scheme approach. It will be possible instead for the new employer, if they wish, to seek "non-associated employer" status within the LGPS, so that transferred staff continue to have access to that pension scheme for their future service. Guidance on this option will be issued along with the proposed *Local Government Pension Scheme (Amendment) Regulations.*'

Nevertheless:

> 'Whichever route is chosen for the protection of staff pensions, local authorities should apply the general principles set out in the Treasury guidance referred to in paragraph 91:

---

1   See para 14.
2   DETR Circular 10/99, para 91.
3   This refers to *Staff Transfers in the Public Sector – Statement of Practice* (see above).
4   DETR Circular 10/99, para 92.
5   SI 1999/3438.

- to treat staff fairly
- to do so openly and transparently
- to involve staff and their representatives fully in consultation about pensions aspects of the transfer at an early stage
- and to have clear accountability within the local authority for the results.'[1]

12.18 New TUPE Regulations are expected (following consultation) in 2000 with a view to addressing the types of TUPE difficulty which have been experienced to date.

BEST VALUE OUTSOURCING

12.19 Whatever type of arrangement is considered, whether it be (for example) the transfer of the service or function to:

– a special purpose vehicle company as part of a Public/Private Partnership or Private Finance Initiative (PFP/PFI);
– a joint venture company;
– an external contractor;
– a service partner;

it will always be necessary to analyse carefully, having regard to all the facts and circumstances, in the light of *Spijkers*[2] and other key case-law, whether an undertaking exists and if so whether it can properly be said to have been transferred. If there is a transfer it will clearly need to be considered who was assigned to the undertaking at the point of transfer.

However, when the legislative infrastructure exists to support the Government's general presumption that TUPE (or the principles of TUPE) will apply on every public sector transfer, the whole process should be much less prone to uncertainty. If (as now expected) the Government makes an order under s 19(1) of the LGA 1999[3] making 'the terms and conditions of employment by contractors of their workers or the composition of, the arrangements for the promotion, transfer or training of or the other opportunities afforded to, their workforces' cease to be a non-commercial matter for the purposes of s 17 of the Local Government Act 1988,[4] then this will considerably advance matters. For then authorities and external contractors or other organisations will be able to agree contractually (amongst other things) that the principles in TUPE will apply.

---

1 DETR Circular 10/99, para 93.
2 See above.
3 See above.
4 'Local and other public authority contracts: exclusion of non-commercial considerations.' See Chapter 10.

Chapter 13

BEST VALUE IN HOUSING

13.1 Satisfactory housing is one of the most basic human needs. For housing gives not merely shelter but a sense of identity and belonging. Good leasehold housing is not merely about sound physical infrastructure and a wholesome environment, but also about the quality of the relationship between landlord and tenant. And as the Government has pointed out in its April 2000 Housing Green Paper,[1] there are 'strong associations between poor housing and poverty, deprivation, crime, educational under-achievement and ill health'.[2]

THE GOVERNMENT'S APPROACH

Introduction

13.2 This is contained in the DETR's *Best Value in Housing Framework* Document ('the Framework Document') issued by the DETR in January 2000. This followed the *Best Value in Housing Framework Consultation Paper* issued by the DETR on 22 January 1999 (and updated on 1 June 1999[3]). The Framework Document applies the law and practice of best value described in the preceding chapters to the specific context of local authority housing. Chris Mullin, Parliamentary Under Secretary of State, in his Foreword pointed out that 'Housing is a key area. Decent Housing is the foundation of social well being. It can affect people's health, educational achievement and job prospects.' However, Mr Mullin also pointed out that the 'document is not a manual on how to achieve Best Value in housing' for it is 'local authorities themselves and their tenants and residents who will make the real difference on the ground'. Also:

> 'Best Value needs to embrace housing in the widest sense – the housing management function on the council housing stock where authorities retain ownership; the strategic and enabling roles that all housing authorities, including Large Scale Voluntary Transfer[4] authorities, must undertake across all housing tenures; and the important role housing has to play in addressing wider cross-cutting issues.'[5]

Further, his remark concerning cross-cutting issues:

> 'underlines the need for local authorities to look beyond traditional service boundaries and to work in partnership with others. By acting together with others,

---

1   *Quality and Choice: A Decent Home for All*, DETR, April 2000.
2   See *Summary and Key Proposals*, ibid.
3   This was to include an analysis of the responses to the Consultation Paper.
4   See the Leasehold Reform, Housing and Urban Development Act 1993, s 135, and ss 32, 34 and 43 of the Housing Act 1985.
5   Foreword to DETR, *Best Value in Housing Framework* (January 2000).

and being clear about the way important service areas like housing can help to address issues which cross traditional service boundaries, authorities can achieve the real and sustainable improvements that Best Value demands.'[1]

In this chapter, paragraph references will be to the Framework Document unless otherwise stated.

Corporate and Strategic Approach

13.3   The statutory duty of best value will affect all local housing authorities and all local authority housing functions. The duty must also be seen as part of the Government's 'wider vision for revitalising public services'.[2] Paragraph 2.6 reminds readers of the 'central purpose of best value' which is 'to make a real and positive difference to services which local people receive from their authority'. Best value gives authorities the opportunities of reassessing their roles and functions and formulating 'innovative ideas for the provision of services which: respond to local community needs and aspirations; maximise the effect and benefit of resources; work effectively in partnership with other agencies; have clear organisational objectives and embrace performance management to confirm accountability'.[3]

A 'clear corporate vision'[4] is needed, flowing from 'a genuinely inclusive community strategy'.[5] Amongst other things, this will entail 'breaking down barriers between local authority departments; cutting out duplication of work; and improving communication both within an authority and with tenants and residents'.[6] As indicated throughout this work, the status quo will be an inadequate base for best value. Authorities will need to be honest about their current performance, to embrace innovation and a culture of comparing with, and learning from others in any sector of business; and in seeking out and applying excellence, above all being determined to do better.[7] Increasingly (as also regularly mentioned in this work) a cross-cutting approach will be needed whereby authorities will 'look across service areas and organisations in addressing issues which face their local communities'.[8]

Whilst a corporate and consultative approach to objectives and performance measures 'will help identify priorities; build on consensus; and show how individual services like housing can contribute to broader cross cutting issues'[9] not all authorities will be starting from the same base. 'Some, through earlier innovation and planning, are better placed to respond to the challenge and opportunity of Best Value and the wider modernisation agenda.'[10] Others 'will need to make more radical changes'.[11] So, as mentioned in Chapter 4 above, the 'self-improvement approach of the Improvement [sic] Development

---

1   Foreword to DETR, *Best Value in Housing Framework* (January 2000).
2   Paragraph 2.1. See, for example, *Modernising Government* (Cm 4310, March 1999).
3   Paragraph 2.8.
4   Paragraph 2.9.
5   Paragraph 2.10.
6   Ibid.
7   Paragraph 2.11.
8   Paragraph 2.12.
9   Paragraph 2.13.
10   Paragraph 2.14.
11   Ibid.

Agency's (IdeA) Improvement Project recognises this by helping local authorities to assess their strengths and weaknesses in achieving Best Value. The IdeA plans to make this available to all local authorities as soon as possible.'[1] The Beacon Councils scheme (referred to in Chapter 3) is similarly 'encouraging authorities to identify the things at which they are particularly good and to promote their successful strategies across local government, speeding up the pace of change'.[2]

Best Value – Functionally Holistic

13.4 Paragraph 4.2 of the Framework Document highlights some of the factors underpinning the importance of best value in housing. These underline the fact that:

- (as indicated above) 'decent housing is one of the fundamentals of life' and that '**all** local housing authorities have important strategic and enabling roles in helping to secure this, whether they have a landlord role or not';
- 'housing provides one of the greatest interfaces with local people and also with other local authority services';
- an important landlord/tenant relationship exists where authorities are providers of housing;
- 'there is, almost uniquely to housing, through the Housing Investment Programme (HIP)[3] a well established central Government mechanism for assessing local authorities' housing strategies and performance which is used in deciding their housing capital allocations';
- 'housing is big business – accounting for nearly a fifth of all local government spending';
- central and local government owe a duty to taxpayers and other local people to make sure resources for housing are spent economically, efficiently and effectively.[4]

13.5 In practice the duty of best value in housing will encompass:[5]

- '[T]he strategic role on housing that all housing authorities (including LSVT authorities) undertake, and cross-cutting links'. This will encompass: housing strategy (including strategic work in partnership with Registered Social Landlords[6] and others); market analysis; resource

---

1 Paragraph 2.14.
2 Paragraph 2.15.
3 The Housing Investment Programme (HIP) is the means by which the Government makes annual capital allocations for housing investment by local authorities. Pursuant to s 55 of the Local Government and Housing Act 1989, in determining the amount of a basic credit approval or a supplementary credit approval to be issued to a local authority, the Secretary of State or other Minister may have regard (subject to provisions set out in s 55) to such factors as appear to him to be appropriate. These factors constitute the criteria governing the annual capital allocation.
4 This material comes from para 4.2, which is also the source of the quotations.
5 This material comes from para 4.3, which is also the source of the quotations.
6 Registered Social Landlords (RSLs) are non-profit-making bodies registered with the Housing Corporation under the Housing Act 1996. The Housing Corporation indicates that most RSLs are constituted as Housing Associations.

planning; enabling; contribution to corporate planning; stock condition (including house condition surveys); housing needs; housing land; homelessness; housing advice; private housing;[1] resident participation; housing register; equalities; cross-cutting links.[2]

- **Where the authority still retains ownership of its own housing stock, the housing management function**. This encompasses matters such as: allocation of tenancies; response repairs; planned maintenance; redevelopment and renewals; tenancy management; estate management; tenant participation; leasehold management/right to buy; energy efficiency; equalities; regeneration; and rent setting and collection.
- **The 'overall activities related to management of housing services'**: procurement; resource allocation; decision making; support services (human resources and information management); and contract management.

Best Value and Other Relevant Organisations

13.6   Registered Social Landlords (RSLs) are 'major providers of low cost rented housing and the main developers of new social housing'.[3] RSLs have already been mentioned and will be looked at in more detail below. However, para 4.7 points out that local authorities 'should have a close working relationship with the RSLs operating in their areas in recognition of the common links and objectives on housing and in maximising the potential for delivering Best Value'. But the precise nature of the relationship will vary 'depending upon local arrangements and responsibilities'. Consistent with authorities' duty to *secure* best value, whoever is providing the service in question, the Government points out that where 'there is a housing management contract, its terms should specify that the RSL (or other body) should follow the local authority's approach to best value. Where there has been a stock transfer, or where the authority has retained housing management, the approach should be one of working in partnership.'[4]

Paragraph 4.9 highlights other organisations operating within the area of housing 'with whom authorities should work closely'. These include:

- tenant and tenant management organisations;
- private sector contractors discharging the housing management and/or related functions as local authority agents;
- private sector contractors who carry out related works such as estate cleaning, repairs and maintenance of housing and support services;

---

1   This includes housing renewal and redevelopment 'including renovation grants; disabled facilities grants; area renewal activity, including clearance; work in relation to HMOs [houses in multiple occupation]; house condition surveys; home improvement agencies; fitness enforcement activity and other enforcement activity in respect of unsatisfactory housing conditions; empty property; and energy efficiency'. (See paragraph 4.3 of *Best Value in Housing Framework*.)
2   The Government points to such links with: care services; community safety; neighbourhood renewal; regeneration; housing and health; sustainable development and social exclusion. (Ibid.)
3   *Best Value in Housing Framework*, para 4.5.
4   Ibid, para 4.8.

- 'other partners (private and voluntary) including those involved with vulnerable groups, such as elderly, young, homeless and disabled people; and with the housing needs of black and other minority ethnic groups';
- 'health and police authorities, for instance in developing strategies to tackle health problems arising from poor housing, crime, and community safety on local authority estates and in problematical areas of private housing'.[1]

THE BROADER CONTEXT

13.7   As indicated in the Guidance 'cross-cutting Reviews which are based on or around clear and recognizable themes or issues and which reflect strategic choices with other partners, are more likely to make a real and lasting difference locally'.[2] So para 4.10 of the Framework Document makes clear that housing 'should not be considered in isolation'. For many of the issues facing local communities will increasingly 'require cross-cutting approaches if they are to be tackled successfully and deliver sustainable improvements'. Partnership is essential – with Registered Social Landlords as well as 'the private and voluntary sectors' and 'other bodies acting locally'.[3] Paragraph 4.14 gives the Government's view as to how pivotal housing is upon individual and social health and integration:

> 'Housing impacts on people's well-being, their sense of worth, the local community and employment. It therefore has a fundamental role to play in addressing wider cross-cutting issues. If people live in decent housing, and are provided with efficient, high quality services needed to sustain that, they are more likely to benefit from good health, higher educational attainment and better-paid work.'

Amongst the areas to which housing 'in co-ordination with other local authority service areas and in partnership with other public, private and voluntary organisations, will have a particularly significant input'[4] are:

- **'Care and support needs of vulnerable people'** so as 'to enable them to live independently within the community'
- **Rough Sleeping**. The Government highlights the report of the Rough Sleepers Unit of the DETR[5] which contains its strategy in this area. The introduction to this publication (harmonising with the theme of co-ordination which is central to best value) notes that the aim of the Government's approach 'is to provide a range of integrated services to help rough sleepers off the streets. This will involve joining up previously fragmented services and filling gaps where appropriate services do not currently exist.' Paragraph 4.15 of the Framework Document indicates that the 'Government's target is to reduce the number of people sleeping

---

1   See generally para 4.9, from which the quotations are also drawn.
2   DETR Circular 10/99, para 21.
3   Paragraph 4.13.
4   Paragraph 4.15. The material and quotations in the following bullet points are drawn from this paragraph unless otherwise indicated.
5   DETR, Rough Sleepers Unit, *Coming in from the cold – Delivering the Strategy* (January 2000).

rough by two thirds by 2002'. Local authorities will be central to the development of 'an integrated local strategy'.

– **Neighbourhood Renewal**. The Government refers to the September 1998 report on Neighbourhood Renewal of its Social Exclusion Unit.[1] This report points out that the poorest 'neighbourhoods are places where unemployment is endemic; crime, drugs, vandalism are rife; and public and private-sector services are second-rate or completely absent. The goal must be to reduce that gap between the poorest neighbourhoods and the rest of the country and bring them for the first time in decades up to an acceptable level'. But:

> 'Delivering this goal requires a huge effort to re-think policies that have failed, and to make Government initiatives work in the poorest places. It will mean learning the lessons of the past and:
>
> – investing in people, not just buildings;
> – involving communities, not parachuting in solutions;
> – developing integrated approaches with clear leadership;
> – ensuring mainstream policies really work for the poorest neighbourhoods;
> – making a long-term commitment with sustained political priority.'

In paragraph 4.15 of the Framework Document the Government indicates that this report on Neighbourhood Renewal 'identified housing as a key element in tackling the problems that beset such neighbourhoods. The Government's national strategy will be published in Summer 2000. But where substantial Registered Social Landlords 'fall within natural neighbourhoods, local authorities will want to explore the scope for coordinated approaches in partnership with RSLs'.

– **Regeneration**. In addition the 'Pathfinder Partnerships set up under the Government's New Deal for Communities and local regeneration initiatives, focus on poor neighbourhoods with severe "joined up" problems where the communities have identified housing condition and management as contributory factors to the wider social and economic problems of the area'. Improvements in these areas are seen to be essential to 'achieving wider neighbourhood renewal and community regeneration'.

– **Housing and Health**. This linkage has already been touched upon. The Government highlight improvements in energy efficiency, tackling unfitness and disrepair and general improvements to the quality and accessibility of housing as amongst the range of 'housing interventions' which can assist in this area. In addition, authorities are urged to participate in or develop strategic approaches through the Health Action Zone initiative[2]

---

1 *Bringing Britain together: a national strategy for neighbourhood renewal* – presented to Parliament by the Prime Minister (Cm 4045, September 1998). See also now *Joining it up locally – National Strategy for Neighbourhood Renewal* (Report of Policy Action Team 17, DETR, April 2000). This can be viewed on http://www.local-regions.detr.gov.uk/pat17/pdf/jiul17.pdf.

2 Health Action Zones (HAZs) are 'partnerships between the NHS, local authorities, the voluntary and private sectors, and community groups. HAZs are co-ordinated locally by a partnership board. Performance management is via NHS Executive regional offices (working with colleagues in social care and government office regions, linking with regional development agencies as appropriate), through those health authority(ies)

(if there is one locally) or informally in partnership with local health and social services authorities (if not).

– **Promoting Equality**. The Government indicates that 'treating people fairly and ensuring equal access to services, whether housing or otherwise, are crucial to Best Value.' Therefore, authorities should: check that the housing service complies with equal opportunities law and remedy any disparities; 'get the best from staff and maximise the potential of the labour market by taking a positive approach on equal opportunities' and make sure that 'black and minority ethnic groups have confidence that they will be treated fairly'. This can be done by top management commitment to racial equality and compliance with the Code of Practice of the Commission for Racial Equality – for example, with commitment to staff training on equal opportunities and 'pursuing anybody guilty of racial harassment'. On this latter point, presumably the Government means taking seriously and investigating every allegation of racial harassment and dealing appropriately with allegations which are upheld. There is clearly a difference between allegation and determination.

Key Players

13.8 The Framework Document identifies the following as key players in the delivery of best value for housing.[1] These are: local authorities; tenants and residents; registered social landlords; Government Offices for the Regions; Regional Development Agencies; the Housing Section of the DETR; the Audit Commission (external auditors and the Housing Inspectorate); the Housing Corporation and housing agencies. Some of the salient features of this section of the Framework Document are noted as follows:

Local Authorities

13.9 Local authorities (with whom the statutory duty of best value resides) are 'best placed to coordinate local partnerships and to deliver the real and sustainable improvements that best value demands'.[2] However, they will 'need to look beyond traditional service boundaries and develop a more corporate and cross service agenda.'[3] Tenant participation compacts (see below) are 'valuable tools in helping landlord local authorities to deliver Best Value for their tenants'.[4]

Paragraph 5.4 contains the following guidance as to what authorities must do in taking forward best value, namely to:

---

covered by the HAZ'. Twenty-six HAZs have been established in England since April 1998 'by the government in areas of deprivation and poor health to tackle health inequalities and modernise services through local innovation'. 'HAZ programmes represent a new approach to public health – linking health, regeneration, employment, education, housing and anti-poverty initiatives to respond to the needs of vulnerable groups and deprived communities.' (See http://www.haznet.org.uk through the Department of Health Website).

1 See Part 5: BVH – key players.
2 Paragraph 5.2.
3 Ibid.
4 Ibid.

'–   ensure time and effort is devoted to training members, staff and tenants and
     residents so that each has a clear understanding of what Best Value is about
     (ethos and process) and so that there is "top to bottom" clarity within the
     authority about leadership, management and service user inputs;

–   fundamentally review their housing strategies and services; examine what
     they are doing and why; and consider whether Best Value is being achieved
     (in the longer as well as shorter term) through current approaches;

–   as part of that, consider whether current approaches are responsive to the
     needs of tenants and residents and will respond effectively to future needs;

–   build in from the start of the BVR process the views of tenants and residents
     and actively encourage tenant and resident involvement in the development
     and implementation of housing strategies and services;

–   search for excellence by comparing performance against national indicators,
     other authorities and the aspirations of tenants and residents; and put into
     practice lessons learnt;

–   look beyond the traditional boundaries of the "housing service" in develop-
     ing and engaging in a more corporate and cross service agenda;

–   develop intelligent procurement strategies on the back of new innovative
     approaches to service provision and delivery;

–   introduce progressive organisational management tools and techniques;

–   develop information and marketing strategies;

–   develop networks with other authorities and alternative service providers.'

13.10   It will be seen that these apply the principles considered in preceding
chapters to the particular context of strategic housing provision; but what role
are elected members to play in the best value housing regime? The Framework
Document sees them as giving strategic management and leadership: 'Members need to understand what changes are required and why they are necessary.
And they need to lead their authority through them'.[1] Paragraph 5.5 points to
the 'invaluable contribution' members have to make through:

'–   representing the interests of local people – the "service users" – and in
     explaining to them how their views will influence the authority's approach;

–   showing commitment to the cultural changes needed, including leadership
     in carrying officers and staff with them;

–   ensuring corporate priorities take account of the broad will of local people
     and can be delivered;

–   linking Best Value to the wider modernisation agenda so that initiatives are
     integrated;

–   setting the overall Best Value strategy;

–   deciding on action following service reviews;

–   looking outwards and taking a constructive attitude to working in partnership
     with the private and voluntary sectors;

–   ensuring arrangements for tenants and residents to participate are safe-
     guarded and enhanced within the new democratic structures;

–   monitoring progress.'

It is clear (and particularly so in the context of the internal structural and other
imminent changes within the Local Government Bill 1999) that the Government wishes completely to recast the traditional role of the elected member. In
many cases, the old orthodoxy saw elected members as the public custodians of
directly provided and owned services and assets. Now they are seen (in the best

---

1   Paragraph 5.5.

value context) as strategic enablers; and as the Government acknowledges, these new expectations require 'new attitudes and new skills'.[1] The traditional minimalist approach to member training needs to change. For even:

> 'longer standing members may find that they need greater depth of expertise in areas like:
>
> – consultation techniques;
> – management of change;
> – performance management;
> – knowledge of service operations;
> – procurement.'

As at present, some members may wish to specialise in particular areas; but there is more to training than attending external courses. For there 'are many other options, for instance – visits to other authorities to learn and share good practice; or working with officers on consultation exercises.'[2] In addition 'consideration should be given to the benefits of this being undertaken jointly with officers and tenants'.[3]

13.11 Regarding officers, the Government considers that 'from front line staff to Directors' they have a vital role to play in putting best value for housing into practice. In particular, services managers will need to:

> '– think corporately and focus on how housing services fit in with their authority's wider corporate objectives;
> – develop skills in organisational management and development (including managing change), information management, procurement, partnership and performance management;
> – recognise staff needs and manage them through the changes, including effective training for staff so that they see Best Value as an opportunity for continuous improvement rather than just a process to be complied with;
> – set challenging but achievable performance targets for housing;
> – make sure services are seen to respond to tenants' and residents' needs and views, engaging them in the design, delivery and monitoring;
> – strike a fair and rational balance between tenants' and residents' views, service standards and costs;
> – direct activity in the housing service to achieving Best Value objectives.'[4]

Front line staff will need to be fully conversant with their authority's ethos in this area and its strategic, detailed and practical approach to best value and their part in the whole process. Such staff will also 'need the skills to deal with tenant and resident participation, even if they do not work directly in this area'.[5] For it 'will help staff who do, and it will reinforce the authority's approach in all its direct contacts'.[6]

---

1   Paragraph 5.6.
2   Paragraph 5.7.
3   Ibid.
4   Paragraph 5.8.
5   Paragraph 5.9.
6   Ibid.

Tenants and Residents

13.12   At the core of best value is the active participation and empowerment of stakeholders; and in this context this means tenants and residents. The Government considers that in the light of the best value regime, tenants and residents should be:

'in a position to:

- –   give an informed view on the type and quality of housing services being provided; on proposals for changing or improving these, and make a constructive, timely input to the authority's decisions on its housing strategy. Such views need to inform the authority's housing BVR process;
- –   reach an informed view on the costs and quality of services they would like to see, but with due regard to the resources available to the authority and priorities that need to be weighed in the face of this;
- –   participate in the locally agreed arrangements for monitoring and reporting on the authority's performance against targets, and for identifying and taking remedial action, where necessary – eg through complaints procedures, customer satisfaction surveys, monitoring panels, etc;
- –   make an informed judgement on the authority's performance which can feed into the authority's continuing review process and reports on performance in the annual BVPP;
- –   feed into the housing inspection process'.[1]

13.13   For active involvement to be meaningful, tenants and residents will need 'good quality and timely information about their local authority's housing services and performance'.[2] However, there needs to be a balance 'which recognises the importance of clear, good quality information but which is not so bureaucratic or burdensome that effort is diverted away from improving services on the ground.'[3] The Framework Document suggests that such arrangements can be negotiated and agreed locally 'as part of tenant participation compacts – agreements between local authorities and tenants on how tenants can get involved in local housing decisions – which are being introduced from April 2000'. These compacts will 'help local authorities and tenants establish mechanisms for tenants to take part effectively in consultation and local housing decisions' which 'goes to the heart of Best Value'.[4] Consequently, compacts are to be regarded as an 'integral part of Best Value as it relates to housing'.[5]

13.14   Compacts will be based on the *National Framework for Tenant Participation Compacts*[6] and on DETR Guidance on *Developing Good Practice in Tenant*

---

1   Paragraph 5.10.
2   Paragraph 5.11.
3   Paragraph 5.12.
4   Paragraph 5.13.
5   Ibid.
6   DETR, June, 1999. This can be viewed at: http://www.housing.detr.gov.uk/information/ compacts/index.htm#contents. This document indicates that 'Compacts are a tool to: help ensure councils become more efficient, transparent and accountable so that people know who exactly will be responsible for decisions and who will be actively involved in helping councils to reach those decisions; implement best value by enabling tenants to make an informed view on their housing services, be involved in planning them, improving them,

Participation.[1] The Government points out in para 5.14 of the Framework Document that:

> 'Compacts need to interact with and inform Best Value in housing through:
>
> – reflecting the outcomes from BVRs in compacts;
> – the arrangements agreed for consulting and involving tenants in the delivery of services – an important area on which authorities will be expected to report in their BVPPs;
> – authorities' performance in delivering what is agreed in compacts which will be subject to independent scrutiny through the strengthened external audit and inspection (ie through the Housing Inspectorate) arrangements under Best Value.'[2]

Further assistance in this area will be available on the publication of the good practice guide *Tenant Involvement in Best Value in Housing* which is 'based on work for the Carrick District Forum of Tenants and experiences in other Best Value pilot authorities'.[3] It is expected during 2000.

The Government recognises that there 'are fewer existing mechanisms for delivering representative opinion from among private housing residents'.[4] Consequently, where possible:

> 'authorities should seek to build on existing structures and look to opportunities they provide for engaging meaningfully with residents, particularly in the context of the wider strategic and enabling roles on housing that all local housing authorities undertake. Focus groups on housing strategic activities; holding stakeholder conferences on all housing activities; and setting up resident panels are examples of possible approaches. Networking with other authorities to share and develop new approaches is also important.'[5]

Registered Social Landlords

13.15 As will be seen below, Registered Social Landlords play an important part in local housing provision and embrace the principles of best value. This can be pursued in partnership with local authorities, for example in:

> '– developing new approaches to improve tenant participation;
> – carrying out reviews of services;
> – establishing benchmarking clubs to compare performance amongst peers, share experiences and spread good practice.'[6]

The DETR – Housing

13.16 The Government indicates that the main role of the DETR is 'to ensure that local housing authorities are clear about what they need to do' and the

---

monitoring and reporting on performance, and identifying and taking remedial action; to help tenants to identify issues of concern and ways of improving their quality of life as part of a wider strategy to tackle poor neighbourhoods.'

1   DETR, 25 August 1999. See http://www.housing.detr.gov.uk/information/tp/goodprac/ index.htm.
2   Paragraph 5.14.
3   Paragraph 5.15.
4   Paragraph 5.16.
5   Paragraph 5.16.
6   Paragraph 5.18.

Framework Document is the 'principal means'.[1] It mentions[2] various of its initiatives in this area including:

- the development of a set of national best value performance indicators for housing within the suite of indicators issued by the DETR in December 1999 (see also Chapter 3);[3]
- taking account of best value and minimisation of 'duplication and bureaucracy' in respect of the Housing Investment Programme;
- the development of 'a protocol on working relationships and information sharing between the key organisations involved in assessing performance of local housing strategies and services';[4]
- the production of the *National Framework for Tenant Participation Compacts*[5] and *Developing Good Practice in Tenant Participation*,[6] referred to above;
- working closely with the Audit Commission on 'arrangements for the establishment and operation of the Housing Inspectorate'.

The DETR intends to continue evolving, updating and evaluating the framework as well as promoting its use 'among local authorities and others'.[7]

The Government Offices for the Regions (GORs)

13.17   The Government Offices for the Regions assess local authority housing performance as part of the Housing Investment Programme (HIP).[8] They will remain involved to assess quality and effectiveness, issuing guidance and advice, encouraging the spread of good practice and making recommendations to ministers on the allocation of housing capital resources.[9] They will also work closely with the Housing Inspectorate as part of the integration of the HIP and best value processes and will be 'a first point of contact for advice and queries on' Best Value and Housing.[10]

Regional Development Agencies (RDAs)[11]

13.18   The Government's HIP assessments are also informed by the assessment of RDAs of local authority housing performance on Single Regeneration

---

1   Paragraph 5.19.
2   See ibid.
3   See *Best Value and Audit Commission Performance Indicators for 2000/2001* (December 1999), Chap 9.
4   Paragraph 5.19.
5   DETR, June 1999.
6   DETR, August 1999.
7   Paragraph 5.19.
8   Part 6 of DETR, *Best Value in Housing Framework* (January 2000) covers the relationship between HIP and best value.
9   Paragraph 5.22.
10   Paragraph 5.23.
11   These were launched formally in the English Regions on 1 April 1999. They are constituted under the Regional Development Agencies Act 1998 and are to 'provide effective, properly co-ordinated regional economic development and regeneration, and will enable the English regions to improve their relative competitiveness.' Their statutory purposes are: economic development and regeneration; business support; investment and competitiveness; skills, training and employment; and sustainable development. They are

Budget[1] funded activities. Together with the GORs they produce regional housing statements 'in consultation with local authorities and other stake-holders'. [2] These 'outline regional priorities and provide a context for local authorities' strategies and the performance assessments which the GOs and Housing Corporation carry out.'[3] Further, 'RDAs need to take account of regional housing statements and housing issues in devising their own regional economic development strategies which look holistically at issues across a region to help create sustainable communities.'[4]

Audit Commission (external audit and the Housing Inspectorate)

13.19 As noted in Chapters 6 and 7, authorities' best value performance plans will be audited annually. In addition there will be scrutiny from the Housing Inspectorate[5] which will be 'less frequent but more intensive'.[6]

Housing Corporation

13.20 The Housing Corporation is the regulatory body for Registered Social Landlords (RSLs – see above) which apart from ensuring best value in the RSL sector also facilitates 'read across between the housing activities of RSLs and local authorities at a national, regional and local level'.[7] The Framework Document highlights various support activities for best value undertaken by the Housing Corporation including: the guidance it issued in February 1999

---

    to develop regional strategies, will work closely with the Government Offices for the Regions and four of the thirteen RDA board members will be drawn from local government. See DETR http://www.local-regions.detr.gov.uk/rda/info/index.htm.

1   The DETR indicates that the 'SRB, which began in 1994, brought together a number of programmes from several Government Departments with the aim of simplifying and streamlining the assistance available for regeneration. SRB provides resources to support regeneration initiatives in England carried out by local regeneration partnerships. Its priority is to enhance the quality of life of local people in areas of need by reducing the gap between deprived and other areas, and between different groups. It supports initiatives which build on best practice and represent good value for money.' See http://www.regeneration.detr.gov.uk/srb/index.htm.

2   Paragraph 5.25.

3   Ibid.

4   Paragraph 5.26.

5   Paragraph 9.1. of *Best Value in Housing Framework* indicates that the 'Housing Inspectorate has been established as a branch of the Audit Commission, as part of the Best Value Inspection Directorate, to assess local authorities' performance in achieving Best Value in the provision of housing services.' It will inspect local housing authorities in three main circumstances, namely following: (as far as possible) the completion of a best value review by an authority covering an aspect of housing or the entire housing service; a referral to the Inspectorate by an authority's external auditors because of concerns regarding the housing service; a direction to inspect from the Secretary of State.

6   Paragraph 5.28.

7   Paragraph 5.29.

(*Best Value for Registered Social Landlords*);[1] its promotion of greater resident involvement; publishing annual performance indicators; running an extensive best value pilot programme and regularly evaluating RSL best value activities; and funding the National Housing Federation[2] to 'support pilots and provide guidance to the RSL sector'.[3]

Housing Agencies

13.21   Other agencies which operate in or have professional expertise in the housing area can also contribute to best value through (amongst other things) 'advice and good practice guidance'; training for local authority elected members, staff, tenants and residents; research 'to help inform or underpin Best Value approaches'; monitoring the effectiveness of approaches to best value and keeping up to date on Best Value developments.[4] Such bodies include the Chartered Institute of Housing, the Chartered Institute of Environmental Health Officers, the Local Government Association and the Improvement and Development Agency.

Protocol on Working Relationships and Information Sharing

13.22   Following the consultation stage which led to the Framework Document, there was 'widespread support' for a protocol to provide 'clarity about the working relationships between the key organisations involved in scrutinising local authorities' housing performance and similarly on information sharing'. This has now been produced and appears at Annex B to the Framework Document.[5] It will be 'reviewed as necessary in liaison with the key organisations covered and the Local Government Association so account can be taken of any legislative or policy changes which impact in the area covered by the protocol, and in light of evolving practice on the ground'.[6] Paragraph 5.34 indicates that it is in two parts, namely:

'–   **Part 1** – provides a commentary on the roles of the key organisations and the main interface with each other;

–   **Part 2** – sets out the information that needs to be shared and between which organisations; how this is brought about and when; the status of the information (eg whether provision is a statutory requirement); and the purpose for which each organisation needs the information. For completeness the key housing information flows from local authorities are also included.'

---

1   See below.
2   As indicated above, this is a not-for-profit company which is set up as the 'voice' of independent social landlords and 'an advocate of decent housing for all'. See the National Housing Federation website on: http://www.housing.org.uk/.
3   Paragraph 5.29.
4   Paragraph 5.30.
5   Paragraph 5.32.
6   Paragraph 5.35.

THE BEST VALUE REVIEW PROCESS IN HOUSING

13.23 Issues concerning reviews in general have been considered in some detail in Chapter 4. Whilst the same principles will apply, Part 6 of the Framework Document outlines some sector specific factors. For instance, in formulating the housing review, authorities will need to decide whether to examine: 'the whole function in one go' or to consider elements separately (for example, allocations or housing management); to undertake a review of the entire housing service in one part of the authority's area or to review as 'part of a wider cross cutting approach such as services to young people; services to the elderly; community safety and so on'.[1] Such decisions 'depend on a number of factors, including authorities' corporate objectives, size of the housing function; the housing strategy and the views of tenants and residents'.[2] Other factors affecting the priority of housing reviews will include satisfaction levels on the part of tenants, residents and other stakeholders with the authority's housing performance; poor performance against national indicators; the size of the housing function compared with the authority's overall budget and 'strategic fit with the authority's review programme'.[3]

Housing, Performance Reviews and the 4Cs

13.24 The 4Cs[4] have been considered in some detail in Chapter 4. Consequently, consideration will be given as follows merely to some of the salient points on local authority housing (including those authorities who have conducted a 'Large Scale Voluntary Transfer' of their stock to another landlord):[5]

- The 4Cs should be viewed as interactive and not linear.
- The **challenge** process should consider the 'underlying rationale for the service(s) under review' and 'why, as well as how and by whom a service is provided; the needs it is intended to address; the method of procurement; the contribution to corporate objectives and priorities; how current objectives and approaches should be changed and whether there are new and better ways of meeting needs.'[6]
- In the nature of best value, authorities must also 'challenge the adequacy and relevance of their strategic and enabling approaches on private housing'. They will also need to examine 'good practice from other

---

1 Paragraph 6.10.
2 Ibid.
3 Paragraph 6.11.
4 Paragraph 2.16 recites the 4Cs as follows: '**challenge** – why, how and by whom a service is being provided; **compare** – with the performance of others across a range of relevant indicators, taking into account the views of service users and potential suppliers; **consult** – local taxpayers, service users, partners, the wider business community and internally in the setting of new performance targets; **competition** – use fair and open competition wherever practicable as a means of securing efficient and effective services'.
5 As indicated above, see the Leasehold Reform, Housing and Urban Development Act 1993, s 135, and ss 32, 34 and 43 of the Housing Act 1985.
6 Paragraph 6.14.

authorities, housing organizations, agencies and private business and what
needs to be done to adapt it to local circumstances'. [1]

- In addition to using 'indicators and benchmarking' to **compare** their
  performance with other authorities, para 6.17 refers to tools 'such as
  HouseMark'[2] which 'provide a way of comparing performance with many
  other organisations through on-line benchmarking'. The **comparison**
  process generally is to 'identify performance gaps and the extent to which
  improvements are needed over the review period' by way of 'an intelligent
  exploration of how analogous services perform'.[3] 'Read across to RSLs' will
  also be important.[4]

- **Consultation** is referred to in para 6.20 as being 'central to best value'. The
  Framework Document refers to the 'joint DETR/Democracy Network
  publication – *Guidance on Enhancing Public Participation* – October 1998'[5]
  which 'provides practical advice on consultation techniques'. Reference is
  also made to the *National Framework for Tenant Participation Compacts*[6] and
  Developing Good Practice in Tenant Participation.[7] Tenants and residents
  should be involved in consultation at an early stage[8] and consultation
  should also include private housing residents concerning 'the strategic
  and enabling roles all local authorities undertake on housing'.[9]

- As to the 4C requirement to **compete**, the Government takes the view that
  'fair and open competition will . . . usually remain the most effective way of
  demonstrating that a function is being carried out competitively'; and
  such 'competition is expected to play an essential and enduring role in
  ensuring Best Value'. Therefore 'reviews will need to consider how this can
  be achieved', which will not happen if 'authorities fail to approach
  competition positively, taking full account of the opportunities for
  innovation and genuine partnership which are available from working
  with others in the public, private and voluntary sectors'.[10] The means by

---

1   Paragraph 6.15.
2   *HouseMark* is a subscription service described by para 7.11 of the Framework Document to
    be an 'Internet based knowledge management system' developed by the Chartered
    Institute of Housing and Arthur Andersen which 'combines validated good practice
    guidance; cross sector benchmarking, discussion forums and links to all housing related
    web sites'. Further information is available from Ross Fraser (e-mail: ross.fraser@cih.org
    (tel: 0207 837 4280)) or Ben Tolhurst (e-mail: ben tolhurst@uk.arthurandersen.com (tel:
    0207 546 9585)).
3   Paragraph 6.18.
4   Paragraph 6.19.
5   Paragraph 6.22.
6   DETR, June 1999. As indicated above, this can be viewed at: http://
    www.housing.detr.gov.uk/information/compacts/index.htm#contents.
7   DETR, August 1999: see http://www.housing.detr.gov.uk/information/tp/goodprac/
    index.htm.
8   Paragraph 6.24: tenants and residents views should input (amongst things) into: the
    drawing up of consultation strategies; the coming to informed judgments about priorities;
    targets and outputs for housing services; the setting, monitoring and reviewing of
    performance targets and standards, and the drawing up of remedial action where agreed
    standards of service are not being met.
9   Paragraph 6.23.
10 See para 6.26.

which 'competition can be tested as a part of deciding the Best Value option for future service delivery' include:

'–   commissioning an independent benchmarking report to enable restructuring or strengthening of the in-house service to match the best public, voluntary and private sector providers;

–   providing core housing services in-house and buying in top-up support from the private sector – eg bringing in private sector organisations to manage specific housing estates or housing advice services for tenants and private householders alike; buying in certain housing services for particular client groups like the elderly;

–   market testing of all or parts of the service (with an in-house bid);

–   the transfer or externalisation of the service to another provider (with no in-house bid);

–   forming a joint venture or partnership following competition for an external partner;

–   re-negotiation of existing arrangements with current providers, where permissible;

–   forming partnerships with tenants to deliver housing management services, including delegating management to tenant groups;

–   tendering all or parts of the housing service with an in-house team bidding against private sector bidders to assess who offers the best quality and value.'[1]

•   Authorities, having regard to the Guidance[2] (and in particular paragraphs 36 to 50 which deal with competition and related issues) will need 'to review and develop their procurement strategies'.[3] 'An intelligent procurement strategy must cover how, and in what circumstances, the authority decides to retain in-house services or to seek competitive tenders, external provision, partnership and so on'; and such a strategy 'needs to be transparent to external auditors, to the staff affected and to trade unions'.[4]

•   In the Government's view, key elements of such a strategy will include:

'–   authority-wide application of good procurement practice;

–   standard tendering and contractual documentation;

–   ensuring standing orders on procurement and tendering are consistent with the statutory requirements of Best Value;

–   procedures for negotiating and developing partnerships and other models of provision;

–   a commitment to fair and equal opportunity in employment policy and to integrate corporate policy objectives into any provider agreements;

–   gaining provider commitment to participate fully in the authority's Best Value approaches;

–   transparent and auditable evaluation methods.'[5]

---

1   Paragraph 6.30. This is a development of para 7.29 of the Government's July 1998 White Paper, *Modern Local Government In Touch with the People*.
2   DETR Circular 10/99, 14 December 1999.
3   Paragraph 6.33.
4   Ibid.
5   Paragraph 6.34.

- A useful 'Action Checklist' for best value housing reviews appears in para 6.34 of the Framework Document, which includes advice to:

  - find out what tenants and residents want and to involve them in the review process
  - keep an open mind about how services should be delivered, for what counts most are the outcomes for tenants and residents
  - involve staff in the review process since 'they have a lot to offer'.

PERFORMANCE INDICATORS

13.25   *The Best Value and Audit Commission Performance Indicators for 2000/2001*[1] have been considered in general terms in Chapter 3. Chapter 9 of this document covers Housing and Related Issues. These will clearly need to be studied with care, particularly by those who will be responsible for meeting the targets contained in them. They cover a range of relevant issues[2] and (as with the other PIs) specify in detail what is required of authorities to meet the targets. For instance, the tenant satisfaction indicator[3] (which is highlighted by para 6.44) is the '[s]atisfaction of tenants of council housing with the overall service provided by their landlord'. The definition is:

> 'Percentage stating that they are very or fairly satisfied with the overall service provided by their landlord.'

> 'Percentage of all council tenants, or a representative random sample of council tenants, stating that they are satisfied with the overall service provided by their landlord. Leaseholders and tenants of other social or private landlords are excluded. The survey should be carried out at least once every three years, starting in 2000/2001, using the National Housing Federation's STATUS[4] standard tenant satisfaction survey methodology. In years when there is no survey, the most recent available year's results will be reported with a note highlighting the date of the survey.'

The STATUS survey approach will also be expected of RSLs by the Housing Corporation which will 'help facilitate read across between local authority and RSL landlords'. Work is being done (and more 'time and resources'[5] will be needed) to facilitate comparability between the local authority and the RSL housing sectors. Paragraph 6.49 of the Framework Document indicates that the *Best Value and Audit Commission Performance Indicators for 2000/2001* are a ' "living" suite retaining the capability to measure performance over time but also needing to evolve in light of policy changes and the development of improved ways of measuring performance – particularly output measures.' Amongst the various measures to be explored with a view to improving housing

---

1   DETR, Audit Commission, Home Office: December 1999.
2   As para 6.43 of the *Best Value in Housing Framework* document indicates, the 'indicators span a wide range of local authority activities recognising that the duty of Best Value applies to strategic and enabling action across all housing tenures as well as to the local authority landlord housing management function'.
3   BVPI74.
4   Standard tenant satisfaction survey methodology.
5   Paragraph 6.47.

performance measures are: cross-cutting issues; the local authority stock repairs backlog; housing management and repair costs; crime, anti-social behaviour, nuisance and related issues; housing mobility and houses in multiple occupation.[1] However, to avoid the number of indicators growing unsustainably, a 'balance will need to be struck between safeguarding stability in national BVPIs (in particular for those against which top quartile targets are set) so that they can measure performance over time, and flexibility to accommodate changes aimed at improving the measurement of performance and/or areas addressed.'[2] In the light of the BVPIs, the Government is to discontinue publication of information which ranks local authorities by 'the number of "management vacants" (ie those properties ready to be let immediately or after minor repairs) and performance in relation to tackling rent arrears.'[3]

13.26 As to local performance indicators, authorities are 'strongly encouraged to develop and use' these 'to supplement those set nationally'.[4] These should cover direct and strategic housing management and should include 'wider cross cutting and other issues' including: 'action to help disabled people and to show the quality of the adaptation service; racial equality and equal opportunities – for example, to measure the level of satisfaction with housing services among black and minority ethnic groups and action to tackle racial harassment; and energy efficiency – for example, to measure the costs of heating properties which impacts particularly on the fuel poor.'[5] Local authorities should also consult with RSLs about the 'number and range of local PIs and explore the scope for developing and agreeing common local performance indicators with RSLs operating in their areas'.[6] A useful Action Checklist for local housing performance indicators appears below para 6.55.

BEST VALUE PERFORMANCE PLANS

13.27 This general area has been covered in some detail in Chapter 5 and is dealt with in the Framework Document at paras 6.56 to 6.64. A useful checklist for performance planning in the housing context appears below para 6.67.

ANNUAL REPORT TO TENANTS

13.28 In the light of the statutory requirement on authorities to produce a best value performance plan,[7] the present statutory framework[8] for an annual

---

1   Paragraph 6.49.
2   Paragraph 6.50.
3   Paragraph 6.51.
4   Paragraph 6.52.
5   Paragraph 6.54.
6   Paragraph 6.55.
7   See s 6(1) of the LGA 1999 and the Local Government (Best Value) Performance Plans and Reviews Order 1999 and Chapter 5.
8   See s 167 of the Local Government and Housing Act 1989 and the Reports to Tenants Determination 1994.

report to tenants on performance against specified indicators is to be repealed. As part of this process, with effect from April 2000, the Reports to Tenants Determination 1994, set out in Annex B to *Department of the Environment Circular 10/94* (which sets out the performance indicators to be included in the annual report to tenants), will be revoked. Circular 10/94 will also be cancelled in its entirety. Instead, authorities will be left with 'the flexibility to decide whether to produce an annual report to tenants.' However, an 'authority should take the views of its tenants into account in reaching a decision.'[1]

BEST VALUE AND THE HOUSING INVESTMENT PROGRAMME (HIP)

13.29 As indicated above, the Housing Investment Programme is the means by which the Government makes annual capital allocations for housing investment by local authorities. The Framework Document points out[2] that there is 'a significant degree of commonality between the requirements of BVH and the existing framework for the operation of the annual housing investment programme'. For the 'main objective of the HIP process is to bring about improvements in the quality of services provided by local housing authorities'.[3] However, the Government indicates that it is committed to ensuring that the HIP regime complements best value in housing and that 'there is no unnecessary duplication in the burdens they place on authorities'.[4] Arrangements for the 2000 HIP process will support this including authorities not being asked to provide HIP data which is already available through the existing performance planning or performance indicator framework.[5] As part of facilitating the HIP and best value in housing inspection frameworks to 'reinforce each other'[6] the Government Offices will use a standard return to provide local authorities with HIP assessment feedback. Information sharing 'among all the key organisations involved in assessing local authorities [sic] housing performance'[7] will also be important and the *Protocol on Working Relationships and Information Sharing* in Annex B to the Framework Document has been 'drawn up to clarify information exchanges'.[8]

The following key features of the HIP process are set out in para 6.68:

> '–   a requirement for authorities to produce a housing strategy for their area covering the whole range of housing issues which sets out broad plans and priorities for tackling the housing needs of the area;
> –   the production of annual plans for their housing capital programme and to progress the longer term objectives;

---

1   Paragraph 6.67.
2   At para 6.68.
3   Paragraph 6.68.
4   Paragraph 6.69.
5   See para 6.69, which also sets out other features of a 'joined-up' housing performance monitoring regime.
6   Paragraph 6.70.
7   Paragraph 6.72.
8   Ibid.

- a strong emphasis on the importance of wide consultation (tenants, residents, RSLs and other housing providers, related service interests (eg health, social services)) in production of the housing strategy and in involving tenants in the preparation and monitoring of the annual plans;
- the assessment, by GOs,[1] of the quality of authorities' housing strategies and their performance in delivering housing services. These assessments are used in determining the allocation of half of the housing capital resources, with higher shares going to the better performers, and in identifying areas where improvements in performance are needed; and
- the use of performance indicators, target setting and a range of other standard information to assess and drive up performance.'

RESOURCE ACCOUNTING

13.30 The Government intends from April 2001 to introduce a 'resource accounting' process which is intended, 'like HIP, to reinforce Best Value and to make local authority housing management more efficient.'[2] Amongst the main objectives of resource accounting are:

- to encourage the more efficient use of housing assets;
- to increase the transparency of the HRA;
- to assist authorities in planning their housing strategy by providing more certainty over future funding for major repairs through the introduction of a new element of subsidy, the Major Repairs Allowance;
- to put housing accounts onto a more business-like basis;
- as part of the new arrangements authorities will have to prepare business plans for the HRA stock. Government Offices will assess these as part of the HIP process. Following consultation, the Department will be issuing guidance in the spring of 2000 in time for authorities to prepare initial business plans for 2001/02;
- primarily the business plan will be a strategic planning tool; the initial preparation and subsequent revision should form part of the authority's overall corporate planning process. The plan should place the future use of the authority's stock in a strategic context and expand in detail on the:

  - means whereby these objectives will be met;
  - income and expenditure projections which support these strategies;
  - assumptions about performance on which these are based;
  - methods and indicators by which performance will be evaluated;

- the business plan will help set the strategic framework (as far as the authority's own stock is concerned) for BVRs;
- housing inspections will be concerned with the quality of the business planning process and how it has been used to improve decision making;
- as with Best Value and HIP, a key principle will be to avoid duplication and bureaucracy by using common data wherever possible.'[3]

---

1   Government Offices for the Regions.
2   Paragraph 6.73.
3   Ibid.

LARGE SCALE VOLUNTARY TRANSFER (LSVT) AUTHORITIES

13.31   Authorities which have transferred their stock to another landlord[1] will also be subject to most of the Framework Document guidance and they will need to understand the principles and practice of best value in the same way as any other authority.[2] 'LSVT authorities retain important strategic and enabling responsibilities in relation to housing as well as responsibility towards prospective tenants in prioritising need for housing and they will be subject to the duty to achieve Best Value in their housing functions and also subject to inspection by the Housing Inspectorate.'[3] Paragraph 6.76 of the Framework Document sets out some particular '4C[4] factors' for authorities in this position.

TENANT MANAGEMENT ORGANISATIONS (TMOS)

13.32   Under powers in the Housing Act 1985,[5] with the consent of the Secretary of State and subject to the other statutory requirements, certain housing management functions can, by way of management agreements, be delegated by a housing authority to a manager who exercises those functions as the authority's agent. Paragraph 6.77 of the Framework Document advises that authorities which have TMOs 'will need to consider how these organisations should reflect and prepare for Best Value'. They should consequently 'consider what advice, guidance, training and support they should give TMOs to help them perform their part. They should also make sure management agreements make clear what TMOs' responsibilities under Best Value will be.'[6] Some key questions on performance review, the 4Cs, local plans 'generated by individual TMOs', and performance monitoring are raised in para 6.77.

THE PRIVATE FINANCE INITIATIVE

13.33   The Framework Document points out[7] that the 'application of PFI to the refurbishment of council housing is currently being piloted in eight

---

1   See the Leasehold Reform, Housing and Urban Development Act 1993, s 135, and ss 32, 34
    and 43 of the Housing Act 1985.
2   Paragraph 6.75.
3   Ibid.
4   As indicated previously, the 'challenge, compare, consult, compete' methodology at the
    core of the best value review process.
5   As amended by the Housing and Planning Act 1986, the Leasehold Reform and Urban
    Development Act 1993 and the Housing Act 1996.
6   Paragraph 6.77.
7   At para 6.79.

pathfinder authorities[1] with the prospect of the first contracts being signed in 2001'; and 'further projects are likely to follow'.[2] Paragraph 6.80 of the Framework Document indicates that as a matter of good contracting: 'Authorities considering PFI should make sure long term contracts are flexible enough to ensure that the arrangements for securing continuous improvement and innovation can be adapted to meet changing local and national priorities and can be improved by agreement'. These themes are also looked at in Chapter 2.[3]

Paragraph 6.81 indicates that many PFI procurement disciplines already reflect best value principles. For example: 'conducting strategic reviews of the need for services as part of appraising options; focusing on objectives, outputs and outcomes; analysing public sector comparators; consulting key stake-holders as part of the commissioning process; and regular performance review and performance payment mechanisms'.

GOOD PRACTICE SOURCES

13.34 Part 7 of the Framework Document contains a useful collection of information in this area and includes: the local authority and RSL pilot programme; the Improvement and Development Agency; the Local Government Improvement Programme; HouseMark;[4] the Housing and Best Value Manual from the Chartered Institute of Housing and the Local Government Association; the Housing Inspectorate; the Housing Corporation and National Housing Federation; the Housing Quality Network;[5] the various quality schemes;[6] and the Beacon Councils Scheme.[7]

AUDIT AND INSPECTION

13.35 Audit of best value performance plans[8] and best value inspections[9] have been considered respectively in Chapters 6 and 7 above. Chapter 12

---

1   Camden LBC, Islington LBC, Leeds City Council, Manchester City Council, Newham LBC, North East Derbyshire DC, Reading BC and Sandwell MBC. Pinsent Curtis has been commissioned to produce guidance on Housing and PFI as part of this project.
2   Paragraph 6.79.
3   See 'Best Value and Contracted-Out Services' within that chapter.
4   See above.
5   The Housing Quality Network, 1 Station Approach, Filey, North Yorkshire YO14 9PF (tel: 01723 515050/516700; fax: 01723 516141; e-mail: hfta@btinternet.com).
6   Paragraph 7.21 of the Framework Document points out that the Government's White Paper, *Modernising Government* (Cm 4310, March 1999), encourages all public sector organisations to make use of one of the four main quality schemes: EFQM Excellence Model®; Investors in People; Charter Mark; and ISO 9000. Further details are contained in DETR Circular 10/99 'including contacts and information on some other commonly used quality schemes'. See also the material on quality schemes on the Cabinet Office website: http://www.cabinet-office.gov.uk/servicefirst/index/library.htm and the Cabinet Office Quality Schemes Taskforce Report on the same website at http://www.servicefirst.gov.uk/2000/report.htm.
7   See Chapter 3 above.
8   See s 7 of the LGA 1999.
9   See ibid, ss 10–13.

(Accounting Issues) is also relevant. Therefore, this section as follows will look only at some of the key issues affecting local authority housing:[1]

– paragraph 8.7 indicates that external auditors will: adopt an open-minded and supportive approach to innovation; support well thought through risk-taking and experimentation;[2] and provide advice and encouragement to authorities by promoting good practice and shared experience;

– CIPFA is examining its *Accounting for Housing Services* guidance 'in the light of Best Value and other current developments'.[3] It 'is considering what further guidance should be given to authorities on accounting for housing to ensure, as far as possible, an objective analysis of expenditure, including that relating to management.'[4]

The Housing Inspectorate

13.36   As noted above, the new Best Value Inspectorate (which incorporates a Housing Inspectorate) has been set up by the Government under the auspices of the Audit Commission. This is to be headed by 'the Chief Inspector of Housing, will have a regional structure and will be part of the Inspection Directorate's regional arrangements'.[5] Regional offices will have a Senior Housing Inspector and a team of housing inspectors.[6] There will also be within regional teams 'tenant inspection advisers' to 'provide a user perspective for inspections that relate to local authority landlord services'.[7] Inspection teams will have a tenant member (although such members will not 'have a role in inspecting their own authority'. To 'gain a broader view on housing across the country' inspection teams will be required to carry out 'a number of inspections in other regions'.[8]

In meeting its core objective of assessing local authorities' performance in achieving best value in the provision of housing services it will adopt the same principles as other parts of the Best Value Inspectorate and will:

'–   inform the public about the performance of local housing services at the time of the inspection and their likely performance in the future, thereby enhancing local accountability;

–   focus on housing services as users experience them;

–   take into account the use of money, (including Housing Revenue Account and General Fund revenue resources as well as capital and special project finance), people and assets and promote economy, efficiency and effectiveness;

---

1   References in this section will be to paragraphs in *Best Value in Housing Framework* unless otherwise indicated.

2   The emphasis here must be on 'well thought through' since unreasonable use of public monies would be unlawful and in breach of the general fiduciary duty of public bodies to those who fund them (see Chapter 1). See also the Audit Commission Act 1998, s 17 (Declaration that an item of account is unlawful) and s 18 (Recovery of amount not accounted for etc).

3   Paragraph 8.13.

4   Ibid.

5   Paragraph 9.8.

6   Paragraph 9.9.

7   Ibid.

8   Paragraph 9.10.

–   act as a catalyst to help housing authorities to improve;
–   identify what works, to inform policy nationally, regionally and locally as well as practice in the local setting;
–   work on the principle that housing inspection will be proportionate to risk; and that the methodology and criteria on which judgements will be based will be explicit and evidence based;
–   as a body independent of Government and local authorities, carry out inspections without fear or favour'.[1]

As indicated earlier in this chapter, there are three main circumstances which will trigger inspection of local housing authorities, namely following:

–   (as far as possible) the completion of a best value performance review by an authority which covers an aspect of housing or the housing service entirely. This will be the standard interaction between the Housing Inspectorate and local authorities;
–   a referral to the Inspectorate by external auditors of an authority because of concerns in respect of the housing service;
–   a direction to inspect from the Secretary of State.[2]

In addition, 'the impact of the service and its current performance' will influence the 'scale and depth of the inspection'.[3]

13.37   The Inspection framework will adopt the following key stages which are amplified in para 9.12 of the Framework Document:

(1)   Initial inspection programme to be agreed with each authority.
(2)   Completion of the best value review to be notified to the Regional Director and agreement on inspection dates to be finalised.
(3)   Request for information of the authority from the Housing Inspectorate covering 'corporate, strategic and service specific issues'.
(4)   First contact between Inspectorate and authority representatives.
(5)   On site inspection to be 'tailored in terms of breadth and depth according to the nature of the service, its performance and the level of resources available for that specific inspection'.[4]
(6)   Interim report to be presented to the authority in private utilising the evidence gathered on: the authority's corporate approach to best value; the housing service strategy and approach to best value; the overall housing service; the housing services covered by the local authority's best value review; compliance with the best value legislation in relation to the use of the 4Cs in the review process.
(7)   Final report, in plain English, which 'will be summarised in a short, publicly accessible version which will be made available to the public through a range of means including the Internet.' It 'will also be produced in the relevant minority languages as advised by the local authority.' But these 'reports will be made available to the authority prior to their general release and before copies are made available to the media.'[5]

1   Paragraph 9.2.
2   Paragraph 9.3.
3   Paragraph 9.11.
4   Paragraph 9.12, subparagraph 5.
5   Paragraph 9.12, subparagraph 7.

(8) The local authority response. The Framework Document indicates that the 'local authority will want to respond thoughtfully to the final inspection report and decide how to proceed depending on the nature and content of the report.'[1] The 'Housing Inspectorate will want to work with the authority on agreeing what action, if required and which has not already been planned by the authority, will be necessary and to be clear what timescales apply and how those actions are to be followed up in subsequent inspections by the Housing Inspectorate.'[2]

The Audit Commission is providing guidance to local authorities 'on the overall approach to inspection'.[3]

INTERVENTION

13.38   This has been dealt with in Chapter 8.

BEST VALUE AND REGISTERED SOCIAL LANDLORDS

13.39   As noted above, Registered Social Landlords (RSLs) are non-profit-making bodies registered with the Housing Corporation under the Housing Act 1996. The Housing Corporation indicates that most RSLs are constituted as Housing Associations. However, whilst as 'independent bodies RSLs will not be subject to the statutory duty of Best Value', nevertheless 'the Housing Corporation and National Housing Federation have made clear that they expect RSLs to fully embrace Best Value'.[4] Consequently, in February 1999, the Housing Corporation issued its Guidance, *Best Value for registered social landlords* (the RSL Guidance). The aim of this is to 'secure continuous improvement in the performance of individual landlords and the sector as a whole'.[5] 'Best Value will help RSLs deliver cost effective services that meet the needs and aspirations of their tenants and residents'.[6] This section will give an overview of some of the key themes in the RSL Guidance; references to paragraphs will be to those in the RSL Guidance unless otherwise indicated.

The RSL Guidance indicates that it is merely one element of the support being given by the Housing Corporation to assist RSLs to deliver best value.[7] In conjunction with the National Housing Federation (NHF)[8] the Corporation has established 23 pilot projects to 'test the methods RSLs can use to deliver

---

1   Paragraph 9.13.
2   Ibid.
3   Paragraph 9.14.
4   *Best Value in Housing Framework*, para 4.6.
5   The Housing Corporation, *Best Value for Registered Social Landlord* (February, 1999) Summary, para 1.
6   Ibid.
7   Paragraph 1.17.
8   As indicated above, this is a not-for-profit company which is set up as the 'voice' of independent social landlords and 'an advocate of decent housing for all'. See the National Housing Federation website on: http://www.housing.org.uk.

Best Value'.[1] Details of these pilots appear in Annex 1 to the RSL Guidance. According to the summary, the objectives of the best value framework in the RSL sector are to:

– strengthen the influence of residents over the design and delivery of the services they receive;
– deliver high-quality and cost effective services; and
– achieve continuous improvement in the services delivered to residents and others.

The practical best value framework in the RSL sector will encompass: comprehensive service reviews (incorporating the 4Cs),[2] the preparation of service statements and the production of performance plans and performance reports. These will be considered briefly below.

STRENGTHENING THE ROLE OF RESIDENTS

13.40   Performance standards in specifying the 'minimum regulatory requirements'[3] will ensure that RSLs 'provide information for residents, consult them, and offer them reasonable opportunities to participate in and influence the management of their own homes'.[4] Under best value:

'residents should be in a position to:

– give an informed view on the range, type and quality of housing services being provided and on proposals for changing or improving these, including options for different approaches to service delivery
– reach and give an informed view on the standards of service to be achieved and targets for service quality and cost to be set by the RSL in its performance plan(s)
– participate – in ways which best meet their needs and aspirations – in the RSL's formal arrangements for monitoring and reporting on performance against targets
– feed their views on performance into the RSL's formal monitoring process (for example, through complaints procedures or satisfaction surveys)
– participate in, and make an informed judgement on, the RSL's performance which will feed into the RSL's continuing review process and its performance plan(s) and report(s).'[5]

Amongst the range of methods which RSLs will need to use are 'focus groups, surveys and resident forums, to ensure that they know residents' priorities for changes in the type, quality and quantity of service offered.'[6] For residents who take the view that their RSL is not pursuing best value with sufficient vigour, the performance review procedures can be used to express concern to the Corporation.[7]

---

1   Paragraph 1.17.
2   See Chapter 4.
3   Paragraph 2.2.
4   Ibid.
5   Paragraph 2.3.
6   Paragraph 2.6.
7   Paragraph 2.8.

So, RSLs should:

'1.   agree with residents the forms of involvement that will ensure effective consumer input into and influence over the implementation of Best Value

2.   involve residents in appropriate ways in the whole process ie

–   drawing up of the programme of comprehensive service reviews
–   the review of each service area
–   the drawing up of service statements, performance plans and reports

3.   agree and fund any training necessary for residents to take part in these activities.'[1]

Achieving Cost Effectiveness

13.41   The RSL Guidance makes the point that rents 'are primarily driven by costs'.[2] Consequently, the Housing Corporation wants to:

'see RSLs bear down on their costs in particular by:

–   using benchmarking techniques to identify areas of comparatively high cost
–   analysing the options for methods of service delivery and their cost implications'.[3]

Competition 'is a traditional means of achieving cost effectiveness'.[4] There is an expectation that RSLs will have competition in place for many of their activities – for example, the development of new homes, accounts audit or building insurance.[5] In addition, RSLs should consider new forms of competition – for example, tendering housing management where an RSL 'owns only a few homes in a given area'.[6] In the case of 'supported housing', where rents are merely one source of cost-covering income, there is 'a more complicated relationship between costs and rents than for general needs housing'.[7] Nevertheless, it will still be necessary for such RSLs to 'examine the efficiency and cost effectiveness of their operations' under best value.[8]

Despite arguments that best value will inevitably increase costs, the Housing Corporation does not accept that 'this will happen over the longer term',[9] particularly bearing in mind 'constant review and improvement' systems and resident participation.[10] 'Experience shows that the long-term benefits of resident participation, if properly conducted, will outweigh any additional costs'.[11]

---

1   Paragraph 2.9.
2   Paragraph 2.10.
3   Ibid.
4   Paragraph 2.14.
5   Ibid.
6   Ibid.
7   Paragraph 2.16. Supported housing is accommodation 'where an individual holds a tenancy at the same time as receiving support (including intensive or supportive housing management) provided by a landlord under the terms of a formal undertaking': see Housing Corporation, *Best Value for registered social landlords* (February 1999), Annex 4, 'Glossary of Terms'.
8   Ibid.
9   Paragraph 2.18.
10   Ibid.
11   Ibid.

13.42 In summary, in:

'achieving cost effectiveness, RSLs should:

1. recognize residents as a vital source of ideas on how to keep costs and rents down
2. develop techniques to identify the costs of individual services and activities
3. make use of benchmarking to know how their costs and performance compare with other organizations
4. use competition wherever appropriate
5. recognize the special features of general needs, supported and leasehold housing, and the need for a flexible and relevant approach'.[1]

Key Ingredients of the Best Value Process for RSLs

13.43 As indicated above, these are:

– Comprehensive Service Reviews;
– Service Statements;
– Performance Plans; and
– Performance Reports.

Comprehensive Service Reviews

13.44 These are analogous to fundamental performance reviews in the local authority sector. However, whilst with RSLs these are carried out by Housing Corporation staff, the processes involved are similar and will include use of the 4Cs.[2] RSLs are advised to 'engage with local authorities undertaking corporate reviews, particularly where they directly affect RSL work'[3] – for example, regeneration, community care or community safety.

Services will need to be divided up into a manageable number of reviews having regard to such matters as: the range of services provided, organisational structures, whether to prioritise support or front line services, whether to adopt a functional or a geographical approach or a combination, and the types of residents to be involved.[4] In drawing up the programme of reviews, including their nature and order, residents should be involved. Other influencing factors include matters such as the performance of the RSL compared with other RSLs and local authority providers (identified through PIs, benchmarking and other means), organisational structure, capacity for improvement and whether a service has been subject to recent review.[5] As with local government, the first round of reviews should be completed within five years.[6]

The conduct of each review should be considered by RSLs and their residents and overall responsibility allocated. Also to be considered is how residents and other stakeholders (including staff) are to be engaged, how the 4Cs are to be applied and the process for monitoring and review.[7]

---

1 Paragraph 2.18.
2 Paragraph 2.21. For the 4Cs, see Chapter 4.
3 Paragraph 2.22.
4 Paragraph 2.23.
5 Paragraph 2.24.
6 Paragraph 2.25. For local government, see the Local Government (Best Value) Performance Plans and Reviews Order 1999, SI 1999/3251. This is dealt with in Chapter 4.
7 Paragraph 2.26.

So, RSLs should:

1. involve residents in drawing up the review programme
2. use PIs and benchmarking outcomes to determine the order of reviews
3. agree as to the conduct of each service area review
4. work to a five-year timetable for review completion
5. agree what will be produced as a result
6. publish the review programme with information as to how reviews will be conducted.[1]

Service Statements

13.45 These constitute an RSL's 'published description' of services provided to their residents and the standards which they aim to achieve in delivering those services.[2] For each service the statement should detail: the service organisational objectives, a description of the services to be provided and the level of service that should be achieved.[3] Statements should be produced as a result of resident consultation, reflecting their 'aspirations, needs and priorities'.[4]

Performance Plans

13.46 These should be based on current RSL service statements and use the results of comprehensive service reviews and performance reports[5] to:

'–   set revised target levels of performance including those covering efficiency savings
–   identify any changes in practice to meet the revised objectives and any new set of targets
–   identify the effect that these changes are likely to have on costs
–   ensure there is a clear timetable and arrangements for action and subsequent review'.[6]

Whilst RSLs may choose to produce such plans annually, it is important that 'performance targets for key areas of activity are set out for each year over a given period of time (say three years).[7] The Corporation believes that all RSLs can potentially improve and 'should be aiming to achieve the standards currently set by the top 25% of performers'.[8] This reflects Government thinking in the *Best Value and Audit Commission Performance Indicators for 2000/2001*.[9] To support this process, the Housing Corporation has started to publish 'the levels of performance for general needs housing achieved by the top 25% for the peer groups that appear in our annual published PI report'.[10]

---

1   Paragraph 2.28.
2   Paragraph 2.19.
3   Paragraph 2.29.
4   Paragraph 2.31.
5   See below.
6   Paragraph 2.33.
7   Paragraph 2.34.
8   Paragraph 2.35.
9   See Chapter 3.
10   Paragraph 2.35. This refers readers to 'Registered Social Landlords in 1998: Performance Indicators'.

So RSLs should be drawing up and publishing, with the involvement of residents, performance plans for service improvement which are clear as to outcome aims and how those are to be achieved. They must also make sure that there 'is a clear timetable and arrangements for action and subsequent review'.[1]

Performance Reports

13.47 These are 'public statements of the levels of performance achieved in the previous period and an explanation of the reasons for this level of achievement'.[2] They should also 'try to identify the causes of any significant shortcomings'.[3] The Housing Corporation suggests that RSLs consider producing performance reports for 'the previous year and performance plans for the following year in the same document'.[4]

Whilst the format of performance reports will be a matter for RSLs, they 'should be as short and simple as possible'[5] but, if following a comprehensive service review, they should reflect the 'aims and changes arising from such a review'.[6] In any case they should contain:

'–   objective assessments of past and current performance
–   comparison with the quantitative and qualitative performance targets set in the last performance plan
–   where published PIs are available and relevant, comparison with the top 25% and 50% performance levels
–   an assessment of the gains achieved and/or the shortcomings experienced
–   details on any changes in the cost of service delivery'.[7]

Supported housing[8] providers will 'need to consider the range of performance reporting required from them by their various funders ... and how far the information in these reports might meet the needs and interests of their residents.'[9]

13.48 Annual performance reports 'for all main services should ideally be produced within six months of the RSL's year end'[10] (by 30 September in most cases). Whilst the Housing Corporation recognises the impact on the ability of RSLs to produce comparative performance data caused by the delay in availability of published performance information and is working to streamline procedures to speed up production, nevertheless it will be for RSLs to consider when to produce these reports given 'the desirability of publishing performance information as soon as possible, the timing of the publication of RSL PIs by the Corporation, and the benefits from combining the production of performance plans and performance reports'.[11]

---

1   Paragraph 2.35. This refers readers to 'Registered Social Landlords in 1998: Performance Indicators'.
2   Paragraph 2.19.
3   Paragraph 2.36.
4   Paragraph 2.36.
5   Paragraph 2.38.
6   Ibid.
7   Paragraph 2.38.
8   See footnote 7 on p 248 above.
9   Paragraph 2.39.
10   Paragraph 2.41.
11   Ibid.

Consequently, RSLs should: involve residents in producing and in reviewing progress concerning performance reports; include performance assessments using published as well as local performance measures and indicators; and publish reports annually, ideally within six months of the year end.[1]

Role of the Housing Corporation

13.49 The Corporation indicates that its primary role is issuing the RSL Guidance and encouraging RSLs to deliver best value. In addition, the Housing Corporation is 'supporting and evaluating' best value activity in the RSL sector through the following:

— Setting up a programme of best value pilots[2] including the provision of grant aid to the National Housing Federation 'to give practical support to the pilot (and other) RSLs involved in best value activity' and the funding of independent evaluation of the pilot programme[3] by the School for Public Policy at the University of Birmingham. The aims of the pilot programme are: to assess the extent to which any improvements in service efficiency and effectiveness have come from best value, to help refine the best value framework and to encourage the spread of good best value practice amongst RSLs.[4]

— Two surveys of RSL best value activity (the first in 1999 and the second in mid 2000) to: provide 'before and after' information to enable assessment of best value progress in the 18-month period following issue of the RSL Guidance, to gather information on the 'extent and type' of best value activities being undertaken and to inform good practice and the further development of best value from issues identified in the implementation of best value.[5]

— An overall assessment of best value in the RSL sector to be undertaken in late 2000.[6]

— Further development of the performance indicator framework. One example is the development of comparative performance indicators by producing a set of standard definitions and publishing the top 25% and 50% levels of performance from the published performance indicator data.[7] Another is the possible development of the existing performance indicator framework to 'make the data more useful under the best value

---

1   Paragraph 2.41.
2   As indicated above, details of the best value RSL pilots appear at Annex 1 to Housing Corporation, *Best Value for registered social landlords* (February 1999).
3   Paragraphs 3.1 and 3.4.
4   Paragraph 3.2.
5   Paragraph 3.7.
6   Paragraph 3.8.
7   Paragraph 3.10.

framework'.[1] The Housing Corporation is 'looking to develop' its performance indicator framework in the areas of: tenant participation; resident satisfaction; shared ownership and leasehold housing; financial resources; development activity; treatment of group structures and supported housing.

– As to supported housing, the Corporation is developing work on performance indicators in this area since, to the date of publication of the RSL Guidance,[2] there has been only a limited number available.[3]

– The Housing Corporation is also minded to develop best value performance indicators 'that are relevant to both the RSL and local authority sectors to enable more direct comparisons between RSLs and local authority housing departments'.[4] This would harmonise with Government thinking concerning 'read across' between the local authority and the RSL sectors.[5]

In addition to the best value RSL pilot programme mentioned, the Housing Corporation is also funding a number of Innovation and Good Practice Programme[6] projects on best value, details of which appear in paras 3.19 to 3.28 of the RSL Guidance.

Regulation

13.50 Although the Housing Corporation has regulatory powers in the Housing Act 1996,[7] the Housing Corporation decided to recommend adoption of a best value framework 'in ways that are appropriate to them and their residents'[8] as a 'voluntary commitment'[9] for RSLs 'with more than 250 homes/bedspaces in ownership or management'.[10] However, the Corporation will 'enforce compliance where RSLs are clearly failing to achieve our minimum Performance Standards requirements' directly relating to best value. These are that RSLs should:

'– have strategies or business plans which include statements of objectives and plans for achieving them

– have a policy on accountability to residents and consult on it

– offer adequate opportunities for resident participation and influence

– provide information on services and standards and rents

– consult on all services and the standards of them

---

1 Paragraph 3.15.
2 February 1999.
3 Paragraph 3.16.
4 Paragraph 3.17.
5 See, for example, para 5.29 of the *Best Value in Housing Framework* document referred to above.
6 The Innovation and Good Practice Programme (IGP) is 'A revenue funded programme administered by the Housing Corporation designed to test new ideas and promote good practice for the benefit of RSLs and their tenants': see Housing Corporation, *Best Value for registered social landlords* (February 1999), Annex 4, 'Glossary of Terms'.
7 See, for example, s 5 which enables the Housing Corporation to set and vary criteria for registration as a social landlord and s 7 (giving effect to Sch 1) which deals with regulation of registered social landlords.
8 Paragraph 4.3.
9 Paragraph 4.2.
10 Paragraph 4.3.

- provide PI information
- ensure general efficiency
- keep rents within reasonable levels.'[1]

13.51 The Housing Corporation will be monitoring progress and will if necessary review its policy that 'Best Value should not become a regulatory requirement'.[2]

Mirroring the interaction in the local authority sector between HIP[3] and Best Value, the Housing Corporation intends 'to enable an RSL's performance under the Best Value Framework to be reflected in funding decisions'.[4]

Although the Housing Corporation is concentrating on 'RSLs with more than 250 homes'[5] that is not to be taken as signifying the Corporation's lack of interest in what smaller RSLs are doing under best value. The Corporation 'will encourage them to adopt the same framework and approach – in ways that make sense to them' since the 'task of ensuring quality and cost effectiveness is just as important to them and their residents as it is for larger RSLs'.[6]

CONCLUSION

13.52 As indicated at the beginning of the chapter, together with food, water and clothing, housing is a basic human need. In addition, it is integral to individual and social identity. Acknowledging this and harmonising with the principles in the *Best Value in Housing Framework Paper*[7] the Government in its April 2000 Housing Green Paper[8] stated amongst its key proposals that of:

'Promoting a stronger role for local authorities in housing to reflect the variations in circumstances around the country and to enable solutions to be tailored to local conditions ... including:

- encouraging all authorities to take a strategic view of needs across all housing, public and private sector;
- encouraging authorities to work in partnership with local communities, registered social landlords and other organisations;
- strengthening the strategic role of authorities which have transferred their housing to registered social landlords; and
- ensuring that authorities link housing policies with planning policies and those for the wider social, economic and environmental well-being of the community.'

The Government is rightly concerned to ensure that public money applied to this sector will add real value to the lives of those for whom it is disbursed. Also integral to best value in housing is that the old power relationship between the

---

1   Paragraph 4.2.
2   Paragraph 4.3.
3   See above – the Housing Investment Programme.
4   Paragraph 4.4.
5   Paragraph 4.5.
6   Ibid.
7   DETR, January 2000.
8   *Quality and Choice: A Decent Home for All* – see Summary and Key Proposals. This Paper can be viewed at: http://www.housing.detr.gov.uk/information/consult/homes/pdf/hous__ gpr.pdf.

dominant and determining public sector landlord and its grateful and subservient tenant should (in the unlikely event that this is not extinct) be completely reconstituted into a relationship of equals, playing complementary and important roles. For with best value it is the user and not the provider which is of paramount importance; and the interests of the user are pivotal to every service.

Chapter 14

BEST VALUE AND THE POLICE

INTRODUCTION

14.1 Failure to comply with the statutory duty of best value will not be a crime – at least in the formal sense of the word, which betokens a breach of the criminal law. Apart from being a dereliction of public service, the specific consequences of failure to give the public the level and type of service they deserve (in accordance with the requirements of Part I of the Local Government Act 1999) have been considered in Chapter 8. If breach of best value is not a crime, nevertheless the duty will certainly apply to the primary agency of crime prevention, investigation and detection – the police service.[1] The work of this service is of major public importance and concern.

As noted frequently throughout this book, gone are the days when institutions of public authority gained unquestioning public acceptance merely by their existence. The public is now a sophisticated and critical consumer of public services and expects stern stewardship of public resources and robust accountability mechanisms.

14.2 With crime figures generally rising,[2] and a widespread public perception of the prevalence of crime and diminution of public safety, the need for an

---

1 It is, of course police *authorities* which are subject to the duty of best value (see s 1(1) of the LGA 1999). However, the Home Office has pointed out that 'Clearly, police authorities will need to work in close partnership with their forces to achieve Best Value: it is the force which will have to deliver Best Value policing. But, ultimately the police authority is accountable to local people for ensuring that they get Best Value from their police service.' (See Home Office, *Best Value – the Police Authority Role* (November 1999), referred to below.)

2 See Recorded Crime Statistics, England and Wales, October 1998 to September 1999 (Home Office, 18 January 2000). In this publication recorded crime figures 'contain details of notifiable offences which are recorded by the police'. New recording rules took effect on 1 April 1998. Under the new system, 'the statistics wherever possible measure one crime per victim ...'. The Home Office notes (amongst other things) that 'an offence relating to the fraudulent use of a credit card would only be recorded by the police if the victim reported the misuse to the police; any misuses that the police discovered during an investigation that had not been reported to them would not be recorded. With the new rules any fraudulent uses would be recorded.' (See Annex A to Recorded Crime Statistics, England and Wales, April 1998 to March 1999.) In addition, new categories of offence are now 'notifiable' including: cruelty to or neglect of children, and possession of controlled drugs and other non-trafficking drug offences. Comparisons made between the current year and the previous year are based on the 'new rules'. According to the January 2000 figures crimes of violence against the person have risen by 5% compared with the previous 12 months. On the same basis, figures for robberies have gone up by 19%, those for sexual offences by 2.2% and criminal damage by 2.4%. However, certain figures have gone down – for example, theft of and from vehicles is down by 1.1% and burglary by 3.9%.

effective police service is a major public concern.[1] So the community will need to be assured that its police authorities and forces are making the best use of the resources available to fight and prevent crime in their areas. Best value, which aims to challenge inefficient, ineffective and uneconomic organisational orthodoxies, will play a vital role in this important area.

BEST VALUE AND THE POLICE SERVICE

14.3   Best value is an all purpose enabling tool to increase service quality and responsiveness to user needs within the public service. So (as with housing and other functions) it can readily be adapted to the particular service environment in question. In the case of the Police Service, the statutory infrastructure outlined in earlier chapters will apply, including DETR Circular 10/99 (the Guidance).[2] To assist with service customisation, on 26 November 1999, Richard Kornicki, Head of the Police Resources Unit at the Home Office, wrote to police authorities and chief police officers with two briefing notes on Best Value: *Best Value – the Police Authority Role*[3] (BVP1) and *Planning Logically*[4] (BVP2). These will be extremely useful to police authorities and forces in their planning for and implementation of best value and are considered below.[5]

The Statutory Position

14.4   By s 1(1)(d) of the LGA 1999,[6] a police authority is a best value authority for the purposes of Part I of that Act. By s 1(4) of the 1999 Act, a police authority is: one established under s 3 of the Police Act 1996; the Common Council of the City of London in its capacity as a police authority; and the Metropolitan Police Authority.

By s 6(1) of the Police Act 1996, every police authority established under s 3 of that Act is required to secure the maintenance of an efficient and effective police force for its area. In discharging its functions it must have regard (amongst other things) to 'any local policing plan issued by the authority under section 8'.[7]

---

1   The Conservative Party has also claimed that crime is rising, according to research it has
     carried out whereby it asked police forces for figures of total notifiable crime between
     1 April and 30 September 1999. Shadow Home Secretary, Ann Widdecombe was reported
     as saying that this survey indicated an increase of 5% compared with the same period last
     year. According to the Conservatives, crime has risen as follows in the following areas: West
     Midlands 26.6%, City of London 19.4%, Bedfordshire 14.5%, Metropolitan Police 14.1%,
     Surrey 10.3% (BBC News, 22 December 1999).
2   See para 3 of DETR Circular 10/99: 'This guidance ... also applies to police and single
     purpose fire authorities in England and Wales.'
3   Home Office, November 1999.
4   Ibid.
5   These documents can be viewed on the Police Resources Unit section of the Home Office
     Website at: http://www.homeoffice.gov.uk/ppd/pru/pru.htm.
6   Section 1(1)(d) of the LGA 1999 came into force in England and Wales on 10 August 1999
     under art 2(1) of the Local Government Act 1999 (Commencement No 1) Order 1999, SI
     1999/2169.
7   Police Act 1996, s 6(2)(d).

Section 7(1) of the Police Act 1996 (amongst other things) requires police authorities before the beginning of each financial year to 'determine objectives for the policing of the authority's area during that year'. Before doing so, authorities must consult the relevant chief constable and consider any views obtained by the authority in accordance with consultation arrangements made under s 96 of the 1996 Act.[1]

14.5 Under s 8(1) of the Police Act 1996, every police authority established under s 3 of that Act must annually, before the start of each financial year, 'issue a plan setting out the proposed arrangements for the policing of the authority's area during the year (the local policing plan)'. This must (amongst other things) 'include a statement of the authority's priorities for the year, of the financial resources expected to be available and of the proposed allocation of those resources'.[2] The plan must also particularise: any objectives determined by the Secretary of State under s 37 of the 1996 Act; any objectives determined by the police authority under s 7; any performance targets established by the police authority, whether in compliance with a direction of the Secretary of State under s 38 of the 1996 Act[3] or otherwise; and (pursuant to s 24(1) of the LGA 1999) 'any action proposed for the purpose of complying with the requirements of Part I of the Local Government Act 1999 (best value)'.

Planning Logically[4] (BVP2), referred to above, indicates that most annual policing plans result from joint working between police authorities and forces[5] and that such plans could also (amongst other things) contain the best value performance plan (BVPP). Since (as noted above) the local policing plan must include details of action proposed for the purpose of complying with the best value requirements of the LGA 1999,[6] this will effectively mean that the BVPP or an accurate summary reflecting the best value review programme will be part of the Annual Policing Plan.[7] Bearing in mind that s 10(2) of the Police Act 1996 requires chief constables to have regard to the policing plan in discharging functions, chief constables will also need to have regard to best value in so doing.

14.6 Police authorities are also required by s 9 of the Police Act 1996 as 'soon as possible after the end of each financial year' to 'issue a report relating to the policing of the authority's area for the year'.[8] This must 'include an assessment of the extent to which the local policing plan' issued under s 8 has been carried out.[9] The report must be published by the police authority 'in such manner as

1   See 'Consultation' below.
2   Police Act 1996, s 8(2), as amended by s 24(1) of the LGA 1999. Pursuant to art 3 of the Local Government Act 1999 (Commencement No 1) Order 1999, SI 1999/2169, s 24(1) of the LGA 1999 came into force in England and Wales on 27 September 1999.
3   Direction by the Secretary of State to police authorities to establish performance targets in respect of policing objectives for police authorities determined by the Secretary of State under s 37 of the Police Act 1996.
4   Home Office, November 1999.
5   Home Office, *Planning Logically* (November 1999), para 4.
6   Police Act 1996, s 8(2).
7   *Planning Logically*, para 7.
8   Police Act 1996, s 9(1).
9   Ibid, s 9(2).

appears to it to be appropriate' and copied to the Home Secretary.[1] Paragraph 20 of *Planning Logically* indicates that there will be 'some overlap between the police authority's Annual Report and the BVPP element of the Annual Policing Plan since BVPPs will have to look back at performance in the previous year'. Chief Constables are required by s 22 of the Police Act 1996 'as soon as possible after the end of each financial year' to 'submit to the police authority a general report on the policing during that year' for their force areas[2] which is to be 'published in such manner as appears to him to be appropriate'.[3]

Planning Logically indicates[4] that whilst most police authorities and forces issue their reports as separate documents 'some do issue them as two documents under the same cover' and at least 'one authority and force have decided to publish both reports together as a single document'. However, this is a matter for the individual authority and force, which may wish to keep the documents separate.[5]

14.7   Section 54 of the Police Act 1996 deals with the appointment and functions of inspectors of constabulary. These are appointed by the Queen on the determination of the Secretary of State with the consent of the Treasury. One of the appointees may be appointed as chief inspector of constabulary.[6] Inspectors of constabulary are already required[7] to 'inspect, and report to the Secretary of State on the efficiency and effectiveness of, every police force maintained for a police area'. Section 24(2)[8] of the LGA 1999 inserts a new s 54(2A) as follows:

> 'The inspectors of constabulary may inspect, and report to the Secretary of State on, a police authority's compliance with the requirements of Part I of the Local Government Act 1999 (Best Value).'

Section 55(1) of the Police Act 1996[9] (subject to considerations of safety or national security) requires the Secretary of State to arrange for the publication 'in such manner as appears to him to be appropriate' of any report received by him under s 54(2) (inspectors of constabulary to inspect, and report to the Secretary of State on the efficiency and effectiveness of, every police force) or s 54(2A) (power to inspect and report to the Secretary of State on police authority's compliance with the duty of best value).

---

1   Police Act 1996, s 9(3).
2   Ibid, s 22(1).
3   Ibid, s 22(2).
4   See para 23.
5   Ibid.
6   Police Act 1996, s 54(1).
7   See ibid, s 54(2).
8   Section 24(2) of the LGA 1999 came into force in England and Wales on 1 April 2000 – see art 4 of the Local Government Act 1999 (Commencement No 1) Order 1999, SI 1999/2169.
9   Section 55(1) of the Police Act 1996 is amended by s 24(3) of the LGA 1999. Section 24(3) of the LGA 1999 came into force in England and Wales on 1 April 2000 – see art 4 of the Local Government Act 1999 (Commencement No 1) Order 1999, SI 1999/2169.

APPLYING BEST VALUE TO THE POLICE SERVICE

14.8 *Best Value – the Police Authority Role*[1] (BVP1) indicates[2] that under 'the Local Government Act 1999, police authorities are responsible for securing Best Value in local policing services'. In 'doing so, they must consult widely with the community including local council tax and business ratepayers, and service users'. But police authorities will have to work in partnership with their forces since 'it is the force which will have to deliver Best Value policing'.[3] Nevertheless, 'ultimately the police authority is accountable to local people for ensuring that they get Best Value from their police service'.[4]

If best value represents a significant test of the police authority role, it also represents a real opportunity since it 'is police authorities who will have to set and drive forward the Best Value agenda locally'.[5] As noted above, the first best value performance plans should have been published by 31 March 2000.

Action for Police Authorities

14.9 BVP1 acknowledges[6] that most police authorities and forces have started planning for the new duty, many of the requirements of which are based on or similar to the existing statutory performance framework which has been operating since 1995. However, the Note also points out that whilst authorities and forces 'should therefore be able to build on their considerable experience of consultation, determining police priorities, target setting, planning and performance monitoring', equally best value 'will mean a step change in the way police authorities operate'. Consequently, authorities 'will need to be much more closely involved in reviewing the quality and effectiveness of every aspect of the performance of their forces'.[7]

One of the key features of the statutory best value framework is that there is no one way of achieving best value. It must always be up to the particular organisation 'to determine its own approach within the legal framework laid down in the Local Government Act 1999 and any statutory and non-statutory guidance'.[8] However, the Note seeks to identify some of the key issues which police authorities will need to address in the lead up to best value. As a starting point the Note suggests that authorities may find it helpful to ask themselves the following questions:

> '– Are all authority members and staff fully conversant with Best Value requirements – if not, what steps need to be taken to bring everyone up to speed?

---

1   As indicated above, this document is one of the two briefing notes accompanying the letter dated 26 November 1999 sent by Richard Kornicki, Head of Police Resources Unit at the Home Office, to police authorities and chief police officers.
2   At para 3.
3   *Best Value – the Police Authority Role*, para 4.
4   Ibid.
5   Ibid, para 5.
6   At para 6.
7   Ibid, para 6.
8   Ibid, para 7.

- How is the authority going to fulfil its Best Value responsibilities? What role will the authority play in key areas such as corporate review (if one is being undertaken); consultation; determining the programme of Best Value reviews; the conduct of individual reviews etc?
- Is there a need to review/adjust the authority's existing decision-making structures to deal with Best Value?
- Is the authority suitably equipped in terms of staffing and other support structures to deal with Best Value? Are there any gaps in existing skills and expertise which need to be supplemented? What training is needed for members and staff?
- Have the authority and Chief Constable discussed how they will work together to achieve Best Value? Is each clear about respective roles and responsibilities?
- Does the authority need to review its techniques for setting targets and its approach to monitoring performance and outcomes?'[1]

By the time best value formally got under way on 1 April 2000, authorities should have had these matters well in hand. However, they do provide a useful checklist of some of the foundation stones.

Working Arrangements and Resources

14.10   Police authorities will also need to make sure they have suitable working arrangements in place to deliver best value. These will, of course, be a matter for individual authorities. However, the Note points out that 'it is essential that whatever working methods are adopted, the authority is in a position to drive forward the best value agenda, in association with the Chief Constable'.[2] As part of this it will be important to ensure that the best value processes of both the authority and the force are properly integrated. 'Authority members and staff may be involved in force-level Best Value steering/working groups and vice versa, as already happens in a number of areas'.[3] It will also be necessary for authorities to ensure they commit appropriate dedicated resources to securing best value, so as to 'achieve a sensible balance between having the support they need to fulfil their responsibilities under Best Value and not replicating work being done in-force'.[4]

Consultation

14.11   Consultation is already part of the operational fabric of police authorities. For instance, s 96 of the Police Act 1996 requires police authorities (after having consulted the chief constable) to make arrangements to obtain the views of local people concerning the policing of the area and to obtain the co-operation of local people with the police in preventing crime in that area. The Crime and Disorder Act 1998 requires chief police officers and local authorities, in formulating their statutory strategy for the reduction of crime

---

1   *Best Value – the Police Authority Role*, para 8. The document points out that the APA (Association of Police Authorities) publication *Can You Manage It?* gives useful advice on this.
2   Ibid, para 9.
3   Ibid, para 11.
4   Ibid, para 13.

and disorder in the area, to obtain the views of persons or bodies in the area on a report of an analysis of a review carried out of the levels and patterns of crime and disorder in the area. The review itself must take 'due account of the knowledge and experience of persons in the area'.[1]

However, as para 15 of BVP1 points out: 'Best Value adds to those responsibilities by requiring police authorities to consult on priorities and service improvements with service users, local business and taxpayers and other partners and agencies'. So 'a strategic and co-ordinated approach to consultation is crucial'[2] and a review of consultation processes will be desirable to ensure that these are meeting the requirements of best value. The Note points out that 'in the light of the Macpherson report'[3] authorities may 'want to pay particular attention to ways of including "hard to reach" groups'. A 'Home Office research project is currently underway on consultation with hard to reach groups' a report from which 'should be available early in 2000'.[4]

A 'key principle of Best Value is that **local people should be the judge of the services they receive**'.[5] Therefore authorities will wish not only to ensure that their arrangements for community consultation include appropriate mechanisms for receiving feedback on public satisfaction with local policing services but also that they are examining 'the extent to which the outcomes of consultation feed into, and influence, service delivery both generally and in the context of individual Best Value reviews'.[6]

Review Programme

14.12 Best value reviews under s 5 of the LGA 1999 have been considered in some detail in Chapter 4. Exactly the same considerations apply to the Police Service. So, pursuant to art 6 of the Local Government (Best Value) Performance Plans and Reviews Order 1999,[7] in conducting its best value review, an authority must:

'(a) consider whether it should be exercising the function;
 (b) consider the level at which, and the way in which, it should be exercising the function;
 (c) consider its objectives in relation to the exercise of the function;
 (d) assess its performance in exercising the function by reference to any best value performance indicator specified for the function;
 (e) assess the competitiveness of its performance in exercising the function by reference to the exercise of the same function, or similar functions, by other best value authorities and by commercial and other businesses, including organisations in the voluntary sector;

---

1 See generally Crime and Disorder Act 1998, ss 5 and 6. See also *Guidance on Statutory Crime and Disorder Partnerships* under the Crime and Disorder Act 1998 (Home Office 1999). This can be viewed at http://www.homeoffice.gov.uk/cdact/actgch1.htm.
2 BVP1, para 16.
3 The Stephen Lawrence Inquiry: Report of an Inquiry by Sir William Macpherson of Cluny, advised by Tom Cook, the Right Rev Dr John Sentamu, Dr Richard Stone. (Presented to Parliament by the Secretary of State for the Home Department by Command of Her Majesty, February 1999.)
4 BVP1, para 17.
5 Ibid, para 18.
6 Ibid, paras 18 and 19.
7 SI 1999/3251.

(f) consult other best value authorities, commercial and other businesses, including organisations in the voluntary sector, about the exercise of the function;

(g) assess its success in meeting any best value performance standard which applies in relation to the function;

(h) assess its progress towards meeting any relevant best value performance standard which has been specified but which does not yet apply;

(i) assess its progress towards meeting any relevant best value performance target'.

All best value authorities must have conducted their first best value review of all functions by 31 March 2005.[1] Police authorities will need to determine in conjunction with their chief constables the approach to be taken to reviews, that is the order of reviews and whether services are to be examined functionally or thematically.[2] Authorities must also be able to 'satisfy themselves that the review processes are thorough, robust and delivering tangible improvements'.[3] A programme will need to be set for the five-year period 'including content, timing and mix' of reviews, a detailed programme for year 1 and 'a review of how the authority itself operates'.[4]

As to individual reviews, authorities will need to consider their role with care and a commonsense approach will be necessary.[5] Some aspects of reviews (for example, those which disclose individual case details) would not be appropriate for the involvement of individual members and in such circumstances other means of seeking assurance about review thoroughness should be used.[6] Since police authorities are 'uniquely placed to balance customer expectations and needs against holding down costs'[7] they will need to consider the reports and recommendations flowing from each review, agree what action needs to be taken and set improvement targets.[8] In addition: 'Authorities may wish to consider whether they need to have mechanisms in place to audit the effectiveness of the overall process on the conduct and resourcing of each review, the results of consultation and the degree of rigour and independence applied to each review topic'.[9]

The 4Cs

14.13 The 4Cs have been considered in detail in Chapter 4. However, para 28 of BVP1 sets out as follows the key role to be played by police authority members 'either as part of the review team or in considering the outcomes of the reviews':

> '**Challenge**: authority members' detachment from day to day involvement with the particular work area under review should mean that they are particularly well-placed to think innovatively and question whether things need to be done in a

---

1   See ibid, art 5.
2   *Best Value – the Police Authority Role* (BVP1), para 23.
3   Ibid.
4   Ibid, para 24.
5   Ibid, para 25.
6   Ibid.
7   Ibid, para 26.
8   Ibid.
9   Ibid, para 27.

particular way or at all. Authority members will also be able to bring to bear their knowledge of the importance placed on any given service by the public.

Consult: authorities will wish to ensure that any consultation carried out in relation to a particular review fits with their consultation strategy or is undertaken as an integral part of it. In particular, members will wish to be satisfied that the public's views as expressed through consultation are being properly taken into account in devising plans for action.

Compare: authority members have a key role to play in scrutinising and comparing the force's performance both with other forces and with other organisations. Members' backgrounds, experience and expertise in other fields may be particularly useful in this respect.

Compete: similarly, authority members should be well-positioned to ask difficult questions about whether better value can be obtained by providing a service in-house or externally. Authorities will wish to satisfy themselves that all sensible competitive options have been properly examined as part of the review process.'[1]

Throughout best value reviews, HMIC[2] would expect authorities and forces to be able to provide demonstrable evidence of how the 4Cs have been addressed. Some means of providing demonstrable evidence are set out in Appendix A to *Best Value: Briefing Notes for the Police Service, Audit and Inspection.*[3]

Benchmarking

14.14 BVP1 indicates that benchmarking and costing are two critical tools to be used in establishing whether best value is being achieved.[4] But the ability to cost activities is identified as being important for the assessment of progress towards best value. The capacity to do this 'varies across the country'. Consequently 'authorities will wish urgently to examine the extent to which their force has costing mechanisms in place and the plans for improving on this'.[5]

Authorities and forces are referred to the *Briefing Note on Benchmarking* which was issued by the Home Office with Richard Kornicki's letter dated 21 September 1999 to police authorities and chief police officers.[6] This analyses benchmarking (for the purpose of reviews) into 'numeric' and 'process' benchmarking. The former compares performance measures such as 'cost, quality and productivity' and the latter 'is a process of searching for, and achieving, excellent levels of performance'. The Benchmarking Note indicates that benchmarking will answer four fundamental questions:

(1) Where are we now?
(2) Where do we want to get to?
(3) How do we get there based on the experience of others?
(4) How do we know we have arrived where we wanted to be?'

---

1   *Best Value – the Police Authority Role* (BVPI), para 27.
2   Her Majesty's Inspectorate of Constabulary.
3   Home Office, *Best Value: Briefing Notes for the Police Service: Audit and Inspection: The Roles of HMIC and the Audit Commission* (21 September 1999) (see below).
4   *Best Value – The Police Authority Role*, para 29.
5   Ibid, para 31.
6   Ibid, para 30. This document can be viewed on the Home Office Website at: http://www.homeoffice.gov.uk/ppd/pru/bv4a.htm.

Amongst the uses to which benchmarking can be put are:

'(1)   Strategic benchmarking (Macro)
       This strategic process aims to establish the strengths and areas for improve-
       ment of business units. It is carried out on the basis of competitive analysis.
 (2)   Functional benchmarking
       The direct comparison of a function with other organisations which may not
       be police related.
 (3)   Operating benchmarking (Macro/micro)
       The review of operations to help establish targets, eg measurement of
       customer satisfaction.
 (4)   Process benchmarking (Micro)
       Provides detailed information on the structure and operational approach of
       any unit within the police service.'

14.15   According to the Benchmarking Note, benchmarking involves planning and organising, the collection and organisation of data as well as an
appropriate response to that analysis, and reviewing and improving performance. It is suggested that potential benchmarking 'targets' or partners can
include: internal units, external organisations, good or best practice and
benchmarking club partners.

Some lessons to be learned from the experience of public sector personnel
are highlighted:

'–   Benchmarking is sometimes used where other simpler techniques would be
      quicker, more effective and more appropriate, eg cause and effect, process
      mapping and value analysis.
 –   It can encourage people within an organisation to "run before they can walk"
      – [t]ime needs to be spent in planning and developing a systematic approach.
 –   Most things can be subject to benchmarking. It is therefore important to
      concentrate on the critical areas of best value services.
 –   To be effective, benchmarking must generate more than numbers.
 –   Pitch the level of the organisation/unit that you are comparing yourself with
      to one that is performing better.
 –   Do not unthinkingly copy other organisations/units. Adapt practices using
      your own strategy, mission statement or culture.
 –   Do not visit other organisations/units just to find out what they are doing.'

The only caveat the writer would place on the above concerns the final bullet
point, where the operative word is considered to be 'just'. It can be valuable to
find out what others are doing *provided* that something positive and demonstrable flows from that information.

Performance Plans

14.16   The content of best value performance plans[1] has been considered in
Chapter 5. The requirement in s 8 of the Police Act 1996 annually to produce a
local policing plan has been amended in a way which will enable the
performance plan to be included in the local policing plan. BVP1 indicates that
police authorities 'will also want to satisfy themselves that [there are]

---

1   The statutory base for best value performance plans is s 6 of the LGA 1999 and arts 3 and 4
    of the Local Government (Best Value) Performance Plans and Reviews Order 1999,
    SI 1999/3251.

appropriate and coherent links between local policing plans and the local crime and disorder strategies, local youth justice plans and the Best Value Performance Plans of other partners such as local authorities'.[1]

It will therefore be for individual authorities and forces to decide how the various planning requirements might link together. But the new duty of best value 'offers an opportunity to reconsider existing systems and ensure that the approach adopted ensures that information flows to the right people at the right time, and that the various plans and improvement targets are complementary to other plans and strategies'.[2] So, whatever approach is taken 'the Annual Policing Plan (which includes the Best Value Performance Plan) should become the vehicle into which the Ministerial Priorities, local Crime & Disorder Reduction strategies and the Efficiency Plan all come together.'[3] All the plans could therefore be published in April as a single document forming a statement of:

- how the authority and force has achieved last year's Best Value targets (from year two);
- what the authority and force intend to do in the coming year;
- how the authority and force intend to achieve the targets set;
- how much money is available to do this;
- how the money will be spent; and,
- what part of the organisation will be reviewed to ensure continuous improvement under Best Value.'[4]

14.17 *Planning Logically* indicates[5] that the Annual Policing Plan 'should also reflect any longer term strategies and the five year review programme as well as the overarching aims and objectives of the police service'. In turn, these could be combined to become a single strategic vision for the Force.[6] However, whatever approach is chosen 'the end result should be a properly co-ordinated approach which allows forces to reduce duplication in processes and costs for each of the different plans'.[7] So, for example, consultation could meet a variety

---

1   *Best Value – the Police Authority Role*, para 35
2   *Planning Logically*, para 25.
3   *Planning Logically*, para 26. This document indicates that: (i) the Home Secretary's Ministerial Priorities (under Police Act 1996, s 37) point to where authorities are expected to focus their development and effort. Annual Policing Plans set out how these priorities are being managed within each area; (ii) (at para 15) 'The Crime and Disorder Act 1998 puts a joint responsibility on police forces and local authorities to formulate Crime and Disorder Reduction Strategies. Police authorities, amongst others, are required to co-operate in the work to formulate these strategies'; (iii) (at para 11) since April 1999 an Efficiency Plan must be included in Annual Policing Plans setting out how the police authority intends to deliver the cumulative 2% efficiency target set by the Government's Comprehensive Spending Review (see *Comprehensive Spending Review: New Public Spending Plans 1999–2002* (Cm 4011, July 1998). Finally, para 13 of *Planning Logically* indicates that: 'The Overarching Aims and Objectives for the police service which were published in August 1998 provide the top down perspective for the Annual Policing Plan. The aims and objectives, together with the Guiding Principles, set out a joint vision of the purpose of policing linking to similar agreed perspectives for the whole criminal justice system. There is no legal requirement to include the Overarching Aims and Objectives in the Annual Policing Plan but clearly they should influence the whole document.'
4   *Planning Logically*, para 26.
5   See para 27.
6   Ibid.
7   Ibid.

of different purposes and 'joined-up thinking' could increase efficiency in other areas, such as budget planning since 'this links with the Annual Policing Plan, the efficiency plans and the Best Value local performance plans'.[1]

Planning Cycle

14.18   *Planning Logically* indicates that the two key dates in the planning cycle are:

–   28 February when the budget and precept is set (although the precept will be expected to be set some weeks earlier)
–   31 March when the Annual Policing Plan must be issued and the best value performance plan must be published.[2]

Audit and Inspection

14.19   This topic for best value authorities generally has been considered in Chapters 6 and 7. Specific to the police function, as noted above, s 24(2) of the LGA 1999 amends s 54 of the Police Act 1996 (which deals with inspectors of constabulary) to enable such inspectors to inspect and report to the Secretary of State on the compliance of a police authority with the best value requirements of Part I of the LGA 1999. Again, the Home Office Police Resource unit has issued guidance on audit and inspection[3] in this context and explains how the inspectors of constabulary (HMIC) will become involved in assisting local auditors in the audit process:[4]

> 'Broadly speaking, the division of responsibility between HMIC and the Audit Commission is that Commission-appointed auditors will check that the BVPP is informed by public consultation, contains comparative performance information, and sets out improvement targets that are realistic and challenging. Auditors will liaise with HMIC before finalising their report on the BVPP and submitting copies to the police authority and the Audit Commission. The auditor's report on the BVPP will be a public document. The auditor may recommend that the authority revise the BVPP to ensure compliance with statutory provision. In exceptional cases, the auditor may have such serious reservations about the BVPP, and the processes underpinning it, that a referral will be made to the Audit Commission or the Secretary of State.'[5]

So 'HMIC must ... be in a position to advise the external auditors, prior to certification, on the rigour which forces and police authorities have applied to the process'.[6]

14.20   As to process, HMIC 'will undertake analysis and limited inspection work'[7] between the publication of forces' plans and the publication of the audit report in June. To ensure consistency of process across forces, HMIC 'will apply

---

1   *Planning Logically*, para 29.
2   See para 33.
3   Home Office, *Best Value: Briefing Notes for the Police Service, Audit and Inspection: The Roles of HMIC and the Audit Commission* (21 September 1999).
4   Ibid, para 8.
5   Ibid, para 5.
6   Ibid, para 6.
7   Ibid, para 7.

a generic Best Value protocol' by means of a 'predominantly desk-based analysis, supplemented by a short visit to the authority/force between April and early June for reality checking'.[1] The Audit and Inspection Publication[2] indicates that 'reality checking' will take the following two forms:

'–   Between April and June each year, HMIC will test and confirm that the BVPP's main elements, (information on current service performance; targets for improvement; the extent and use of consultation etc), reflect reality and can be delivered. For example:

–   has the force the managerial capacity and commitment to secure improvement?

–   have resources been deployed in a way that will enable objectives to be achieved?

–   A second type of reality check will test whether customer perceptions of service delivery match claims made about performance. They will be carried out during both the annual assessment of the BVPP and during any subsequent inspection and will include:

–   detailed examination of processes used to learn about customer views (surveys, public focus groups, analysis of complaints, etc);

–   assessment of how the force analyses and uses such information, and action plans to improve services;

–   detailed examination of processes used to involve the public in Best Value reviews (public attitude surveys, focus groups, etc);

–   interviews with representatives of the users of policing services and organisations with whom the police work in partnership;

–   letters to representatives of key stakeholder groups;

–   interviews with police staff at all levels;

–   structured and unscheduled visits to police/public interface sites, e.g. station counters, control rooms and custody suites;

–   unscheduled visits to operational units and work shadowing.'

In carrying out the 'reality check' the Inspectorate will expect the police authority to provide evidence that:

'–   a corporate review[3] or similar has been undertaken (see Preparing for Best Value – the Corporate Review)

---

1   *Best Value: Briefing Notes for the Police Service, Audit and Inspection: The Roles of HMIC and the Audit Commission*, para 8.
2   See para 12.
3   Per para 13 of *Best Value: Briefing Notes for the Police Service, Audit and Inspection: The Roles of HMIC and the Audit Commission*, the Inspectorate will expect 'to find evidence that the Best Value regime is underpinned by a vision for the force and objectives set that are consistent with achieving it', that 'the approach to Best Value and the proposed methodology and programme for reviews are coherent and appropriate' and that 'the vision, objectives, approach to Best Value and selection of reviews has been determined through consultation and thorough research'. Per para 14 (ibid) a full corporate review may be necessary which would be expected to: establish a clear picture of the police force's strengths and weaknesses; review the vision for the police force; review and set practical corporate objectives for achieving the over-arching vision; involve the community in reviewing and setting overall priorities; consider future issues such as changes in statute or regulation; provide a clear link to the selection of best value reviews; demonstrate a clear understanding of the needs and aspirations of local people in terms of cost and quality of the services provided and the future priorities.

- the corporate review has identified strengths and weaknesses of the organisation;
- the selection of services for Best Value Review has been based on appropriate criteria;
- the performance data in the plan is accurate;
- there are mechanisms in place to ensure that targets are set at an appropriate level ie challenging but realistic;
- the schedule for the Best Value Reviews is appropriate and has been determined using an appropriate methodology; and
- effective community consultation has taken place and that there is a clear link between the community consultation and the selection of services for Best Value reviews.'[1]

The Home Office points out that since the 'customer view is paramount' 'reality checks will be a core feature of the inspection/audit approach'.[2]

14.21   The Home Office Audit and Inspection Note indicates[3] that from April 2000, best value inspections will form part of the HMIC inspection programme which will then be based on need and risk assessment. Each summer, 'following the BVPP audit process and the availability of the latest performance data, HMIC will undertake a risk assessment of all forces to determine the schedule for subsequent inspections'.[4] There will be a number of inspection triggers including 'poor overall performance and specific incidents that cause concern'.[5] Amongst these will be 'a serious failure to comply with BVPP requirements as assessed during the audit process'.[6] The audit process will also 'link into the risk assessment and provide the trigger for Best Value inspections undertaken by HMIC later in the year'.[7] The Note indicates that the purpose of a best value inspection is to 'validate the rigour and challenging nature' of authority best value reviews.[8] Inspections will include: further reality checks, a full evaluation of the best value review which has been undertaken[9] and an examination of the authority's management of best value as a whole.[10]

As mentioned above, the Inspectorate will expect 'to find evidence that the Best Value regime is underpinned by a vision for the force and objectives set that are consistent with achieving it',[11] which may necessitate a full corporate review.[12]

Whether or not there has been a corporate review, the Inspectorate will expect a police authority to be able to demonstrate that:

---

1   *Best Value: Briefing Notes for the Police Service, Audit and Inspection*, para 8.
2   Ibid, para 19.
3   Ibid, para 9.
4   Ibid.
5   Ibid.
6   Ibid, para 10.
7   Ibid.
8   Ibid, para 11.
9   Ibid, per para 17: 'HMIC will expect police authorities to be able to evidence their answers to the following: What criteria determined the choice of a Best Value Review carried out? What is the involvement of the police authority in the review? What is the composition of the review team? What methodology was used for the review? How did the Review address the 4Cs ie challenge, compare, compete and consult?'
10   Ibid, para 11.
11   Ibid, para 13.
12   See footnote 3 on page 269 above.

'– the authority has undertaken thorough community consultation;

– the overall vision and strategic objectives reflect the priorities of local people and service users;

– the authority's overall vision is available in a publicly accessible form;

– the authority has determined the approach that it will adopt for the implementation of Best Value;

– the authority has a performance management framework in place to enable the measurement of continuous improvement;

– the authority has an appropriate methodology in place for measuring the strengths and weaknesses of all the services it provides in a rigorous and objective way;

– the authority has set out a clear programme for reviewing all of the services that it provides over a five year period;

– the programme of reviews was determined using a clear methodology which prioritised those services for early review on the basis of appropriate criteria such as: cost, quality, user satisfaction, performance.'[1]

14.22   For each subsequent year, the Inspectorate will expect to see 'demonstrable evidence that the corporate review or other methods for providing the under-pinning of the Best Value process have been revisited and updated where appropriate'.[2] There should also be processes in place for determining when a full corporate review is necessary.[3]

Inspections will also examine overall management of best value, and in particular: best value leadership, the involvement of the police authority in best value, and how the implementation of action plans following best value reviews is managed.[4]

14.23   The scope of inspection is to widen and deepen, for on 14 February 2000 the Home Secretary, Jack Straw, announced a new 'five-year strategy to cut crime and measure police performance'.[5] From April 2000, 'all police authorities will include challenging crime reduction targets[6] in their Best Value Performance Plans, aiming to cut domestic burglary and vehicle crime rates at a local level'.[7] In addition 'five large metropolitan authorities (... Greater Manchester, Merseyside, West Midlands and West Yorkshire) which account for 70% of all robberies, will set targets to cut robbery.'[8] The Government hopes that if these targets can be delivered, at national level vehicle crime will be cut by 30% and domestic burglary by 26%. Whilst HMIC has previously inspected at force level, inspection was announced to commence also at Basic Command Unit (BCU) level as from April 2000. Jack Straw said that:

'Inspections will also be carried out at BCU level as well as force level by HMIC who will be working with the Audit Commission, and about 50 police divisions, to identify the critical success factors that make for a good police division. From April 2001, HMIC hope to extend this to all 320 BCUs ... Tackling crime and disorder is

---

1   *Best Value: Briefing Notes for the Police Service, Audit and Inspection*, para 15.
2   Ibid, para 16.
3   Ibid.
4   Ibid, para 18.
5   Home Office Press Release, 14 February 2000.
6   Copies of the provisional targets for each authority are available from the Home Office and were also placed in the House of Commons Library on 14 February 2000.
7   Home Office Press Release, 14 February 2000.
8   Ibid.

at the heart of the Government's commitment to build a better Britain. By modernising the system and raising performance we can make a real difference in the fight against crime and disorder.'[1]

Performance Indicators

14.24 This area has been examined in Chapter 3 above. In addition, on 8 February 2000, the Home Office wrote to Chief Police Officers and Clerks to Police Authorities (with a copy to Police Authority Chairs) with 'some further non-statutory guidance on the BVPIs,[2] their definitions and issues around data collection'. Whilst all 'the actual indicators have remained the same', since the publication of the performance indicators on 22 December 1999, the Home Office has 'received a large number of queries from forces and authorities seeking clarification on particular points' which the tabular guidance is intended to answer.[3]

Beacon Scheme for the Police Service

14.25 The general scheme has also been mentioned in Chapter 3. However, in respect of the Police Service, on 7 June 1999, the Home Secretary, Jack Straw, wrote to Chief Police Officers and Clerks to Police Authorities (with copies to the Association of Chief Police Officers,[4] the Association of Police Authorities[5] and all Chairs of police authorities) with an invitation to 'police forces and authorities jointly to bid against a £1 million "challenge fund" in 1999/2000 for projects to improve efficiency'. The letter also indicated that the 'challenge fund will be combined with a requirement to disseminate best practice, forming a "beacon" scheme for the police service along the lines of that introduced by the Department of the Environment, Transport and the Regions for local councils'. Although the deadline for applications expired on 9 July 1999, the Prospectus[6] gives a useful insight into the nature of the scheme. For example, the:

> 'criteria for all efficiency projects under the police beacon scheme are:
>
> – they should be likely to produce results capable of being usefully disseminated to other forces and to other BCUs to spread best practice;
> – gains are not to be made by cuts in delivery of frontline policing or at the expense of partnership working;
> – they should be completed briskly – and in any case by no later than 29 February 2000 – so that the results can be evaluated and disseminated to other police forces and police authorities to complement the introduction of Best Value in April 2000.'

Also:

> 'Ideally projects should meet at least one of the following conditions:

---

1   Home Office Press Release, 14 February 2000.
2   Best value performance indicators.
3   This guidance can be viewed at http://www.homeoffice.gov.uk/ppd/pru/guidance.htm.
4   25 Victoria Street, London SW1H 0EX, tel 0207 227 3400.
5   Local Government House, Smith Square, London SW1P 3 HZ.
6   This can be viewed on http://www.homeoffice.gov.uk/ppd/pru/beaconp.doc.

– they encourage innovation beyond the areas set out for efficiency gains in the efficiency guidance issued by the Home Secretary on 4 November 1998;
– they are focused at local level (BCU or more locally);
– they focus on and deliver savings or gains for the benefit of frontline policing'.[1]

Intervention

14.26 Intervention in general has been dealt with in Chapter 8. Mirroring the Protocol on Intervention Powers,[2] a protocol as to how intervention powers will be used has also been agreed between the Home Office, the Association of Police Authorities and the Association of Chief Police Officers. This is entitled *Home Office/Police Service: Protocol on Intervention Powers*. It covers similar ground to the DETR Protocol (although with adaptations to meet the specific service and statutory context) and was circulated to police authorities and chief officers on 2 November, under cover of a letter from Richard Kornicki, Head of the Police Resources Unit at the Home Office.

Paragraph 3 of the *Protocol* gives a useful summary of the police best value context:

'The Best Value legislation requires police authorities to secure continuous improvement in the economy, efficiency and effectiveness of local policing services. It is the responsibility of the police authority to set clear standards and targets for these services in the local policing plan and local performance plan. Chief constables [which term for these purposes includes the Commissioner of the Metropolitan Police and the Commissioner of the City of London police] ... are responsible for the day to day direction and control of policing. They should address the need to deliver continuous improvement in the economy, efficiency and effectiveness of local policing services when drafting the local policing plan and local performance plan. As now, both police authorities and chief constables must have proper regard to cost and quality in delivering local policing services.'

Further Guidance

14.27 The Association of Police Authorities[3] has issued specific guidance and support for police authorities on their best value role.

CONCLUSION

14.28 So (as with all other public services) there is much to be done to improve accountability and the classic 3 'E's of economy, efficiency and effectiveness. Changing to a *service* rather than an autocratic mindset can be challenging for all public services, where it has often been service providers rather than consumers who have 'called the shots'.

Although the Sergeant in *The Pirates of Penzance*,[4] bemoaned that:

---

1   Beacon Scheme for the Police Service: Prospectus.
2   DETR, September 1999 (reproduced in Annex D to DETR Circular 10/99).
3   Local Government House, Smith Square, London SW1P 3HZ.
4   1879 – libretto by W S Gilbert.

'When constabulary duty's to be done –
　　　　　　To be done,
The policeman's lot is not a happy one ...'

the duty of best value was not then in contemplation. Nowadays, if approached in the right way, best value should not make anyone's lot unhappy. So police authorities and forces will need to ensure that those at the sharp end who will be turning best value into reality are suitably engaged with the whole process[1] – for movement without motivation can signify a runaway train.

1　See Chapter 4 above, where Wendy Thomson, former Chief Executive of Newham LBC (at the time of writing, Director of Inspection at the Audit Commission), is quoted as indicating that Newham's first year of best value as a pilot was 'very challenging but also exciting and fun'. Clearly, unless the entire organisation is motivated and engaged it will be impossible to make best value happen in any meaningful way.

Chapter 15

THE CROCK OF GOLD – FUTURE THOUGHTS

INTRODUCTION

15.1 'Tomorrow', advises the proverb, 'never comes'. But if the future is the anticipated unexpired span of our individual and collective lives, most of us are likely to have a place in at least part of it, since the future unfolds by the second. So assuming the future has a future, we all need to be doing what we can to make it a good place to be.

Although Confucius[1] advised us to 'Study the past, if you would divine the future',[2] what is to come rarely takes precisely the shape we expect. For each new subjective experience aggregates and amplifies to alter objective reality. And if the world is no more than how each of us and all of us sees it, the world must ever be changing, since it is seen ever anew. So change is the only constant.

BEST VALUE IN THE FUTURE

15.2 But on a practical level we do need to learn from our past mistakes if we are to enable future improvement. And best value, of course, demands *continuous* improvement. We also need to be perennially sensitive to change (and the need for it) externally, in ourselves (and what we do and fail to do) as well as in the ambit of our control and influence. So as the perception of what has been and what is to be merges as always into the instantly perceived moment, here are some thoughts about the shape of best value in the future:

- Local government needs to make sure that it is (or becomes) and remains an indispensable part of people's lives. It will be assisted in this by the proposed new powers for authorities to do anything likely to achieve the promotion or improvement of local economic, social and environmental well-being.[3] Local government will need to be ready to embrace the new possibilities opened up by these powers. For its wings have been strapped back for so long, some may have forgotten it can fly. Local government must become fast and flexible and abandon any ponderous ways.

---

1   551–479 BC.
2   *Analects.*
3   See the Local Government Bill 1999, introduced in the House of Lords on 25 November 1999.

- Local government will have a future only if it does this and commands the confidence of those who pay for it and for whom it exists. It must therefore be able to adapt to changing perceptions, needs and expectations. If it will not seize the initiative then others will.

- Providing local government achieves these things, public participation and engagement will be an increasing demand as more and more people become involved and see this as mainstream rather than a patronising and meaningless concession. Authorities will need to plan and programme their functions and activities accordingly.

- Listening to the public is a voyage of discovery for which only the adventurous and adaptable need apply. For listeners are likely to hear what they would rather not. This can upset ordered perceptions of the world; but listening has the potential to make that world a better place – provided the listener is prepared to change within and without.

- Enhanced democratic participation should not mean local abdication. For government is there to lead, inspire, enable and of course govern.[1] More democracy should mean better rather than negative government. This does not simply mean taking soundings and going with the majority view. Government and leadership can involve unpopular decisions for the greater good.

- Members and officers will have to adapt to ever new roles to meet the changing environment. Change has been charted by the Local Government Bill 1999;[2] but it will not stop there. What will be the position of officers as executive members become ever more executive? Will there be fewer but better qualified and remunerated members? How can membership of a local authority be made compatible with a career and/or family and domestic responsibilities? How can membership be opened up to a more representative selection of the community? Are local politics a constraint upon local democracy?

- New executive freedoms will need to be balanced by robust responsibility and accountability. For liberation of thought does not mean unbridled licence and care must be taken to maintain proper stewardship of public resources.

- Local authority employees need to be and feel fully and properly engaged and to have a real stake in the authority and its business. They will need to be empowered to make a difference in their ambit of control and influence and appropriately to alter their working patterns and environment to facilitate, promote and enhance best value.

- Also, local authority employees will need new status and remuneration structures. For under best value (with its joined-up output focus) the sun will (if it has not already) set upon territorial empire building with its traditional reward emphasis upon how many infantry there are fighting under a particular chief officer's flag.

---

1   Amongst the definitions offered by *The Chambers Dictionary* (1998) are: 'To direct; to control; to rule with authority; to determine'. However, firm but inclusive leadership will clearly need to be conducted within a modern social context if it is to gain ownership and acceptance from those for whom it is applied.

2   See above.

- best value is already urging authorities to 'plan positively for diversity'.[1] 'Cold war' barriers between public, private and voluntary sectors are already breaking down. Residual suspicions will need to disappear as the best way of achieving objectives for the benefit of communities rather than the means of their achievement becomes the prime local focus.
- Local authorities, their members and staff will need to have with them on their flight to the future:
    - an energetic and positive outlook
    - an open mind
    - a focus on what is to be achieved
    - a passion for doing and making things better.
- However, accountability processes will need to be structured so that the creativity and enthusiasm needed by those who have to deliver best value is not extinguished. The Government has a responsibility here (in partnership with best value authorities) as the regime unfolds.

CONCLUSION

15.3 Best value can be seen as the crock of gold at the end of the rainbow which will be eternally travelled towards but never captured. For there can be no perfection in an imperfect world; and if *best* value were ever to be achieved, this would negate the future continuous improvement which is at the heart of the concept. If best value is a journey rather than a destination, it must bring increasingly *better* value at each step of the way.

Robert Louis Stevenson[2] once advised us that 'To travel hopefully is a better thing than to arrive, and the true success is to labour.'[3] If this is so, best value is likely to yield much success and many well-travelled local authority labourers. Bon voyage!

---

1   DETR Circular 10/99 (14 December 1999), para 10.
2   1850–1894.
3   *Virginibus Puerisque* (1881), Chap VI, El Dorado.

Appendices

CONTENTS

Appendix 1

LOCAL GOVERNMENT ACT 1999, PART I

An Act to make provision imposing on local and certain other authorities requirements relating to economy, efficiency and effectiveness; and to make provision for the regulation of council tax and precepts. [27th July 1999]

PART I

BEST VALUE

Best value authorities

Duties

Audit of best value performance plans

Best value inspections

Exercise of functions by best value authorities

PART I

BEST VALUE

Best value authorities

1   Best value authorities

(1) For the purposes of this Part each of these is a best value authority –

  (a) a local authority;
  (b) a National Park authority;
  (c) the Broads Authority;
  (d) a police authority;
  (e) a fire authority constituted by a combination scheme and a metropolitan county fire and civil defence authority;
  (f) the London Fire and Emergency Planning Authority;
  (g) a waste disposal authority;
  (h) a metropolitan county passenger transport authority;
  (i) Transport for London;
  (j) the London Development Agency;

(2) In relation to England 'local authority' in subsection (1)(a) means –

  (a) a county council, a district council, a London borough council, a parish council or a parish meeting of a parish which does not have a separate parish council;
  (b) the Council of the Isles of Scilly;
  (c) the Common Council of the City of London in its capacity as a local authority;
  (d) the Greater London Authority so far as it exercises its functions through the Mayor.

(3) In relation to Wales 'local authority' in subsection (1)(a) means a county council, a county borough council or a community council.

(4) In subsection (1)(d) 'police authority' means –

  (a) a police authority established under section 3 of the Police Act 1996;
  (b) the Common Council of the City of London in its capacity as a police authority;

  (c) the Metropolitan Police Authority.

(5) In subsection (1)(g) 'waste disposal authority' means an authority which –

  (a) is a waste disposal authority for the purposes of Part II of the Environmental Protection Act 1990, or
  (b) is established under section 10 of the Local Government Act 1985 (joint arrangements).

2 Power to extend or disapply

(1) The Secretary of State may by order provide that any of the authorities and bodies mentioned in subsection (2) is a best value authority for the purposes of this Part.

(2) The authorities and bodies are –

  (a) a local precepting authority within the meaning of section 39(2) of the Local Government Finance Act 1992;
  (b) a levying body within the meaning of section 74(1) of the Local Government Finance Act 1988;
  (c) a body to which section 75 of that Act applies (special levies).

(3) An order under subsection (1) providing for an authority or body to be a best value authority may provide for section 7 to have effect in relation to that authority or body with specified modifications.

(4) The Secretary of State may by order provide for the Greater London Authority to be a best value authority for the purposes of this Part in relation to –

  (a) specified functions of the Authority which it does not exercise through the Mayor;
  (b) specified functions which are not functions of the Authority but are functions of another best value authority;

and an order may provide for this Part to have effect in relation to those functions with specified modifications.

(5) The Secretary of State may by order provide that a best value authority specified, or of a description specified, in the order is not to be subject, in relation to such functions as may be specified, to a duty –

  (a) which is specified in the order, and
  (b) to which the authority would otherwise be subject under this Part.

(6) No order shall be made under this section unless a draft has been laid before, and approved by resolution of, each House of Parliament.

Duties

3 The general duty

(1) A best value authority must make arrangements to secure continuous improvement in the way in which its functions are exercised, having regard to a combination of economy, efficiency and effectiveness.

(2) For the purpose of deciding how to fulfil the duty arising under subsection (1) an authority must consult –

    (a) representatives of persons liable to pay any tax, precept or levy to or in respect of the authority,

    (b) representatives of persons liable to pay non-domestic rates in respect of any area within which the authority carries out functions,

    (c) representatives of persons who use or are likely to use services provided by the authority, and

    (d) representatives of persons appearing to the authority to have an interest in any area within which the authority carries out functions.

(3) For the purposes of subsection (2) 'representatives' in relation to a group of persons means persons who appear to the authority to be representative of that group.

(4) In deciding on –

    (a) the persons to be consulted, and

    (b) the form, content and timing of consultations,

an authority must have regard to any guidance issued by the Secretary of State.

4   Performance indicators and standards

(1) The Secretary of State may by order specify –

    (a) factors ('performance indicators') by reference to which a best value authority's performance in exercising functions can be measured;

    (b) standards ('performance standards') to be met by best value authorities in relation to performance indicators specified under paragraph (a).

(2) An order may specify different performance indicators or standards –

    (a) for different functions;

    (b) for different authorities;

    (c) to apply at different times.

(3) Before specifying performance indicators or standards the Secretary of State shall consult –

    (a) persons appearing to him to represent the best value authorities concerned, and

    (b) such other persons (if any) as he thinks fit.

(4) In specifying performance indicators and standards, and in deciding whether to do so, the Secretary of State –

    (a) shall aim to promote improvement of the way in which the functions of best value authorities are exercised, having regard to a combination of economy, efficiency and effectiveness, and

    (b) shall have regard to any recommendations made to him by the Audit Commission.

(5) In exercising a function a best value authority must meet any applicable performance standard specified under subsection (1)(b).

5   Best value reviews

(1) A best value authority must conduct best value reviews of its functions in accordance with the provisions of any order made under this section.

(2) The Secretary of State may by order specify a period within which an authority is to review all its functions, and an order may –

    (a) apply to one authority or more;

    (b) make different provision in relation to different authorities;

    (c) require specified functions to be reviewed in specified financial years.

(3) In conducting a review an authority –

    (a) shall aim to improve the way in which its functions are exercised, having regard to a combination of economy, efficiency and effectiveness, and

    (b) shall have regard to any guidance issued by the Secretary of State under this section.

(4) The Secretary of State may by order specify matters which an authority must include in a review of a function under this section; and in particular an order may require an authority –

    (a) to consider whether it should be exercising the function;

    (b) to consider the level at which and the way in which it should be exercising the function;

    (c) to consider its objectives in relation to the exercise of the function;

    (d) to assess its performance in exercising the function by reference to any performance indicator specified for the function under section 4 or under subsection (6)(a) below;

    (e) to assess the competitiveness of its performance in exercising the function by reference to the exercise of the same function, or similar functions, by other best value authorities and by commercial and other businesses;

    (f) to consult other best value authorities and commercial and other businesses about the exercise of the function;

    (g) to assess its success in meeting any performance standard which applies in relation to the function;

    (h) to assess its progress towards meeting any relevant performance standard which has been specified but which does not yet apply;

    (i) to assess its progress towards meeting any relevant performance target set under subsection (6)(b).

(5) The Secretary of State may issue guidance on –

    (a) the timetable for a review;

    (b) the procedure for a review;

    (c) the form in which a review should be recorded;

    (d) the content of a review.

(6) In particular, guidance may state that an authority should –

    (a) specify performance indicators in relation to functions;

    (b) set targets for the performance of functions ('performance targets') by reference to performance indicators specified under section 4 or under paragraph (a);

    (c) set a plan of action to be taken for the purposes of meeting a performance target.

(7) Guidance may state the matters which should be taken into account in setting performance targets; and these may include the range of performances expected to be attained by best value authorities.

6   Best value performance plans

(1) A best value authority must prepare a best value performance plan for each financial year in accordance with any order made or guidance issued under this section.

(2) The Secretary of State may by order specify matters which an authority must include in a plan for a financial year; and in particular an order may require an authority –

    (a) to summarise the authority's objectives in relation to the exercise of its functions;
    (b) to summarise any assessment made by the authority of the level at which and the way in which it exercises its functions;
    (c) to state any period within which the authority is required to review its functions under section 5;
    (d) to state the timetable the authority proposes to follow in conducting a review;
    (e) to state any performance indicators, standards and targets specified or set in relation to the authority's functions;
    (f) to summarise the authority's assessment of its performance in the previous financial year with regard to performance indicators;
    (g) to compare that performance with the authority's performance in previous financial years or with the performance of other best value authorities;
    (h) to summarise its assessment of its success in meeting any performance standard which applied at any time in the previous financial year;
    (i) to summarise its assessment of its progress towards meeting any performance standard which has been specified but which does not yet apply;
    (j) to summarise its assessment of its progress towards meeting any performance target;
    (k) to summarise any plan of action to be taken in the financial year to which the plan relates for the purposes of meeting a performance target;
    (l) to summarise the basis on which any performance target was set, and any plan of action was determined, in relation to a function reviewed under section 5 in the previous financial year.

(3) An authority must publish its plan for a financial year before –

    (a) 31st March of the previous financial year, or
    (b) such other date as the Secretary of State may specify by order.

(4) The Secretary of State may issue guidance on the form and content of plans and the manner in which they should be published.

Audit of best value performance plans

7   Audit

(1) A performance plan published by a best value authority for a financial year under section 6 shall be audited by the authority's auditor.

(2) An audit of a performance plan is an inspection for the purpose of establishing whether the plan was prepared and published in accordance with section 6 and any order or guidance under that section.

(3) Subsections (1), (2) and (4) to (7) of section 6 of the Audit Commission Act 1998 (auditor's right to documents and information) shall have effect in relation to an

auditor's functions under this Part as they have effect in relation to his functions under that Act.

(4) In relation to an authority's performance plan the auditor shall issue a report –

(a) certifying that he has audited the plan,

(b) stating whether he believes that it was prepared and published in accordance with section 6 and any order or guidance under that section,

(c) if appropriate, recommending how it should be amended so as to accord with section 6 and any order or guidance under that section,

(d) if appropriate, recommending procedures to be followed by the authority in relation to the plan,

(e) recommending whether the Audit Commission should carry out a best value inspection of the authority under section 10, and

(f) recommending whether the Secretary of State should give a direction under section 15.

(5) An auditor shall send a copy of his report relating to an authority's performance plan –

(a) to the authority,

(b) to the Audit Commission, and

(c) if the report recommends that the Secretary of State give a direction under section 15, to the Secretary of State.

(6) Copies of a report shall be sent in accordance with subsection (5) –

(a) by 30th June of the financial year to which the relevant performance plan relates, or

(b) by such other date as the Secretary of State may specify by order.

(7) Subject to subsection (8), the reference in subsection (1) to an authority's auditor is, in respect of a financial year, a reference to the auditor or auditors appointed to audit the authority's accounts for the previous financial year.

(8) If a person who would by virtue of subsection (7) be an authority's auditor in respect of a financial year or one of an authority's auditors in respect of a financial year –

(a) is no longer eligible for appointment under section 3 of the Audit Commission Act 1998, or

(b) is not willing to act,

the reference in subsection (1) to the authority's auditor is, in respect of that financial year, a reference to an auditor or auditors appointed by the Audit Commission.

(9) Section 3 of the 1998 Act shall apply to an appointment under subsection (8) as if it were an appointment of a person to audit the authority's accounts under section 2(1) of the 1998 Act.

8   Code of practice and fees

(1) An auditor carrying out an audit under section 7 shall have regard to any code of practice under this section.

(2) The Commission shall prepare, and keep under review, a code of practice prescribing the way in which auditors are to carry out their functions under section 7.

(3) Section 4(3) to (6) of the Audit Commission Act 1998 (code of audit practice) shall have effect in relation to a code of practice under this section.

(4) The Audit Commission shall prescribe a scale or scales of fees in respect of the audit of performance plans which are required to be audited in accordance with this Part.

(5) Section 7(3) to (8) of the Audit Commission Act 1998 (fees for audit) (read with section 52(1) and (3) of that Act (orders and regulations)) shall have effect in relation to fees under subsection (4).

(6) Before preparing or altering a code under subsection (2) or prescribing a scale of fees under subsection (4) the Commission shall consult –

   (a) the Secretary of State, and
   (b) persons appearing to the Commission to represent best value authorities.

(7) Before making any regulations under section 7(8) of the Audit Commission Act 1998 as it has effect in relation to fees under subsection (4) the Secretary of State shall consult –

   (a) the Commission, and
   (b) persons appearing to the Secretary of State to represent best value authorities.

9   Response to audit

(1) A best value authority shall publish any report received in accordance with section 7(5)(a).

(2) The following subsections apply where a best value authority receives a report under subsection (4) of section 7 which contains a recommendation under any of paragraphs (c) to (f) of that subsection.

(3) the authority shall prepare a statement of –

   (a) any action which it proposes to take as a result of the report, and
   (b) its proposed timetable.

(4) A statement required by subsection (3) shall be prepared –

   (a) before the end of the period of 30 working days starting with the day on which the authority receives the report, or
   (b) if the report specifies a shorter period starting with that day, before the end of that period.

(5) The authority shall incorporate the statement in its next best value performance plan.

(6) If the statement relates to a report which recommends that the Secretary of State give a direction under section 15, the authority shall send a copy of the statement to the Secretary of State –

   (a) before the end of the period of 30 working days starting with the day on which the authority receives the report, or
   (b) if the report specifies a shorter period starting with that day, before the end of that period.

(7) For the purposes of this section a working day is a day other than –

   (a) a Saturday or a Sunday,

(b) Christmas Day or Good Friday, or

(c) a day which is a bank holiday under the Banking and Financial Dealings Act 1971 in England and Wales.

Best value inspections

10 Inspections

(1) The Audit Commission may carry out an inspection of a best value authority's compliance with the requirements of this Part.

(2) If the Secretary of State directs the Commission to carry out an inspection of a specified best value authority's compliance with the requirements of this Part in relation to specified functions, the Commission shall comply with the direction.

(3) Before giving a direction under subsection (2) the Secretary of State shall consult the Commission.

(4) In carrying out an inspection, and in deciding whether to do so, the Commission shall have regard to –

(a) any relevant recommendation under section 7(4)(e), and

(b) any guidance issued by the Secretary of State.

11 Inspectors' powers and duties

(1) An inspector has a right of access at all reasonable times –

(a) to any premises of the best value authority concerned, and

(b) to any document relating to the authority which appears to him to be necessary for the purposes of the inspection.

(2) An inspector –

(a) may require a person holding or accountable for any such document to give him such information and explanation as he thinks necessary, and

(b) may require that person to attend before him in person to give the information or explanation or to produce the document.

(3) A best value authority shall provide an inspector with every facility and all information which he may reasonably require for the purposes of the inspection.

(4) An inspector shall –

(a) give three clear days' notice of any requirement under this section, and

(b) must, if so required, produce documents identifying himself.

(5) A person who without reasonable excuse fails to comply with a requirement of an inspector under this section is guilty of an offence and liable on summary conviction to a fine not exceeding level 3 on the standard scale.

(6) Any expenses incurred by an inspector in connection with proceedings for an offence under subsection (5) alleged to have been committed in relation to an inspection of a best value authority are, so far as not recovered from any other source, recoverable from the authority.

(7) In this section 'inspector' means an officer, servant or agent of the Audit Commission carrying out an inspection under section 10.

12 Fees

(1) The Audit Commission shall prescribe a scale or scales of fees in respect of inspections carried out under section 10.

(2) An authority inspected under section 10 shall, subject to subsection (3), pay to the Commission the fee applicable to the inspection in accordance with the appropriate scale.

(3) If it appears to the Commission that the work involved in a particular inspection was substantially more or less than that envisaged by the appropriate scale, the Commission may charge a fee which is larger or smaller than that referred to in subsection (2).

(4) Before prescribing a scale of fees under this section the Commission shall consult –

(a) the Secretary of State, and
(b) persons appearing to the Commission to represent best value authorities.

13 Reports

(1) Where the Audit Commission has carried out an inspection of an authority under section 10 it shall issue a report.

(2) A report –

(a) shall mention any matter in respect of which the Commission believes as a result of the inspection that the authority is failing to comply with the requirements of this Part, and
(b) may, if it mentions a matter under paragraph (a), recommend that the Secretary of State give a direction under section 15.

(3) The Commission –

(a) shall send a copy of a report to the authority concerned, and
(b) may publish a report and any information in respect of a report.

(4) If a report recommends that the Secretary of State give a direction under section 15, the Commission shall as soon as reasonably practicable –

(a) arrange for the recommendation to be published, and
(b) send a copy of the report to the Secretary of State.

(5) If a report states that the Commission believes as a result of an inspection that an authority is failing to comply with the requirements of this Part, the next performance plan prepared by the authority under section 6 must record –

(a) that fact, and
(b) any action taken by the authority as a result of the report.

14 Inspections: housing benefit and council tax benefit

(1) The following shall be substituted for section 139A(1) and (2) of the Social Security Administration Act 1992 (reports on administration of housing benefit and council tax benefit) –

'(1) The Secretary of State may authorise persons to consider and report to him on the administration by authorities of housing benefit and council tax benefit.

(2) The Secretary of State may ask persons authorised under subsection (1) to consider in particular –

(a) authorities' performance in the prevention and detection of fraud relating to housing benefit and council tax benefit;
(b) authorities' compliance with the requirements of Part I of the Local Government Act 1999 (best value).

(2A) A person may be authorised under subsection (1) –

(a) on such terms and for such period as the Secretary of State thinks fit;
(b) to act generally or in relation to a specified authority or authorities;
(c) to report on administration generally or on specified matters.'

(2) In section 139C(1) of that Act (reports) for the words from 'in particular' to the end there shall be substituted 'in particular –

(a) in the prevention and detection of fraud relating to benefit, or
(b) for the purposes of complying with the requirements of Part I of the Local Government Act 1999 (best value).'

15 Secretary of State's powers

(1) This section applies in relation to a best value authority if the Secretary of State is satisfied that it is failing to comply with the requirements of this Part.

(2) Where this section applies in relation to an authority the Secretary of State may direct it –

(a) to prepare or amend a performance plan;
(b) to follow specified procedures in relation to a performance plan;
(c) to carry out a review of its exercise of specified functions.

(3) Where this section applies in relation to an authority the Secretary of State may direct a local inquiry to be held into the exercise by the authority of specified functions.

(4) Subsections (2) to (5) of section 250 of the Local Government Act 1972 (inquiries) shall apply in relation to an inquiry which the Secretary of State directs to be held under this section as they apply in relation to an inquiry which a Minister causes to be held under that section.

(5) Where this section applies in relation to an authority the Secretary of State may direct the authority to take any action which he considers necessary or expedient to secure its compliance with the requirements of this Part.

(6) Where this section applies in relation to an authority the Secretary of State may direct –

(a) that a specified function of the authority shall be exercised by the Secretary of State or a person nominated by him for a period specified in the direction or for so long as the Secretary of State considers appropriate, and
(b) that the authority shall comply with any instructions of the Secretary of State or his nominee in relation to the exercise of that function and shall provide such assistance as the Secretary of State or his nominee may require for the purpose of exercising the function.

(7) The Secretary of State may by regulations make provision which –

(a) relates to an enactment which confers a function on him in respect of a function of a best value authority, and
(b) he considers necessary or expedient for the purposes of cases in which he makes a direction under subsection (6)(a).

(8) Regulations under subsection (7) may, in relation to the cases mentioned in subsection (7)(b) –

(a) disapply or modify an enactment of the kind mentioned in subsection (7)(a);
(b) have an effect similar to the effect of an enactment of that kind.

(9) Subject to subsection (11), before giving a direction under this section the Secretary of State shall give the authority concerned an opportunity to make representations about –

(a) the report (if any) as a result of which the direction is proposed, and
(b) the direction proposed.

(10) Subject to subsection (11), before giving a direction under this section following a recommendation in a report under section 7(4)(f) the Secretary of State shall have regard to any statement under section 9(2) which the authority concerned sends to him before the expiry of the period of one month starting with the day on which the authority received the report.

(11) The Secretary of State may give a direction without complying with subsection (9) or (10) if he considers the direction sufficiently urgent.

(12) Where the Secretary of State gives a direction without complying with subsection (9) or (10) he shall inform –

(a) the authority concerned, and
(b) such persons appearing to him to represent best value authorities as he considers appropriate,

of the direction and of the reason why it was given without complying with subsection (9) or (10).

(13) A direction given under this section shall be enforceable by order of mandamus on the application of the Secretary of State.

Exercise of functions by best value authorities

16   Power to modify enactments and confer new powers

(1) If the Secretary of State thinks that an enactment prevents or obstructs compliance by best value authorities with the requirements of this Part he may by order make provision modifying or excluding the application of the enactment in relation to those authorities.

(2) The Secretary of State may by order make provision conferring on best value authorities any power which he considers necessary or expedient to permit or facilitate compliance with the requirements of this Part.

(3) An order under this section may –

(a) impose conditions on the exercise of any power conferred by the order (including conditions about consultation or approval);
(b) amend an enactment;
(c) include consequential, incidental and transitional provision;
(d) make different provision for different cases.

(4) No order shall be made under this section unless a draft has been laid before, and approved by resolution of, each House of Parliament.

(5) In exercising a power conferred under subsection (2) a best value authority shall have regard to any guidance issued by the Secretary of State.

17 Orders under section 16: procedure

(1) Before the Secretary of State makes an order under section 16 he shall consult such authorities or persons as appear to him to be representative of interests affected by his proposals.

(2) If, following consultation under subsection (1), the Secretary of State proposes to make an order under section 16 he shall lay before each House of Parliament a document explaining his proposals and, in particular –

(a) setting them out in the form of a draft order, and
(b) giving details of consultation under subsection (1) above.

(3) Where a document relating to proposals is laid before Parliament under subsection (2), no draft of an order under section 16 to give effect to the proposals (with or without modification) shall be laid before Parliament until after the expiry of the period of sixty days beginning with the day on which the document was laid.

(4) In calculating the period mentioned in subsection (3) no account shall be taken of any time during which –

(a) Parliament is dissolved or prorogued, or
(b) either House is adjourned for more than four days.

(5) In preparing a draft order under section 16 the Secretary of State shall consider any representations made during the period mentioned in subsection (3) above.

(6) A draft order laid before Parliament in accordance with section 16(4) must be accompanied by a statement of the Secretary of State giving details of –

(a) any representations considered in accordance with subsection (5) above, and
(b) any changes made to the proposals contained in the document laid before Parliament under subsection (2) above.

18 Contracting out

(1) Section 70 of the Deregulation and Contracting Out Act 1994 (contracting out functions of local authorities) shall apply in relation to functions of any best value authority (other than excluded functions within the meaning of section 71) as it applies in relation to certain functions of local authorities.

(2) An order under section 70 as applied by subsection (1) above may be made only –

(a) by the Secretary of State, and
(b) if he considers the order necessary or expedient for the purpose of permitting or facilitating compliance with the requirements of this Part.

19 Contracts: exclusion of non-commercial considerations

(1) The Secretary of State may by order provide, in relation to best value authorities, for a specified matter to cease to be a non-commercial matter for the purposes of section 17 of the Local Government Act 1988 (local and other public authority contracts: exclusion of non-commercial considerations).

(2) An order under this section may –

(a) provide for a matter to cease to be a non-commercial matter for specified purposes or to a specified extent;

(b) apply in relation to specified authorities, functions or contracts;

(c) make different provision for different cases;

(d) include consequential or transitional provision (including provision amending an enactment).

(3) No order shall be made under this section unless a draft has been laid before, and approved by resolution of, each House of Parliament.

(4) In exercising a function regulated by section 17 of the Local Government Act 1988 with reference to a matter which is the subject of an order under this section a best value authority shall have regard to any guidance issued by the Secretary of State.

20   Publication of information

At the end of section 2(1) of the Local Government, Planning and Land Act 1980 (duty of authorities to publish information) there shall be inserted –

'; and any other authority which is a best value authority for the purposes of Part I of the Local Government Act 1999 (best value).'

General

21   Transition from compulsory competitive tendering to best value

(1) The following provisions shall cease to have effect on 2nd January 2000 –

(a) Part III of the Local Government, Planning and Land Act 1980 (direct labour organisations);

(b) Part I of the Local Government Act 1988 (competition);

(c) section 32 of and Schedule 6 to that Act (direct labour organisations);

(d) sections 8 to 11 of and Schedule 1 to the Local Government Act 1992 (competition).

(2) The Secretary of State may issue to best value authorities guidance which –

(a) concerns the exercise of their functions between 2nd January 2000 and the date on which any provision of this Part comes into force, and

(b) is designed to secure or facilitate compliance with the requirements of the provision after it comes into force.

(3) A best value authority shall have regard to any guidance issued by the Secretary of State under this section.

22   Audit Commission

(1) In this Act a reference to the Audit Commission is a reference to the Audit Commission for Local Authorities and the National Health Service in England and Wales.

(2) The Audit Commission may delegate any of its functions under this Part to –

(a) a committee or sub-committee established by the Commission (including a committee or sub-committee including persons who are not members of the Commission), or

(b) an officer or servant of the Commission.

(3) The Audit Commission Act 1998 shall be amended as follows.

(4) In section 33 (studies by Commission) –

(a) in subsection (1)(a), for 'the provision of local authority services and of other services provided by bodies subject to audit' substitute 'the exercise of the functions of best value authorities and the provision of services provided by other bodies subject to audit', and
(b) in subsection (6)(a) for 'local authorities' substitute 'best value authorities'.

(5) In section 49(1) (restrictions on disclosure of information) –

(a) after 'any provision of this Act' insert 'or of Part I of the Local Government Act 1999', and
(b) at the end of paragraph (b) insert 'or under Part I of the 1999 Act'.

(6) In section 53(1) (interpretation) after the definition of 'auditor' insert –
' "best value authority" means a best value authority for the purposes of Part I of the Local Government Act 1999;'.

(7) After section 75(1)(e) of the Housing Associations Act 1985 (Housing Corporation and, in relation to Wales, Secretary of State: general functions) there shall be added –

'(f) to provide on request, to such extent as the Relevant Authority considers appropriate, advice and assistance to the Audit Commission for Local Authorities and the National Health Service in England and Wales in relation to the Commission's functions under Part I of the Local Government Act 1999 (best value).'

(8) The Audit Commission may make payments to the Housing Corporation or the Secretary of State in respect of advice and assistance provided under section 75(1)(f) of the Housing Associations Act 1985.

23 Accounts

(1) The Secretary of State may make regulations about the keeping of accounts by best value authorities.

(2) The regulations may –

(a) require accounts and statements of accounts to be prepared, kept and certified in such form or manner as the regulations may specify;
(b) require accounts to be deposited at such places as the regulations may specify;
(c) require the publication of information about accounts and of statements of accounts;
(d) make provision (which may include provision requiring the payment of fees) entitling specified classes of person to inspect and to make or receive copies of specified documents.

(3) The regulations may –

(a) make provision in relation to best value authorities generally or in relation to one or more particular authorities;
(b) make different provision for different cases.

(4) Before making regulations under subsection (1) the Secretary of State must consult –

(a) the Audit Commission,

(b) the authorities concerned or persons appearing to him to represent them, and

(c) such bodies of accountants as appear to him to be appropriate.

(5) If –

(a) a person contravenes a provision of regulations under subsection (1) without reasonable excuse, and

(b) the regulations declare that contravention of the provision is an offence,

the person is liable on summary conviction to a fine not exceeding level 3 on the standard scale.

(6) Any expenses incurred by an auditor (within the meaning of section 7) in connection with proceedings in respect of an offence under subsection (5) which is alleged to have been committed in relation to the accounts of an authority are recoverable from the authority so far as they are not recovered from any other source.

24 Police Act 1996

(1) Section 8(2) of the Police Act 1996 (local policing plans) shall be amended by –

(a) the omission of the word 'and' after paragraph (b), and

(b) the insertion of the following after paragraph (c) –
     ', and
        (d) any action proposed for the purpose of complying with the require-
             ments of Part I of the Local Government Act 1999 (best value).'

(2) In section 54 of that Act (inspectors of constabulary) after subsection (2) there shall be inserted –

'(2A) The inspectors of constabulary may inspect, and report to the Secretary of State on, a police authority's compliance with the requirements of Part I of the Local Government Act 1999 (best value).'

(3) In section 55(1) of that Act (publication of reports) after 'section 54(2)' there shall be inserted 'or (2A)'.

25 Coordination of inspections etc

(1) In arranging for or carrying out –

(a) inspections of best value authorities, or

(b) inquiries or investigations in relation to best value authorities,

a person or body to whom this section applies shall have regard to any guidance issued by the Secretary of State for the purposes of securing the coordination of different kinds of inspection, inquiry and investigation.

(2) This section applies to –

(a) the Audit Commission;

(b) an inspector, assistant inspector or other officer appointed under section 24(1) of the Fire Services Act 1947 (inspectors of fire brigades);

(c) Her Majesty's Chief Inspector of Schools in England;

(d) Her Majesty's Chief Inspector of Schools in Wales;

(e) a person carrying out an inquiry under section 7C of the Local Authority Social Services Act 1970 (inquiries);

(f) a person carrying out an inspection under section 48 of the National Health Service and Community Care Act 1990 (inspection of premises used for provision of community care services);

(g) a person conducting an inspection under section 80 of the Children Act 1989 (inspection of children's homes, &c.) or an inquiry under section 81 of that Act (inquiries in relation to children);

(h) a person authorised under section 139A(1) of the Social Security Administration Act 1992 (reports on administration of housing benefit and council tax benefit);

(i) an inspector appointed under section 54 of the Police Act 1996 (inspectors of constabulary).

(3) The Secretary of State may by order provide for this section to apply to a person or body specified in the order.

26   Guidance

(1) This section has effect in relation to any guidance issued by the Secretary of State under this Part.

(2) The Secretary of State –

(a) may issue guidance to or in respect of best value authorities generally or to or in respect of one or more particular authorities;

(b) may issue different guidance to or in respect of different authorities;

(c) must, before he issues guidance, consult the authorities concerned or persons appearing to him to represent them;

(d) must arrange for guidance to be published.

(3) Before issuing guidance under section 10 the Secretary of State shall, in addition to the consultation required by subsection (2)(c) above, consult the Audit Commission.

(4) Before issuing guidance under section 25 the Secretary of State shall, in addition to the consultation required by subsection (2)(c) above, consult the persons or bodies concerned.

27   Commencement

(1) Subject to subsections (2) and (3), sections 1 to 20 and 22 to 26 shall come into force at the end of the period of 12 months beginning with the day on which this Act is passed.

(2) The Secretary of State may by order provide for –

(a) any of sections 1 to 13, 15, 19, 20, 22, 23, 25 and 26 to be brought into force in relation to England before the time appointed by subsection (1);

(b) any of those sections, in so far as it relates to an authority falling within section 1(1)(d) or (e), to be brought into force in relation to Wales before that time;

(c) any of sections 14, 16 to 18 and 24 to be brought into force before that time.

(3) The National Assembly for Wales may by order provide for any of the sections mentioned in subsection (2)(a), except in so far as it relates to an authority falling within

section 1(1)(d) or (e), to be brought into force in relation to Wales before the time appointed by subsection (1).

(4) An order under subsection (2) or (3) may appoint different days for different purposes.

28 Orders and regulations

(1) An order or regulations under this Part –

    (a) shall be made by statutory instrument, and
    (b) may include supplementary, incidental, consequential and transitional provisions.

(2) An order under section 4, 5, 6, 7 or 25, and regulations under section 15 or 23, shall be subject to annulment in pursuance of a resolution of either House of Parliament.

29 Modifications for Wales

(1) In its application to Wales this Part shall have effect with these modifications –

    (a) for each reference to the Secretary of State there shall be substituted a reference to the National Assembly for Wales;
    (b) sections 2(6), 19(3) and 28(2) shall be omitted.

(2) But subsection (1) shall not apply –

    (a) in relation to an authority falling within section 1(1)(d) or (e), or
    (b) in relation to any of sections 14, 16 to 18, 24 and 27.

(3) In exercising a power under section 16 the Secretary of State –

    (a) shall not make any provision which has effect in relation to Wales unless he has consulted the National Assembly for Wales, and
    (b) shall not amend, or modify or exclude the application of, legislation made by the National Assembly for Wales, unless the Assembly consents.

(4) Section 15(7)(a) shall apply to Wales as if the reference to a function conferred on the Secretary of State were a reference to a function conferred on the National Assembly for Wales or the Secretary of State; but the Assembly may not make regulations under section 15(7) which relate to a function conferred on the Secretary of State without his approval.

Appendix 2

LOCAL GOVERNMENT ACT 1999 (COMMENCEMENT NO 1) ORDER 1999 SI 1999/2169

Made   .   .   .   .   *28th July 1999*

The Secretary of State, in exercise of the powers conferred on him by sections 27(2) and (4) of the Local Government Act 1999 and of all other powers enabling him in that behalf, hereby makes the following Order –

1 Citation and interpretation

(1) This Order may be cited as the Local Government Act 1999 (Commencement No. 1) Order 1999.

(2) In this Order 'the Act' means the Local Government Act 1999.

2 Provisions coming into force on 10th August 1999

(1) Sections 1(1)(d), (e), (4)(a) and (b) and 17 of the Act shall come into force in relation to England and Wales on 10th August 1999.

(2) The provisions of the Act specified in column 1 of Schedule 1 to this Order (which relate to the matters specified in column 2 of that Schedule) shall come into force on 10th August 1999 –

    (a) in relation to England;
    (b) in relation to Wales in so far as those provisions relate to an authority falling within section 1(1)(d) or (e) of the Act.

3 Provisions coming into force on 27th September 1999

(1) Sections 16, 18 and 24(1) of the Act shall come into force in relation to England and Wales on 27th September 1999.

(2) The provisions of the Act as specified in column 1 of Schedule 2 to this Order (which relate to the matters specified in column 2 of that Schedule) shall come into force on 27th September 1999 –

    (a) in relation to England;
    (b) in relation to Wales in so far as those provisions relate to an authority falling within section 1(1)(d) or (e) of the Act.

4 Provisions coming into force on 1st April 2000

(1) Sections 14 and 24(2) and (3) of the Act shall come into force in relation to England and Wales on 1st April 2000.

(2) The provisions of the Act specified in column 1 of Schedule 3 to this Order (which relate to matters specified in column 2 of that Schedule) shall come into force on 1st April 2000 –

(a) in relation to England;

(b) in relation to Wales in so far as those provisions relate to an authority falling within section 1(1)(d) or (e) of the Act.

SCHEDULE 1   Article 2(2)

PROVISIONS COMING INTO FORCE ON 10TH AUGUST 1999

(1) Provisions of the Act	(2) Subject matter of provisions
Section 1(1)(a), (b), (c), (g), (h), (2)(a), (b) and (c) and (5)	Best value authorities: definition.
Section 3(2), (3) and (4)	The general duty: consultation, definition of 'representatives', and guidance.
Section 4(3) and (4)	Performance indicators and standards: consultation and specification requirements.
Section 12(4)	Fees: consultation.
Section 23(4)	Accounts: consultation.
Section 26(2)(c), (3) and (4)	Guidance: consultation requirements.

SCHEDULE 2   Article 3(2)

PROVISIONS COMING INTO FORCE ON 27TH SEPTEMBER 1999

(1) Provisions of the Act	(2) Subject matter of provisions
Section 2 except subsection (4)	Power to extend or disapply.
Section 4(1) and (2)	Performance indicators and standards: orders.
Section 5(2), (4), (5), (6) and (7)	Best value reviews: orders and guidance.
Section 6	Best value performance plans.
Section 8(2), (3), (4), (5), (6) and (7)	Code of practice and fees: preparation by the Audit Commission of code of practice and prescription of fees.
Section 10(4) for the purposes of the issue of guidance by the Secretary of State	Inspections: guidance.
Section 12(1)	Fees: prescription of fees by the Audit Commission.
Section 15(7) and (8)	Secretary of State's powers: Regulations.
Section 19	Contracts: exclusion of non-commercial considerations.
Section 20	Publication of information.
Section 22	Audit Commission.
Section 23, except subsection (4)	Accounts.
Section 25	Coordination of inspections, &c.
Section 26(1) and (2)(a), (b) and (d)	Guidance: general.

SCHEDULE 3   Article 4(2)

PROVISIONS COMING INTO FORCE ON 1ST APRIL 2000

(1) Provisions of the Act	(2) Subject matter of provisions
Section 3(1)	The general duty.
Section 4(5)	Best value authorities' duty to meet performance standards.
Section 5(1) and (3)	Best value authorities' obligation to conduct reviews.
Section 7	Audit of best value performance plans.
Section 8(1)	Auditor's obligation to have regard to any code of practice issued under section 8.
Section 9	Response to audit.
Section 10(1), (2), (3) and (4) so far as not already in force	Best value inspections by the Audit Commission.
Section 11	Inspectors' powers and duties.
Section 12(2) and (3)	Fees payable for best value inspections.
Section 13	Inspection reports.
Section 15 except subsections (7) and (8)	Secretary of State's powers: Enforcement.

Appendix 3

LOCAL GOVERNMENT ACT 1999 (COMMENCEMENT) (WALES) ORDER 1999 SI 1999/2815

Made   .   .   .   .   *28th September 1999*

The National Assembly for Wales makes the following Order in exercise of the powers given to it by section 27(3) and (4) of the Local Government Act 1999 –

1   Citation and interpretation

(1) This Order may be cited as the Local Government Act 1999 (Commencement) (Wales) Order 1999.

(2) In this Order 'the Act' means the Local Government Act 1999.

2   Provisions coming into force on 1st October 1999

The following provisions of the Act shall come into force in relation to Wales on 1st October 1999 –

section 1(1)(a), (b) and (g), (3) and (5)(a),
section 2(1), (2), (3) and (5), 9
section 3(2), (3) and (4),
section 4(1), (2), (3) and (4),
section 5(2), (4), (5), (6) and (7),
section 6,
section 8(2), (3), (4), (5), (6) and (7),
section 10(4),
section 12(1) and (4),
section 19(1), (2) and (4),
section 20,
section 22,
section 23,
section 25(1), (2)(a), (d), (e), (f), (g) and (h) and (3).
section 26.

3   Provisions coming into force on 1st April 2000

The following provisions of the Act shall come into force in relation to Wales on 1st April 2000 –

section 3(1),
section 4(5),
section 5(1) and (3),
section 7,
section 8(1),
section 9,

section 10(1), (2) and (3),
section 11,
section 12(2) and (3),
section 13,
section 15.

Appendix 4

DETR CIRCULAR 10/99
Local Government Act 1999: Part I
Best Value

SUMMARY

This best value circular is divided into **four** sections.

1. **An Overview** from paragraphs **1–14**
   This section contains:
   - A summary of the scope of the guidance, with an overview of the Government's agenda for modernising local authorities.
2. **Guidance** from paragraphs **15–60**
   This section contains guidance to best value authorities made under the provisions in Sections 5 and 6 of the Act.
   - BEST VALUE REVIEWS
     The timing of Reviews, the required elements for successful Reviews, the 4Cs, partnerships, processes and outcomes.
   - BEST VALUE PERFORMANCE PLANS
     The purpose of plans and the audience they address. Form, content and publication issues.
3. **Other Guidance** from paragraphs **61–94**
   This section contains further non-statutory guidance for best value authorities on:
   - AUDIT AND ACCOUNTING
     Audit reports, the role of auditors and proper accounting practice.
   - INSPECTION
     Inspection arrangements under best value, and the role of the Inspectorates.
   - TACKLING FAILING SERVICES
     The scope of the Secretary of State's powers where authorities fail to achieve best value.
   - FAIR EMPLOYMENT
     the Government's agenda for fair employment and its relationship to best value.
4. **Annexes A–E**
   These contain additional information on:
   - BEST VALUE PILOTS
   - BEST VALUE PUBLICATIONS
   - QUALITY SCHEMES
   - PROTOCOL ON INTERVENTION POWERS
   - BEST VALUE INSPECTORATE FORUM

. . .

SCOPE OF THE GUIDANCE

1.   This circular provides guidance to best value authorities in England and to police and fire authorities in Wales on how they might meet the requirements of Part I of the Local Government Act 1999. It includes guidance made under provisions in Sections 5 (Best Value Reviews) and 6 (Best Value Performance Plans), and guidance in respect of other matters which affect the way in which authorities carry out their responsibilities under Part I.

2.   In preparing this guidance, the Government has drawn on the experience of the best value pilot authorities, the pilot partnership networks and many others who have sought to apply the key principles of best value over the last two years. The Government is grateful to them and to the Local Government Association, the Improvement and Development Agency, the Audit Commission, the CBI, TUC and others who have, working often in partnership together, supported the development of the policy and its application on the ground. Where relevant, boxed examples of the way some best value authorities are applying policy on the ground are provided. These are designed to be illustrative as a possible approach rather than indicative of one to be followed exactly.

3.   This guidance applies to all principal local authorities in England defined as best value authorities in Section 1 of the 1999 Act. It also applies to police and single purpose fire authorities in England and Wales. It will also apply in due course to bodies that are defined in the Greater London Authority Act 1999 such as Transport for London and the London Development Agency. For the fire service, the guidance will apply directly to those county councils that are fire authorities, and so far as is practical to single-purpose authorities including the London Fire and Emergency Planning Authority when established as a functional body of the Greater London Authority. The Home Office is to supplement this guidance by means of fire service circulars and a series of briefing notes for police authorities on the key aspects of best value as they affect the police service. Separate guidance will be provided for parish and town councils.

MODERN PUBLIC SERVICES

4.   Section 3 of the 1999 Act requires best value authorities to make arrangements to secure continuous improvement in the way in which they exercise their functions, having regard to a combination of economy, efficiency and effectiveness. This is a broad remit, and one that provides local government with a considerable challenge and a major opportunity. It also recognises local government as an equal partner with central government in the drive to modernise the way in which public services are provided.

5.   The Government's vision for public services into the next century is described in the *Modernising Government* White Paper (Cmmd. 4310), published in March this year. All of the five main themes of the White Paper are relevant to best value authorities:

- ensuring that public services are responsive to the needs of citizens, not the convenience of service providers
- ensuring that public services are efficient and of a high quality
- ensuring that policy making is more joined-up and strategic, forward looking and not reactive to short-term pressures

- using information technology to tailor services to the needs of users
- valuing public service and tackling the under-representation of minority groups.

6.   Best value is about delivering these commitments at the local level. It has been designed to make life better for people and for business, and will be mirrored in the way in which policies and programmes are developed amongst other public bodies responsible for delivering public services locally. But local authorities are in the forefront of these changes, and giving such changes effect will strengthen their capacity for community leadership, as envisaged in the *Modern Local Government: In Touch with the People* White Paper (Cmmd. 4014), published in July 1998. Legislation in the current Parliamentary session will underpin that role.

7.   The leadership role will entail the development of a **community strategy**, which sets out the broad objectives and vision for the community in the area. Such strategies need to reflect the contribution which the authority and its partners expect to make to improve the social, economic and environmental well-being of their areas, both immediate and longer-term. They should also reflect local aspirations and recognise the potential for others to contribute ideas and resources and to participate in service delivery. It should provide the starting point for the first step under best value – the setting of **strategic objectives and corporate priorities**. Elected members (and all members in the case of police authorities) have a key role to play in the setting of these objectives and priorities – as they do in all matters to do with achieving best value – and in ensuring that all sections of the community are properly engaged in their definition.

8.   The development of a community strategy will require consultation processes which identify and balance the needs of the community as a whole. These should include measures designed to embrace those who may be hard-to-reach, such as those for whom English is not a first language, young people, the elderly and the homeless, for whom best value provides a real opportunity to shape the pattern of local services.

9.   The **performance management framework** at Figure 1 [*see page 308*], taken from the 1998 White Paper, should already be familiar to all local authorities. It presents the key elements of the best value process clearly and simply. It places Best Value Reviews and Performance Plans in a wider context and as a logical sequence of steps that each authority can recognise and replicate. But the real world will not always be quite so ordered or so predictable. What matters most is that authorities carry out Reviews and approach the preparation of Performance Plans in such a way that they do not lose sight of the central purpose of best value – to make a real and positive difference to the services which local people receive from their authority.

10.   The Government is committed to this outcome. It matters far more than who is providing the service or indeed how it is provided. What matters is what works. What works will depend critically on whether local services are able to respond quickly and imaginatively to peoples' needs and aspirations on the one hand, and to technological and organisational change on the other. The Government takes the view that rising expectations amongst the public for efficient high quality services, together with significant advances in the way in which services can be delivered, make it unlikely that any one provider can guarantee best value by itself. Rather authorities should draw from the best providers, whether in the public, private or voluntary sector, and plan positively for **diversity**: diversity in the way in which services are delivered; and diversity in their choice of provider. In this way, real flexibility can be built into local services, making them better able to respond to the demands and opportunities of the future.

11.   This is why the Government emphasises the importance of **partnership** in delivering best value. Partnership with the private and voluntary sectors; partnership with other public bodies acting locally; partnership with central government itself.

Figure 1 – The Best Value Performance Management Framework

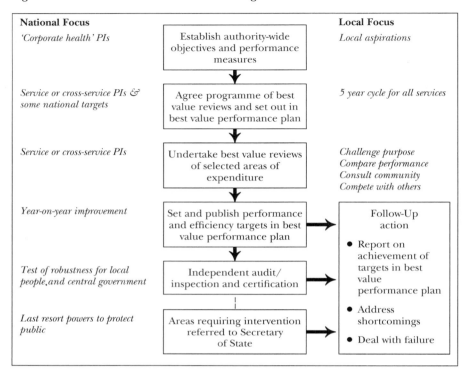

Acting together with others, authorities can add real value to their communities: through sustainable improvements in the quality of life for all, and through the higher quality and more efficient services that local people seek. But partnership also requires clarity about the contribution expected from each of the partners at different stages of policy development and implementation, and new management structures that recognise the challenge that working with others brings. All authorities need to consider how best such clarity can be achieved as part of their community and corporate strategies, and how to give it effect through a considered and far-reaching approach to the commissioning and procurement of services.

12.   A council-wide approach to partnership under best value is essential. It should flow from the broader community leadership role envisaged for local councils, and reflect discussions with key partners. Such an approach will enable local authorities to position themselves as one of several service providers in their area, equipped to set out a clear picture of their potential contribution and the way in which they intend to exercise it. In turn, this will translate into a set of corporate objectives for the authority itself, together with clear strategies for community consultation, procurement and staff development, as well as a programme designed to deliver the key Reviews required by the legislation.

13.   Best value is much more than a statutory framework. It will succeed insofar as it produces significant and continuous improvements to every service for which authorities are responsible. Without such improvements the processes that give effect to the framework will wither. The performance management framework around which the new statutory regime is structured will, in the Government's view, only deliver real improvements if it is followed imaginatively and in the spirit in which it has been designed. If it is used as a technical device operated by specialists it will fail to live up to its

potential for delivering substantial change. That is why best value requires the engagement of the **political leadership** of the authority and of other members, as well as that of officers. Elected members need to be involved not only in the processes associated with best value but in owning the outcomes which those processes are designed to deliver.

14. The self-improvement approach of the Improvement and Development Agency's Improvement Project, whereby authorities are helped to assess their strengths and weaknesses in the context of achieving best value, recognises this, and the Government welcomes the intention to make this available to all local authorities as soon as possible. It is important that authorities take full advantage of it. Similarly the first stage of the beacon council scheme will encourage councils to identify the things that they are good at and to promote these in the wider local government community, thus accelerating the momentum for change which modernisation requires.

BEST VALUE REVIEWS

15. Section 5 of the 1999 Act requires authorities to conduct **Best Value Reviews** of their functions in accordance with the provisions of any order made under that section and empowers the Secretary of State to issue guidance on the timetable, procedures, form and content of such Reviews. In particular, and as required by SI 1999/3251, a best value authority will need to:

- consider whether it should be exercising the function
- consider the level at which and the way in which it should be exercising the function
- consider its objectives in relation to the exercise of the function
- assess its performance in exercising the function by reference to any performance indicators specified for the function
- assess the competitiveness of its performance in exercising the function by reference to the exercise of the same function, or similar functions, by other best value authorities and by commercial and other businesses including organisations in the voluntary sector
- consult other best value authorities, commercial and other businesses, including organisations in the voluntary sector, about the exercise of the function
- assess its success in meeting any performance standard which applies in relation to the function
- assess its progress towards meeting any relevant performance standard which has been specified but which does not yet apply
- assess its progress towards meeting any relevant performance target.

16. These requirements can be summarised as follows: authorities should in carrying out Reviews

- **challenge** why, how and by whom a service is being provided
- secure **comparison** with the performance of others across a range of relevant indicators, taking into account the views of both service users and potential suppliers
- **consult** local taxpayers, service users, partners and the wider business community in the setting of new performance targets

- use fair and open **competition** wherever practicable as a means of securing efficient and effective services.

Where carried through successfully, such Reviews will meet the purpose for which they have been designed: to be the principal means by which authorities consider new approaches to service delivery and set the demanding performance targets which will deliver continuous improvements.

17.   The experience to date of the best value pilot authorities and others suggests that such Reviews have the potential to make a real difference to performance on the ground. If that potential is to be realised, then Reviews will need to:

- **take a sufficiently long-term perspective.** Reviews will be unlikely to set targets that reflect best value unless they look far enough ahead to anticipate prospective changes in the demand for services and the means by which such services might be delivered. As far as possible, sufficient flexibility should be built into all delivery arrangements, particularly those with a term in excess of 3 years, to ensure that there are measures to secure continuous improvement and innovation and which can be adapted to meet changing local and national priorities. This flexibility must be balanced against a reasonable degree of certainty over the length of any contract to allow start-up costs, risk and investment to be managed at sensible cost.
- **involve elected members.** Elected members – whether with executive or non-executive roles once the provisions in the Local Government Bill 1999 are in force – have a key responsibility to ensure that Reviews reflect from the start the strategic objectives and corporate priorities of the authority and focus on the perspective of actual and potential service users, including those that are typically hard-to-reach. Elected members will also need to monitor action plans following the completion of Reviews.
- **seek advice from outside the authority.** Authorities with a track record of working with partners in the public, voluntary or private sectors recognise the benefits of involving them in the review process as an additional source of advice or as a sounding board for new ideas. Other external advice can be tapped by setting up expert panels or forums, perhaps involving service users (or potential service users). And the same principle can be applied through involving members and officers who are not directly involved in the particular service or group of services being reviewed.
- **involve those currently delivering services.** This applies to all employees, but particularly to frontline staff whose experience of face-to-face contact with the public and service users can bring an important perspective as to how a service is perceived and valued, and how it can be improved. Their support is critical to successful implementation.
- **question existing commitments.** Where authorities are committed to longer-term contracts, there are usually provisions that enable improvements to be made in agreement with the parties concerned. Where this is not the case, authorities should still consider the scope for changes – perhaps by measures complementing the contract – and where these are justified cost any such adjustments as part of their appraisal of service delivery options.
- **engage with users and potential users of services.** A customer focus to Reviews is essential. It is important that authorities seek out the views of all potential users, especially those who have traditionally been under-represented. Those that fail

to engage local people fully from the outset – including hard-to-reach groups – will carry little conviction when it comes to explaining decisions on service targets and selected providers, and invariably overlook real opportunities to bring about lasting change.

- **address equity considerations.** Reviews should consider the way in which services impact on all sections of the community, including minority groups, and set targets to redress disparities in the provision of services to those that are socially, economically or geographically disadvantaged. Issues of social exclusion and isolation will be important ones for many authorities, and a service cannot be effective under best value unless it addresses equity considerations. Reviews should explicitly consider whether the authority complies with the relevant legislation.[1]

- **give effect to the principles of sustainable development.** New performance targets generated by Reviews need to reflect the principles of sustainable development, set out in *A better quality of life – a strategy for sustainable development for the UK* (May 1999), and summarised in *The Government's sustainable development strategy: What does it mean for local authorities?* published in July this year. Where authorities have LA21 and any community strategies in place, Reviews will provide an opportunity to give such principles practical effect through the setting of consistent performance targets.

18.   Authorities need to include in their Performance Plans a programme of Reviews in accordance with SI 1999/3251, which stipulates that best value authorities conduct Reviews of all functions within a 5 year period ending 31 March 2005, and within consecutive five year cycles thereafter. As a general rule, the Government does not intend to prescribe a common Review timetable. The timetable should be practical and realistic and take into account the resources available to the authority, the opportunity for tackling cross-cutting issues, and the demands placed on it by other statutory, financial and contractual requirements. This approach may need to be adapted to meet particular circumstances. For example, in the case of fire authorities, the Government is intending to set a prioritised programme of Reviews in the early years of the first cycle for the specific functions of communications and control, training and procurement, in order to promote joint working and co-operation between authorities.

19.   Authorities will need to establish a clear audit trail as to how the Review programme has been drawn up. They will be expected to demonstrate that the programme flows from any community strategy they may have, from their corporate vision for the authority and from a clear analysis of current performance – based on a comparison using the best value and other indicators – as well as from consultation with local people, business and employees. Poorly performing services should normally be reviewed early in the 5 year cycle, but the Government recognises that exceptionally this may not always be the right course, particularly where achieving significant improvements in one service area may be dependent on developments in another already under review. Even so, authorities must be able to justify a Review timetable which does not

---

1   Local authority service provision is covered by the Sex Discrimination Act 1975, the Race Relations Act 1976 and the Disability Discrimination Act 1995 which prohibit direct and indirect discrimination in the provision of services. Local authorities have a duty under section 71 of the Race Relations Act to make appropriate arrangements with a view to securing that their various functions are carried out with due regard to the need to eliminate unlawful racial discrimination and to promote equality of opportunity, and good relations, between persons of different racial groups. The Children Act 1989 requires authorities to take account of a child's race, religion, cultural and linguistic background in arranging both day and foster care. The NHS and Community Care Act 1990 also obliges service providers to take account of the differing needs of various ethnic communities.

tackle the poorest performing services in the early years. That would not rule out a Review of a well performing service where there may be useful lessons to be learnt for the conduct of Reviews, including the factors that contribute to a successful outcome. And in the first year in particular, authorities may also wish to consider whether the Review programme can be aligned ahead of inspections where these are already programmed or expected.

20.   The Government also recognises that it will not be possible to set out a Review programme over five years which anticipates all eventualities. Priorities will change over any single period, and flexibility is needed to reflect local political as well as other considerations. Nevertheless, firm proposals are needed for the first two or three years to assure local people that their concerns will be addressed and auditors and inspectors that there is a sound basis for forward planning. Authorities will need to justify changes to the Review programme each year in their Performance Plans, and in particular any variations which have the effect of postponing Reviews of poorly performing services.

21.   The Review programme should be built around a mix of service specific and cross-cutting Reviews. Service specific Reviews can provide focus and clear account-ability, and provided they are sufficiently ambitious and on a large enough scale are likely to ensure that authorities make early improvements in efficiency and service quality. On the other hand, cross-cutting Reviews which are based on or around clear and recognisable themes or issues and which reflect strategic choices with other partners, are more likely to make a real and lasting difference locally. Authorities proposing to carry out Reviews based only on service specific programmes will need to explain why they have passed over the potential benefits of tackling at least one cross-cutting issue in each year of the Review cycle. Either way it is important that Reviews are completed to a rigorous timetable, and structured and approached in a way that maximises the potential for innovation. For example, authorities might look at investment and service requirements together, and should recognise the importance of support services to effective front-line performance.

22.   Authorities will need to consider a number of other factors in structuring their Review programme. Important changes in legislation or national policy could set a clear agenda for a particular service or group of services, as did legislation and policy on crime prevention. In other cases, authorities might wish to review services around a theme such as partnership or customer care, or integrated service delivery to a particular social group such as the elderly. Some authorities might usefully address concerns about access to services in rural areas, or in specific neighbourhoods. Other Reviews might be triggered by the need to free up significant resources for specific new priorities. In deciding the appropriate mix of service and cross-cutting Reviews, authorities will need to balance the different resource implications and, regardless of the mix adopted, all Reviews can and should be demanding in terms of targets set for future performance.

23.   The Government expects authorities to take a realistic view of the numbers of Reviews they can sensibly undertake in any one year and over a five year cycle. It would be helpful if authorities were to include an assessment of their capacity to carry out each Review early in their programme, and were able to demonstrate that all Reviews will be properly resourced and deliverable within the proposed timescale. One approach demonstrating how an authority has in practice tackled this task is set out below. Further advice will be available from Warwick Business School's evaluation of the best value pilots, and from the Improvement and Development Agency.

Choosing a Review Programme

One authority developed a scoring matrix to prioritise services for the first year of Reviews, each service being scored on a 1–5 scale against the following criteria:

- public satisfaction
- importance to the public
- user satisfaction
- size of budget
- performance on national PIs and other benchmarks
- cost
- potential for market delivery
- strategic fit with Council objectives
- quality accreditation

Services selected for the first year of Reviews were those which were:

- relatively important to the public
- poor performers (and publicly seen as such)
- relatively high cost
- a major part of the budget
- central to the Council's objectives and priorities
- and open to market delivery

---

24. Whatever the focus of a Review under best value, common considerations apply to the way in which the review process should be conducted under the provisions of SI 1999/3251. The 4Cs – **challenge, compare, consult and compete** – reflect these key considerations and can be addressed in different ways. Many authorities have already used them in reviewing services and in other planning processes. Their experience suggests that the 4Cs should be viewed not as a linear process but as interactive elements, each essential for a penetrating and comprehensive Review.

25. Without the element of **challenge** there can be no effective Review: it is the key to significant improvements in performance and without it authorities are unlikely to reach the targets which the Government will set for authorities, and those which are set locally. Challenging why and how a service is provided requires a fundamental rethink, asking basic questions about the needs that each service is intended to address and the method of procurement that is used. Challenge is therefore intrinsically tied up with the competition element as well as those of comparison and consultation.

26. Authorities will be expected to show evidence that they have considered the underlying rationale for the service(s) under review and the alternative ways in which it might be provided. The potential for utilising new technology in service provision should be explored, and a capacity developed whereby authorities can analyse the effects of demographic, social and economic changes on local service needs. Although the past can provide useful lessons as to what works and does not work it will usually point to incremental rather than fundamental change: that may be insufficient to secure the step-change in performance that the Government expects from Reviews and which local people may be seeking. So it is critical that authorities look forwards and outwards in reviewing their services: forwards to identify the significant changes in what local people want from their authority; outwards to identify the alternative ways in which those demands can be met and by whom.

27.   Authorities will recognise that success in identifying these factors will flow from a close engagement with the community – often through and driven by locally elected members – and with the market – principally through a capacity for market analysis and dialogue with the private and voluntary sectors, as well as with other local authorities. Guidance on these matters is in paragraphs 33–35 on consultation and paragraphs 36–48 on competition.

28.   Informed **comparison** is the basis of performance management, and is also critical to an effective Review. Authorities will recognise that as from next year (2000/2001) they will be expected to set targets within the range specified for the national best value indicators when these are published later this year. These targets will reflect an authority's position in relation to other authorities nationally, and in respect of cost and efficiency in relation to similar types of authority, such as County Councils. Authorities will also wish to reflect on their performance against the national corporate health indicators, relevant Audit Commission indicators, and those used by Government Departments. Such indicators will provide a good starting point from which authorities can consider and compare their performance. Many of them are already in use, and over time authorities will become more familiar with those indicators that matter most. In the first year in particular, authorities will need to take a sensible and realistic view as to what is readily available, and concentrate on putting in place the mechanisms that will build comparison into their normal performance management arrangements.

29.   Authorities should aim to compare their current and prospective performance against other public sector bodies, and those in the private and voluntary sectors. This will rarely be a process of exact comparison, rather the intelligent exploration of how analogous services or elements of such services perform: this needs to be sufficient to enable authorities to identify the significant performance differences and the reasons for them, and thus the extent to which improvements are needed over the review period. Of the different performance indicators required for this purpose, national best value performance indicators (BVPIs) set by the Government and those identified by the Audit Commission will enable a rounded view to be taken. These will be published shortly. Authorities may also wish to use for comparative purposes any indicators which they have developed, for example with neighbouring authorities or similar types of authority. Comparison with other authorities will be necessary to set:

- quality targets that are, as a minimum, consistent with the performance of the top 25% of all authorities
- cost and efficiency targets over 5 years that, as a minimum, are consistent with the performance of the top 25% of authorities of the type to which they belong and which are consistent with the overall target of 2% p.a. efficiency improvement set for local government spending as a whole.

The way in which these general principles will apply to police authorities is being considered by the Home Office in consultation with the police service.

30.   As far as possible comparisons should be made on the basis of outcomes, although detailed comparisons of inputs and outputs will be required to assess the scope for greater efficiency consistent with the Government's overall target of 2% p.a. efficiency improvements for local government as a whole. This does not mean that each Review is expected to identify efficiency improvements of 2% a year. Some Reviews may identify much greater opportunities for improved efficiency, others less so, and in some cases such improvements will be difficult to quantify precisely. Nor is it expected that improved efficiency will be used to reduce overall spending. The Government is committed to ensure that resources freed up through greater efficiency are made available to meet nationally and locally agreed priorities.

31.   Selective and informed benchmarking can also be useful in identifying the scope for efficiency improvements, by analysing processes which help to deliver better performance and outcomes. Some authorities have secured real gains from bench-marking with other authorities and the Government is supportive of them. However, it will look to evidence of a wider approach from authorities as part of the Review process, and will encourage other public sector bodies and those in the private and voluntary sectors to share and debate performance information more widely.

32.   Quality schemes too have an important role to play through the contribution each can make to securing effective comparison and continuous service improvements. Many authorities have made use of a variety of accredited schemes to improve the quality and efficiency of their services and thereby prepare for best value. Such schemes are not sufficient in themselves to deliver best value. But they can support the necessary cultural changes required, ensure staff and members are fully involved, and create a commit-ment to quality and efficiency which fosters a determination to make a difference, which is the hallmark of best value. The key quality schemes are listed at **Annex C**. Although they serve different purposes they should be considered as complementary to each other. A report on how the different schemes can work together in the public sector to enhance their overall impact is to be issued by the end of the year by the Modernising Government Quality Schemes Task Force. The Government will at the same time publish a guide, following consultation with local government and the different scheme promoters, to help authorities assess how each scheme might assist in preparing for and achieving best value.

33.   Section 3 of the 1999 Act requires authorities to **consult** a wide range of local and other interests as to the way in which they fulfil their duties to secure best value. Section 5 and SI 1999/3251 place specific requirements in respect of the carrying out of Reviews. These are complementary provisions which reflect the importance the Government attaches to the place of the citizen – as user and taxpayer – in best value, and to the role of the private and voluntary sectors in contributing to the overall health of the local community.

34.   The Government has no current plans to issue guidance under Section 3(4) of the 1999 Act. It takes the view that authorities are best placed to decide whom to consult and in what way, taking account of other statutory requirements as well as good practice. It believes nonetheless that authorities should take a strategic approach to consultation and ensure that adequate arrangements are in place to meet their responsibilities to consult both on the general requirements for best value under Section 3 and also for the specific purposes of the Review process required under Section 5. Arrangements under Section 5 will need to address:

- **co-ordination with other best value authorities and other public bodies undertaking consultation at the same time.** This will be particularly important where there is a two-tier structure of local government, and/or where there is a well-developed network of partnership working. Maximum use needs to be made of existing consultation exercises, and new forms of consultation should be designed with regard to economy and corporate priorities. Without such an approach there are risks of alienating those whose views have been sought and of incurring substantial cost to little effect.
- **within a broad framework of general principles, a mix of techniques available for the full range of services and consultees.** It will be important to develop techniques appropriate for the different services and for communicating with groups within the local community that are typically hard-to-reach, whether because written English is not their usual or favoured mode of comunication or for a variety of other reasons.

- **a process for selecting the appropriate approaches for each specific Review.** Each Review is likely to require a different approach to consultation depending upon its focus and projected outcome.

- **arrangements for informing consultees of the purpose of the consultation, how the information they supply will be used, details of the timetable and decision-making process, and feedback on the outcome and the reasons for it.** It is important that Reviews are not embarked upon without a clear indication being given to local people and potential partners as to what they should expect at the different stages, including feedback.

35.   Practical advice on how to consult in different circumstances is best provided from within the local government community itself. Advice on consultation techniques, for example, is available from the I&DeA and from the joint DETR/Democracy Network publication *Guidance on Enhancing Public Participation* (October 1998). Experience in consulting people on LA21 strategies will also be valuable.

36.   Reviews are also required to assess the competitiveness of different functions by reference to the performance of other bodies, including best value authorities and private and voluntary sector providers. The 1999 Act does not require authorities to subject their functions to competition in the way in which legislation on compulsory competitive tendering did. Even so, fair and open **competition** will, in the Government's view, most often be the best way of demonstrating that a function is being carried out competitively. Such competition is expected to play an essential and enduring role in ensuring best value, and Reviews will need to consider how this can best be achieved. It will not be achieved if authorities fail to approach competition positively, taking full account of the opportunities for innovation and genuine partnership which are available from working with others in the public, private and voluntary sectors.

37.   The Government has made it clear that the future for public service provision is one where there is real variety in the way services are delivered and genuine plurality among service providers. It is opposed to any single supplier dominating the provision of services either locally or nationally: the public is not best served where this occurs. It takes the view that local government, the trade unions and the private and voluntary sectors share a responsibility with Government itself to make this a reality.

38.   The first step is to create a climate in which all parties can contribute to a discussion of the issues in a spirit of trust and co-operation. Local authorities have a key role to play by putting the needs of service users uppermost and by adopting an open mind as to how a service might be provided and by whom, and by being prepared to seek out and listen to the views of others. The trade unions and the voluntary and private sectors can also help to develop the conditions under which services are run for the benefit of those that require them, and where diversity can flourish. The Government welcomes the steps that each party has taken to create such a climate, and has acted to support them through its fair employment agenda (see paragraphs 84–93). Authorities that give insufficient weight to the merits of a healthy and genuine partnership between public, private and voluntary sectors, are unlikely to achieve the sustained improvements that local people will rightly expect under best value.

39.   Authorities should therefore analyse the structure of supply markets for the different services, and the way in which they are developing, and draw upon such market intelligence in carrying out their Reviews. They should consider, in discussion with current and potential suppliers in the public, private and voluntary sectors, suppliers' capacity to meet the improvements which consultation has highlighted, and identify the benefits that can arise from bringing new providers into the market. Services which are currently provided to a uniform standard for example, could be restructured to

encourage variety and choice: alternatively, similar services which are currently delivered by different authorities could be amalgamated to deliver economies of scale.

Developing Markets: Researching the Options

In researching supply markets authorities should explore:

- the service developments that are anticipated in response to best practice, legislation or user views
- the current market for the provision of the service(s)
- new combinations of service which the marketplace suggests could deliver best value
- the alternative ways to procure the service(s)

This will require engagement with the markets, perhaps though:

- holding discussions with selected private and voluntary sector providers
- sending a questionnaire to suppliers to ask how they could add value
- discussing existing experience with other authorities who have contracted the service from an external provider
- holding a contractors' briefing day to explain the objectives of the authority and to elicit their views

---

40.   The process of researching markets in this way is important, but further action by authorities is required:

- to secure improved performance from mature markets
- to create the conditions in which new suppliers might take root where the current market is demonstrably weak, poorly developed and offers no credible alternative to the current supplier.

The objective in both cases is not to favour one supplier against another but to encourage diversity, innovation and the competitiveness of the supply base.

41.   Amongst the steps which authorities should consider in order to create the conditions in which new suppliers might take root or existing suppliers might become more competitive are:

- basing requirements on outcomes to allow for and encourage innovative methods of provision
- grouping activities to reflect prospective market competencies. This too can help generate interest from innovative providers
- packaging work appropriate to the market. In some areas of activity larger packages may generate more interest than smaller ones; in others authorities may wish to encourage small and medium-sized companies to bid
- being clear about intentions. Authorities need to make clear where they want long-term relationships with potential suppliers, and demonstrate a genuine interest in using the best suppliers, regardless of the sector from which they come
- developing an understanding of the potential sources of supply. Early discussions with prospective suppliers can help in shaping the optimum size, composition and length of contracts, whilst ensuring the fairness, openness and transparency required by EC procurement rules
- being clear in advance whether there will be an in-house bid for the work.

42.   These developments will require authorities to develop new capacities, either alone or with others:

- to analyse supply markets and identify what such markets can provide
- to select the best suppliers
- to manage new forms of relationship designed to achieve whole life value for money, continuous improvement and the sharing of risks and rewards.

43.   The fact that a service is currently provided internally or externally following a competitive process is not in itself sufficient to demonstrate best value, particularly where the contract is of a long duration and has been in operation for several years. Authorities need to consider whether the service meets current and future needs, rather than those assumed at the time the original choice was made. Contracts with the private sector should be examined to see if they permit, and provide incentives for, innovation and continuous improvement. Where this is not the case, authorities need to discuss with providers how best to accommodate these improvements, taking into account the scope for agreeing or negotiating new contract arrangements, and their willingness to finance service improvements and share any risks and rewards.

44.   Reviews which give full consideration to the four Cs – challenge, comparison, consultation and competition – will set demanding targets for service improvement, and action plans to deliver these to a realistic timetable, including decisions on the **best value option for future service delivery**. The main options include, for example:

- the cessation of the service, in whole or in part
- the creation of a public–private partnership, through a strategic contract or a joint venture company, for example
- the transfer or externalisation of the service to another provider (with no in-house bid)
- the market-testing of all or part of the service (where the in-house provider bids in open competition against the private or voluntary sector)
- the restructuring or re-positioning of the in-house service
- the re-negotiation of existing arrangements with current providers where this is permissible
- the joint commissioning or delivery of the service.

45.   The choice amongst these options will depend on an objective analysis of what has emerged from the Review. This will flow from a corporate perspective which embraces both a clear procurement strategy and a written policy on evaluation and appraisal. In each Review authorities will be expected to demonstrate that they have explored the full range of practical alternatives and selected the options most likely to deliver best value to the public. External auditors will expect a clear audit trail and proper justification for the preferred choice.

46.   This will apply as much to work which is to be carried out in-house by the authority itself as it does to work undertaken under contract by the private or voluntary sectors, or in partnership. Services should not be delivered directly if other more efficient and effective means are available. Retaining work in-house will therefore only be justified where the authority can show it is competitive with the best alternative. The way in which this is demonstrated is for an authority to determine in accordance with its procurement strategy and evaluation policy, but where there is a developed supply market this will most often be through fair and open competition. The changes to accounting practice referred to in paragraph 68 should help ensure that the costs of work carried out in-house are fully transparent, so that in considering options for service delivery there is an improved basis for comparison, evaluation and auditing.

47.   Authorities should revisit their standing orders on procurement and tendering to ensure that they are consistent with the statutory provisions of the 1999 Act and the requirements of this guidance.

48.   The Government recognises that moving towards a more plural and partnership based form of service provision may be challenging for many authorities and is considering with the Local Government Association and others what further measures are needed to equip authorities for the new forms of procurement which best value demands.

49.   Improvements to service quality and efficiency arising from individual Reviews will need to be within a range set by the Secretary of State in respect of the national best value indicators. They will be supplemented by local improvement targets developed through consultation with local people. Either way, the targets and the **action plans** for delivering them will form the basis upon which local people will assess their authority's performance year on year. It is therefore essential that authorities put in place the necessary monitoring and scrutiny arrangements, involving both members and officers, to provide a regular check on performance: these need to give an early warning of potential slippage against targets or the emergence of unintended outcomes.

50.   Authorities will recognise that these Reviews have the potential to demonstrate that best value is owned by local government itself. That is why inspection under best value will as far as possible follow Reviews rather than precede them. Paragraphs 72–78 describe the steps which the different Inspectorates are taking to address the implications for their inspection programme and for their approach to inspection itself.

BEST VALUE PERFORMANCE PLANS

51.   The Best Value Performance Plan likewise provides authorities with the opportunity to engage with local people, and with others with an interest, around their record of delivering local services and their plans to improve upon them. They are intended as the principal means by which an authority is held to account for the efficiency and effectiveness of its services, and for its plans for the future.

52.   Performance Plans should reflect the strategic objectives and corporate priorities of the authority, and act as a bridge between these and the service specific and financial plans which are required for resource allocation and other purposes. They will bring together performance information of corporate relevance from these different sources in a form which is accessible to local people. Such plans are therefore more than summaries of information provided elsewhere: they offer the potential to add real value by bringing together information on authorities' performance and budgeting across all services. This will facilitate a genuine dialogue with local people on local priorities, and also influence the response local authorities receive from the private and voluntary sectors, who will be looking to Performance Plans to provide an indication of service delivery opportunities and of an authority's commitment to engage in constructive partnership.

53.   Section 6 of the 1999 Act and SI 1999/3251 lay down the matters which must be included in the Performance Plan. These amount to a clear statement about:

- what services an authority will deliver to local people
- how it will deliver them
- to what levels services are currently delivered
- what levels of service the public should expect in the future

- what action it will take to deliver such levels of service and over what timescale.

54.   Plans must include:

- **a summary of the authority's objectives in respect of its functions.** These will derive from the authority's overall vision and community strategy, and from any corporate planning processes which give effect to that vision. The summary will also reflect nationally set objectives, any medium term financial strategy, and identify service priorities.

- **a summary of current performance.** This will need to include performance against the national best value indicators, and might usefully draw upon any indicators that are identified by the Audit Commission or required by Government for planning or programme purposes. It should also include performance against local sustainable development indicators and especially those developed locally to reflect community preferences. The summary should also include any commentary that authorities might wish to make which would help place their performance in context. For example, comparative information can be presented in the form of a schematic diagram showing performance against the average nationally or by type of authority.

- **a comparison with performance in previous financial years.** Authorities will need to provide an historic context for local people to understand the performance data for the year in question. Fully audited indicators from the preceding financial year and, where practicable, a consideration of comparative information from other best value authorities should be included. Discrepancies that occur between estimated outturn and actual audited figures for each performance indicator should be highlighted.

- **a summary of the authority's approach to efficiency improvement.** Authorities need to take a corporate approach to improving efficiency, as well as to improving quality and effectiveness. The Performance Plan should set out how authorities have assessed the scope for improvements in efficiency, both in individual services and in the way the authority manages itself and its assets; how they propose to deliver better performance; and the level of efficiency improvement that they expect to achieve. The Government accepts that the scope for efficiency improvements will vary year-on-year and between authorities and services, but authorities should ensure that over time their proposed aggregate efficiency gains are consistent with the 2% per annum target currently set for local authority expenditure as a whole.

- **a statement describing the Review programme.** Authorities will need to explain and justify their Review programme, together with the commencement and completion dates for the early Reviews and the resources they intend to devote to them. Where there are critical areas of uncertainty that might affect a Review's timetable then these should be identified clearly. Otherwise, authorities should explain variations to previous Review programmes, and highlight where the Secretary of State or an Inspectorate has required a Review to be carried out at their request.

- **the key results of completed Reviews.** All Reviews that have been completed in the previous year should be reported on in summary form, and the Plan should include where possible information from those that are in train. The results of consultation, the alternatives considered, an explanation of the agreed outcome and a plan of action to achieve the new targets should be summarised clearly and, where necessary, should include a cross-reference to the source material.

- **the performance targets set for future years.** The Performance Plan will normally roll forward the targets set for both local and national indicators in previous years for the majority of services, adjusted as necessary in the light of the resources available and the authority's priorities. Where variations are included – especially if the targets were set following earlier Reviews – an authority would need to include a full justification for its actions and an assurance that the new targets would comply with best value. Authorities should highlight any new targets derived from Reviews and their implications, if any, for other service targets: this might be particularly important following those Reviews that have considered cross-cutting themes. In the first Performance Plan authorities will need to set targets against those BVPIs which mirror existing Audit Commission indicators. Authorities will not be expected to set targets against new indicators for 2000/01, given the lack of historic data, but will need to do so in their subsequent Performance Plans. Authorities will also wish to set other targets which reflect local priorities and build wherever possible on relevant historic data, such as recorded crime.

- **a plan of action.** Targets which involve a substantial departure from previous targets or performance, or which are set following a Review in the last year, should be accompanied by an action plan explaining how they are to be met. Similarly, when authorities have had to respond to an auditor or inspector's report, then there should be a clear response from the authority as to the steps it has taken or intends to take to address the issues raised. All action plans should include measurable milestones against which progress can be monitored.

- **a response to audit and inspection reports.** Recommendations from the previous year's audit report must be included. Authorities should also highlight any changes that have been made, or are expected to be made, following audit or inspection reports, or because of directions given by the Secretary of State.

- **a consultation statement.** A brief statement should be included explaining how the authority has complied with its duty to consult under Sections 3 and 5 of the 1999 Act. This could usefully comment on the forms and types of consultation carried out over the previous year, the numbers or types of groups, bodies and individuals involved and an analysis of the results. The statement could refer to previous consultations that have informed the Performance Plan, include contact details for those who wish to make representations, and provide information on how or where local people can remain involved or provide feedback. Any changes planned over the coming year to secure improved results from consultation should be highlighted.

- **financial information.** In summarising the level at which it exercises its functions and to assist local people in understanding how well it has performed, an authority should provide suitable financial information that places cost indicators in a wider context. A summary of its financial performance during the past year will be required and this should include the budgeted income of the authority with an analysis of budgeted expenditure for the year ahead. Other information such as details of major capital projects and investments, and changes to purchasing proposals should also be included. Paragraphs 68–71 describe plans to enhance the comparability of local authority financial information, and give further guidance on additional financial information that authorities should consider including in their first Plan.

55. Authorities are required to publish their first Performance Plans no later than 31 March 2000 and no later than 31 March in each subsequent year. The Plans will be subject to audit, normally by the same team auditing the previous year's financial accounts. Since the first Plan will report on performance and preparations made prior to the statutory introduction of the duty of best value, auditors will take this into account in their assessment which is to be completed by 30 June 2000. SI 1999/3251 requires, for the first Performance Plan, the inclusion of information for 1999/2000 as specified in the Audit Commission's Direction of 1998. The auditor will look to establish that the

necessary statutory requirements have been complied with as well as at actual and planned performance. Information contained within the Plan will be scrutinised to ensure it is reasonable and robust. The first Performance Plan is likely to provide clear evidence of an authority's approach to the introduction of best value and the steps it has taken to embrace the challenge of the years ahead. Auditors may refer Plans to the Secretary of State where they are not persuaded that an authority has made a serious attempt to address the issues in such a way as to ensure best value for local people. The Audit Commission will issue guidance to auditors later this year: this will include the circumstances which might trigger referral.

56.   Performance Plans will look both forwards and backwards. It will look backwards at the performance of the authority for the financial year just ending. For this, the use of provisional data – which may include estimates and projections – will be necessary. It will also contain the audited performance information for the year before that. The robustness and breadth of performance information available is expected to improve as authorities establish better performance management procedures, but local people will rightly look for information of the highest possible standard and authorities are responsible for its accuracy. The Plan will also look forwards in identifying the targets that authorities have set themselves for the next and future years, and a concise course of action for achieving these targets. The Government will set out in guidance shortly the factors which authorities should take into account when setting targets against the national BVPIs (see paragraphs 28–29). Home Office guidance on target-setting for certain of the police authority indictors on recorded crime will be issued next year following consultation with the police service. The Home Office have already written to police authorities and forces on this issue.

57.   The published Plan will enable authorities to demonstrate to a wider audience the effectiveness of the authority itself and its relations with the community of which it is a part. There is a balance to be struck between explaining the content of all the other plans, programmes and initiatives in which the authority is involved, and providing local people with sufficient information to reach a rounded view on the performance and aims of the authority. It will not be possible – nor would it be desirable – to include the details of all individual service plans, inspectors' reports and Reviews. Nevertheless, a clear summary of such information – focussing on the key outcomes and targets – is necessary, together with an audit trail of supporting information.

58.   The Government accepts that there are many different ways of presenting the required performance information and that authorities will wish to explore the various options over time. An authority might, for example, choose to present the relevant details within service specific chapters, or list all the performance information targets within a separate section, with another section explaining the service strategy and review work of the authority. Alternatively, some authorities may take as a starting point the results of the year's Reviews and provide information in later sections. Other authorities might adopt an approach focusing on particular neighbourhoods, urban or rural areas, sections of the community, or based on cross-cutting themes. Much will depend on an authority's corporate stance on these matters, as in the case of the selection of services for Reviews.

59.   Although the Government does not intend to specify the precise format of Performance Plans, it expects authorities to adopt a clear and accessible style and an attractive design. It is working with the Audit Commission, the LGA and the I&DeA to identify good practice in presenting auditable Performance Plans to a wider audience

and will discuss its proposals with those representing service customers, providers and employees.

60. Published Performance Plans will need to balance the specific requirements of the legislation in respect of audit against the general requirements of transparency and accessibility. The Government views both requirements as consistent with real accountability to local people. It accepts, however, that to engage local people and local interests fully in best value and in the outcomes which are presented in Performance Plans, authorities will need to supplement these Plans by providing summarised information to local households and other places of residence, and to service users and local business and voluntary interests. Any such summaries should offer a fair and accurate reflection of information within the Plans themselves. Authorities will be free to select which indicators and targets they might highlight alongside other information, but should have regard to key national and local priorities and any action which they have in hand to tackle performance weaknesses. Summaries should also include a guide as to how the complete documentation might be viewed or accessed (in libraries or on the Internet, for example), and what arrangements are in place to handle queries and comments. Both Plans and summaries should be available by 31 March each year in as many forms as necessary to ensure fair access for the whole local community.

AUDIT AND ACCOUNTING

61. The independent audit of Performance Plans is designed to reassure local people first and foremost that their authority's account of its own performance and its targets for the future are reasonable and robust. It is not intended as a commentary on the policies of the authority as such, and neither does it purport to cover the ground principally envisaged for an inspection under best value. It is an important check on an authority's capacity to achieve best value, and will complement the financial audit and the inspection process.

62. The external auditor is required to prepare a report on an authority's published Performance Plan, and local authorities must ensure appropriate publicity for that report as soon as possible following its receipt by 30 June each year. Copies will be sent to:

- the authority
- the Audit Commission
- the Secretary of State for the Environment, Transport and the Regions (where the report recommends that a direction should be given)

63. In completing the report, the auditor will seek to ensure that the Performance Plan has been prepared and published in accordance with the statutory requirements and guidance. This will include an assessment of whether the Plan includes all the required information, whether the authority has in place proper arrangements to ensure that the Plan presents a fair and accurate reflection of its performance for that year and the targets set are realistic and achievable. The Government recommends that authorities include a 'statement of responsibility' in the Performance Plan. Such a statement might take the following form:

'The Authority is responsible for the preparation of the Performance Plan and for the information and assessments set out within it, and the assumptions and estimates on which they are based. The Authority is also responsible for setting in place appropriate performance management and internal control systems from which the information and assessments in the Performance Plan have been derived. The Authority is satisfied that the information and assessments included in the plan are in all material respects accurate and complete and that the plan is realistic and achievable.'

64.   Auditors will also consult the relevant Inspectorates before reaching a view. They will also, where appropriate, make recommendations as to:

- the way in which the Plan should be amended
- any procedures to be followed by the authority in relation to the Plan
- whether or not there should be a special inspection of the authority
- whether or not the Secretary of State should give a direction.

65.   In carrying out the audit of Performance Plans, auditors will act within the spirit of statements provided by the Public Audit Forum, particularly that included in the *Modernising Government* White Paper (Cmmd. 4310) whereby auditors will:

- adopt an open-minded and supportive approach to innovation
- support well thought through risk-taking and experimentation
- provide advice and encouragement to authorities by promoting good practice and shared experience.

The Audit Commission will also shortly publish guidance to auditors carrying out the audit of Performance Plans with a view to securing consistency in the interpretation of legislation and the advice in this circular.

66.   It will be the responsibility of the local authority to ensure that all reports produced by the external auditor are published as quickly as possible following their receipt. Where the auditor's report contains a recommendation for action, the authority must prepare a statement explaining the action that it intends to take as a result of the report and its proposed timetable for doing so. This statement should be prepared within 30 working days of receipt of the report, or within any shorter period specified by the auditor, and sent to the Secretary of State where required. The auditor will assess whether the action taken is appropriate and make further recommendations where necessary. The finalised statement and relevant explanations must be incorporated within the following year's Performance Plan.

67.   External auditors are likely to look for any significant differences between projected and actual returns and, where these occur, they should be explained and corrected in the following year's Performance Plan. Authorities' internal auditors have a key role to play in all aspects of best value, and the Audit Commission expect to publish guidance shortly as to how that role might be enhanced.

68.   CIPFA's *Best Value Accounting – Code of Practice* is being prepared to provide local authorities with accounting guidance which will enhance the comparability of local authority financial information. The Code will help authorities comply with the provisions of Sections 5 and 6 of the 1999 Act and the order made under these sections, and be recognised as proper practice for all best value authorities. The Code, upon which there has already been wide consultation, will be published in early 2000 and will apply to the accounting arrangements supporting March 2001 Best Value Performance Plans. A series of documents on the detailed work on the Code can be found on CIPFA's website at **http://www.cipfa.org.uk/pt/bestvalue.html**

69.   For the first Performance Plan, and prior to the introduction of the *Best Value Accounting – Code of Practice*, the Government recommends that authorities include a summary disclosure note listing the nature, turnover and profit/loss of any significant trading operations engaged in by the authority for which separate accounts are maintained. For this, where balances on trading accounts are significant such that

relevant performance indicators would be materially misstated, the balances should be re-apportioned to services. The apportionments should be disclosed as part of the summary disclosure note. The forthcoming Code will provide further guidance on this.

70. Any such information included in the Performance Plan will require the use of provisional accounting returns and wherever possible authorities should aim to draw upon regular monthly or quarterly returns to enhance its credibility. Authorities will need in any case to develop in-house accounting and budgeting systems to ensure the accuracy of any financial information required for inclusion in Plans in subsequent years.

71. Section 23 of the 1999 Act provides the Secretary of State with powers to make regulations about the keeping of accounts by best value authorities, following consultation with the appropriate bodies. The Secretary of State will decide whether he should exercise those powers after publication of the *Best Value Accounting – Code of Practice.*

INSPECTION

72. All functions will be subject to inspection under best value. Many are already scrutinised by the existing specialist Inspectorates: the Benefit Fraud Inspectorate; HM Fire Services Inspectorate; HM Inspectorate of Constabulary; the Social Services Inspectorate; and the Office for Standards in Education (OFSTED). The Audit Commission has been given the scrutiny role for those areas not previously subject to inspection, and will work in partnership with the existing specialist Inspectorates where it is sensible to do so.

73. The Local Government Act 1999 contains a number of new provisions regarding inspection. Section 10 provides for the Audit Commission to carry out inspections for best value purposes and for the Secretary of State to direct inspections to be carried out should he so decide. Further provisions give the Commission the necessary access to documents and premises, as well as providing for fees to be set, grant to be received from central government and for reports to be issued. Section 25 provides for the Secretary of State to issue guidance to the relevant Inspectorates for the purpose of securing the co-ordination of inspection work under best value, and he will do so should the need arise.

74. The new inspection arrangements will have a key role to play in delivering best value. Inspection reports will:

- enable the public to see whether best value is being delivered
- enable the inspected body to see how well it is doing
- enable the Government to see how well its policies are working on the ground
- identify failing services where remedial action may be necessary
- identify and disseminate best practice.

Reports will also be published, and details of publication arrangements will be provided to authorities during the course of inspections.

75. Inspection will not remove the responsibility for delivering best value from local authorities. That is why best value inspections will, as far as possible, and where legal and

resource considerations permit, follow authorities' own Reviews. Authorities can make a significant difference to the inspection process by ensuring that their Reviews show clearly how the statutory guidance has been followed and how outcomes have been and will be secured. This will avoid duplication of effort between the Review and the inspection processes, and in turn minimise pressure on the inspected body. Authorities should be clear, however, that inspection is not limited to the information generated by a Review: it will also probe the current state of service provision, particularly from the viewpoint of users. Details of the Review programme provided in annual Performance Plans will increasingly be taken into account in the programming of inspections. As a transitional arrangement for the first year of best value, authorities have been asked to provide such information to their external auditors ahead of completing their first Performance Plans.

76.   The frequency of best value inspections is at the discretion of the Inspectorates carrying them out. The Audit Commission's expectation is that, as with the Reviews themselves, inspections of all functions will take place at least once within any five year period, and be aligned as far as possible with the Review cycle. In addition, the Secretary of State may at any time direct that an inspection should be carried out wherever there is a cause for concern about the performance of the authority, following an annual audit report for example. Such inspections may necessarily take place ahead of an authority's own Review and will typically be more fundamental and searching in order to reach a proper diagnosis of the problems.

77.   Each Inspectorate will adapt its working methods to accommodate its own new role and the new role of inspected authorities under best value. Existing Inspectorates will incorporate the best value role alongside their existing responsibilities. The Audit Commission has already consulted on a set of principles for public inspection which received widespread endorsement. Important principles include those that confirm that inspection should inform the public and focus on services as users experience them, and that the scale of inspection should be proportionate to risk. The outcome of a further Audit Commission consultation on inspection methodology *From principles to practice* will be published shortly. It will confirm that authorities will have an opportunity to own the findings of inspection – because inspections will build upon Reviews and share an interim view with the authority, for example – and that the relevant report will be clear and simple, and addressed to all the key audiences, including local people. The issues raised by these proposals will be discussed by the different Inspectorates collectively.

78.   The Best Value Inspectorate Forum has been set up to act as a focus for such discussions. It will also provide a channel of communication between local authorities, Inspectorates and central government, and be an important vehicle for sharing best practice. The Terms of Reference of the Forum[2] are at **Annex E**. The Forum's priorities for the year ahead are as follows:

- to consider the scope for co-ordinating programmes of audit and inspection
- to develop and enhance arrangements for working together.

The inspection process will evolve in line with the experience gained by both the Inspectorates and the inspected bodies. The Forum will, from time-to-time, publish reports and papers for discussion and will welcome views from those with an interest in improving public services.

---

2   A separate Inspectorate Forum, with broadly similar Terms of Reference, exists for Wles. HM Inspectorate of Constabulary and HM Fire Service Inspectorate are also members of that Forum in order to ensure consistency between inspection arrangements for the police and fire services in England and Wales.

TACKLING FAILING SERVICES

79. Section 15 of the 1999 Act provides the Secretary of State with powers to act where authorities are failing to deliver best value. The Government is committed to working with best value authorities and others to ensure that the incidence of such failure is minimised and has made clear that intervention will be the exception. However, it will not hesitate to act where necessary to protect the interests of local people and the users of services.

80. The powers of the Secretary of State are flexible and wide-ranging in order to ensure that the most appropriate form of action is available, including the removal of responsibility for a function from an authority altogether. The legislation provides for an authority to make representations before a decision is taken to intervene, except where the Secretary of State considers it urgent to do so under Section 15(11) – such circumstances might arise, for example, when services to vulnerable people are seriously deficient.

81. A protocol has been agreed with the Local Government Association setting out the principles under which these wide-ranging powers will be used and the procedures that will be followed at each stage. Amongst the key principles are that:

- the Secretary of State will only act on clear evidence of failure
- the form and extent of intervention should reflect the type and seriousness of failure and the need for effective improvement
- except in cases of serious service failure or unless there is a need for urgent intervention, the authority will normally be given the opportunity to make the necessary improvement itself
- best value authorities will provide accurate and timely responses to requests for information, and co-operate with such action as the Secretary of State may direct in accordance with his powers and the protocol.

82. The full text of the protocol is at **Annex D**. This recognises that responsibility for standards of performance rests with authorities themselves. Where improvement is needed, authorities are encouraged to seek help from other authorities, the LGA and the I& DeA.

83. The Home Office has agreed a separate protocol with the Association of Police Authorities and the Association of Chief Police Officers setting out the principles under which the new intervention powers will be used under the tripartite structure of policing. The Home Office has issued this protocol separately to all police authorities.

FAIR EMPLOYMENT

84. The Government recognises the importance of fair employment and that a well-motivated and well-trained workforce is vital to the provision of public services whether employed in the public, private or voluntary sectors. Sustained improvement under best value depends on employees being committed to providing the public with high quality and cost-effective services.

85. The Government has acted to enhance employees' rights and promote fairness in the labour market. These measures include:

- the implementation of the National Minimum Wage which establishes minimum standards for all employees
- the Employment Relations Act 1999 which implements the measures proposed in the White Paper *Fairness at Work* (Cmmd. 3968) and contains important reforms extending good practice in the workplace, so that all employees enjoy decent basic standards at work, and helps people to combine their work and family responsibilities
- the Working Time and Young Workers Directives which provide fair minimum standards for workers.

86.   Getting the best from staff and maximising the potential of the labour market generally involves more than compliance with minimum standards. It also depends on a positive and effective approach to **equal opportunities**. This applies throughout the process of delivering services, but authorities should consider corporately, and as part of their Performance Review programme, the extent to which their recruitment and management practices achieve the standards set out in the codes of practice on employment issued by the Commission for Racial Equality and the Equal Opportunities Commission, as well as guidance issued by DfEE in respect of the Disability Discrimination Act 1995. The Commission for Racial Equality's *Standard for Racial Equality for Local Government* and the Equal Opportunities Commission's *Mainstreaming gender equality in local authorities* will both assist authorities in securing an effective approach to equal opportunities.

87.   The Government is committed to a competitive economy with a flexible labour market underpinned by the fair treatment of those involved. New forms of partnership with the private and voluntary sectors and other public bodies will co-exist with, and often supersede, the way in which authorities have tendered previously. In either case, if it is to be effective, competition must be fair, seen to be fair and conducted in a spirit where employees' rights are fully respected.

88.   Both employers and employees need to have confidence in the fairness of the competitive process. The Government will amend Part II of the Local Government Act 1988 in such a way as to enable local authorities to take into account appropriate workforce matters in the selection of tenderers and the award of contracts, consistent with its EC obligations and the achievement of value for money. A consultation paper will be issued shortly and the Government expects to make the necessary Regulations ahead of 1 April 2000.

89.   The Government will also act to bring greater certainty to the processes involved in transferring staff to new employers. It will amend the *Transfer of Undertakings (Protection of Employment) Regulations 1981* (TUPE) in order to implement the revised *Acquired Rights Directive* and to improve their operation. The intention is that TUPE will apply to all staff transfers under best value, and will protect employees during the life of a contract. This will build upon the definition of a transfer secured in the revised Directive, adopted during the UK Presidency in 1998, in order to achieve as great a degree of certainty and clarity as possible in the Regulations' application (including the reassignment of contracts). The Government expects to publish a consultation paper early next year with a view to having new Regulations in place by the summer of 2000.

90.   The Government has also published a *Statement of Practice on Staff Transfers in the Public Sector*. This makes clear that public/private partnerships and contracting exercises (including re-tendering) in the public sector, will be conducted on the basis that staff will transfer and that TUPE will apply, unless there are genuinely exceptional reasons for their not doing so – for example where an activity is an essentially new or one-off project. The Government expects all public sector organisations to adopt this

statement of practice. It is available from the Cabinet Office website at www.cabinet-office.gov.uk

91.   The Government also wishes to see that employees' pension entitlements are secured in staff transfers to the private sector. The Statement of Practice includes HM Treasury guidance entitled *Staff Transfers from Central Government: A Fair Deal for Staff Pensions.* That guidance was drafted with specific reference to staff transfers from central Government Departments and Agencies, on whom it was binding immediately, but Ministers said at the time that they also wanted other public sector contracting authorities to make arrangements to meet the standards of protection for staff pensions which it set out, consistent with the law and good procurement practice.

92.   As set out in the guidance, there are two separate but related aspects to protection of pensions in a staff transfer. First, to ensure continuity of pension accrual where the transferred staff leave the public pension scheme they should be offered membership of an alternative scheme by the new employer which is actuarially certified as being 'broadly comparable' with the public service scheme. This certification should be by reference to the criteria for 'broad comparability' set out by the Government Actuary, meaning that no identifiable employees should suffer material detriment overall in terms of future pensions accrual. Secondly, there should be a 'bulk transfer' agreement with the new employer's pension scheme providing that staff will be able to transfer their accrued service credits into that scheme on a day-for-day, or equivalent, basis.

93.   In the case of employees who are members of the Local Government Pension Scheme (LGPS), there will be an alternative to the requirement to the broadly comparable scheme approach. It will be possible instead for the new employer, if they wish, to seek 'non-associated employer' status within the LGPS, so that transferred staff continue to have access to that pension scheme for their future service. Guidance on this option will be issued along with the proposed *Local Government Pension Scheme (Amendment) Regulations.* Whichever route is chosen for the protection of staff pensions, local authorities should apply the general principles set out in the Treasury guidance referred to in paragraph 91:

•   to treat staff fairly
•   to do so openly and transparently
•   to involve staff and their representatives fully in consultation about pensions aspects of the transfer at an early stage
•   and to have clear accountability within the local authority for the results.

94.   Enquiries about this circular should be addressed to Local Government Competition and Quality Division, Department of the Environment, Transport and the Regions, Zone 5/B5, Eland House, Bressenden Place, London SW1E 5DU (Tel: 020 7890 4107) or emailed to bv_circular@detr.gov.uk

J.R. Footitt, Assistant Secretary

ANNEX A

THE BEST VALUE PILOT PROGRAMME

Background

Since April 1998, 38 best value pilot projects have been under way. These include projects run by 34 individual local authorities, two joint projects by local authorities, and two police authorities. The pilots were granted exemptions from the requirements of compulsory competitive tendering (CCT) where this was possible. In addition, there are also six pilot Partnership Networks. These are made up of authorities that are experimenting with various forms of partnership, particularly with the private sector.

The pilots are playing a key role in working up best practice and providing practical experience of successful approaches. They have adopted a range of interesting and innovative approaches to best value and have learnt valuable lessons. Their experience is playing an important part in helping to shape the detail of best value.

A research team led by Warwick University Business School has been evaluating and monitoring the best value pilot programme on behalf of the Department. Researchers visited the pilots during the spring to identify the lessons learned during the first year and have now produced an interim evaluation report.

THE BEST VALUE PILOTS IN ENGLAND

Birmingham City Council

Birmingham's pilot project involves a comprehensive review focussed on: services for tenants, benefits service, services for older people and catering. All four areas of the pilot were chosen because of their performance, issues arising from public consultation and their impact on each other. They centre on working across departmental and organisational boundaries. Together the project represents 22% of the City Council's budget.

Bradford City Council

Bradford's pilot draws on one of the five priorities identified in their Community Plan, 'Fighting Crime for a Safer District.' The returns to the public consultation exercise mounted during the development of the Community Plan identified crime as a matter of public concern. The ten services selected for the pilot scheme contribute to community safety, as well as providing a balanced approach to best value.

Braintree District Council

Braintree is using the opportunities provided by best value to completely revisit their approach to strategy formulation and service delivery. They had a well-developed corporate approach to service planning and the best value programme was designed to build on that. They are reviewing all their services in a four year cycle, making sure that they address the community-based principles of Local Agenda 21, sustainability, quality and equality.

London Borough of Brent

Brent's pilot focuses on Kilburn, an area of social, economic and cultural diversity, which attracts SRB and URBAN funding and for which the authority is developing a local area strategy. Best value is being pursued in the context of the cross boundary issues of social exclusion, community safety and regeneration. The services covered are: housing related services, refuse and cleansing services, highways enforcement, council benefits services and community safety issues.

Brighton and Hove Council

Brighton and Hove's whole authority pilot includes a 5-year review programme. The reviews aim to achieve improvements in service performance and cost reduction or containment, which reflect the priorities of the community. Brighton and Hove have mainstreamed best value through an approach to reviews which are managed departmentally, whilst retaining a corporate steer by member involvement and an officers' cross-departmental steering group.

Bristol City Council

Bristol's pilot project contains four elements. The first is the development of the corporate framework for undertaking best value work in the authority. The second is the integration of the City Centre strategy with the Council's corporate priorities, particularly those that relate to young and elderly people. The third project involves providing free community access to electronic information, building on the success of the Digital City Bristol initiative. The fourth examines the use of in-house transport provision and the options for rationalisation.

London Borough of Camden

Camden's pilot is an all-authority project, covering fifteen services in the first year. The services chosen for review were a mixture of in-house and externally provided services, giving a mixture of the good, the bad and the average. Each service in the pilot bid was expected to text itself against the five principles of best value for Camden.

Carrick District Council

Carrick's pilot covers all housing services: management, maintenance, homelessness and housing advice, enabling and allocations, housing services to the elderly, private sector housing and grants. Housing was identified as a key service because of an acute shortage of affordable housing and a need for investment in public and private housing stocks.

Cleveland Police Constabulary

The pilot is based on a whole organisational approach, focused on how the Middlesbrough police district delivers front line police services to the community and how such front-line services are supported by the organisation. Middlesbrough district was chosen to permit comparison with the force as a whole. It also provides challenges in terms of delivering police services.

Cumbria County Council

The pilot project focuses on issues of disability and mental health. The services covered are: residential facilities; supported housing; day care; home care; sheltered employment, and education. Cumbria Council developed a purchaser/provider split for the provision of care services, and the pilot project sought to apply the lessons learned to the complex area of disability and mental health. They are seeking to achieve a negotiated joint commissioning strategy with the Health Authorities.

CWOIL (Cambridge, Welwyn Hatfield, Oxford, Ipswich and Lincoln)

The CWOIL pilot is a collaborative project between five authorities concentrating on housing and revenues services. The approach is based on benchmarking and continuous improvement. 12 specific service areas were identified for fundamental service reviews. The first year areas were homelessness, housing advice, repairs, local taxation, benefits and cashiers.

Exeter City Council

Exeter chose an area covering 6 of the 18 wards in the north of the city to pilot the project. Services covered are: housing, including housing benefits and private sector housing; environmental services, and social services including care in the community, community safety, health promotion and community facilities. The authority proposed to work in partnership with Devon County Council, North and East Devon Health Authority and Exeter Council for Voluntary Services.

Gosport District Council

As part of their Local Agenda 21 initiative, Gosport undertook a major consultation exercise. The three pilot projects: housing, building control and food safety were chosen because consultation identified the importance of the relationship between service users and the Council. The Council recognised that these services were in different stages of development.

Great Yarmouth Borough Council

The Council developed a social strategy in partnership with Norfolk County Council, East Norfolk Health Authority and the local Association of Voluntary Organisations. The aim is to reduce current levels of social deprivation in Great Yarmouth. The Council chose to pilot services that contributed to this aim. The services piloted were seven in housing, two in finance, planning, economic development, environmental health, amenities, leisure, recreation, welfare rights, refuse collection and street cleansing.

Greater Manchester Police

The force decided to pilot its approach to best value in four inner city sub-divisions in Manchester and Salford. These were chosen as typical areas of the organisation which undertake a wide range of front line services. These services can be broadly divided into five main categories: crime management, traffic management, public reassurance and public order management, responding to and dealing with calls from the public, and community relations and community problem solving.

London Borough of Greenwich

The Greenwich pilot covered eight services: advice and benefits, domiciliary care, early years services, education inspectorate and advice, housing repairs, libraries, property management and passenger transport. These provided a variety of service types, covered the majority of Council directorates, and presented a range of different problems and potential solutions. In terms of overall expenditure, these services amounted to some £60 m.

London Borough of Harrow

The Harrow pilot comprises four specific fundamental reviews that are path-finding a whole-authority approach to best value that aims to examine all functions over a three-year period. The major pilots are: domiciliary care, special needs transport, education administration and financial services.

Ipswich Borough Council

Ipswich embarked on a 5-year best value programme to review all council services. The first phase of the programme identified 20% of services, which form the pilot project. A number of criteria were used to select the services included in the pilot. The services are: tax and benefits; development control, building and design services, theatre and museums, Corporate Directors Team, town centre management, Town Hall and Corn Exchange, community safety, and transportation.

Leeds City Council

The project focuses on the delivery of integrated services that meet local needs in the most efficient and effective way. It covers two contrasting wards in the south of the city, Middleton and Rothwell. The services proposed for review include some subject to CCT and some provided directly. They are: advice and benefits, social services, training, street cleaning, community sport, grounds maintenance, libraries, housing, refuse collection, street lighting and highways maintenance. A specific focus of the project is to examine how services can improve the levels of service to older people and make an impact on community safety in the area.

London Borough of Lewisham

Lewisham's bid has three main elements. The first is increasing accountability to residents and involving the community through a community plan, a new business panel and a Lewisham citizens panel. The second is introducing new council-wide performance and quality systems. The third is a strategic review of services during the three years of the pilot, representing more than 20% of the Council's budget. The major service areas reviewed in the first year of the project include education standards, housing benefits and housing company, passenger transport, community safety, leisure, environmental services, catering PFI, revenues, construction and property services.

Lincolnshire County Council

The aim of Lincolnshire's pilot is to build upon its established track record of securing alternative methods of service delivery. A corporate review of services was carried out to identify priority service areas for review. The priority services, being covered in year one of the pilot project represent 21% of the Council's budget. They include: waste disposal, corporate parent and looked-after-children, highways maintenance, student and school services, home care, community services, Fire Brigade services, and finance and resources.

Manchester City Council

Manchester's pilot aims to build sustainable communities in three localities with different characteristics. It identifies three areas of improvement on which the Council wishes to concentrate: physical environment, educational standards, parenting skills and family support, vandalism, disorder, crime and fear of crime. The focus is on early, preventive intervention and on cross-service improvements across departmental and agency boundaries.

Newark and Sherwood District Council

Following a corporate organisational review, the Council submitted a Best Value bid comprising a mixture of internal and external services. These were: revenues, benefits, legal, housing, information technology and environmental and direct services. The objectives of the programme are: to encourage active citizenship, to continuously improve customer service, and to demonstrate innovation in local governance.

City of Newcastle-upon-Tyne

Newcastle has a twin track approach to Best Value. The first element is the development of a corporate framework for best value. The second consists of two pilot projects: integrated environmental services and Council Tax collection. The Council's overall aims are to improve services, reduce costs where possible and to bring about a democratic revival and real meaning to the involvement of local people in their services.

London Borough of Newham

Newham proposed that all the authority's services would be reviewed over the three years of the pilot programme, with 27 services being considered within the first year. They aimed to achieve cost savings, improve service quality levels and increase externally supplied services. This was an ambitious and wide ranging bid from an authority located in an area confronted by formidable problems of social and economic deprivation. The breadth of the programme provided a challenge to the authority's capacity to undertake a large volume of reviews within a tight timetable.

Northamptonshire County Council

The overall strategy for the pilot stems from the review of the Council structure and management processes and is based on the implementation of a performance plan. The pilot bid comprises four service areas from each major department. These are highways and transportation, residential care for the elderly, waste management, and youth services. The performance planning process is designed to include consultation with other agencies and the public.

Oldham MBC

Oldham's project is aimed at improving the quality of life within the Chadderton area of the Borough by providing residents with improved services and the opportunity to influence those services. It seeks to integrate the services of housing management, buildings maintenance, grounds maintenance, highways and street lighting, refuse collection and street cleaning.

Portsmouth City Council

Portsmouth has selected eight projects for review, on the basis of four residents surveys backed up by community consultation meetings. They are: reducing high levels of school exclusion, providing a better service for pupils with learning difficulties, responding to concern about crime and the safety of parks, improving support for young people leaving care, obtaining better value for money in residential care, improving job prospects through economic development, enhancing partnerships with the private sector and achieving value for money in asset management.

Reading Council

The purpose of Reading's pilot is to examine how working in partnership can improve the range and quality of services available to the public. Reading proposed to: develop a mechanism to improve service delivery in partnerships, develop a wider range of partnerships and publish a guide to partnership opportunities.

Redcar and Cleveland Council

Redcar and Cleveland's pilot covers all the services provided by the authority, but incorporates five individual projects. These are: a training and development initiative, a local estates service initiative, the Occupational Therapy Service project, a Council Tax collection project and a housing/council tax benefit joint service delivery project. The local estates service initiative is a multi-agency scheme, targeted at Grangetown, aimed at developing a model for service delivery with direct community and stakeholder involvement.

Southampton City Council

The Council's best value pilot concentrates on the quality of life facing older people and how it could be improved by joint action within the city. It was devised in partnership with a range of organisations within the city and focused on the needs of the more vulnerable members of the older population. Three initiatives to be explored in the first year were: a crisis prevention and support scheme, 'night watch' services for older people at night, and a 'Home Safe' package to enable vulnerable old people to remain at home. Housing services play a key part in all these projects.

South Norfolk District Council

South Norfolk chose to review services that would contribute to the authority's aim to tackle social exclusion. The services include: increasing employment opportunities, sustaining rural community viability, housing and leisure for all, welfare rights and rural transport.

Sunderland City Council

Sunderland's pilot involves sixty young people moving from social exclusion to inclusion in the world of work through a structured programme of real work experience, vocational training and personal development. The pilot is testing service provision in youth justice, after care, housing, leisure, adult education, youth and personnel services.

Surrey County Council

Surrey's best value pilot has four elements: community profiling, community planning, community commissioning and community indicators. These processes involve the authority working jointly with the community in identifying service needs, planning, commissioning and monitoring services. Community Co-ordinators and Community Service managers have been appointed to identify and co-ordinate local needs and priorities. The bid focuses on Epsom and Ewell and on three services: library, adult education and youth services, which are being integrated with a community focus.

Tandridge and Wealden Councils

Tandridge and Wealden joined together to deliver Council Tax, Business Rates, and Housing and Council Tax Benefits as a consortium. The partners argued that, if joint working in Council Tax and Benefit processing could deliver efficiencies of scale, the national savings could be significant. The councils considered the options for a jointly delivered service and are evaluating the option of a centralised process centre with local enquiry facilities.

Warwickshire County Council

The pilot programme covers all services and aims to secure across-the-board benefits by a comprehensive regime of performance management and continuous improvement. All services are being reviewed and improved every year. The involvement of customers, citizens and other stakeholders is being increased.

Watford District Council

The pilot seeks to illustrate a comprehensive strategic process that applies to all elements of the Council's activities. It includes: community planning, ethical procurement, delivery partnerships, organisational development, performance management and policy-led resource allocation. The service areas cover: keeping the town clean and recycling, traffic congestion, building and development control, environmental health, Housing and Council Tax Benefits youth services and improving the quality of life in Leavesden Green.

City of York

The aim of the pilot is to generate savings, improve services and working with other public and private organisations. The services covered in the bid are: street lighting, school meals, commercial waste, libraries, personnel and payroll, independent living, transport procurement, and leisure services.

The best value pilots have undertaken a wide variety of projects relating to best value. The following examples, in the pilots' own words, have been selected to demonstrate the different aspects of best value. Some pilots have concentrated on collaboration and partnership, others have emphasised the consultation process. Other aspects highlighted are benchmarking, performance reviews, all-service reviews and cross-cutting issues.

CAMDEN COUNCIL

Putting the customer first

Background

'In October 1997, Camden Council published the *Camden Plan*. This laid out our goals for the future of the borough, and our aim to provide quality services and to be a leading, progressive borough. We have achieved most of the targets in the plan and we now intend to update it. We have already produced a Best Value Performance Plan (BVPP) and we are consulting on a new community plan, which we will publish in June 2000.

In Camden, we are striving to make our services as efficient and as cost-effective as possible. We believe that the best way to check our progress is to ask local people what they think. The *Camden Plan* committed the Council to survey local residents every two years and to use the information to improve public satisfaction with council services. This year, we have also set up a Citizens' Panel with Camden and Islington Health Authority. This involves 1,500 Camden residents who are representative of the borough as a whole. We will consult the panel regularly on a range of issues and proposals.

Access to all views

Children's views count too. We have produced a pioneering guide to consulting and involving young people, and have worked with them to draw up a strategy for young people in Camden. School Councils are being developed in every Camden school. Camden was also chosen by the Local Government Association to launch Local Democracy Week 1999. This had a particular focus on involving young people in local politics. We have launched a new website – www.camden.gov.uk – and we are piloting touch-screen kiosks to give everybody access to the website. Residents will be able to use it to find out everything from details of council services to places of interest in Camden.

Best Value reviews

Fifteen services, representing roughly 26 per cent of Camden's budget, were the subject of Best Value reviews in 1998–99. These services were chosen for various reasons. Many were already improving; some were known to be "failing services"; some offered us opportunities to develop partnerships with the private sector and other external providers. This would bring in investment and help to ensure that services were delivered effectively. We learned a lot.

For example, the review of the school meals service shows our approach to putting the customer first. There were concerns that the current service, although cheap, did not offer best value. The review surveyed parents and pupils (both users and non-users of the service) in a representative sample of eight schools. The key findings were:

- 21% of users said that they were always satisfied with the service in general;
- only 2.7% of users were always dissatisfied; and
- 55% were usually satisfied.

Mostly, people wanted to see an increase in the number and range of choices each day; they wanted catering and school staff to be more pleasant and helpful; and food serving temperatures to be increased. Parents and carers in particular also wished to see healthier food on the menu. For the Council's part, we wanted to make sure that more of the meals were eaten rather than wasted.

Targets for improvement

As a result of best value, all these issues have been built into a new contract, and we are confident that the appointed contractor (Serviceteam) will achieve them to the satisfaction of users. The target is that, after one year of operation, the number of customers who are always satisfied should increase to 25% and the number always dissatisfied should decrease to 2%. Since the start of the new contract in April 1999, the amount of school meals eaten has increased by 16.2%.'

Camden London Borough Council, Camden Town Hall, Judd Street, London WC1H 8LE, tel: 020-7278 4444, web http://www.camden.gov.uk

CARRICK DISTRICT COUNCIL

Measuring the quality and cost of housing

Background

'Carrick District Council in Cornwall was keen to give its customers the opportunity not just to suggest improvements to Council housing, but to measure the cost and quality of the housing, and then to judge whether we were delivering best value.

In housing services, our tenants can comment on "where things are going wrong" and "how things could be improved". But to make a judgement about best value, tenants needed more information about what tenants in other housing organisations were getting for their rent money.

Comparing costs and performance

We termed this "benchmarking" from the customer's perspective. We compared our costs, performance, employment practices and other factors with two other housing organisations. One was Pinnacle Ltd, the best and largest supplier of housing management services. The other was Penwith Housing Association, a neighbouring housing association of similar size and with similar commitments to social inclusion, resident involvement and customer care.

We gave our tenants information about the costs and qualities of the three organisations. We also provided an independent advisor to help tenants in their analysis, and to bring other information to the table.

The final part of the analysis was a joint conference of tenants from Carrick District Council and Penwith Housing Association. This allowed tenants to ask various "why" questions:

- Why do we do less of this?
- Why does this cost more at Carrick?
- Why do we spend this much when they spend that much?

An improving debate

This open debate required honesty and openness from the two landlords but gave the consumers real power – power to seek improvements, to challenge the status quo, and to confirm that their rent money was giving them best value.

After this exercise, tenants confirmed that we provided good value in a number of housing services, particularly rent recovery, neighbour nuisance, repairs and empty property management. But tenants sought improvements in tenant participation, the provision of rent account information, and staff absence owing to ill health. We agreed an improvement plan for these weaknesses which we are currently monitoring.'

Carrick District Council, Carrick House, Pydar Street, Truro, Cornwall, TR1 1EB (01872 224400)

EXETER CITY COUNCIL

Staff involvement in best value

Background

'Staff at Exeter City Council play an essential part in the best value process. Our view is that the customers who use the service and the staff who provide them are the people who know our services best. It was therefore essential from the outset of the pilot project to involve staff in the best value process, alongside the local community and partner agencies.

Training in best value

By providing best value training to every member of staff, we promoted awareness and a general understanding of the meaning of the term. The training set out to address both the technical and practical implications of best value. It encouraged staff to think about how their own service areas could be improved through better arrangements for consultation and partnership working. We followed up the training sessions with a series of lunchtime "drop in" sessions. These were available for staff to attend informally to discuss any queries or concerns about best value.

In September 1998, we carried out a staff satisfaction survey based on the Business Excellence Model. The survey was comprehensive. It covered areas from staff's general satisfaction with their jobs and working environment, to their views on policy and strategy. We achieved an excellent response rate and fed back the results in full to every member of staff. Afterwards, we analysed the findings by service area and used our information to identify issues to consider for each service review. We are doing another survey this year to see how staff perceptions have changed during the first twelve months of best value.

Involving staff in reviews

Our model for service reviews is staff involvement throughout. At the start of each review, all staff working in the service area met with the review group to discuss what the review covers, how staff may be affected and how they could be involved. Staff had direct involvement in the service review process through staff groups set up for each service review. The groups consisted of 8 to 10 members of staff and union representatives nominated by the wider workforce within the unit under review. Staff groups met regularly throughout the review process. Initially, they brainstormed the positive and negative aspects of the service, before going on to look at ways of improving service delivery. Finally, they looked at proposals of the full review group and fed back their comments. We consulted staff during the development of action plans which arose from reviews and encouraged them to set milestones and targets.

A number of service reviews have involved suggestion schemes for all staff working within the service under review or related services. We asked staff to anonymously provide as much or as little information as they chose about where they felt improvements were needed. This was from a service delivery and an employment point of view. Again, response rates were extremely high. Constructive staff ideas have helped to shape the service reviews and programmes for improvements.

Other reviews used a "staff case study" approach. We invited staff working within the service under review to prepare a diary of a typical week and to use this as the basis to discuss how we could address issues within the service review concerning the service provided, or working conditions.

Benefits to the Council

This approach has brought great benefits to the Council. Staff feedback has been positive and constructive. Ideas for service improvements have ranged from day-to-day operational matters, through strategic thoughts on joint service delivery and better customer focus. Staff groups have brought staff together from areas that were traditionally separate to address how to improve the services that customers receive. Ultimately, by taking part in the review process, staff have taken part in the decision-making process. They understand the reasons behind the decisions made and have a shared sense of ownership in improving the services that they provide.'

Exeter City Council – Civic Centre, Paris Street, Exeter, Devon, EX1 1JN (01392-277888)

LONDON BOROUGH OF LEWISHAM

Best Value Review of Education

Background

'In 1998, the London Borough of Lewisham decided to create a select committee as the main instrument for a best value review of education. The review concerned raising GCSE achievement. We decided that a select committee was the most direct way of carrying out this important review, and would also test the best value way of working.

The select committee was cross-party. It was chaired by a then backbench councillor, and included eight other councillors and a business representative. It worked on the parliamentary model and was supported by a range of officers and an external facilitator.

The review was evaluated through feedback from participants. Members felt empowered because they had come to grips with a difficult subject, and were able to make a real contribution. They pursued their own line of questioning rather than relying on officer reports. The real challenge was to maintain focus on one strand – what makes a difference to GCSE achievement – within a very broad policy area.

Full consultation and evidence-taking

The select committee certainly introduced challenge and commissioned a full programme of consultation. The committee held five meetings in public, between October and December 1998, and heard evidence and questioned witnesses as follows:

- Reports and presentations on stakeholder and community consultation including conference, focus groups, questionnaires to parents, governors and heads, residents and citizens' panel surveys.
- Witness statements and written evidence from London Borough of Lewisham Chair and Director of Education, Leader and Chief Executive; oral evidence from four Head Teachers and four Chairs of Governors.
- Oral and written evidence from the Director of Education, London Borough of Newham.
- Oral presentation by Greg Wilkinson, formerly of the Audit Commission and lead member for Education in the London Borough of Hammersmith & Fulham.
- Oral presentation by the Forum for Raising the Achievement of African and Afro-Caribbean Pupils, and from teachers unions.

The committee also considered a wide range of statistical and other written information. The programme allowed them to pursue issues from a variety of perspectives. They held sessions in schools, which were attended by a few but very interested and vocal members of the public.

A range of recommendations

At the end of the review the committee reached 33 recommendations. These covered accountability for targets, creating a culture of achievement, support and training for governors, and practical support for schools. These were reported to the Education Committee who responded and produced an action plan which has since been agreed by full council. We have published the select committee report, *Making a difference*, and distributed this widely in the borough.'

Lewisham London Borough Council, Lewisham Town Hall, London SE6 4RU, tel 020-8314 6000, web: http://www.lewisham.gov.uk

NEWCASTLE UPON TYNE

Integrating environmental services

Background

'At the start of the best value pilot project in Newcastle, we had a relatively high level of public dissatisfaction with a number of services. These included refuse collection, street cleansing, grounds maintenance, street lighting and road and footpath repairs.

We conducted an extensive consultation process with stakeholders in the four pilot wards. This included special forum meetings in each ward to find out about local needs and concerns. As a result, we identified residents' priorities for service improvement. These were better maintenance of roads and footpaths, reduction of dog mess and better street cleansing.

We drew up an action plan to try out new approaches to delivering services. Our aim was to achieve greater flexibility, integration and efficiency and to move to an approach driven by the needs and wishes of users and local communities. A review of service delivery challenged the compulsory competitive tendering (CCT) approach, which involved rigid specifications, pre-determined frequencies of provision and strict demarcation between services. We decided to remove the client/contractor split and put in place an integrated environment maintenance budget which allows a more flexible use of resources.

Specific project initiatives

The scheme has involved a number of special initiatives:

- A dedicated customer call centre (Envirocall), to respond to all enquiries for front-line environmental services. It monitors progress and provides management information which helps us to improve services.
- A wheeled bin refuse collection service. We tested this in the pilot area and are extending the service across the city over the next two years. We estimate 19% savings in unit costs by 2002/2003.
- New equipment to deal with community priorities of chewing gum and dog fouling. There is also stricter enforcement of dog fouling legislation and a better dog warden service.
- Improved integration between street cleansing and grounds maintenance. This involves "multi-tasking" to ensure more effective removal of litter from shrub beds and grassed areas. This permits reductions in staff and introduces a street cleansing approach, based on required standards, that focuses on customer needs.
- A simplified process for dealing with requests for tree work, based on consultation with Council tenants.
- Regular meetings between operational managers to co-ordinate service delivery and to produce an Environmental Maintenance Calendar circulated to households.

Achievements

- We project a 10% reduction in the combined unit cost of street cleansing and grounds maintenance services for the city from 1997/98 to 1999/2000.
- There are early indications of improved service quality: an increase from 64 to 69 in the Tidy Britain index for the pilot area; and local people have reported improved performance.
- There is enthusiasm from staff doing the jobs: they enjoy greater responsibility and flexibility which has led to greater job satisfaction and a better service for local residents.

Issues and lessons

- We do not think we can sustain the way we consulted with local communities across the whole city, although we are applying some elements of the process which worked well.
- It will take time to "change the culture" and to overcome the legacy of CCT.
- It is important that we involve the workforce and trade unions fully in discussions about changes in the way we deliver services.'

Newcastle City Council, Civic Centre, Newcastle Upon Tyne, NE99 2BN (0191-232-8520).

NEWHAM COUNCIL

More for less

Background

'The major dynamic behind Newham Council's best value project has been the unification of front-line services to the customer, while streamlining the "back office" costs.

Once we have carried out the best value plans following our first year's reviews, early in 2002, we expect the quality of the service to have improved by 6% while costs will have reduced by 2.5% (or £7.3 million at today's prices). We expect similar improvements from the second and third year reviews.

By unifying front-line services and reducing back office costs in this way, we believe we can achieve several millions more in savings by developing this strategy further. For example, we will introduce alternative working and rationalise our back office buildings.

Other savings from the programme

We have identified other savings, for example:

- Due to greatly improved collection rates, the Council Tax service is on target to break even in this financial year (1999/2000), having previously had a subsidy of £175,000.
- After taking account of client costs, the housing benefits service is on course to save some £2 million by the end of 2001/2002. This follows from externalising back office processing, and from moving the customer care of applicants to new local service centres which offer unified front-line services.

Taken together, the Elders Residential and Home Support services should also deliver some £2 million in savings by 2001/2002 by market-testing and externalising services.

- Environmental management will save around £300,000 over three years by a combination of restructuring the service to focus on generic enforcement teams, and by market-testing particular services like Pest Control.
- School Meals will save £300,000 per year over three years by phasing out transport kitchens, and by increasing income from growing take-up and market testing.'

Newham London Borough Council, Town Hall, East Ham, London E6 2RP. Tel 020-8472 1430, web http://www.newham.gov.uk

OLDHAM MBC

Improving responsiveness of services to the public

Background

'At Oldham, our best value pilot project focuses on the geographical area of Chadderton, in the west of the borough. The area has around 13,000 properties, some 4,000 of which are public housing.

The main objectives of the pilot are to:

- promote better inter-departmental co-ordination, and increase our service quality and responsiveness to local residents;
- reduce unit costs of services resulting from "duplication and bureaucracy" under compulsory competitive tendering (CCT); and
- introduce choice for residents and improve consultative arrangements with them.

The seven services included in the pilot were selected because they have a direct impact on the quality of life of local residents. They include housing repairs and management; highway repairs; street lighting; grounds maintenance; street cleansing; and refuse collection. We have integrated these into a new "holistic" service delivery model, the Service Co-ordination Team (SCT).

Key Achievements

Service Co-ordination Team

- This is a "one-stop-shop" for the services included in the pilot. The team acts as an "agent" for the local community, co-ordinating the activities of the relevant service departments.
- The new arrangements for service delivery developed by the SCT have reduced bureaucracy and delivery time and improved quality.
- There are now cross-functional inspections.

Housing repairs

- Housing repair operatives have been empowered; they receive repair requests directly and respond without the need for client processing and pre-inspection.
- Tenants are acting as post inspectors.
- There is a reduction in service response times from 18 days to three.

Highways Maintenance

- There are twice as many highways inspections.
- We are testing new materials to improve the life of repairs.
- We have reduced the maximum time from discovery to repair of a non-emergency fault.

Grounds Maintenance

- We have reduced response times and have co-ordinated with the street cleansing service to improve litter clearance.
- There is better consultation and communication with local residents, helping to improve services further.
- We have empowered ground worker teams to carry out minor work up to an agreed value to reduce time delays, bureaucracy and improve responsiveness.
- We have reintroduced permanent gardeners into parks with apprentices and mobile park patrols.

Environmental Services

We formed the Environmental Action Unit (EAU) which is empowered to operate across traditional departmental boundaries. It provides a rapid response to reported problems of litter, graffiti, fly tipping etc.

- There is now a Street Calendar advising when streets will be swept, and residents act as post inspectors.
- There is an appointments system for clearing bulky household waste.
- We have improved the inter-departmental co-ordination of landscaping of new roads and highways improvement schemes.

Encouraging results

We have phased in these innovative ways of delivering services over the life of the pilot. A complete assessment of the costs and benefits is not yet available. However, there is evidence of benefits from the new housing repairs model. Feedback from people doing the work shows an increase in job satisfaction. There is also a good deal of positive feedback from tenants and elected members.'

Oldham Metropolitan Council, Civic Centre, West Street, Oldham, OL1 1UG (0161-911-3000)

BEST VALUE PARTNERSHIP NETWORK PILOTS

Background

The six successful Best Value Partnership Network Pilots were announced on 24 September 1998 and have run parallel to the best value pilots. The six are:

- **Crossing the Boundaries** (trading standards);
- **Institution of Civil Engineers Best Value Taskforce** (developing procurement practice in built environment services);
- **North Yorkshire Audit Partnership** (internal audit);
- **Payroll Partnership Network** (payroll-related services);
- **Public Sector plc** (public–private partnerships); and
- **The Hub** (local franchise partnerships).

Of these final six projects, two are led by the private sector, one by a professional body and three by local authorities. The pilots include over 55 local authorities, some 44 private sector companies, and three trade unions.

The evaluation of the six Pilot Partnership Networks (PPNs) is being conducted over a three-year period and involves a baseline, interim and final stage evaluation. The evaluation of the PPNs has the objectives of understanding and sharing good practice on the:

- Process of partnership development and operation
- Impact of the partnership on service delivery.

The baseline study was conducted in the period March to May 1999 and has been very recently reported to DETR. The interim and final stages will commence in March 2000 and 2001 respectively. The baseline report provides a brief outline of the purpose and progress of each of the six PPNs and information on the initiation of the PPNs, implementation issues, consultation and management arrangements.

The six PPNs are quite different in terms of the number, scope and types of partners involved the organisational forms of partnership, the timetable of activity and the agreed objectives. The three main types of partnership networks are:

- Cross border service delivery through local authority led partnerships, involving primarily local authorities. PPNs of this type are Crossing the Boundaries (Trading Standards joint working), Payroll Partnership and the North Yorkshire Audit Partnership.
- Private sector led partnerships that involve a number of private sector organisations that are looking to engage and work in partnership with individual local authorities. PPNs are Public Sector Plc and the Hub.
- Networks of local authorities and private sector/voluntary sector participants working to develop good practice in advancing best value. There is one PPN of this type, the Institute of Civil Engineers Taskforce.

The monitoring and evaluation of the Partnership Networks is within a wider three year programme of research on local authority partnerships. This is being carried out on behalf of the DETR by Newchurch & Company. The study comprises five interlocking elements:

- Literature Review of relevant partnership material culminating in the generation of a working definition of Partnership for the purposes of this Study
- three-year evaluation of the six Pilot Partnership Networks
- Postal Survey of partnership arrangements in all local authorities in England
- a Mapping Study of a sample of ten authorities in order to clarify generic issues emerging from the postal survey
- 2+ year Case Study of the management and development of partnership arrangements in a sample of six local authorities in the light of Best Value considerations and other current issues e.g. Governance.

This will be complemented by a parallel examination of a sample of partner organisations and their experiences.

A brief description of each Partnership Network.

Crossing the Boundaries is a partnership between five County Trading Standards Departments: Warwickshire, Gloucestershire, Oxfordshire, Shropshire and Worcestershire. The partnership's main objectives are to optimise resources, to share best practice for the provision of Trading Standards, and to ensure measurable improvements in the quality and standards of the service. The partnership was initiated in Spring 1996, and a formal memorandum of understanding was signed at the end of 1998. This PPN has developed a 1999/2000 joint service plan, detailing improvements and projects to be undertaken during the financial year, and each of the partners have begun to focus on their responsibilities outlined in the plan.

The **Institute of Civil Engineers Best Value Taskforce** has been formed to achieve two main objectives. Firstly, to provide an opportunity for public and private sector organisations to meet in a non-confrontational environment in order to discuss and develop best practice guidance for the 'Built Environment' and secondly, to publish a definitive guide to best practice in advancing Best Value in the Built Environment. The Institute of Civil Engineers ('ICE') instigated the partnership in March 1998, with 25 public sector organisations and 12 private sector organisations. Due to the wide publicity of the PPN it has grown in membership to a total of 64 organisations. The partners have all signed an agreement to openly share information, compare experiences and practices, explore alternative approaches, and work constructively for the development of the guide and the network. The guide will be published in early 2000.

The **North Yorkshire Audit Partnership** ('NYAP') involves Scarborough Borough Council, Selby and Ryedale District Councils and most recently the City of York. The partnership was initiated in the summer 1998 as a result of problems with the retention and recruitment of internal audit staff at Selby and Ryedale District Councils. The three authorities have adopted a separate contractor unit that comprises internal audit staff from all three authorities and that provides internal audit services to each. The main objectives for the PPN include providing economies-of-scale as well as improvements in service quality and performance. A formal agreement was signed and the partnership went fully operational in February 1999.

The **Payroll Partnership** involves Bath & Northeast Somerset and South Gloucestershire. Bristol City Council was also involved, during the initial stages, but withdrew in March 1999. The partnership was instigated in Spring 1998 and developed in order to explore the opportunities available for jointly outsourcing payroll services and achieve reductions in costs through productivity savings. Following Bristol's departure progress with the remaining authorities became slow owing to resource pressures on other considerations, such as the introduction of a millennium payroll system and the implementation of the fair funding regime in schools. After careful consideration both authorities have decided to put the Payroll Partnership on hold.

The **Public Sector Plc** ('PSP') is a private sector led partnership that seeks to establish an alternative service delivery model that fills the gap between resources available to the local authority and the resources required to deliver the level and quality of services demanded, with resources from the private sector. There are three main elements to PSP; two pathfinder projects, one in the London Borough of Havering and the other at Portsmouth City Council and a third element that involves the testing of PSP in other service areas such as leisure, housing and home care.

A network of organisations (the Private Sector Partners) has been established to assist local authorities in evaluating its service planning priorities through exploration of what and how services can be delivered, providing an understanding of market dynamics and those factors that will stimulate market interest. The Network is keen to examine the form of contracting relationship which might arise when the authority's own internal resources become an integral part of the contract activity.

The Hub is an alternative model of service delivery for Council Tax, National Non-Domestic Rates, Housing Benefit and Council Tax Benefit administration. ICL and Barony Consulting developed the concept, although Barony withdrew from the partnership earlier this year. The Hub is designed to provide comprehensive service delivery for authorities through a jointly managed partnership between private sector organisations and local authorities. The concept requires the re-engineering of services that will allow local authorities to remain responsible for front-line engagement with customers whilst much of the work shifts to a call centre located in the administrative hub with only the highly complex enquiries being passed to 'experts'.

In addition to the administrative hub, it is proposed there will be a technology hub where ICL provide technology-based solutions to the administrative process. ICL is at a late stage of discussion with a large Metropolitan authority to finalise the details of the first partnership. Once joint commitment is secured the work packages to develop the end-to-end service model will be agreed and the project plan developed.

Partnership Formation – Evidence from the Partnership Networks

This section is an extract on the experiences of the PPNs taken from a wider research paper, *Local Authorities, Partnership and Best Value* written by Newchurch & Company. This drew from the baseline evaluation interviews with each of the networks and an exchange of good practice seminar held in July 1999 with members of the PPNs (and the Joint Revenue Services best value pilot) on issues around partnership formation. The full version of this paper, and others in the series, are available on the DETR website.

The findings of the evaluation work on the PPNs (and the wider research work on partnership) concentrate on the issues surrounding the formation and structure of partnerships and the measurement methodologies and broad headline issues that require further probing in the balance of the study. At a time when most councils are actively considering the issue of the use of partnerships for the best value delivery of services these findings, especially in relation to the preconditions for sound partnerships, are of some importance.

Initiation

Three main reasons for local authorities exploring the possibility of partnership working have emerged:

- To share risk
- To access new resources and specialist skills
- To review service delivery options.

Increasing budgetary pressures, problems with recruiting and retaining staff (particularly those with specialist skills) and the duty of best value have all prompted authorities to investigate alternative routes to providing their services in order to reduce costs and improve the quality of service.

The private sector is concerned with improving relationships between the public and private sectors, sharing knowledge and expertise and exploring new business opportunities.

The initial development process depends on who leads. Local authority led partnerships have tended to grow from informal relationships between officers. Whilst private sector led partnerships have similarly exploited existing relationships, they have also targeted and approached potential partner organisations. Typically, the private sector encounters some difficulty in persuading local authorities to pilot partnership arrangements because of propriety problems related to public sector competition rules, often necessitating extensive discussions with officers and councillors.

The key objectives and parameters of partnerships need to be established at the start. This will also include defining the tasks, roles and responsibilities of each partner. The development of a Memorandum of Understanding, a formal document that addresses the objectives, membership, management arrangements, values and responsibilities of partners can give additional momentum to partnership development and progress.

A number of factors and conditions for developing and sustaining effective partnership relationships are:

- A shared understanding of the aims and objectives of the partnership

- A sustained interest in and commitment to the development and success of the partnership
- Open and trustworthy relationships to enable partners to share information
- An overall driving force and leadership to ensure the partnership maintains a momentum and focus
- Regular, well organised communication between partners and within each partner organisation
- Clearly understood objectives and responsibilities for each individual partner
- The demonstration of progress and individuals contributions.

Benefits realised during the initial and developmental stages of the PPNs were reported to be:

- Improved knowledge of others' experiences and sharing best practice
- Reduced duplication of effort
- Improved access to resources (particularly specialist skills)
- Increased ability to network
- Improved understanding of the issues facing local authorities
- Increased profile for the individual authorities and organisations involved.

Implementation

The length of time needed for development and implementation of the partnerships reflects the complexity of the concept and service area, the number of partners, and the commitment of partner organisations. Relationships between partners can change during the development of the partnership.

The main changes perceived were a greater openness and willingness to exchange good practice and a greater commitment to the overall success of the partnership. Generally partners believe that relationships continue to change over the lifetime of the partnership. The expected changes are as follows:

- Introduction or redefinition of client/contractor roles for delivery of services
- Larger partnerships having some partners becoming less involved
- Closer working relationships in other service areas
- Collaboration between partners for other local authority contracts
- Competition between partners for local authority contracts
- Spin-off partnerships between alliances formed in the PPN.

This evolutionary aspect of partnership is very important in the context of long term partnering relationships such as PFI.

Prior to implementation, authorities need to undertake detailed service reviews to understand the functions, process and performance of services. This is necessary to identify inconsistencies between partners, objectives, priorities and performance targets for services, and ensure a common starting point. Once the baseline position is established the partnerships need to develop a Service Plan/Trading Agreement outlining the programme of activity, performance targets for the partnership and each partner. The final stage prior to implementation is to ensure the legal and personnel requirements are satisfied.

Consultation

During the development and exploration stages of the partnership, significant consultation is required. This includes consultation to identify the interest of potential partners; to agree the scope and potential of partnership activity; to assess different practices and systems and to agree aims, objectives and requirements of service areas. Consultation is also required to assess political, staff and service recipient's support for partnership working and the impact of new arrangements for service delivery.

Consultation with service recipients and users tends to depend on the nature of the service area (whether a front-line or support service). Where the partnership is concerned with support services and the clients are largely internal, consultation on an annual basis to gain an overall opinion of the service seems to be adequate. More evidence is required about consultation with external customers.

Management Arrangements

The management arrangements appear to change as partnerships move from the developmental to the operational stage.

The management structure during the development stages of a partnership tends to have one key individual who acts as the overall partnership leader, and ensures the partnership achieves progress against an agreed timetable. In addition, each partner organisation needs a lead officer to drive the process within the partner organisation. These individuals are also responsible for reporting to their organisations, and as such, need to be of a fairly senior position.

At an operational stage the management arrangements are likely to reflect structures that would otherwise be in place for a typical contractual relationship, the operation of specialist projects or the management of a company. Further evidence and discussion is required in respect of the issue of elected member involvement in partnership management.

Constraints on Partnership

All of the PPNs have experienced difficulties during the partnership preparation period, primarily in relation to legal, cultural and technological difficulties.

A major area of concern is the tension between the process of developing partnership arrangements and the current EU procurement legislation. Regulations in respect of negotiated procurement route and anti-competitive behaviour (arising in cases where partnership develops from an exclusive relationship with one contractor) appear to be major hurdles to innovative working not only because of these regulatory requirements but also within the context of accountable councils and their relationships with their external auditors, and existing contract standing orders.

These problems seem likely to emerge in their most acute form where a private sector organisation or consortium with an innovative idea seeks an exclusive relationship with a local authority that will result in a contractual relationship that would normally be subject to the requirement for competition. While EU rules do offer some limited scope to avoid competition in certain specific situations e.g. major housing renewal projects, and permit the selection of a partner without a fully competitive process there seems a general acknowledgement that exclusive relationships for the provision of public services agreed without a competitive process challenge existing procurement law. In the same way they will usually run counter to local authority standing orders for contracts.

A further concern is agreeing the distribution of power and the structure, scope and responsibilities of special purpose vehicles, companies and partnerships boards within a local authority structure and the associated vires issues.

Technological difficulties have frustrated attempts to access accurate, reliable data to establish the baseline position of services. The use of different systems or applications, variations in operational practice and reporting as well as differences in the knowledge and training of staff have hindered partner organisations seeking to deliver cross border services. Process mapping exercises and the involvement of service provider and IT staff have proved essential in exploring and developing standardised approaches.

Cultural difficulties have caused the most concern. Cultural change has been necessary at three levels within local authorities, with Members, staff and service recipients. Reactions to partnership proposals have varied by PPN and by local authority. These reactions have tended to reflect past experiences of the authorities of partnership working and particularly of CCT.

Engaging and sustaining the interest of Members and agreeing their level of participation has been challenging, particularly where more than one authority is involved in the partnership or where there may have been a change in political control during the life of the partnership. This problem has a sharp edge where it is necessary for the council to commit often substantial resources to the start-up of partnerships.

Keeping staff, Members and service recipients well informed, consulted and involved in the decision-making process throughout the development and implementation of partnership arrangements is seen as critical to the development of partnerships beyond initiation.

Cultural changes are not just required in local authorities, and the experiences of the PPNs are that partner organisations also need to examine how they operate and how they may need to adapt to work in partnership with local authorities. Suspicion about the public sector and unease about embarking on long term partnering relations with authorities is a continuing theme of private sector partners.

Further constraints in the implementation of partnership are the time and cost implications to partners. Typically, partnerships require senior officers and managers to invest time and effort to ensure the partnership maintains momentum both within their organisation and the partnership as a whole. Some partners believed that by discussing the partnership early on with Members and Company Directors or Partners, it is possible to understand the requirement and make a judgement early on as to whether it would be worth pursuing and, if so, to allocate resources to it.

Problems of Measurement

In the initial work with PPNs the difficulty of fixing reliable benchmarks against which subsequent performance can be judged is a recurrent theme. The same problems emerged with the Best Value Pilots. In the case of PPNs much work is needed by them to get to a point where they are all able to demonstrate quantifiable improvements in the cost quality and efficiency of partnership services.

It is recognised that existing performance indicators (PIs) are of some assistance but they may not be sufficiently focussed to lend themselves to direct use. Even where they are there remain the problems of establishing methodologies for measuring the new arrangements.

There is some evidence to suggest that this is an easier task where all the partners are local authorities; where they are uniting for the provision of a well established and measured service provided on an almost identical basis in each of the partner councils and where the client is internal. Where the partnership involves a service being undertaken by a private partner not only will there be need to develop a common frame of reference for comparison but also the need to develop different methodologies to allow for such things as the transfer of risk.

Further difficulties arise where the subject of partnering is not easily definable. ICE is a good example. Its objective is to produce a guide to good practice for best value in the built environment. This raises difficult conceptual questions about what can be measured. One approach would be to measure the subsequent performance of those using the guide. However, changes in performance might not necessarily be wholly attributable to the guide itself.

Yet another problem arises when there is a clash between the need for hard data to show improvements and the understandable reluctance of private partners to reveal information about operations that they regard as commercially sensitive. To a degree this could be avoided by relying on local authority financial data but the manner in which this should be approached will be a topic of study in the next phases of the project. At present the issues of objective measurement in the PPNs and probably in many existing local authority partnerships remain to be clarified.

When Things Don't Work Out

An important element of all policy making is the capacity to learn from experience. Both in relation to the PPNs and in the forthcoming Mapping and Case Study work it is important to understand why partnerships fail to get started either at all or in one location as opposed to another and cease to work once they have been operational.

Early indications from direct PPN experience (The Hub and Payroll Partnership) point interestingly to typical problems facing the private and public sectors. Barony withdrew from The Hub because of conflicts between partnership activity and their core consultancy activity. Payroll Partnership is 'on hold' because without the momentum given to the project by three members and confronted with other pressures arising directly out of Government policy and requirements the remaining two authorities did not have the resources to carry on.

Over and above those specific examples, there is evidence that failures can arise from changes in political make-up, personality and resource availability. Some of these matters can be prevented; understanding and being able to recognise and deal with them can attenuate some. More evidence will be obtained in later stages of the study.

ANNEX B

LIST OF CURRENT ADVICE ON BEST VALUE

Publication	Produced by	Status
Modernising Local Government – Improving Local Services through Best Value	DETR (March 98)	Consultation paper
Modern Local Government – In Touch with the People	DETR (March 98)	White Paper
Local Government Act 1999 Local Government Act 1999: Explanatory Notes	Stationery Office (July 99)	Act
Modernising Government	Cabinet Office (March 99)	White Paper
Local Leadership, Local Choice (including draft Local Government (Organisation and Standards) Bill and Explanatory Notes)	DETR (March 99)	Consultation paper
Guidance on Enhancing Public Participation	DETR (October 98)	Management paper
Involving Users: Improving the Delivery of Local Public Services	Cabinet Office/ Consumer Congress/ National Consumer Council (March 99)	Report
Best Value in Housing Framework	DETR (January 99)	Consultation paper
National Framework for Tenant Participation Compacts	DETR (June 1999)	Guidance
Developing Good Practice in Tenant Participation	DETR (August 1999)	Guidance
A New Approach to Social Services Performance	Dept of Health (February 99)	Circular
A New Approach to Social Services Performance: Consultation Responses and Confirmation of Performance Indicators	Dept of Health (July 1999)	Circular

Publication	Produced by	Status
Promising Beginnings	Audit Commission (September 98)	Compendium
Better by Far – Preparing for Best Value	Audit Commission (December 98)	Management paper Councillor's briefing
Developing Principles of Public Inspection	Audit Commission (January 99)	Consultation paper
Measure of Success – setting and monitoring local performance indicators	Audit Commission (February 99)	Management paper
A Modernised Framework for Local Authority Accounting – accounting for best value	CIRFA (March 99)	Consultation paper
Best Value Series: Achieving BV through: – Performance review (No 5) – Competition, benchmarking and performance networks (No 6) – Partnership (No 7) – Public engagement (No 8) – Quality management (No 9) – Authority-wide approaches (No 10)	Local Government Centre (Warwick Business School)/ DETR (December 98)	Research evaluation of early experiences of BV pilot projects
Interim evaluation of best value pilots	DETR	Research
Newchurch/DETR Partnership Series: – Partnership: A Working Definition (No 1) – Local Authority Partnerships: A Review of Literature (No 2) – Baseline Evaluation of Pilot Partnership Networks (No 3) – Summary Baseline Evaluation of Pilot Partnership Networks (No 4) – Service Delivery Partnerships in English Local Authorities: Survey Findings (No 5) – Exchange of Good Practice Briefing: Partnership Initiation, Selecting Partners & Organisational Change (No 6) – Local Authorities, Partnership and Best Value (No 7)	Newchurch & Company/DETR	Research

Publication	Produced by	Status
Improving From Within	LGA (January 99)	Report on the Improvement Project
Best Value – an introductory guide	LGMB (1999)	Guide
Integrating Sustainable Development into Best Value	LGA/LGMB (1998)	Report
A better quality of life – a strategy for sustainable development in the UK	DETR (May 1999)	White Paper
No Quality without Equality – Best Value and Equalities	LGA/LGMB (1998)	Report
Racial Equality means Quality – A Standard for Racial Equality in England and Wales	Commission for Racial Equality (1995)	Guidance
Mainstreaming gender equality in local government	Equal Opportunities Commission (1999)	Guidance/Report
Best Value Initiatives: Database Survey Report	LGA/IDA	
Planning to Succeed: service and financial planning in local government	Audit Commission (1999)	Management Paper
Starting to Modernise – achieving best value	New Local Government Network (1999)	Report
Partnerships for best value	New Local Government Network (1999)	Report
How to Improve your Services – a guide to quality schemes for the public sector	Cabinet Office (January 1999)	Guide (covering Excellence Model, IiP, Charter Mark and ISO 9000)
Assessing Excellence – A guide to using self-assessment against the Excellence Model, Charter Mark and IiP to achieve performance improvement in the public sector	Cabinet Office (March 1999)	Guide

Publication	Produced by	Status
Public Sector Benchmarking Project – Brochure of Services Available	Cabinet Office (July 99 version 3)	Brochure
Towards Best Practice – an evaluation of the first two years of the Public Sector Benchmarking Project 1996–1998	Cabinet Office (January 1998)	Report
There are also a range of other publications on best value available through the LGA/ I&DeA	I&DeA publications 020 7296 6516	

ANNEX C

QUALITY SCHEMES

The *Modernising Government* White Paper, published in March 1999, encourages all public sector organisations to make use of one of the four main quality schemes. These are the EFQM Excellence Model®, Investors in People, Charter Mark and ISO 9000. All these schemes are useful tools which could be employed for a local authority's Best Value strategy:

The EFQM Excellence Model®:

The EFQM Excellence Model® (formerly the Business Excellence Model) provides a framework against which organisations can carry out a self-assessment to identify strengths and areas for improvement, in order to identify those areas of their internal operation where improvement will have the greatest impact on their ability to meet their targets. The Model examines results and the processes needed to achieve them, which permits some degree of forward prediction of results and enables organisations to understand the reasons for the level achieved.

The Cabinet Office runs a Public Sector Benchmarking Project which offers assistance to all public sector organisations which use the Model. Public sector organisations can access reduced rate training and consultancy and free database services including analysis of results, a partner search service and the sharing of best practice.

Contact: Cabinet Office   tel: 020 7270 6440
             Website: www.cabinet-office.gov.uk/eeg/1999/benchmarking.htm
             British Quality Foundation   tel: 020 7654 5000

Investors in People:

Investors in People is a national Standard for effective investment in the training and development of people in order to achieve organisational goals. It is based on four key principles:

- A commitment, from the top, to develop all employees;
- A regular review of the training and development needs of employees and a plan to meet those needs;
- Action to train and develop individuals throughout their employment;
- The measurement of the organisation's success in suing its investment in training and development effectively.

Contact: Investors in People UK   tel: 020 7467 1900

Charter Mark:

Charter Mark is the Government's award scheme recognising and encouraging excellence in public service. It is unique among quality schemes because it concentrates on results; i.e. the service the customer actually receives. Appropriate public sector organisations can measure their service against the ten Charter Mark criteria and make an application. This is subject to expert scrutiny, and in most cases involves a visit by an assessor. Based on the evidence provided, detailed feedback is given to help the organisation improve service further and the organisation learns whether they have won an award.

Charter Mark is open to all public sector organisations that deal directly with the public. It has also been extended to include voluntary organisations providing a service to the public and receiving at least 50% of their income from public sector funds.

Contact: Cabinet Office   tel: 020 7270 6343
              Website: www.servicefirst.gov.uk/index/guidhome.htm

ISO 9000:

ISO 9000 is a tool to help organisations ensure that their processes and documentation enable them consistently to meet their customers' needs. To become registered to the standard an organisation needs to review and document its procedures in accordance with the requirements of this international standard, then prepare a quality manual and submit its management system to a third party for assessment. In other words organisations must:

- Say clearly what they do;
- Capture this in a quality manual;
- Ensure they do what they say;
- Make sure their actions are effective;
- Make improvements to what they do.

Once the quality system is in place and established, there is an independent assessment by a certified body to check conformity with the requirements of the standard and to ensure that declared procedures are working in practice.

Contact: British Standards Institution   tel: 020 8996 9000

Some other commonly used schemes are:

Value Management:

Provides a framework with a range of tools to show how a product can best meet user needs and expectations.

Contact: Institute of Value Management   tel: 01908 234 774

The Local Government Improvement Programme:

This peer review programme was established to provide support for local authorities in addressing the Government's proposals for the wider modernisation of local government, including for best value. The programme is offered to all local authorities through the Improvement and Development Agency for Local Government (I&DeA).

The programme covers political and management arrangements, as well as a consideration of an authority's performance and its ability to engage with its local community. It centres upon a one week review by a team of councillors, senior local government officers and one external team member in order to give a rounded insight of the authority and its capacity for change.

The Improvement Model consists of:

- A review against a benchmark of the 'Ideal Local Authority of the Future'
- A consideration of the extent to which performance needs to be improved to meet the ideal
- Evidenced feedback to the authority, verbally and subsequently in writing, along with recommendations for action to secure improvement
- Help in developing an Improvement Plan
- Ongoing monitoring of the agreed programme for change
- access to further specific support from the I&DeA

Contact: Improvement & Development Agency   tel: 020 7296 6600

Local Authority EC Eco-management and Audit Scheme (LA-EMAS)

The local authority management system for securing continuous improvement in managing resources and environmental impacts, and reporting publicly on performance

Contact: EMAS helpline   tel: 020 7296 6598

ISO 14001

The international standard for environmental management systems which local authorities may use to help them manage the environmental impacts of activities.

Contact: British Standards Institution   tel: 020 8996 9000

This list is not exhaustive, nor is it designed to be a checklist. Authorities will wish to consider the extent to which other schemes complement the way in which they manage performance and assist them in complementing the national framework of performance indicators with those which they develop locally. These for instance might include the range of schemes which have been developed with the aid of Agencies such as Sport England and the Countryside Commission, and those which focus on assessing the quality of voluntary organisation, which may have a key role to play in delivering best value at the local level.

The Cabinet Office can provide further advice on all these schemes.

ANNEX D

PROTOCOL ON INTERVENTION POWERS

Preamble

I.   This Protocol derives from the Framework for Partnership signed in November 1997 by the Deputy Prime Minister on behalf of the Government and the Chairman of the Local Government Association (LGA) on behalf of local authorities. The Framework provides for the Government and the LGA to discuss policy for the use of intervention powers, including how best to facilitate a supportive role for the LGA.

II.   The Protocol gives expression to the shared aim of central and local government to raise standards in public service, to support and assist local authorities in improving services, to provide a clear framework for intervention by central government in cases of service failure, and an orderly process for resumption of service by local authorities following intervention.

Purpose

III.   The Protocol sets out the general principles that would underpin the exercise of the Secretary of State's intervention powers in England under section 15 of the Local Government Act 1999, and the role of the LGA. the term 'Secretary of State' is used throughout to mean the appropriate Secretary of State.

IV.   Local authorities have a responsibility to deliver to local people services to clear standards. Local authorities should set those standards – covering both cost and quality – for all the services for which they are responsible. But in those areas, such as education and social services, where the Government has key responsibilities and commitments, the Government will itself set national standards. The best value legislation requires councils to improve continuously their economy, efficiency and effectiveness in delivering services and meeting standards.

Role of the LGA in helping authorities at risk of failure

V.   Where evidence and experience show that a local authority is at risk of failing in that duty in respect of a service or services, there are several ways of achieving improvements. Councillors, officials and contractors have the prime responsibility for delivering quality services and addressing shortcomings and failings. The LGA and the Improvement and Development Agency are committed to work with local authorities to support improvement where problems exist, and the LGA encourages its member authorities to give early warning of potential problems emerging from inspections, draft reports, complaints, reviews or other sources so that advice and support can be offered. Support may be offered by other authorities through networks, or the authority may be helped to identify and procure other external advice and assistance.

Principles governing intervention by the Secretary of State

VI.   The Secretary of State will exercise intervention powers under section 15 of the Local Government Act 1999 only when there is clear evidence that an authority is failing either to discharge its functions adequately or failing to meet its statutory obligations.

VII.   The Secretary of State will inform the authority of the reasons for intervention whenever using his powers under this legislation.

VIII.   The form and extent of intervention will reflect the type and seriousness of failure and the need for effective improvement.

IX.   Except in cases of serious service failure or unless there is a need for urgent intervention, the authority will normally be given the opportunity to make the necessary improvements itself.

X.   Best value authorities will provide accurate and timely responses to requests for information, and co-operate with such action as the Secretary of State may direct in accordance with his powers and this protocol.

XI.   In cases where a function is exercised by the Secretary of State or a person acting on his behalf, both the Secretary of State and his nominee will be subject to the statutory duties that the authority would normally be subject to in respect of that function.

Process

Identification of problems
XII.   Intervention powers will be invoked on the basis of clear evidence. Such evidence may emerge, for example, from:

- annual audits of financial accounts
- audit of local performance plans
- Audit Commission inspections of fundamental reviews
- inspection reports
- public interest reports
- reports of inquiries, Ombudsman investigations or judicial findings
- concerns raised about serious danger or harm to the public

Examples of triggers are at Appendix A
XIII.   Before the decision to intervene is taken, the authority will have had the opportunity to make representations about any report that is the basis for a proposed intervention. If necessary, and as urgently as the case requires, the Secretary of State would make further investigations to ensure he has all relevant information.

Exercise of intervention powers
XIV.   Once the Secretary of State decides that the facts of the case mean that intervention is likely to be necessary, he will formally notify the authority and the LGA. The usual sequence of action would be as follows:

- the authority will be notified in writing of the improvements the Secretary of State judged necessary;
- the authority will be given until a specified deadline to produce and publish a statement of action for making such improvements;

- the statement of action will need to set out clearly the actions to be carried out, the people responsible, the costs involved, the intended outcomes, the dates by which they are to be achieved and the authority's own proposals for monitoring and implementing the statement of action;
- if the statement of action is acceptable to the Secretary of State, the authority will be notified, informed how implementation will be monitored, and given a deadline by which specific improvements must be completed;
- if the statement of action is unacceptable, the Secretary of State will notify the authority and the LGA of his decision to direct the authority under the powers contained in section 15 of the Local Government Act 1999;
- the authority will be given the opportunity to make representations about the direction proposed.

XV.   If monitoring of the statement of action shows that it is not being implemented effectively, or if the outcomes are not met on time, the Secretary of State will inform the authority and intervene as necessary to secure improvements.

XVI.   If during monitoring of a statement of action evidence emerges that the authority is failing adequately to discharge one or more of its other functions, the Secretary of State will inform the authority of how he intends to proceed in line with this protocol.

Intervention in cases of urgency
XVII.   Although the above arrangements will be the norm, there may be exceptional cases where the severity or persistence of failure, or the continuing risk of harm or financial loss, show that urgent intervention is necessary. If these circumstances prevail, and an authority could reasonably be expected to be aware of these problems and has failed to take adequate action to address them, then the Secretary of State retains the discretion to abbreviate the procedures outlined above as he sees necessary. When exercising his powers in this way, the Secretary of State will notify the authority and the LGA of the intervention that is necessary and the reasons for intervention, and will provide a full explanation of his reasons for curtailing the procedures.

Nature of the intervention
XVIII.   The Secretary of State may take such action he judges necessary to secure compliance by the authority with the requirements of Part 1 of the Local Government Act. This may require, for example, directing the local authority to act within a specified period to:

- prepare or amend a performance plan;
- follow specified procedures in relation to a performance plan;
- carry out a review of its exercise of specified functions;
- make sure a function is carried out so as to achieve specified objectives;
- secure advice/consultancy on the performance of that function;
- secure the function from a specified provider or put the function out to tender.

The Secretary of State may also direct a local enquiry to be held.

A list of the forms of intervention that might be used are at Appendix B.

Media relations and exchange of information
XIX.   Any announcements, publications or press releases issued in relation to any part of the procedures for intervention covered under this protocol will be subject to the

agreement set out in the section titled 'Public Announcements and Exchange of Information' in the Schedule for Arrangements for the conduct of Central-Local Relations under the Framework for Central Local Partnership.

An extract from the relevant section of the schedule is at Appendix C.

Monitoring and review

XX.   In cases where a function is exercised by the Secretary of State or a person acting on his behalf, the Secretary of State will aim to return that function to the control of the local authority as soon as is practicable. To that end he will regularly monitor the function involved and consider whether the authority is in a position to resume and sustain effective responsibility for the function, and will notify the authority and the LGA of his decision and the reasons for it.

Where intervention is based on a direction which leaves responsibility for the function with the local authority, the direction will be lifted when the Secretary of State is content that the objectives of the intervention can be met on a sustainable basis. Lifting the direction will not nullify any contracts that resulted from it.

APPENDIX A

Examples of triggers

I.   The following lists provide examples of failures of process and failures of substance in relation to best value. Although the Secretary of State reserves the right to exercise his powers in any of these circumstances, his intention is to intervene proportionately to the seriousness of the failure. A single failure of process, for example, is unlikely to trigger intervention by the Secretary of State, whereas a failure of substance is more likely to attract intervention.

Failure of process

- a failure to consult or to consult adequately as identified by the external auditor
- a failure to produce a best value performance plan, or a failure to include any of the prescribed elements within it
- a failure to agree, publish, or carry out a programme of fundamental performance reviews in compliance with the statutory framework
- unreasonable neglect of alternative options for service provision when conducting performance reviews
- a failure to set performance targets or publish details of performance against them
- a failure to set performance targets, which, in the opinion of the external auditor are sufficiently challenging
- a failure to publish details of how performance compares with that of others
- a failure to publish performance information as prescribed (in respect of content, form or timing)
- a failure to make adequate information available to local people about the comparative performance of other bodies

Failure of substance

- failure to meet any single nationally prescribed standard of performance
- persistently high unit costs (by comparison with other councils or, where appropriate, with private and voluntary sector providers) which are not satisfactorily accounted for by higher quality service or greater level of need
- failure to improve service standards or a deterioration in standards
- failure to draw up and implement an action plan following a critical inspection report

APPENDIX B

Local Government Act 1999

II.   The form of intervention might include a direction by the Secretary of State:

- to prepare or amend a performance plan
- to follow specified procedures in relation to a performance plan
- to carry out a review of its exercise of specified functions
- to take such other action as in the Secretary of State's opinion is necessary or expedient to secure compliance with
- to make sure a function is carried out so as to achieve specified objectives
- to secure advice/consultancy on the performance of that function
- to secure the function from a specified provider or put the function out to tender to expose a particular service or work of a particular description to competition (with or without an in-house bid to carry out the work)
- to accept external advice from a specified source relating to the performance of a management function
- to obtain a function from a specified provider
- to transfer responsibility to another authority or third party

III.   The Secretary of State may direct a local inquiry to be held into the exercise by the authority of specified functions.

APPENDIX C

A Framework for Partnership

Public Announcements and Exchange of Information
IV.   **The Government** will always convey announcements (i.e. Parliamentary statements, publications, and news releases) directly concerning local government to **the LGA** no later than to the media. Where announcements are provided to the media on an embargoed basis, in advance of publication or as soon after as Parliamentary protocol permits, they will be provided to **the LGA** on the same terms. Announcements by **the LGA** concerning central Government will always be conveyed to the Departments concerned no later than to the media. Where announcements are provided to the

media on an embargoed basis, in advance of publication, they will be provided to **the Government** on the same terms.

V. **The Government and the LGA** will keep each other informed of their activities and of their proposals and policies. Where policies and proposals are founded upon consultants' or research reports each will, wherever practicable, provide copies of those reports and other factual analysis (but not necessarily advice based on them) to the other.

ANNEX E

TERMS OF REFERENCE FOR BEST VALUE INSPECTORATE FORUM FOR ENGLAND

The Inspectorate Forum will meet to consider strategic issues relating to the inspection of best value authorities in England. It will be an effective channel of communication for Inspectorates: with central government, with best value authorities and other interested parties. The Forum will act to increase the effectiveness of inspection on behalf of service users while minimising the demands on inspected bodies.

The Forum will:

- consider the scope for co-ordinating programmes of audit and inspection;
- develop arrangements to inspect across organisational boundaries including the identification of thematic issues for cross cutting inspection;
- ensure a consistent approach to best value arrangements by different Inspectorates and auditors and that they do not provide conflicting evaluations of the same arrangements;
- build on and develop joint inspection methodologies and develop protocols and similar agreements to facilitate working together and information sharing;
- consider the scope for involving users more in the inspection process;
- consider ways of targeting resources on those areas where the risks involved are the greatest;
- identify and promote best practice in best value inspection.

In making recommendations about inspection and intervention issues the Forum will have regard to the different forms of statutory underpinning that supports each Inspectorate. Where they believe it is appropriate they may recommend that the Secretary of State issue guidance under Section 24 of the Local Government Act 1999.

Appendix 5

FRAMEWORK AGREEMENT ON BEST VALUE[1]
(National Joint Council for Local Government Services, 16 October 1999)

1. This is an agreement between the National Employers and the recognised unions (GMB, TGWU, UNISON) which sets out our joint views on the employee relations implications of Best Value.

2. Best Value aims to produce continuous improvement in all local government services by considering the full range of options available to councils. This involves:

- Comprehensive and careful consultation with the community about their wants and needs;
- Establishing how these can best be addressed;
- Considering how far existing arrangements meet the requirements;
- Assessing what changes, if any, are needed to current provisions.

The process will be challenging and will involve comparisons outside the organisation. It may consider new forms of partnership.

3. Employees and the representative unions have a direct, legitimate interest in all Best Value reviews. They have a deep knowledge and understanding of how their services work and of the people they serve. They are themselves service users. For many members of the public, the council is in practice represented by the employees who serve them. The directness of this relationship means that front line employees are one of the best channels through which councils can find out what the public want and how best to deliver it. The National Joint Council encourages authorities to make the maximum use of this resource and in the process encourage employee ownership of the Best Value outcomes.

4. The National Joint Council's guiding principles as embodied in Part 1 of the Green Book (the Single Status agreement) are to support and encourage

- 'high quality services delivered by a well-trained, motivated workforce with security of employment ...
- equal opportunities in employment; equality as a core principle which underpins both service delivery and employment relations ...
- a flexible approach to providing services to the community, which meets the needs of employees as well as employers
- stable industrial relations and negotiation and consultation ...'

---

1   The NJC will ask the Joint Working Group to reconvene in due course to consider DETR guidance and any accompanying changes in legislation. Further advice on conditions of service, transfer of pensions, and TUPE may be required at that stage.

The provision of quality direct services, which deliver Best Value, sits four-square with these principles.

5.   To succeed, Best Value needs the active support of the workforce. To gain this support, it is essential:

- That employers and trade unions work together in co-operation, based on a clear commitment to high quality direct services to the communities we serve;
- That employees and their unions are involved at the start and throughout the process of strategic review e.g. on review teams;
- That employees and their trade unions are involved in the process of consulting the community;
- That employees and their unions are involved in the process of implementation;
- To ensure that employees are treated fairly and that Best Value is not used as a mechanism to drive down terms and conditions of service.

This approach should be seen as a partnership to achieve the quality services provided by a quality workforce that both Sides of the National Council are committed to. The NJC recognises the importance and benefit of joint working by the authority and employees and their unions to get the best results, acknowledging that the public interest needs to come first. For the partnership to develop and flourish, it is important for momentum to be maintained by all concerned – undue delays can be detrimental to the process. Authorities may also need to use imaginative ways to involve 'hard to reach' employees e.g. part-time peripatetic employees, where their experience is essential in evaluating and improving service provision.

6.   The NJC recognises that Best Value reviews could lead to the reorganisation of in-house services. The NJC agrees that it is essential that the workforce and the trade unions are fully involved from the outset and that issues are dealt with in a transparent and co-operative manner. This may include changing working arrangements and work content to improve service delivery. Change can often be difficult, but it offers opportunities to explore different ways of working which can be of benefit to both employees and authorities. Change should aim to bring about better services and better jobs. Among matters likely to be addressed are:

- The need to acquire additional skills to enhance the flexibility of the workforce, with the implications for training which accompany it;
- An examination of working hours (which will need to be reviewed regularly) to ensure that they suit the needs of service users;
- The introduction of more family friendly working arrangements to complement new patterns of service delivery;
- Ensuring the fair and non-discriminatory treatment of individuals;
- Ensuring that proper standards of health and safety are maintained.

7.   Councils may decide to outsource services. This may mean transfer to another public, private or voluntary agency. The NJC would wish to add its voice in stressing the importance of high standards and transparency in local government's approach to public procurement. Where it is proposed that a service is outsourced, the need to ensure that the workforce has a full understanding of and involvement in the process is crucial. Use of the authority's joint consultative arrangements to achieve understanding is important. An example of involvement in the process would be the participation of employees in discussions with external bidders. Moreover, the Council as transferor has

a duty to safeguard, as far as it lawfully can, the rights and interests, including in relation to pay, conditions and pensions, of the transferred employees.

8. The NJC encourages local authorities and their unions to enter into local negotiation in the spirit of this agreement and to reflect this agreement in their Best Value policies and procedures. Such policies and procedures should focus on the general matters considered above and also cover specific issues, such as changes to working practices and reasonable trade union facilities.

© National Joint Council for Local Government Services.

Appendix 6

PINSENT CURTIS SUITE OF PERFORMANCE INDICATORS FOR LEGAL DEPARTMENTS

These indicators cover the following areas:

Part 1   Outcomes
A.   Corporate Value
B.   Community Value
C.   Service Outcomes

Part 2   Enabling and facilitating outcomes
D.   Operational Performance
E.   Client Satisfaction
F.   People Satisfaction
G.   Innovation
H.   Service Review

A.   CORPORATE VALUE

1.   Number of upheld ombudsman complaints or legal challenges caused by shortcomings in legal or administrative process or advice.

2.   Number of customer complaints caused by shortcomings in legal or administrative process or advice.

3.   Evidence that the department has added value to corporate propriety process and practice.

4.   Evidence that the department has added value to corporate strategic and service outcomes.

B.   COMMUNITY VALUE

1.   Evidence that the department has added value to community outcomes.

2.   Evidence of the department's support for or participation in community initiatives.

3.   Evidence that the department's service is provided in a way which will meet the needs of all the inhabitants in the area.

C. SERVICE OUTCOMES

1.   Number of matters (per annum or other specified period) where the desired outcome has been achieved against number where the desired outcome has not been achieved through the ascertainable shortcoming of the service provider.

2.   Evidence of added value to service outcomes by:

(a) individual;
(b) team;
(c) department.

3.   Evidence of involving other departments, authorities and organisations in joined-up service provision.

D. OPERATIONAL PERFORMANCE

1.   Percentage of target chargeable hours achieved by:

(a) individual;
(b) team;
(c) department.

2.   Percentage chargeable as against non-chargeable hours by:

(a) individual;
(b) team;
(c) department.

3.   Number and type of matters referred opened and closed (per annum or other specified period) by:

(a) individual;
(b) team;
(c) department.

4.   Number (per annum or other specified period) of debt collection matters referred by:

(a) individual;
(b) team.

5.   Number (per annum or other specified period) of debt collection matters processed (ie opened, dealt with and concluded) by:

(a) individual;
(b) team.

6.   Amount of debt recovered against amount of debt instructed to be recovered (per annum or other specified period) by:

(a) individual;
(b) team.

7.   Number (per annum or other specified period) of right to buy matters referred by:

(a) individual;
(b) team.

8.   Number (per annum or other specified period) of right to buy matters processed (ie opened, dealt with and concluded) by:

(a) individual;
(b) team.

9.   Number (per annum or other specified period) of matters where no action taken by department for eight weeks or more by:

(a) individual;
(b) team;
(c) department.

10.   Number (per annum or other specified period) of cases conducted by unit cost by:

(a) individual;
(b) team;
(c) department.

11.   Number (per annum or other specified period) of such cases which were concluded at less than the unit cost by:

(a) individual;
(b) team;
(c) department.

12.   Number (per annum or other specified period) of such cases which were concluded at more than the unit cost by:

(a) individual;
(b) team;
(c) department.

13.   Average caseload (per annum or other specified period) by:

(a) individual;
(b) team;
(c) department.

14.   Number of file audits for adherence to Law Society's Practice Management Standards and/or Office Manual and/or other quality procedures conducted in respect of each fee earner (per annum or other specified period).

15.   Number of such file audits identifying good practice in respect of the same fee earner on more than one occasion.

16.   Number of such file audits identifying breach, default or poor practice in respect of the same fee earner on more than one occasion.

17.   Number of concluded matters (per annum or other specified period) where client satisfied that the matter was well-handled throughout by:

(a) individual;

(b) team;

(c) department.

E.   CLIENT SATISFACTION

1.   Number of client complaints of dissatisfaction against number of jobs completed per annum or other specified period.

2.   Number of such clients still dissatisfied after conclusion of the complaints process.

3.   Number of jobs (against number of jobs completed per annum or other specified period) where clients satisfied with (a) the services provided and (b) the way they were provided.

4.   Number of jobs (against number of jobs completed per annum or other specified period) where customers more than satisfied with (a) the services provided and (b) the way they were provided.

5.   Number of public complaints against the Council arising out of the work of the department (discounting those accepted by Chief Executive as being frivolous or vexatious).

6.   Positive public comments arising out of the work of the department.

7.   Evidence of integrating client/stakeholder needs into the service.

F.   PEOPLE SATISFACTION

1.   Evidence that most individuals know, understand and feel they have a stake in departmental objectives.

2.   Evidence of regularly held staff review and development meetings where performance against target is reviewed, new targets set and a development plan for the forthcoming period set.

3.   Evidence of fair and effective training policy, procedure and practice.

4.   Evidence of integration of all staff fully into Best Value policy procedure and practice.

5.   Evidence of effective staff supervision processes.

6.   Evidence that most staff feel their views count within the department.

7.   Evidence that most staff feel they can make a difference in the work of the department.

8.   Evidence that all staff have satisfactory access to senior management when necessary.

9.   Evidence that most staff are motivated in their working environment.

10.   Number of upheld grievances or other staff complaints.

G. INNOVATION

1. Examples of new products introduced within the department.

2. Examples of new ways of doing things introduced within the department.

3. Examples of new products or ways of doing things introduced corporately on the advice of the department.

4. Examples of new processes which have added value within the department or council.

5. Examples of innovations introduced within the department which have been adopted outside the Council.

H. SERVICE REVIEW

1. Evidence of objective challenge (incorporating representatives from outside the department) as to what we do, why and how we do it at levels of:

    (a) individual;
    (b) team;
    (c) department.

2. If the review determines that the Council needs the service or function we provide, evidence of objective challenge as how the service should best be provided.

3. Evidence of effective and appropriate consultation with all those who have a stake in the outcomes of our service and of taking that consultation properly into account in the way the service is delivered.

4. Evidence of comparison processes with outside public, private or voluntary organisations which have yielded demonstrable improvements in departmental policy, process and practices.

5. Evidence that all or part of the department's services:

    (a) have been subjected to competitive tender; and/or
    (b) are provided by an external provider; and/or
    (c) are being carried out in Best Value Partnerships with suitable external providers; and/or
    (d) have been through a suitable market testing process which has demonstrated its competitiveness; and/or
    (e) has been reviewed rigorously and in detail by managers outside the department and/or external consultants; and/or
    (f) where provided externally are subject to key Best Value principles including the need for regular review and continuous improvement.

Appendix 7

PINSENT CURTIS BEST VALUE HEALTHCHECK

FOREWORD

Pinsent Curtis wishes to support Local Government in its drive to modernise. To give practical help to authorities in introducing the Best Value regime and to ensure that they are well-positioned to deal with Best Value reviews, we have put together a Best Value toolkit.

This will provide a detailed Healthcheck and enable action planning to promote continuous improvement in line with the duty of Best Value in the Local Government Act 1999.

The Healthcheck is in two parts:

Part 1 – Outcomes
Part 2 – Enabling and facilitating outcomes

This is important since the whole purpose of Best Value is to improve the end product and 'to make a real and positive difference to the services which local people receive from their authority'.[1]

The idea is not necessarily to go through the Healthcheck exhaustively. Its purpose is to help you devise an improvement action plan on a reasonable phased basis to accommodate key areas of identified development need.

We will be pleased to assist you with conducting your own reviews using the Healthcheck to build on your existing strengths and to meet any shortfalls which become apparent.

This Healthcheck particularly is focussed on Legal Services Departments. However, it can readily be adapted to accommodate other functions.

Nicholas Dobson
National Head of Local Government Law
Pinsent Curtis

---

1   *DETR Circular 10/99, 14 December 1999.*

INTRODUCTION

To say that Best Value is radical is an understatement. It demands a fundamental shift in culture to enable (as the Government has put it) 'the real and positive difference to the services which local people receive from their authority'.[1]

The prime focus is making continuous improvements to outcomes. For support service managers this means essentially two things:

–   Ensuring that their operation and its approach to service outcomes is demonstrably economic, efficient and effective in line with the reconfigured expectations of Best Value

–   Ensuring that their service adds real value to corporate and community outcomes.

The role of legal services departments is set to change as new powers become available e.g. under section 16 of the Local Government Act 1999 (where the Secretary of State can confer new powers or remove existing legal impediments to Best Value) or the proposed new powers to promote the economic, social and environmental well-being of Council areas. We may for instance see some authorities being able to provide legal services directly to local people under the Community Legal Service proposals. So legal and support services departments need to make sure they are fit for the future.

This Healthcheck is designed to help you to achieve this through conducting a rigorous service review before the statutory review takes place. An improvement plan can then be drawn up tailored to your particular requirements. In so doing it will be vital to engage staff so that their individual motivation is unlocked into achieving Best Value. The aim is to enable a first class service contributing to excellent corporate and community outcomes.

---

1   *DETR Circular 10/99.*

BEST VALUE HEALTHCHECK

The Healthcheck covers the following areas:

Part 1 Outcomes
A.   Corporate Value
B.   Community Value
C.   Service Outcomes

Part 2 Enabling and facilitating outcomes
D.   Operational Systems
E.   Client Satisfaction
F.   Financial Systems
G.   People Issues
H.   General Management
I.   Strategic Planning

A. CORPORATE VALUE

Please consider how accurately each proposition describes what the Department does at the time this Healthcheck is completed and grade accordingly by ticking one of the three boxes on the right hand side of the page. These will enable you to plot your Department's current position on a three point spectrum:

1.   not in place and no plans to do so;
2.   not in place but moving towards;
3.   fully in place.

Some of the questions cover ground already covered elsewhere in the Healthcheck. This is deliberate as part of an holistic Best Value approach.

Wherever used within this Healthcheck 'client' means the person asking the Department to provide a service on behalf of the Council. 'Client' will include officers, members, the Council, its committees, sub-committees, other democratic structures, agreed public bodies and any other persons having a stake in what the Department does.

The Department has in place and fully operational an efficient, effective, integrated and comprehensive approach to:

1.   Ensuring so far as reasonably practicable that the Council at all times acts properly, lawfully and reasonably.

1	2	3

2.   Ensuring so far as reasonably practicable that all decisions taken by or on behalf of the Council are (and are seen to be) properly, lawfully, and reasonably founded.

1	2	3

3.   Ensuring that all decisions taken by or on behalf of the Council are properly, accurately and clearly recorded.

1	2	3

		1	2	3
4.	Training officers and members so that they understand, own and are familiar with the law, practice, procedure and internal rules governing probity, propriety and due process.	☐	☐	☐

5. Ensuring that in particular, officers and members have had training in:

		1	2	3
5.1	the Council's constitution document/ standing orders/financial regulations;	☐	☐	☐
5.2	the law and procedure governing members interests;	☐	☐	☐
5.3	(until it is replaced) the National Code of Local Government Conduct;	☐	☐	☐
5.4	the 'General Principles of Conduct';	☐	☐	☐
5.5	the Council's Codes of Conduct (for members and officers);	☐	☐	☐
5.6	the Council's Whistleblowing Policy.	☐	☐	☐

		1	2	3
6.	Taking into account in every decision the legal, financial, corporate and human rights implications.	☐	☐	☐
7.	Raising corporate awareness of the need for lawfulness, reasonableness and procedural propriety and in all the Council's actions.	☐	☐	☐
8.	Dynamically supporting the operation of the Standards Committee and the related propriety infrastructure.	☐	☐	☐
9.	Discharging or supporting as appropriate the monitoring officer role in a proactive but preventative way.	☐	☐	☐
10.	Ensuring that all requisite codes, procedures and protocols are properly in place and applied throughout the Authority.	☐	☐	☐
11.	Ensuring staff access when the Department considers it necessary, desirable or appropriate to the highest decision making vehicles of the Council both at officer and member levels.	☐	☐	☐

12. Ensuring that departmental staff are treated properly and courteously throughout the Council organisation.

    1   2   3
    ☐   ☐   ☐

13. Ensuring that departmental strategic objectives support the Council's corporate and strategic objectives.

    1   2   3
    ☐   ☐   ☐

14. Ensuring that the Council's strategic objectives are integrated into team improvement processes at team and individual levels.

    1   2   3
    ☐   ☐   ☐

15. Ensuring that the Department adds demonstrable value to corporate objectives and outcomes.

    1   2   3
    ☐   ☐   ☐

16. Ensuring that the Department is integrated into the Council's decision making processes.

    1   2   3
    ☐   ☐   ☐

17. Driving and supporting the Council's modernisation agenda and infrastructure and in particular:

    1   2   3
    ☐   ☐   ☐

    17.1   Best Value;

    1   2   3
    ☐   ☐   ☐

    17.2   democratic renewal;

    1   2   3
    ☐   ☐   ☐

    17.3   new democratic structures;

    1   2   3
    ☐   ☐   ☐

    17.4   new ethical framework.

    1   2   3
    ☐   ☐   ☐

18. Ensuring that the Department has sound and effective two way lines of communications with the corporate centre of the authority.

    1   2   3
    ☐   ☐   ☐

19. Ensuring that the Department has sound and effective relations with elected members founded upon mutual trust and respect.

    1   2   3
    ☐   ☐   ☐

20. Ensuring that all advice and support has regard to the Authority's legal, political, policy and management contexts.

    1   2   3
    ☐   ☐   ☐

21. The provision of client (including officer/ member) training to add real value to corporate outputs.

    1   2   3
    ☐   ☐   ☐

22.   Being constantly alert to the opportunities for recasting approaches to service provision and service outputs in the light of the changing legal and policy environment.

1   2   3

☐   ☐   ☐

B. COMMUNITY VALUE

Please consider how accurately each proposition describes what the Department does at the time this Healthcheck is completed and grade accordingly by ticking one of the three boxes on the right hand side of the page. These will enable you to plot your Department's current position on a three point spectrum:

1.   not in place and no plans to do so;
2.   not in place but moving towards;
3.   fully in place.

Some of the questions cover ground already covered elsewhere in the Healthcheck. This is deliberate as part of an holistic Best Value approach.

Wherever used within this Healthcheck 'client' means the person asking the Department to provide a service on behalf of the Council. 'Client' will include officers, members, the Council, its committees, sub-committees, other democratic structures, agreed public bodies and any other persons having a stake in what the Department does.

The Department has in place and fully operational an efficient, effective, integrated and comprehensive approach to:

1.   Liaising with other relevant departments, directorates and where appropriate external agencies to ensure that the Council receives a 'joined-up' service.

1   2   3

☐   ☐   ☐

2.   Proposing cross-cutting solutions to corporate and community issues.

1   2   3

☐   ☐   ☐

3.   Ensuring and/or supporting as necessary and appropriate the Authority's community planning processes.

1   2   3

☐   ☐   ☐

4.   Ensuring that the interests of the local community and the Department's stakeholders in general are integrated into departmental strategy, processes and procedures.

1   2   3

☐   ☐   ☐

5.   Ensuring that all actions taken within the Department are focused on the fact that the Council exists to serve the local community.

1   2   3

☐   ☐   ☐

6.   Ensuring that the services we provide are of the highest quality in the interests of the local community and to maintain trust in the Council as the centre of local governance.

1   2   3

☐   ☐   ☐

7. Consulting with the community in an accessible and meaningful manner where appropriate to the nature of the service.

    1 ☐ 2 ☐ 3 ☐

8. Supporting the Council in community consultation, for example through creation of suitable consultation media, generating new ideas, drafting consultation documents, producing newsletters and participation in consultation.

    1 ☐ 2 ☐ 3 ☐

9. Proposing cross-cutting solutions to corporate and community issues.

    1 ☐ 2 ☐ 3 ☐

10. Ensuring that our service delivery is consistent with the needs of all the inhabitants of the Council's area.

    1 ☐ 2 ☐ 3 ☐

11. Ensuring that our service delivery meets the requirements of the Disability Discrimination Act 1995.

    1 ☐ 2 ☐ 3 ☐

11. Making full use of existing and developing legal powers to add real community value.

    1 ☐ 2 ☐ 3 ☐

12. Being constantly alert to the opportunities for recasting approaches to service provision and service outputs in the light of the changing legal and policy environment.

    1 ☐ 2 ☐ 3 ☐

C. SERVICE OUTCOMES

Please consider how accurately each proposition describes what the Department does at the time this Healthcheck is completed and grade accordingly by ticking one of the three boxes on the right hand side of the page. These will enable you to plot your Department's current position on a three point spectrum:

1. not in place and no plans to do so;
2. not in place but moving towards;
3. fully in place.

Some of the questions cover ground already covered elsewhere in the Healthcheck. This is deliberate as part of an holistic Best Value approach.

Wherever used within this Healthcheck 'client' means the person asking the Department to provide a service on behalf of the Council. 'Client' will include officers, members, the Council, its committees, sub-committees, other democratic structures, agreed public bodies and any other persons having a stake in what the Department does.

The Department has in place and fully operational an efficient, effective, integrated and comprehensive approach to:

1.   Ensuring that the outcomes of our services:

    1.1   meet in every particular the needs of those   1   2   3
           for whom our services are provided;   [   ] [   ] [   ]

    1.2   are consistent with the Council's corporate   1   2   3
           strategies.   [   ] [   ] [   ]

2.   Taking careful initial instructions and clarifying in   1   2   3
      detail the outcomes required and how and when   [   ] [   ] [   ]
      they will be achieved.

3.   At the outset making clear:

    3.1   the charging/cost basis;   1   2   3
                                                         [   ] [   ] [   ]

    3.2   who will be dealing with the matter;   1   2   3
                                                         [   ] [   ] [   ]

    3.3   confirming this information in writing.   1   2   3
                                                         [   ] [   ] [   ]

4.   Monitoring all work being carried out to ensure   1   2   3
      that each matter is handled soundly and   [   ] [   ] [   ]
      satisfactorily, in accordance with the client's
      instructions, the Law Society's Practice
      Management Standards (where applicable) and in
      the overall interests of the Council.

5.   Notifying the client promptly of any change in   1   2   3
      circumstances and any resulting cost   [   ] [   ] [   ]
      consequences.

6.   Reviewing individual matters with out clients   1   2   3
      following the completion to identify any ways in   [   ] [   ] [   ]
      which the matter could have been better handled.

7.   Ensuring that any such feedback is properly taken   1   2   3
      into account in the continuous improvement   [   ] [   ] [   ]
      processes.

8.   Ensuring that other departments and agencies are   1   2   3
      involved where appropriate to ensure a joined-up   [   ] [   ] [   ]
      and cross-cutting approach.

9.   Applying creative thinking to the services we   1   2   3
      provide and how we provide them.   [   ] [   ] [   ]

10. Considering new joined-up ways of providing legal
services eg some regional provision with other
authorities.

    1   2   3

11. Ensuring that all our services clearly enhance the
role of the Council in making a real and positive
difference to the services which local people
receive from the Authority.

    1   2   3

12. Considering the role of quality systems, for
example the Business Excellence Model in
contributing to Best Value.

    1   2   3

13. Being constantly alert to the opportunities for
recasting approaches to service provision and
service outputs in the light of the changing legal
and policy environment.

    1   2   3

D. OPERATIONAL SYSTEMS

Please consider how accurately each proposition describes what the Department does at the time this Healthcheck is completed and grade accordingly by ticking one of the three boxes on the right hand side of the page. These will enable you to plot your Department's current position on a three point spectrum:

1. not in place and no plans to do so;
2. not in place but moving towards;
3. fully in place.

Some of the questions cover ground already covered elsewhere in the Healthcheck. This is deliberate as part of an holistic Best Value approach.

Wherever used within this Healthcheck 'client' means the person asking the Department to provide a service on behalf of the Council. 'Client' will include officers, members, the Council, its committees, sub-committees, other democratic structures, agreed public bodies and any other persons having a stake in what the Department does.

The Department has in place and fully operational an efficient, effective, integrated and comprehensive approach to:

1. Capturing all time spent on each activity in the
Department as it happens.

    1   2   3

2. Processing the time captured into a
comprehensive range of practical and useful
management and client reports.

    1   2   3

3. At the outset, opening files and recording the
client, the nature of the matter, the fee earner
and the fee earner's supervisor.

    1   2   3

4. Taking and recording client instructions (having
careful regard to the overall corporate interests of
the Council).

    1   2   3

		1	2	3
5.	What we are to do for the client, how we are to do it and in what timescale	☐	☐	☐
	5.1 the name and contact details of lead fee earner ('fee earner' refers to staff who carry out professional work on behalf of the council);	☐	☐	☐
	5.2 the name and contact details of any ancillary fee earners;	☐	☐	☐
	5.3 charging information;	☐	☐	☐
	5.4 how to complain;	☐	☐	☐
	5.5 key information at the outset and throughout the matter.	☐	☐	☐
6.	How to address any conflict of interest (eg with corporate strategy, other departments, for legal considerations or for any other reason).	☐	☐	☐
7.	Supervising all work undertaken and ensuring that it is being carried out well and at the appropriate level.	☐	☐	☐
8.	Ensuring that files are maintained in a clear logical and orderly matter and appropriate to the particular type of matter.	☐	☐	☐
9.	Regular and random file audits conducted by an independent manager to check on the quality of the work being produced and the efficiency and orderliness of the file and the administration arrangements for the matter.	☐	☐	☐
10.	Regular programmed supervision of each employee.	☐	☐	☐
11.	Dealing effectively with situations where work falls below a satisfactory standard.	☐	☐	☐
12.	Setting and monitoring performance targets agreed with clients.	☐	☐	☐
13.	Engaging Counsel, external solicitors and other consultants (consultants).	☐	☐	☐

14. Noting and recording comments on the performance of the consultant and in particular whether the consultant met the prescribed output objectives.

1	2	3

15. Dealing effectively and satisfactorily with complaints both internally and externally.

1	2	3

16. Assessing and recording client satisfaction at regular stages throughout and at the end of the matter.

1	2	3

17. Taking immediate and effective action to address any identified performance shortfalls.

1	2	3

18. Sound equal opportunities practice in all systems, processes and procedures.

1	2	3

19. Ensuring that appropriate professional and physical resources are available to every fee earner to ensure high quality outputs.

1	2	3

20. Ensuring key stages in all matters are noted, diarised and properly dealt with.

1	2	3

21. Maintaining effective and operational back up systems to ensure that no key stage is ever missed.

1	2	3

22. Ensuring that all service outcomes are monitored for quality, timeliness, compliance with the clients' objectives and the Council's strategic objectives.

1	2	3

23. Setting and monitoring performance indication and targets.

1	2	3

24. Ensuring a joined-up and cohesive service to clients.

1	2	3

25. Compliance with the Law Society's Practice Management Standards.

1	2	3

E. CLIENT SATISFACTION

Please consider how accurately each proposition describes what the Department does at the time this Healthcheck is completed and grade accordingly by ticking one of the three boxes on the right hand side of the page. These will enable you to plot your Department's current position on a three point spectrum:

1.   not in place and no plans to do so;
2.   not in place but moving towards;
3.   fully in place.

Some of the questions cover ground already covered elsewhere in the Healthcheck. This is deliberate as part of an holistic Best Value approach.

Wherever used within this Healthcheck 'client' means the person asking the Department to provide a service on behalf of the Council. 'Client' will include officers, members, the Council, its committees, sub-committees, other democratic structures, agreed public bodies and any other persons having a stake in what the Department does.

The Department has in place and fully operational an efficient, effective, integrated and comprehensive approach to:

		1	2	3
1.	Regularly assessing client satisfaction both generally and in respect of specific matters.	☐	☐	☐
2.	Allocating specific individual overall responsibility for client satisfaction at team and departmental levels.	☐	☐	☐
3.	Regularly testing the satisfaction of different categories of client eg the chief executive; officers; members at different functional levels (eg executive/scrutiny) and outside bodies.	☐	☐	☐
4.	Ensuring that the outputs from team client satisfaction processes feed into departmental client satisfaction processes.	☐	☐	☐
5.	Maintaining records of regular client satisfaction surveys and ensuring that:	☐	☐	☐
	5.1 these are taken properly into account in departmental strategic planning;	☐	☐	☐
	5.2 these are regularly inspected by senior management and all those who have a stake in them;	☐	☐	☐
	5.3 prompt and effective action is taken at all stages to remedy any shortcomings identified in client satisfaction processes;	☐	☐	☐
	5.4 all remedial actions are agreed with the client;	☐	☐	☐
	5.5 the nature of the action that has been taken to remedy the shortcomings by reference to specific documentary records;	☐	☐	☐

5.6   client satisfaction is demonstrably an integral part of departmental continuous improvement processes;

   1   2   3

5.7   at all times the Department is solution and outcome-focussed and avoids the 'its not *my* problem' approach.

   1   2   3

6.   Integrating client and stakeholder needs into the service eg by holding 'open days'.

   1   2   3

7.   Constantly considering what new 'products' and services it can offer to meet changing clients' needs.

   1   2   3

F.   FINANCIAL SYSTEMS

Please consider how accurately each proposition describes what the Department does at the time this Healthcheck is completed and grade accordingly by ticking one of the three boxes on the right hand side of the page. These will enable you to plot your Department's current position on a three point spectrum:

1.   not in place and no plans to do so;
2.   not in place but moving towards;
3.   fully in place.

Some of the questions cover ground already covered elsewhere in the Healthcheck. This is deliberate as part of an holistic Best Value approach.

Wherever used within this Healthcheck 'client' means the person asking the Department to provide a service on behalf of the Council. 'Client' will include officers, members, the Council, its committees, sub-committees, other democratic structures, agreed public bodies and any other persons having a stake in what the Department does.

'Fee Earner' – refers to staff who carry out chargeable professional work on behalf of the Council.

The Department has in place and fully operational an efficient, effective, integrated and comprehensive approach to:

1.   Identifying the nature, amount and cost of all work undertaken by each fee earner and the person(s) for whom that work is carried out.

   1   2   3

2.   Identifying in respect of each fee earner the nature and cost of all non-productive work.

   1   2   3

3.   Following up with individual fee earners any areas of concern or other matters identified by these financial systems.

   1   2   3

4. Regularly reviewing the amount of target
    chargeable hours for different categories of fee
    earner to promote continuous improvement in
    the light of economy, effectiveness and efficiency.

    1   2   3
    [ ] [ ] [ ]

5. Reporting regularly to clients on all financial
    aspects of work undertaken for them tailored to
    their departmental structures including the cost
    by reference to any time period of:

    1   2   3
    [ ] [ ] [ ]

    5.1 all work of a particular type;

    1   2   3
    [ ] [ ] [ ]

    5.2 all work for a particular team;

    1   2   3
    [ ] [ ] [ ]

    5.3 all work by a particular team;

    1   2   3
    [ ] [ ] [ ]

    5.4 all work by a particular fee earner;

    1   2   3
    [ ] [ ] [ ]

    5.5 all work on a particular project;

    1   2   3
    [ ] [ ] [ ]

    5.6 all general advice given.

    1   2   3
    [ ] [ ] [ ]

6. Ensuring that any corporate or statutory financial
    targets are effectively and satisfactorily met.

    1   2   3
    [ ] [ ] [ ]

7. Monitoring all revenue income and expenditure.

    1   2   3
    [ ] [ ] [ ]

8. Producing financial monitoring information for
    the Council on the cost of the department and its
    financial performance.

    1   2   3
    [ ] [ ] [ ]

9. Allocating sufficient resources for capital
    expenditure.

    1   2   3
    [ ] [ ] [ ]

10. Costing and financially maintaining the physical
    fabric of the premises.

    1   2   3
    [ ] [ ] [ ]

11. Monitoring capital income and expenditure.

    1   2   3
    [ ] [ ] [ ]

G. PEOPLE ISSUES

Please consider how accurately each proposition describes what the Department does at the time this Healthcheck is completed and grade accordingly by ticking one of the three boxes on the right hand side of the page. These will enable you to plot your Department's current position on a three point spectrum:

1. not in place and no plans to do so;
2. not in place but moving towards;
3. fully in place.

Some of the questions cover ground already covered elsewhere in the Healthcheck. This is deliberate as part of an holistic Best Value approach.

Wherever used within this Healthcheck 'client' means the person asking the Department to provide a service on behalf of the Council. 'Client' will include officers, members, the Council, its committees, sub-committees, other democratic structures, agreed public bodies and any other persons having a stake in what the Department does.

The Department has in place and fully operational an efficient, effective, integrated and comprehensive approach to:

		1	2	3
1.	Identifying the skills, experience and personal attributes required when staff are recruited.	☐	☐	☐
2.	Ensuring that all recruitment is conducted in the light of a detailed, sound, fair and effective code of recruitment practice which sets out clearly what is to be done by whom and by when at each stage of the recruitment and selection process.	☐	☐	☐
3.	Ensuring that sound and effective equal opportunities practice is integrated fully into our processes and practice.	☐	☐	☐
4.	Monitoring and verifying that recruitment processes are conducted properly and fairly in the light of the above processes.	☐	☐	☐
5.	Ensuring that a comprehensive, effective and up to date recruitment pack is prepared for every recruitment exercise and supplied to all candidates.	☐	☐	☐
6.	Providing new employees with friendly, effective and comprehensive induction into the department including:	☐	☐	☐
6.1	an up to date and comprehensive information pack with signposts to key contacts, locations and office procedures;	☐	☐	☐
6.2	the provision of suitable accommodation and equipment.	☐	☐	☐

7. Ensuring that management training is provided to all staff with management or supervisory responsibilities to ensure a high level of competence in core management skills, abilities and attributes including: delegation, empowerment, coaching and staff support, strategic skills, decision making, political skills, equal opportunities, negotiation skills and leadership, co-operative working and joined-up thinking.

1	2	3
☐	☐	☐

8. Regularly assessing staff morale in a structured way and taking any necessary positive action in the light of the outcome of the assessment.

1	2	3
☐	☐	☐

9. Obtaining and taking meaningfully into account at departmental management level the views of staff concerning practical and key aspects of the department and its management.

1	2	3
☐	☐	☐

10. Specifying the departmental policy and approach to training with clear links to departmental objectives.

1	2	3
☐	☐	☐

11. Recognising that training is wider than attendance on courses and can encompass (for example):

1	2	3
☐	☐	☐

    11.1   coaching;

1	2	3
☐	☐	☐

    11.2   shadowing;

1	2	3
☐	☐	☐

    11.3   on the job;

1	2	3
☐	☐	☐

    11.4   involvement in projects.

1	2	3
☐	☐	☐

12. Recording all training undertaken by each employee as necessary with separately identifiable recording of continuing professional development training.

1	2	3
☐	☐	☐

13. For each member of staff who has undergone any training events to report in writing as to:

    13.1   what was learnt on a particular training event;

1	2	3
☐	☐	☐

		1	2	3
13.2	how this will help the employee to do his/her job better;	☐	☐	☐
13.3	how this will contribute to the overall success of the Council;	☐	☐	☐
13.4	whether there were any shortcomings in the training and if so what they were;	☐	☐	☐
13.5	how those shortcomings are to be remedied by the employee;	☐	☐	☐
13.6	the arrangements by which the employee will be making available to other relevant employees the skills and knowledge acquired on the training;	☐	☐	☐
13.7	on at least a regular six monthly basis setting objectives for each employee and agreeing with each employee development needs and how these should most effectively be met linked to departmental strategic objectives;	☐	☐	☐
13.8	ensuring that all staff at all levels are trained to give them the skills, abilities and experience to discharge their duties so as to enable them to yield high quality outputs consistent with departmental and corporate objectives.	☐	☐	☐
14.	Maintaining a database of the skills, experience of all staff (including those which go beyond the operational role of staff).	☐	☐	☐
15.	Involving all staff in best value policy, procedure and practice.	☐	☐	☐
16.	Setting personal and team development goals with team improvement plans which feed into the departmental, directorate and corporate best value strategy.	☐	☐	☐
17.	Monitoring and reporting the carrying out of team improvement plans.	☐	☐	☐
18.	Encouraging joined-up thinking.	☐	☐	☐

		1	2	3
19.	Ensuring staff are motivated and enaged into contributing positively to service outputs.	☐	☐	☐
20.	Supporting and empowering staff to make their own creative contribution to Best Value.	☐	☐	☐

H.   GENERAL MANAGEMENT

Please consider how accurately each proposition describes what the Department does at the time this Healthcheck is completed and grade accordingly by ticking one of the three boxes on the right hand side of the page. These will enable you to plot your Department's current position on a three point spectrum:

1. not in place and no plans to do so;
2. not in place but moving towards;
3. fully in place.

Some of the questions cover ground already covered elsewhere in the Healthcheck. This is deliberate as part of an holistic Best Value approach.

Wherever used within this Healthcheck 'client' means the person asking the Department to provide a service on behalf of the Council. 'Client' will include officers, members, the Council, its committees, sub-committees, other democratic structures, agreed public bodies and any other persons having a stake in what the Department does.

The Department has in place and fully operational an efficient, effective, integrated and comprehensive approach to:

		1	2	3
1.	Providing firm, fair, responsive and sensible people and sensitive management.	☐	☐	☐
2.	Ensuring that all key decisions and actions are, wherever appropriate, SMART ie specific, measurable, accountable, realistic and time based.	☐	☐	☐
3.	Periodic programmed strategy meetings to ensure that the wider context is fully accommodated and integrated into decision making.	☐	☐	☐
4.	Regular departmental management meetings to enable an integrated and cohesive approach to departmental issues.	☐	☐	☐
5.	Following up and monitoring the implementation of strategic and departmental management decisions.	☐	☐	☐
6.	Ensuring that the maximum information possible is made available to all staff following strategy and departmental management meetings.	☐	☐	☐
7.	Regular team briefings (at least fortnightly) to enable information to flow rapidly and effectively and to enable all staff to be fully and properly informed.	☐	☐	☐

8. Regular one to one management/supervisory meetings between each member of staff and their line manager/supervisor.

1	2	3

9. Enabling all staff to have proper and effective access to senior management whenever necessary.

1	2	3

10. Dealing speedily and effectively with discipline and grievance issues.

1	2	3

11. Dealing speedily and effectively with personal harassment issues.

1	2	3

12. Ensuring that all managers are appropriately supported and resourced to enable them efficiently and effectively to carry out their duties.

1	2	3

13. Taking a pro-active and responsive response to service delivery and integrating customer responses into departmental systems and procedures.

1	2	3

14. Making work a pleasant and enjoyable place to be for all staff.

1	2	3

I. STRATEGIC PLANNING

Please consider how accurately each proposition describes what the Department does at the time this Healthcheck is completed and grade accordingly by ticking one of the three boxes on the right hand side of the page. These will enable you to plot your Department's current position on a three point spectrum:

1. not in place and no plans to do so;
2. not in place but moving towards;
3. fully in place.

Some of the questions cover ground already covered elsewhere in the Healthcheck. This is deliberate as part of an holistic Best Value approach.

Wherever used within this Healthcheck 'client' means the person asking the Department to provide a service on behalf of the Council. 'Client' will include officers, members, the Council, its committees, sub-committees, other democratic structures, agreed public bodies and any other persons having a stake in what the Department does.

The Department has in place and fully operational an efficient, effective, integrated and comprehensive approach to:

1. Determining strategy for operational matters; products to be offered; manner of service provision, marketing; potential client groups; internal procurement; demand/supply management.

1	2	3

		1	2	3
2.	Keeping under constant review, what we are here for, where we need to get to, by when, and how we intend to get there.	☐	☐	☐
3.	Deciding when to change direction, where we are heading and why.	☐	☐	☐
4.	Communicating our strategy clearly, accessibly and meaningfully at all levels.	☐	☐	☐
5.	Integrating the principles of best value fundamentally into departmental strategy and operations.	☐	☐	☐
6.	Ensuring that all operations are carried out so as to be consistent with and promote departmental strategy.	☐	☐	☐
7.	The Department has consequently carried out a rigorous service review involving stakeholders, other managers and external organisations and in so doing has:	☐	☐	☐
7.1	**challenged** what we do (ie all our activities and functions) and whether all parts are objectively necessary for the Council;	☐	☐	☐
7.2	**challenged** how we do what we do and whether there are better ways of providing all or any part of the service.	☐	☐	☐
8.	Consequently considering:			
8.1	what other ways are there of meeting the Council's needs in the service areas in question?	☐	☐	☐
8.2	the importance of the service to the provision of other authority services;	☐	☐	☐
8.3	whether each aspect of the service is being provided at times and locations suitable to those who need them;	☐	☐	☐
8.4	the effectiveness of operational processes underpinning service delivery;	☐	☐	☐
8.5	whether these processes are being properly complied with across the operation;	☐	☐	☐
8.6	whether any aspect of the service could be delivered more economically;	☐	☐	☐

		1	2	3
8.7	to what extent service quality can be improved in each of the key activities undertaken;	☐	☐	☐
8.8	any parts of the service which attract general corporate and individual user esteem;	☐	☐	☐
8.9	the impact of equal opportunities in service delivery.	☐	☐	☐
8.10	the extent to which departmental practice and procedure add value to effective service outputs.	☐	☐	☐

9. The Department has:

		1	2	3
9.1	regularly **consulted** with representatives of our service users at appropriate levels;	☐	☐	☐
9.2	**consulted** all others who have a stake in the outcomes of our Department (stakeholders).	☐	☐	☐

9.3 We have considered the following consultation methods:

		1	2	3
9.3.1	user satisfaction surveys;	☐	☐	☐
9.3.2	intranet feedback;	☐	☐	☐
9.3.3	user groups;	☐	☐	☐
9.3.4	surgeries;	☐	☐	☐
9.3.5	open days;	☐	☐	☐
9.3.6	including stakeholders in review process;	☐	☐	☐
9.3.7	focus groups;	☐	☐	☐
9.3.8	regular meetings with key stakeholders.	☐	☐	☐

10. The Department has:

    10.1 regularly and systematically **compared** our systems, procedures, processes and costs with similar organisations in the public, private and (as appropriate) the voluntary sectors;

          1   2   3 ☐ ☐ ☐

    10.2 action planned continuing improvements from the comparison process on a continuing basis and monitored the carrying out of those action plans.

          1   2   3 ☐ ☐ ☐

11. The Department has:

    11.1 demonstrated a **competitive** approach to the provision of departmental services in that Departmental management has:

          1   2   3 ☐ ☐ ☐

        11.1.1 ensured it has all necessary information to enable the carrying out of a rigorous analysis of outputs and the taking of all necessary action;

          1   2   3 ☐ ☐ ☐

        11.1.2 arranged for the department to be reviewed rigorously and in detail by managers outside the department or other suitable external persons;

          1   2   3 ☐ ☐ ☐

        11.1.3 where a review process demonstrates that it is necessary or desirable to do so periodically, subjected parts of the Department to competition or to further profound and rigorous service review;

          1   2   3 ☐ ☐ ☐

    11.2 enaged external service providers for some services and taken the opportunity to benchmark with the external supplier or otherwise to seek challenging opportunities for continuous improvement;

          1   2   3 ☐ ☐ ☐

    11.3 engaged in best value partnerships with suitable external service providers.

          1   2   3 ☐ ☐ ☐

11. Involving staff and key stakeholders in our strategic planning processes.

          1   2   3 ☐ ☐ ☐

INDEX

References are to paragraph numbers